SPANISH
MADE SIMPLE

BY

EUGENE JACKSON, A.B.

Chairman of Foreign Languages (Ret.)
Samuel J. Tilden H. S., Brooklyn, N.Y.

AND

ANTONIO RUBIO, Ph.D.

Chairman, Dept. of Modern Languages (Ret.)
DePaul University, Chicago, Ill.

MADE SIMPLE BOOKS
DOUBLEDAY & COMPANY, INC.
GARDEN CITY, NEW YORK

ABOUT THIS BOOK

Spanish for Tourist, Traveler, and Business Man

Do you wish to attain rapidly and easily the ability to pronounce Spanish well, to engage in everyday conversation, to read simple Spanish text,—in short, do you wish to acquire enough knowledge of Spanish to meet your needs as tourist, traveler, or businessman in a Spanish-speaking country? SPANISH MADE SIMPLE is the book for you.

The bilingual text which eliminates the burdensome and time-consuming looking up of words in the dictionary, the dialogues dealing with common topics, the word building exercises, the Spanish questions and the answer-key for self-checking, all these will enable you to attain your goal pleasantly and effectively.

The important words and expressions and many cultural facts are easily remembered because they appear naturally in a series of conversations between the Mexican teacher Mr. Lopez and his pupil Mr. Adams, a businessman of New York, who like you is about to take a trip to Latin America and wishes to be able to get along in Spanish.

Spanish for Students

Do you wish a thorough grounding in the Spanish language for secondary school or college? SPANISH MADE SIMPLE will enable you to attain your goal. The essential grammatical facts of Spanish grow naturally out of the conversation and reading texts. The facts are clearly explained. Non essentials are omitted. The numerous illustrative drills and exercises and the answer key for self-checking will enable you to gain a thorough knowledge of the elements of Spanish and lay the foundation for advanced study of the language.

SPANISH MADE SIMPLE thus meets the needs of the self-learner, whether his aim is the practical conversation and comprehension ability needed by the tourist, traveler, or businessman, or a thorough grounding in the fundamentals of the Spanish language desired by the high school or college student. It can also serve as an excellent refresher course for those who already have had some study of the language.

Spanish Text for Classroom Use

Although primarily designed for self-study, SPANISH MADE SIMPLE can serve as a textbook in Spanish classes in secondary schools or college. The material is practical; the conversational approach is simple and interesting; and the cultural aspects are closely integrated with the language elements. The book offers an easy method for acquiring vocabulary, everyday expressions, and even grammatical facts which are generally a bugbear to students. SPANISH MADE SIMPLE is a refreshing change from the conventional textbook with its academic approach and over-emphasis on grammar.

—Eugene Jackson
—Antonio Rubio

TABLE OF CONTENTS

CAPÍTULO 1 (UNO)—CHAPTER 1

MEET THE SPANISH LANGUAGE

1. *Spanish is not a complete stranger.*

On your introduction to the Spanish language you will be glad to learn that you already know or can guess the meaning of many Spanish words.

First of all there are those words which are spelled alike and have the same meaning in Spanish and English. For example:

actor	color	doctor	gratis	canal	conductor	hospital
hotel	error	piano	animal	auto	principal	director

Then there are many Spanish words whose spelling is only a bit different from like words in English, and whose meaning is easily recognized. Thus:

aire	arte	centro	barbero	mula	profesor	conversación
air	*art*	*center*	*barber*	*mule*	*professor*	*conversation*

Many Spanish verbs differ from corresponding English verbs only in the matter of ending. Thus:

declarar	adorar	admirar	usar	informar	defender	dividir
declare	*adore*	*admire*	*use*	*inform*	*defend*	*divide*

English has borrowed words directly from the Spanish with or without changes in spelling. Thus:

adobe	rodeo	fiesta	lazo	patio	tomate	siesta	rancho
adobe	*rodeo*	*fiesta*	*lasso*	*patio*	*tomato*	*siesta*	*ranch*

Spanish has borrowed words directly from the English. This is especially true in the field of sports. You will recognize these words even in their strange spellings.

rosbif	mitin	pudín	tenis	béisbol	fútbol	básquetbol
roastbeef	*meeting*	*pudding*	*tennis*	*baseball*	*football*	*basketball*

The similarities between the Spanish and English vocabularies will be a great help to you in learning Spanish. However, you must bear in mind that words of the same or similar spelling in the two languages are pronounced differently. Also you must be on the lookout for some Spanish words which are alike or similar in spelling to English words, but different in meaning.

2. *Spanish is not difficult to pronounce and spell.*

Spanish is a phonetic language. This means that words are spelled as they are pronounced. There are no silent letters in Spanish except **h**, which is always silent, and **u** which is silent under certain circumstances. How much simpler this is than English, where such words as *height, knight, cough, rough, rogue, weigh, dough,* and a host of others, give so much difficulty to the foreigner learning English.

When you see the letter **a** in Spanish words like **Ana, mapa, sala,** you know it is pronounced like *a* in *father,* because Spanish a is always like *a* in *father.* It is never like *a* in *cat, all,* or *fame.* Like **a,** the other letters of the Spanish alphabet are an accurate guide to the pronunciation of the words.

In Chapter 2, the pronunciation of the Spanish sounds and their spelling is explained in detail. Most of the Spanish sounds have like sounds in English, or sounds so similar that they are easy to learn. The description of the sounds should enable you to pronounce them quite well. If possible you should get some Spanish speaking person to help you with your pronunciation, for it is important for you to hear the sounds correctly spoken and to have your own pronunciation checked.

You can improve your pronunciation and understanding of the spoken word by listening to Spanish recordings and radio broadcasts. The "commercials" are particularly valuable for this purpose, because they contain so much repetition and emphatic expression. At first a few minutes of listening each day will suffice. As you progress in your study of Spanish you should increase the amount.

3. *Our Good Neighbors to the South Speak Spanish.*

Spanish speaking countries of the Western Hemisphere include: All the republics of South America with the exception of Brazil; all the republics of Central America; Cuba, Puerto Rico, and the Dominican Republic in the West Indies; and our nearest neighbor Mexico. They include some 80 million people. The Spanish which they speak differs in some respects from Castilian Spanish, the official language of Spain. The chief differences are in the pronunciation of z, and c (before e and i). In Castilian these letters are pronounced like *th* in *think*. In the Spanish of Spanish America they are pronounced like *s* in *see*.

This book teaches the pronunciation of our Good Neighbors in Spanish America. This is desirable because of the ever-growing business and cultural intercourse between our country and the peoples in the southern half of our hemisphere. Mexico in particular has become a favorite country for business men and tourists from the United States, thousands of whom visit it every year.

CAPÍTULO 2 (DOS)

SPANISH PRONUNCIATION

This chapter contains many useful words and expressions. If you follow the instructions for pronunciation practice carefully, you will acquire many of these without difficulty. It is not necessary to try to memorize all of them at this point as they will appear again in later chapters when you will have the opportunity to learn them thoroughly. However, it is desirable to memorize at once the numbers and the days of the week as these serve to illustrate most of the Spanish sounds.

PARTE PRIMERA (PART FIRST)

The Numbers 1 to 21—The Days of the Week

Among the most important words in any language are the numbers. Let us start by learning the Spanish numbers 1 to 21. These numbers illustrate many of the Spanish sounds.

Pronounce each number aloud five times. Stress (emphasize) the syllables in heavy type.

1. **uno** (*oo-noh*) Spanish **u** is like *oo* in *boot*. Symbol, *oo*.

   Spanish **o** is like *o* in *bone*. Symbol *oh*.

2. **dos** (*dohs*) Spanish **s** is like *s* in *see*.

3. **tres** (*trays*) Spanish **e** is like *ay* in *day*. Symbol, *ay*.

   Remember: **s** is like *s* in *see*.

4. **cuatro** (*kwah-troh*) In the combination ua, the **u** is pronounced like *w*. **ua** = *wah*. There is no letter *w* in Spanish.

   Spanish **r** is like *r* in *three*. It has a slight trill.

5. **cinco** (*seen-koh*) Spanish **i** is like *ee* in *seen*. Symbol, *ee*.

   c is pronounced as in English; like *s*, before *e* or *i* (*ceiling, cinder*); like *k*, before any other letter. There is no letter *k* in Spanish.

6. **seis** (*sayees*) The combination **ei** is pronounced *ayee*. Pronounce the first part (*ay*) stronger than the second part (*ee*).

7. **siete** (*syay-tay*) In the combination **ie**, the **i** is pronounced like *y* in *yes*. Thus **ie** = *yay*.

8. **ocho** (*oh-choh*) **ch** is like the English *ch* in *choke*. In Spanish, **ch** is considered a single letter and follows **c** in the alphabet and dictionary.

9. **nueve** (*nway-vay*) The combination **ue** is pronounced *way*.

10. **diez** (*dyays*) Spanish **z** equals *s* as in *see*. It is not like English *z*.

11. **once** (*ohn-say*)

12. **doce** (*doh-say*)

13. **trece** (*tray-say*)

14. **catorce** (*kah-tor-say*) The letter **o** is sometimes pronounced as in the English word *for*. In such cases **o** is used as a symbol instead of *oh*.

15. **quince** (*keen-say*) **qu** always equals *k*. **qu** is found only before **e** and **i**.

16. diez y seis (*dyays ee sayees*)   19. diez y nueve (*dyays ee nway-vay*)
17. diez y siete (*dyays ee syay-tay*)   20. veinte (*vayeen-tay*)
18. diez y ocho (*dyays ee oh-choh*)   21. veinte y uno (*vayeen-tay ee oo-noh*)

NOTE: The letter y as a vowel is pronounced *ee*. As a consonant it is like *y* in *you*. The word y means *and*.

Practice aloud and memorize:

1. uno (*oo-noh*)   8. ocho (*oh-choh*)   15. quince (*keen-say*)
2. dos (*dohs*)   9. nueve (*nway-vay*)   16. diez y seis
3. tres (*trays*)   10. diez (*dyays*)   17. diez y siete
4. cuatro (*kwah-tro*)   11. once (*ohn-say*)   18. diez y ocho
5. cinco (*seen-ko*)   12. doce (*doh-say*)   19. diez y nueve
6. seis (*sayees*)   13. trece (*tray-say*)   20. veinte (*vayeen-tay*)
7. siete (*syay-tay*)   14. catorce (*kah-tor-say*)   21. veinte y uno

Summary of Spanish Vowels and Vowel Combinations Learned Thus Far

		Vowels					Vowel Combinations		
Spanish letters	a	o	u	e	i (y)	ua	ue	ie	ei
Symbols	ah	oh[1]	oo	ay[1]	ee	wah	way	yay	ayee

NOTE: 1. *oh* and *ay* are not exact equivalents of Spanish o and e but they are near enough for practical purposes.

Days of the Week and Months of the Year

Practice aloud and memorize. The names of the days and months contain only one sound not found in the numbers 1–21; namely j. Spanish j is something like a strong English *h*.

domingo (*doh-meen-goh*)	Sunday	jueves (*hway-vays*)	Thursday
lunes (*loo-nays*)	Monday	viernes (*vyayr-nays*)	Friday
martes (*mahr-tays*)	Tuesday	sábado (*sah-bah-doh*)	Saturday
miércoles (*myayr-koh-lays*)	Wednesday		

enero (*ay-nay-roh*)	January	julio (*hoo-lyoh*)	July
febrero (*fay-bray-roh*)	February	agosto (*ah-gos-toh*)	August
marzo (*mahr-soh*)	March	septiembre (*say-tyaym-bray*)	September
abril (*ah-breel*)	April	octubre (*ok-too-bray*)	October
mayo (*mah-yoh*)	May	noviembre (*noh-vyaym-bray*)	November
junio (*hoo-nyoh*)	June	diciembre (*dee-syaym-bray*)	December

NOTE: The combination io is pronounced *yoh*.

PARTE SEGUNDA (PART SECOND)

Useful Expressions for the Traveler

Here are some key words which every traveler needs:

1. por favor (*por fah-vor*) please. This is most handy for introducing a question or request.

2. señor (*say-ñor*) Mr., sir; señora (*say-ño-rah*) Mrs., madame; señorita (*say-ño-ree-tah*) Miss. It's polite to follow your **por favor** with one of these. **Por favor, señor,** etc.

NOTE: ñ is like *n* in *onion*. Everyone knows this sound in **mañana** tomorrow. ñ follows n in the alphabet and dictionary.

3. ¿Cuánto cuesta? (*kwahn-toh kways-tah*) How much does it cost? For short, ¿**Cuánto?** will do.

In this connection the following words are handy: Es caro (*ays kah-roh*) It is dear. Más barato (*mahs bah-rah-toh*) cheaper.

NOTE: Spanish questions begin with an inverted question mark.

4. **¿Dónde está —?** (*dohn-day ays-tah*) Where is —?

5. **Quiero** (*kyay-roh*), I want. **Deseo** (*day-say-oh*) I want. If you begin with **Por favor,** you won't sound too abrupt.

6. **¿A qué hora** (*ah kay oh-rah*) At what time? The Spanish says: At what hour?

NOTE: h in Spanish is always silent.

7. **Muchas gracias** (*moo-chahs grah-syahs*) Many thanks. Thank you very much.

NOTE: The combination ia is pronounced *yah.*

8. **De nada** (*day nah-dah*) or **No hay de qué** (*ahee day kay*). Don't mention it or you're welcome. You'll hear either of these in reply to your gracias.

9. **¿Cómo se llama usted?** (*koh-moh say yah-mah oos-tayd*) What's your name? The Spanish says: What do you call yourself?

NOTE: ll is pronounced like *y* in *you.* ll is considered a single letter in Spanish and follows l in the alphabet and dictionary.

10. **Me llamo . . .** (*may yah-moh*) My name is . . . The Spanish says: I call myself . . .

Some Useful Words

Repeat aloud, three times, the words listed under each heading. Then repeat each word with the heading under which it is listed. Thus:

¿Cuánto cuesta el sarape? etc.

¿Dónde está la Calle A? etc.

¿Cuánto cuesta . . .?

1. **el sarape** (*sah-rah-pay*) blanket
2. **el rebozo** (*rray-boh-soh*) shawl
3. **el sombrero** (*sohm-bray-roh*) hat
4. **la blusa** (*bloo-sah*) blouse
5. **la camisa** (*kah-mee-sah*) shirt
6. **el vestido** (*vays-tee-doh*) dress

7. **la cesta** (*says-tah*) basket
8. **el plato** (*plah-toh*) plate
9. **el jarro** (*hah-rroh*) pitcher
10. **el automóvil** (*ow-toh-moh-veel*) automobile

NOTE:

1. Pronounce el like *ell* in *bell.*
2. au = *ow* as in *how.*
3. r at the beginning of a word, and rr are strongly trilled, like the *r* of the telephone operator in *thrrr-ee.* rr is a letter in Spanish but no word begins with rr.
4. el = *the* before a masculine noun and la = *the* before a feminine noun. You will learn more about these later.

¿Dónde está . . .?

1. **la Calle Gante** (*kah-yay gahn-tay*) Gante Street
2. **la Avenida Juárez** (*ah-vay-nee-dah hwah-rays*) Juarez Avenue
3. **el hotel** (*oh-tel*) hotel
4. **el lavabo de señores** (*lah-vah-boh*) men's room

5. **el lavabo de señoras** ladies' room
6. **el correo** (*koh-rray-oh*) post office
7. **el museo** (*moo-say-oh*) museum
8. **el agente** (*ah-hayn-tay*) agent
9. **la oficina** (*oh-fee-see-nah*) office
10. **el garage** (*gah-rah-hay*) garage

NOTE: g, before e or i, is pronounced like Spanish j. Before any other letter it is hard as in *goat.*

Quiero . . . Deseo . . .

1. **un cuarto con baño** (*kwahr-toh kon bah-ñoh*) a room with bath
2. **agua caliente** (*ah-gwah kah-lyayn-tay*) hot water
3. **el jabón** (*hah-bohn*) soap
4. **toallas** (*toh-ah-yahs*) towels
5. **el menú** (*may-noo*) menu

6. **la cuenta** (*kwayn-tah*) bill
7. **la revista** (*rray-vees-tah*) magazine
8. **el diario** (*dyahr-yoh*) newspaper
9. **telefonear** (*tay-lay-foh-nay-ahr*) to telephone
10. **cambiar dinero** (*kahm-byahr dee-nay-roh*) to change money

Me llamo . . .

1. **el señor Gómez** (*goh-mays*) Mr. Gomez
2. **la señora de Gómez** Mrs. Gomez
3. **Pablo** (*pah-bloh*) Paul
4. **Felipe** (*fay-lee-pay*) Philip
5. **Roberto** (*rroh-ber-to*) Robert
6. **José** (*hoh-say*) Joseph
7. **Juan** (*hwahn*) John
8. **Isabel** (*ee-sah-bel*) Isabelle
9. **Ana** (*ah-nah*) Anna
10. **María** (*mah-ree-ah*) Mary

The Numbers 20 to 100

Practice aloud:

20	veinte (*vayeen-tay*)	50	cincuenta (*seen-kwayn-tah*)	80	ochenta (*oh-chayn-tah*)
22	veinte y dos	55	cincuenta y cinco	88	ochenta y ocho
30	treinta (*trayeen-tah*)	60	sesenta (*say-sayn-tah*)	90	noventa (*noh-vayn-tah*)
33	treinta y tres	66	sesenta y seis	99	noventa y nueve
40	cuarenta (*kwah-rayn-tah*)	70	setenta (*say-tayn-tah*)	100	ciento (*syayn-toh*), cien
44	cuarenta y cuatro	77	setenta y siete		(*syayn*)

Practice aloud:

10	diez sarapes	50	cincuenta camisas	80	ochenta platos
20	veinte rebozos	60	sesenta vestidos	90	noventa jarros
30	treinta sombreros	70	setenta cestas	100	cien garages
40	cuarenta blusas				

NOTE: **cien** is used instead of **ciento** before a noun.

SUMMARY OF THE SPANISH CONSONANTS

Most of the Spanish consonants are pronounced like or almost like corresponding English consonants. The following however deserve special attention:

b,v There is no difference between these sounds. Both are made with the lips slightly open. **sábado, lavabo**

c[1] is like English *c*, that is, it is pronounced like a hissing *s* before **e** or **i**, and like *k* before any other letter. **cinco** (*seen-koh*). **cc** = *ks*. **lección** = *layk-syohn*

d,t like the English sounds, but tongue is against the teeth. Between vowels, **d** is more like *th* in *this*. **nada** (*nah-thah*)

h always silent. **hay, hoy**

j like a strong English *h*. **jueves** (*hway-vays*)

g like hard *g* in *go*. Before **e** or **i** it is like Spanish **j**. **garage** (*gah-rah-hay*)

ll[1] like *y* in *you*. **llamo** (*yah-moh*)

ñ like *n* in *onion*. **mañana** (*mah-ñah-nah*)

rr pronounced with a strong trill as in *thrrrr-ee*. **jarro** (*hah-rroh*)

r pronounced like **rr**, at the beginning of a word. At other times it has a slight trill. **reboso** (*rray-boh-soh*) **sombrero** (*sohm-bray-roh*)

s,z[1] like hissing *s* in *see*. **sesenta** (*say-sayn-tah*) **diez** (*dyays*)

qu like *k*. **quince** (*keen-say*)

NOTE: 1. In Castilian Spanish, **c** (before **e** and **i**) and **z**, are like *th* in *think;* and **ll** is like *ll* in *million*.

PARTE TERCERA (PART THIRD)

The Stress in Spanish Words

The stressed syllable of a word is the syllable which is emphasized. In the word *father*, the syllable *fa-* gets the stress; in *alone*, *-lone* gets the stress; in *education*, the stressed syllable is *-ca*. There are no good rules for stress in English.

In Spanish there are three simple rules by means of which you can tell which syllable of a word is stressed. They are:

RULE 1.   If a word ends in **a o u e i n** or **s,** the next to the last syllable is stressed.

som-bre-ro   a-ve-ni-da   sie-te   quin-ce   lu-nes   se-ño-ra   re-bo-so

RULE 2.   If a word ends in any consonant except **n** or **s,** the last syllable is stressed.

se-ñor   ho-**tel**   fa-vor   I-sa-**bel**   us-ted   cam-**biar**   te-le-fo-ne-**ar**

RULE 3.   If the stress does not follow Rules 1 or 2, an accent mark shows which syllable is stressed.

sá-ba-do   miér-co-les   Gó-mez   ja-bón   Jo-sé   au-to-mó-vil

Dialogues for Pronunciation Practice

Directions for Study of Dialogues.

1. Read the Spanish text silently, sentence by sentence, using the English translation to get the meaning.

2. Practice aloud the words which follow the text under the heading "Practice These Words."

3. Finally read the whole Spanish text aloud several times.

Diálogo 1 (*dee-ah-loh-goh*)

¿Cómo Está Usted?

1. **Buenos días, señor López. ¿Cómo está usted?**

2. **Muy bien, gracias. ¿Y usted?**

3. **Muy bien, gracias. ¿Y cómo está la señora de López?**

4. **Muy bien, gracias. ¿Y cómo están su papá y su mamá?**

5. **Muy bien, gracias. Hasta la vista, señor López.**

6. **Hasta mañana, Felipe.**

How Are You?

1. Good day, Mr. Lopez. How are you?

2. Very well, thank you. And you?

3. Very well, thank you. And how is Mrs. Lopez?

4. Very well, thank you. And how are your father and mother?

5. Very well, thank you. Good-bye, Mr. Lopez.

6. Until tomorrow, Philip.

Practice These Words

1. **Buenos días** (*bway-nohz dee-ahs*). Pronounce the **s** of buenos like the English **z** instead of like the usual **s** sound.

2. muy bien (*mwee byayn*) gracias (*grah-syas*)

3. cómo (*koh-moh*) están (*ays-tahn*)

4. papá (*pah-pah*) mamá (*mah-mah*)

5. hasta la vista (*ahs-tah lah vees-tah*)

6. usted (*oos-tayd*)

7. hasta (*ahs-tah*)

Diálogo 2

Los Días de la Semana

1. **¡Oiga Jaime! ¿Cuántos días hay en una semana?**

2. **Hay siete días en una semana.**

3. **Bueno. Dígame, por favor, los siete días.**

4. **Los siete días de la semana son lunes, martes, miércoles, jueves, viernes, sábado y domingo.**

5. **Muy bien. ¡Oiga Jorge! ¿Qué día es hoy?**

6. **Hoy es lunes. Mañana es martes.**

7. **Carlos, ¿sabe usted los números desde uno hasta doce?**

The Days of the Week

1. Listen, James. How many days are there in one week?

2. There are seven days in one week.

3. Good. Tell me, please, the seven days.

4. The seven days of the week are Monday, Tuesday, Wednesday, Thursday, Friday, Saturday and Sunday.

5. Very good. Listen, George. What day is today?

6. Today is Monday. Tomorrow is Tuesday.

7. Charles, do you know the numbers from one to twelve?

8. Sí, señor, los números son uno, dos, tres, cuatro, cinco, seis, siete, ocho, nueve, diez, once, doce.

9. Muy bien, Carlos.

8. Yes sir, the numbers are one, two, three, four, five, six, seven, eight, nine, ten, eleven, twelve.

9. Very good, Charles.

Practice These Words

1. Oiga (*oi-gah*) oi in Spanish is like *oi* in *oil*.
2. hoy (*oy*) oy in Spanish is like *oy* in *boy*.
3. hay (*ay*) ay and ai are like *ai* in *aisle*.
4. semana (*say-mah-nah*)

5. dígame (*dee-gah-may*)
6. Jorge (*hor-hay*)
7. sabe (*sah-bay*)
8. desde (*dayz-day*)

Diálogo 3

¿Habla Usted Español?

1. ¿Habla usted español, Claudio?
2. Sí, señor, yo[1] hablo español.
3. ¿Habla Pancho español?
4. Sí, señor, él habla español bien.
5. ¿Habla Paulina español?
6. Sí, señor, ella habla español bien.
7. ¿Habla ella inglés también?
8. No, señor, ella no habla inglés.
9. ¿Es Pablo de México?
10. Sí, señor, él es de México. Es mexicano.

Do You Speak Spanish?

1. Do you speak Spanish, Claude?
2. Yes, sir, I speak Spanish.
3. Does Frank speak Spanish?
4. Yes, sir, he speaks Spanish well.
5. Does Pauline speak Spanish?
6. Yes, sir, she speaks Spanish well.
7. Does she speak English also?
8. No, sir, she does not speak English.
9. Is Paul from Mexico?
10. Yes, sir, he is from Mexico. He is a Mexican.

NOTE: 1. The subject pronouns yo I, él he, ella she, are usually omitted in Spanish. They are used here for emphasis. You will learn more about this later.

Practice These Words

1. español (*ays-pah-ñol*)
2. hablo (*ah-bloh*), habla (*hah-blah*)

3. yo (*yoh*), él (*el*), ella (*ay-yah*), usted (*oos-tayd*) or (*oos-stay*)
4. Paulina (*pow-lee-nah*)

5. México (*may-hee-coh*). The x in México is pronounced like Spanish j. Outside the country of México the name is often spelled Méjico. The usual pronunciation of Spanish x is as in English.

Diálogo 4

¿Cómo Se Llama Ud.?

1. ¿Cómo se llama Ud., joven?
2. Me llamo Pablo Rivera.
3. ¿Dónde vive Ud.?
4. Vivo en la calle 23 (veinte y tres).
5. ¿Cuántas personas hay en su familia?

6. Hay cinco personas, mi padre, mi madre, mi hermano Carlos, mi hermana Ana, y yo.

7. Ud. habla bien el español. ¿Estudia Ud. la lengua en la escuela?
8. Sí, señor. Además hablamos español en casa. Mis padres son puertorriqueños.
9. Adiós, Pablo.
10. Adiós, señor.

What Is Your Name?

1. What is your name, young man?
2. My name is Paul Rivera.
3. Where do you live?
4. I live on 23d Street.
5. How many persons are there in your family?

6. There are five persons, my father, my mother, my brother Charles, my sister Anna, and I.

7. You speak Spanish well. Are you studying the language in school?
8. Yes, sir. Besides, we speak Spanish at home. My parents are Puerto Ricans.
9. Good-bye, Paul.
10. Good-bye, sir.

NOTE: Ud. or Vd. are abbreviations of usted.

Practice These Words

1. llama (*yah-mah*) calle (*kah-yay*)
2. joven (*hoh-vayn*) Rivera (*rree-vay-rah*)
3. vive (*vee-vay*) vivo (*vee-voh*)
4. personas (*per-soh-nahs*) familia (*fah-mee-lyah*)
5. padre (*pah-dray*) madre (*mah-dray*)
6. mi hermana (*mee er-mah-nah*)

7. estudia (*ays-too-dyah*) lengua (*layn-gwah*)
8. en la escuela (*ayn lah ays-kway-lah*)
9. hablamos (*ah-blah-mohs*)
10. además (*ah-day-mahs*)
11. puertorriqueños (*pwer-toh-rree-kay-ñohs*)
12. adiós (*ah-dyohs*)

CAPÍTULO 3 (TRES)

You now have a good working knowledge of Spanish pronunciation and are ready for a more intimate study of the language. However, pronunciation must at no time be neglected. Practice conscientiously the pronunciation aids after each conversational text and follow all directions for reading aloud and speaking. Remember: the only way you can learn to speak a language is by speaking it.

This chapter will introduce you to Mr. Adams, a New York businessman who is as eager as you are to learn Spanish. You will also meet his congenial teacher, Señor López, a Mexican living in New York. As he teaches Mr. Adams he will also teach you in a pleasant and interesting way.

So Buena Suerte (Good Luck) and Buen Viaje (Happy Voyage) as you accompany Mr. Adams on the road which leads to a practical knowledge of the Spanish language.

PARTE PRIMERA

¿Quién Es El Señor Adams?
Instrucciones para estudiar.

Who Is Mr. Adams?
Instructions for study.

1. Read the Spanish text silently, referring to the English only when necessary to get the meaning.
2. Cover up the English text and read the Spanish text silently.
3. Study the Pronunciation and Spelling Aids which follow the text. Then read the Spanish text aloud, pronouncing carefully.
4. Study the section "Building Vocabulary."
5. Do the exercise "Completion of Text."
6. Proceed to Parte Segunda (Part Second).
7. Follow these instructions with the conversational texts in succeeding chapters.

1. El señor Adams es un comerciante de Nueva York. Es norteamericano.

2. Vive con su familia en uno de los suburbios de la ciudad.

3. En la familia Adams hay seis personas: el padre, el señor Adams; la madre, la señora Adams; dos hijos, y dos hijas. El señor Adams es un hombre de cuarenta años de edad. La señora Adams es una mujer de treinta y cinco años.

4. Los hijos se llaman Felipe y Guillermo. Las hijas se llaman Rosita y Anita.

5. La casa del señor Adams tiene siete cuartos: el comedor, la sala, la cocina, tres dormitorios, y un cuarto de baño. Hay también un zaguán.

6. Es una casa particular, y todos los cuartos están en un piso.

1. Mr. Adams is a business man of New York. He is a North American.

2. He lives with his family in one of the suburbs of the city.

3. In the Adams family there are six persons: the father, Mr. Adams; the mother, Mrs. Adams; two sons, and two daughters. Mr. Adams is a man forty years of age. Mrs. Adams is a woman of thirty-five years.

4. The sons are named Philip and William. The daughters are named Rosie and Annie.[1]

5. The house of Mr. Adams has seven rooms: the dining room, the living room, the kitchen, three bedrooms, and a bathroom. There is also a vestibule.

6. It is a private house and all the rooms are on one floor.

7. La oficina del señor Adams está en la calle Whitehall.

8. Está en el décimo piso de un edificio muy grande.

9. El lunes, el martes, el miércoles, el jueves, y el viernes, el señor Adams va por tren a su oficina en la ciudad.

10. Allí trabaja diligentemente todo el día.

7. The office of Mr. Adams is on Whitehall Street.

8. It is on the tenth floor of a very big building.

9. On Monday, Tuesday, Wednesday, Thursday and Friday, Mr. Adams goes by train to his office in the city.

10. There he works diligently all day.

NOTE: 1. Literally (word for word): The sons call themselves Philip and William. The daughters call themselves Rosie and Annie. *Lit.* will be used hereafter as an abbreviation for literally.

Pronunciation and Spelling Aids

1. Practice Aloud:

ins-truc-**cio**-nes	su-**bur**-bios	par-ti-**cu**-lar
co-mer-**cian**-te	co-**me**-dor	o-**fi**-ci-na
fa-**mi**-lia	dor-**mi**-to-rios	**ca**-lle (cah-yay)
nor-te-a-me-**ri**-ca-no	Gui-**ller**-mo (gee-yer-moh)	za-**guán** (sah-gwahn)

2. The **u** in gui (Gui-ller-mo) is silent. Its purpose is to show that the **g** is hard as in *gold*. Without silent **u**, it would be like **g** in gente (*hayn-tay*). Remember: **g** before **e** or **i** is pronounced like Span. **j.**

Building Vocabulary

A. La Familia   The Family

el padre	the father	el hermano	the brother
la madre	the mother	la hermana	the sister
el hijo	the son	el tío	the uncle
la hija	the daughter	la tía	the aunt
el niño	the child (little boy)	el señor	the gentleman
la niña	the child (little girl)	la señora	the lady, Mrs.
el muchacho	the boy (teen age)	el hombre	the man
la muchacha	the girl (teen age)	la mujer	the woman

B. Los Cuartos de la Casa   The Rooms of the House

el comedor	the dining room	el dormitorio	the bedroom
la sala	the living room	la recámara (Mex.)	the bedroom
la cocina	the kitchen	el cuarto de baño	the bathroom
el cuarto	the room	el zaguán	the vestibule

Expresiones Importantes   Important Expressions

por tren	by train	todo el día	all day

Exercise No. 1—Completion of Text

For maximum benefit follow these instructions carefully in all "Completion of Text" exercises.

1. Complete each sentence by putting the English words into Spanish. Where you can, do this from memory.

2. If you do not remember the words refer to the Spanish text. There you will find the words in the order of their appearance in the sentences. You have only to reread the text to find them easily.

3. When you have completed the sentence with the needed words, read the complete sentence aloud in Spanish.

4. It will be a great help to your memory if you write each completed sentence. This is true for all exercises.

5. The correct Spanish words for the "Completion of Text Exercises" are in the Answer Section of this book, along with the answers to all other exercises. Check all your answers.

WARNING: Never refer to the English Text when you do the Completion of Text Exercise.

Ejemplo (Example): 1. **El señor Adams es un comerciante de Nueva York.**

1. **El señor Adams es un** (business man) **de Nueva York.**
2. **¿**(Who) **es el señor Adams?**
3. **Vive** (with) **su familia.**
4. **El señor Adams es el** (father)**.**
5. **La señora Adams es la** (mother)**.**
6. (There are) **seis personas.**
7. **Los hijos** (are called) **Felipe y Guillermo.**
8. **En** (his) **familia hay seis personas.**
9. **Es una casa** (private)**.**
10. (All the rooms) **están en un piso.**
11. **La oficina está en el décimo** (floor)**.**
12. **Está en la** (street) **Whitehall.**
13. **El edificio es** (big)**.**
14. (There) **trabaja el señor Adams** (all day)**.**
15. **Su oficina está en la** (city)**.**

PARTE SEGUNDA

Grammar Notes

1. *The Definite Article.* Note the four forms of the definite article.

	masculine			feminine	
Singular:	**el** padre	*the* father		**la** madre	*the* mother
Plural:	**los** padres	*the* fathers		**las** madres	*the* mothers

The definite article has four forms. These agree with their nouns in number and gender.

2. *The Gender of Nouns*

a. Nouns are either masculine or feminine in gender. This is true for thing-nouns as well as person-nouns. Thus:

el señor	el hijo	el cuarto	el piso	el comedor
la señora	la hija	la sala	la calle	la casa

b. Nouns ending in -o are usually masculine. Nouns ending in -a are usually feminine.

c. The definite article must be repeated before each noun to which it refers. Thus: **el padre y la madre** *the* father and mother.

d. Many nouns for persons have a masculine form in -o and a feminine form in -a. Thus: **el hermano** the brother, **la hermana** the sister; **el muchacho** the boy, **la muchacha** the girl; **el tío** the uncle, **la tía** the aunt; **el esposo** the husband, **la esposa** the wife.

3. *The Plural of Nouns.* Note the singular and plural of the following nouns.

el padre	el hermano	la casa	la mujer	el señor	la ciudad
los padres[1]	los hermanos	las casas	las mujeres	los señores	las ciudades

To form the plural of nouns add **-s** if the nouns end in a vowel. Add **-es** if the nouns end in a consonant.

NOTE: 1. **los padres** means either *the fathers*, or *the parents*; **los hermanos** *the brothers*, or *brother(s) and sister(s)*; **los hijos** *the sons, son(s) and daughter(s)*, or *children*. In such words the plural masculine may include both genders.

4. *The Indefinite Article.* Note the four forms of the indefinite article.

un cuarto	*a* room		**una** casa	*a* house
unos cuartos	*some* rooms		**unas** casas	*some* houses

un *a* or *one*, is used before a masculine noun; **una** *a* or *one*, before a feminine noun; **unos,** *some*, before a masculine plural; **unas** *some*, before a feminine plural.

5. *Some Common Verbs*

es	(he, she, it) is	**vive**	(he, she, it) lives
está	(he, she, it) is (located)	**tiene**	(he, she, it) has
están	(they) are (located)	**se llaman**	they are named, or their names are
hay	there is, there are		(*Lit.* they call themselves)

NOTE: The subject pronouns corresponding to *he, she, it* and *they,* are usually omitted in Spanish, since the ending of the verb indicates the subject pronoun quite clearly.

PARTE TERCERA

Ejercicios (Exercises) No. 2A-2B-2C

2A. Replace the English articles by the correct Spanish articles.

Ejemplo: (La) familia Adams vive en Nueva York.

1. (The) familia Adams vive en Nueva York.
2. Nueva York es (a) ciudad grande.
3. (The) casa está en (the) suburbios.
4. (The) padre es el señor Adams; (the) madre es la señora Adams.
5. Anita es (a) hija; Felipe es (a) hijo.
6. (The) dormitorio es grande.
7. (The) cuartos están en (one) piso.
8. (Some) muchachos están en (the) sala; (some) muchachas están en (the) cocina.
9. (The) niños están en (the) calle.
10. (The) hermanos y (the) hermanas están en (the) ciudad.

2B. Change the following nouns into the plural.

1. la calle
2. el comedor
3. el cuarto
4. el señor
5. la recámara
6. la cocina
7. la madre
8. el padre
9. la sala
10. la hija
11. la ciudad
12. el año
13. la mujer
14. el hombre
15. el tío

2C. Translate into Spanish.

1. Mr. Adams is a North American.
2. He lives in New York.
3. There are six persons in the family.
4. The house has six rooms.
5. It is a private house.
6. Mrs. Adams is the mother.
7. Mr. Adams is the father.
8. The office is in Whitehall Street.
9. He goes by train to the city.
10. There he works all day.

Exercise No. 3

Preguntas Questions Respuestas Answers

Study and read aloud the questions and answers. Note: a) the questions words. b) the inverted question mark which begins all Spanish questions. c) the omission of subject pronouns in Spanish.

1. ¿Quién es el señor Adams?
   Es un comerciante de Nueva York.
2. ¿Es norteamericano?
   Sí, señor, es norteamericano.
3. ¿Dónde vive el señor Adams?
   Vive en los suburbios de la ciudad.
4. ¿Cuántas personas hay en su familia?
   Hay seis personas en su familia.
5. ¿Cómo se llaman sus hijos?
   Se llaman Felipe y Guillermo.
6. ¿Cómo se llaman sus hijas?
   Se llaman Rosita y Anita.
7. ¿Cuántos cuartos tiene la casa del señor Adams?
   Tiene siete cuartos.
8. ¿Dónde están todos los cuartos?
   Están en un piso.
9. ¿En qué calle está la oficina del señor Adams?
   Está en la calle Whitehall.
10. ¿Es grande el edificio?
    Sí, señor, es muy grande.

1. Who is Mr. Adams?
   He is a business man of New York.
2. Is he a North American?
   Yes, sir, he is a North American.
3. Where does Mr. Adams live?
   He lives in the suburbs of the city.
4. How many persons are there in his family?
   There are six persons in his family.
5. What are the names of his sons?
   They are named Philip and William.
6. What are the names of his daughters?
   They are named Rosie and Annie.
7. How many rooms has the house of Mr. Adams?
   It has seven rooms.
8. Where are all the rooms?
   They are on one floor.
9. In what street is the office of Mr. Adams?
   It is in Whitehall Street.
10. Is the building big?
    Yes, sir, it is very big.

CAPÍTULO 4 (CUATRO)

PARTE PRIMERA

¿Por qué estudia el Sr. Adams el español?

Why is Mr. Adams studying Spanish?

Instrucciones para estudiar. (See Chapter 3)

1. El Sr. Adams es importador.

2. Importa objetos de arte y otros artículos de México y de Guatemala.

3. En la primavera el Sr. Adams va a hacer un viaje a México. Desea visitar a su agente en la ciudad de México. Desea hablar con él en español.

4. También desea ver unos lugares de interés en México. Espera además ir a Guatemala, y tal vez a Colombia.

5. El Sr. Adams sabe leer el español un poco. Pero no habla español. Por eso estudia la lengua.

6. Su maestro es el Sr. López.

7. El Sr. López, amigo del Sr. Adams, es mexicano. Es un hombre de cuarenta y cinco años de edad.

8. Los martes y los jueves los dos señores tienen una cita, casi siempre en la casa del Sr. Adams. Allí hablan español.

9. El Sr. López es un maestro bueno.

10. El Sr. Adams es muy inteligente y aprende rápidamente.

11. En la primera conversación aprende de memoria este diálogo:

12. Buenos días, Sr. López. ¿Cómo está Ud?
Muy bien, gracias. ¿Y Ud?
Muy bien, gracias.

13. El Sr. Adams aprende también unos saludos y unas despedidas.

14. Buenos días. Buenas tardes. Buenas noches.

15. Adiós. Hasta la vista. Hasta luego. Hasta mañana.

1. Mr. Adams is an importer.

2. He imports art objects and other articles from Mexico and Guatemala.

3. In the spring Mr. Adams is going to make a trip to Mexico. He wants to visit his agent in the City of Mexico. He wants to speak with him in Spanish.

4. He also wants to see some places of interest in Mexico. He expects, moreover, to go to Guatemala, and perhaps to Colombia.

5. Mr. Adams knows how to read Spanish a little. But he does not speak Spanish. Therefore he is studying the language.

6. His teacher is Mr. Lopez.

7. Mr. Lopez, a friend of Mr. Adams, is a Mexican. He is a man forty-five years old.

8. On Tuesdays and Thursdays the two gentlemen have an appointment, almost always in the house of Mr. Adams. There they speak Spanish.

9. Mr. Lopez is a good teacher.

10. Mr. Adams is very intelligent and learns rapidly.

11. In the first lesson he learns this dialogue by heart.

12. Good day, Mr. Lopez. How are you?
Very well, thank you. And you?
Very well, thank you.

13. Mr. Adams also learns some salutations and farewells.

14. Good day. Good afternoon. Good night.

15. Good-by. Until we meet again. So long. Until tomorrow.

NOTE: All the expressions in sentence 15 are ways of saying *"Good-by."*

Pronunciation and Spelling Aids

1. Practice:

im-por-ta-**dor**	Gua-te-ma-la	rá-pi-da-men-te	a-llí (*ah-yee*)	a-de-**más**
im-**por**-ta	Co-**lom**-bia	de-**se**-a	in-te-li-**gen**-te	(*in-tay-lee-hayn-tay*)
ar-**tí**-cu-los	ciu-**dad** (*syoo-dahd*)	es-**tu**-dia	sa-**lu**-dos	a-**gen**-te
pri-ma-**ve**-ra	ma-**es**-tro	es-**pe**-ra	des-pe-**di**-das	**lue**-go

2. el = the   él = he or him

3. The name of countries are capitalized. The names of nationalities, languages (**español**, Spanish), days of the week, and months are written with small letters.

Building Vocabulary

A. Synonyms (Words of the Same Meaning)

1. **el negociante = el comerciante** business man   2. **también = además** also, moreover
3. **el maestro = el profesor** teacher (*m*) **la maestra = la profesora** teacher (*f*)

B. Antonyms (Words of Opposite Meaning)

1. **grande** big **pequeño** small   2. **bueno** good **malo** bad   3. **allí** there **aquí** here
4. **importador** importer **exportador** exporter   5. **el saludo** greeting **la despedida** farewell

C. Lenguas (Languages)

1. **el español** Spanish   3. **el francés** French   5. **el alemán** German
2. **el inglés** English   4. **el portugués** Portuguese   6. **el italiano** Italian

Expresiones Importantes

1. **Buenos días** Good morning (day)
2. **Buenas tardes** Good afternoon
3. **Buenas noches** Good evening (night)
4. **adiós** goodbye
5. **hasta la vista** until we meet again
6. **hasta luego** so long
7. **hasta mañana** until tomorrow
8. **de memoria** by heart
9. **por eso** therefore
10. **tal vez** perhaps

Exercise No. 4—Completion of Text

Follow carefully the instructions given in Exercise No. 1.

1. ¿(Who) es el Sr. Adams?
2. Es (a business man of New York).
3. (His office) **está en Nueva York.**
4. **Importa objetos de arte y** (other) **artículos.**
5. **En la primavera** (he is going) **a hacer un viaje.**
6. (He wants) **visitar la ciudad de México.**
7. **Espera** (moreover) **ir a Guatemala.**
8. (But) **no habla español.**
9. (He is studying) **la lengua.**
10. **Los** (Tuesdays) **y los** (Thursdays) **tienen una cita.**
11. **El Sr. Adams aprende** (rapidly).
12. **Es** (very intelligent).
13. **El Sr. López es** (Mexican).
14. **Es** (a good teacher).
15. **El Sr. Adams aprende un diálogo** (in the first conversation).

PARTE SEGUNDA

Grammar Notes

1. The Use of **es** and **está.**

In Spanish there are two words for *to be*, **ser** and **estar**. The form **es** comes from **ser**. The form **está** comes from **estar**. Both mean *he, she,* or *it is*.

a. The form **es** and other forms of **ser** are used in such questions and answers as:

¿Quién es el Sr. Adams?	Who is Mr. Adams?
Es un comerciante de Nueva York.	He is a New York business man.
¿Qué es el Sr. López?	What is Mr. Lopez?
Es un maestro de español.	He is a Spanish teacher.

b. The form **está**, and other forms of **estar**, are used in questions and answers that have to do with place. They really mean *is* or *are located*. Thus:

¿Dónde está la Sra. Adams?	Where is Mrs. Adams?
Está en casa.	She is at home.

Later you will learn more about the uses of **ser** and **estar.**

2. Some Common Verbs

habla	(he, she, it) speaks	sabe	(he, she, it) knows how
hablan	they speak	hablar	to speak
no habla	(he, she, it) does not speak	visitar	to visit
importa	(he, she, it) imports	leer	to read
estudia	(he, she, it) studies	ver	to see
desea	(he, she, it) wants	ir	to go
espera	(he, she, it) expects	va a hacer	he is going to make
aprende	(he, she, it) learns		

NOTE: The verb endings -a and -e mean *he, she,* or *it.* The verb endings -ar, -er, and -ir mean *to.*

3. Special Uses of the Definite Article

a. Use the definite article before titles when speaking about a person. Omit it when speaking to a person.

El Sr. Adams va a México.	Mr. Adams is going to Mexico.
Buenos días, Sr. Adams.	Good day, Mr. Adams.

b. Use the definite article before a language. Omit it if the language is used after the verb **hablar** or after **en.**

El francés es la lengua de Francia.	French is the language of France.
El Sr. Adams no habla francés.	Mr. Adams does not speak French.
en español *en* francés *en* inglés	*in* Spanish *in* French *in* English

PARTE TERCERA

Ejercicios (Exercises) No. 5A-5B-5C

5A. Complete the sentences with es or está as the sense requires.

Ejemplo: 1. El Sr. Adams es importador.

1. El Sr. Adams ―― importador.
2. ¿Dónde ―――― su oficina?
3. ¿Qué ――― el Sr. López?
4. La familia ――― en la sala.
5. ¿Quién ―――― norteamericano?
6. ¿―――― Carlos mexicano?
7. Su agente ――― en México.
8. La ciudad de Nueva York no ― en México.
9. ¿Qué ――― el Sr. Adams?
10. Carlos ―――― norteamericano.

5B. Select from Column II the word groups that best complete the sentences begun in Column 1.

Ejemplo: (1 d) El Sr. Adams desea hablar con su agente en español.

Column I	Column II
1. El Sr. Adams desea hablar	a) aprende rápidamente.
2. El Sr. Adams sabe leer	b) de México y Guatemala.
3. Es muy inteligente y por eso	c) en la casa del Sr. Adams.
4. Importa objetos de arte	d) con su agente en español.
5. Los dos señores tienen una cita	e) de cuarenta y cinco años de edad.
6. El Sr. López es un hombre	f) el español un poco.

5C. Find the corresponding Spanish words in the text or in "Building Vocabulary" and write them.

1. and	5. to	9. there	13. How are you?	17. small
2. in	6. perhaps	10. here	14. very well	18. good
3. with	7. but	11. almost	15. thank you	19. bad
4. also	8. therefore	12. always	16. big	20. rapidly

Exercise No. 6—Preguntas y Respuestas

Study and read aloud the questions and answers. Note: a) the word order.   b) the omission of subject pronouns.   c) that all question words have an accent mark.

1. ¿Quién es el maestro?
   El Sr. López es el maestro.
2. ¿Habla español?
   Sí, señor, habla español.
3. ¿Quién es el comerciante?
   El Sr. Adams es el comerciante.
4. ¿Habla español?
   No, señor, no habla español.
5. ¿Dónde está la oficina del Sr. Adams?
   Está en la calle Whitehall.
6. ¿Importa automóviles?
   No importa automóviles.
7. ¿Aprende rápidamente?
   Sí, señor, aprende rápidamente.
8. ¿Cuándo tienen los señores una cita?

   Los martes y los jueves tienen una cita.

9. ¿Es inteligente el Sr. Adams?
   Es muy inteligente.
10. ¿Por qué[1] estudia el español?
    Porque desea hacer un viaje a México.

1. Who is the teacher?
   Mr. Lopez is the teacher.
2. Does he speak Spanish?
   Yes, sir, he speaks Spanish.
3. Who is the merchant?
   Mr. Adams is the merchant.
4. Does he speak Spanish?
   No, sir, he does not speak Spanish.
5. Where is the office of Mr. Adams?
   It is in Whitehall Street.
6. Does he import automobiles.
   He does not import automobiles.
7. Does he learn rapidly?
   Yes, sir, he learns rapidly.
8. When do the gentlemen have an appointment?
   On Tuesdays and Thursdays they have an appointment.
9. Is Mr. Adams intelligent?
   He is very intelligent.
10. Why is he studying Spanish?
    Because he wants to make a trip to Mexico.

NOTE: 1. **por qué** means *why*.   **porque** means *because*.

CAPÍTULO 5 (CINCO)

PARTE PRIMERA

En la Sala del Señor Adams

1. **Es martes, 5 (cinco) de enero de 1954.**[1]
2. **Son las 8 (ocho) de la noche.**
3. **El señor Adams está sentado en la sala de su casa. El señor López está sentado cerca de él.**
4. **El señor López dice al señor Adams—Alrededor de nosotros hay muchas cosas; en la casa, en la calle, en la oficina, en el parque, en la ciudad y en el campo.**
5. **En los Estados Unidos y en Inglaterra es necesario saber los nombres de las cosas en inglés. En España y en Hispano-América es necesario saber los nombres de las cosas en español.**

6. **Estamos en la sala de su casa. Dígame, por favor ¿Qué es esto?**
7. **Es un piano. Mi esposa toca bien el piano.**
8. **Bueno. ¿Y qué está encima del piano?**
9. **Una lámpara y un libro de música.**

1. It is Tuesday, January 5, 1954.
2. It is eight o'clock in the evening.
3. Mr. Adams is seated in the living room of his house. Mr. Lopez is seated near him.
4. Mr. Lopez says to Mr. Adams. "Around us there are many things: in the house, in the street, in the office, in the park, in the city and in the country."
5. In the United States and in England it is necessary to know the names of things in English. In Spain and in Spanish America it is necessary to know the names of things in Spanish.

6. We are in the living room of your house. Tell me, please, "What is this?"
7. It is a piano. My wife plays the piano well.
8. Good. And what is on the piano?
9. A lamp and a music book (*Lit.* a book of music).

10. ¿Y qué está en la pared sobre el piano?
11. Es el retrato de mi esposa.
12. Excelente. Dígame, por favor, los nombres de otros objetos en la sala y dónde están.

13. Con mucho gusto.
14. El estante está delante de una ventana. El escritorio está cerca de la puerta. Una silla está cerca del escritorio. Encima del escritorio están un lápiz, una plumafuente, unos papeles, y unas cartas. Unos libros están en la mesita.
15. Bueno. Basta por hoy. Hasta la vista, señor Adams.
16. Hasta el jueves, señor López.

10. And what is on the wall over the piano?
11. It is the picture of my wife.
12. Excellent. Tell me, please, the names of other objects in the living room and where they are.
13. With pleasure.
14. The bookcase is in front of a window. The desk is near the door. A chair is near the desk. On the desk are a pencil, a fountain pen, some papers, and some letters. Some books are on the little table.
15. Good. Enough for today. So long, Mr. Adams.
16. Until Thursday, Mr. Lopez.

NOTE: 1. 1954 = mil novecientos cincuenta y cuatro

Pronunciation and Spelling Aids

1. Pronounce carefully.

al-re-de-dor	a-quí (*ah-kee*)	plu-ma-fuen-te	es-tan-te	Es-ta-dos U-ni-dos
es-cri-to-rio	ne-ce-sa-rio	ex-ce-len-te	dí-ga-me	In-gla-te-rra
lá-piz	via-ja	es-ta-mos	His-pa-no-A-mé-ri-ca	Es-pa-ña

2. All question words in Spanish have an accent mark.

quién (sing.)	who	cuándo	when	cuánto	how much
quiénes (plur.)	who	qué	what	cuántos	how many
dónde	where	cómo	how	por qué	why

Building Vocabulary

A. **En La Sala**   In the Living Room

la carta	letter	la mesa	table	la puerta	door
el escritorio	desk	la mesita	little table	el retrato	portrait
el estante	bookcase	el papel	paper	la silla	chair
la lámpara	lamp	la pared	wall	el sillón	armchair
el libro	book	la plumafuente	fountain pen	la ventana	window
el lápiz	pencil	la pluma	pen	el sofá	davenport

B. Some Common Prepositions

a	to, at	debajo de	under	con	with
de	of, from	delante de	in front of	en	in, on, at
alrededor de	around	detrás de	behind	entre	between
cerca de	near	encima de	on top of	sobre	over, above

Expresiones Importantes

1. está sentado	is seated	5. con mucho gusto	with pleasure
2. es necesario	it is necessary	6. basta por hoy	enough for today
3. por favor	please	7. son las ocho	it's 8 o'clock
4. dígame	tell me	8. cinco de enero	January 5

Exercise No. 7—Completion of Text

1. El señor (is seated) en la sala.
2. (There are) muchas cosas en la calle.
3. Es necesario (to know) los nombres.
4. (Tell me) — ¿Qué es esto?
5. (My wife) toca bien el piano.
6. El retrato está (over the piano).
7. En el escritorio están (a pencil, a pen, and some papers).
8. Algunos libros (are on the little table)
9. (Enough) por hoy.
10. (Until Thursday) Sr. López.

PARTE SEGUNDA
Grammar Notes

1. The Contractions **del** and **al**

   a. The preposition **de** (*of, from*) contracts with **el** and forms **del** (*of, from the*)

   ¿Dónde está la oficina *del* comerciante?   Where is the house *of the* merchant?

   b. The preposition **a** (*to*) contracts with **el**, and forms **al** (*to the*).

   El maestro habla *al* comerciante.   The teacher speaks *to the* merchant.

   c. The other forms of the definite article do not contract with **de** or **a**.

   El padre *de los* niños está aquí.   The father *of the* children is here.

   Los niños van *a la* escuela.   The children go *to* school.

2. Possession

   a. Possession is indicated by a phrase with **de**, never by means of an apostrophe.

   la casa del maestro   the house *of the teacher*   the teacher's house
   el tío de María   the uncle *of Mary*   Mary's uncle

   b. de quién, de quiénes   whose, of whom

   ¿De quién es la oficina?   Whose office is it?
   Es la oficina del Sr. Adams.   It is Mr. Adams' office.
   ¿De quiénes son estos libros?   Whose are these books?
   Son los libros de los alumnos.   They are the students' books.

3. Omission of the Indefinite Article

   Omit the indefinite article with words indicating professions and occupations after the verb **ser** *to be*. If such words are modified, the indefinite article is not omitted.

   El Sr. Adams es negociante.   Mr. Adams is a business man.
   Es un negociante bueno.   He is a good business man.

PARTE TERCERA
Ejercicios (Exercises) No. 8A-8B-8C-8D

8A. Write the singular, plural, and meaning of the following nouns. Use the definite article.

Ejemplo: **el edificio los edificios** building

1. calle	3. pared	5. señor	7. papel	9. estante
2. oficina	4. silla	6. mesa	8. puerta	10. ventana

8B. Complete in Spanish. First review "Building Vocabulary B."

Ejemplo: **1. El lápiz está debajo de los papeles.**

1. **El lápiz está** (under) **los papeles.**
2. **Un parque está** (near) **la casa.**
3. (On top of the) **escritorio hay muchas cartas.**
4. **Un retrato está** (above) **el piano.**
5. **Un sillón está** (between) **las ventanas.**
6. **Un automóvil está** (in front of the) **edificio.**
7. **Las sillas están** (around) **la mesa.**
8. **¿Qué está** (behind) **la puerta?**
9. **¿Qué está** (under) **la mesa?**
10. **¿Qué está** (near the) **escritorio?**

8C. Use **del, de la, de los, de las, al, a la, a los,** or **a las** as required. First review "Grammar Notes 1."

Ejemplo: **1. La sala de la casa es grande.**

1. **La sala** (of the) **casa es grande.**
2. **María habla** (to the) **maestro.**
3. **La señora de Gómez es la maestra** (of the) **muchachas.**
4. **El Sr. López es un amigo** (of the) **negociante.**
5. **Los señores van** (to the) **puerta.**
6. **Felipe es un amigo** (of the) **niños.**

7. **El maestro habla** (at the) **alumnos.**

8. **El negociante va por tren** (to the) **ciudad.**

9. **¿Quién habla** (to the) **padre?**

10. **¿Quién habla** (to the) **alumnas?**

8D. Practice the Spanish aloud.

1. **¿De quién es este sombrero?**
   Es el sombrero de Juan.

2. **¿Es este estante de Carlos o de Maria?**
   Es de María.

3. **¿Es esta plumafuente de él o de ella?**
   Es de ella.

4. **¿De quién es el retrato?**
   Es el retrato de la señora Adams.

5. **¿De quiénes son estos papeles?**
   Son los papeles de los maestros.

1. Whose is this hat?
   It is John's hat.

2. Is this desk Charles' or Mary's?
   It is Mary's.

3. Is this fountain pen his or hers? (*Lit.* of him or of her)
   It is hers. (*Lit.* of her)

4. Whose portrait is it?
   It is Mrs. Adams' portrait.

5. Whose are these papers?
   They are the teachers' papers.

Exercise No. 9—Preguntas

Answer in complete Spanish sentences. Consult the text for your answers. The correct answers to these questions and those in all later lessons are given in the Answer Section of the Appendix. Check all your answers.

1. **¿Dónde está sentado el Sr. Adams?**
2. **¿Quién está sentado cerca de él?**
3. **¿Hay muchas cosas alrededor de nosotros?**
4. **¿Hay muchas cosas en la calle?**
5. **¿Quién toca bien el piano?**
6. **¿Dónde está un libro de música?**
7. **¿Dónde está el retrato de la Sra. Adams?**
8. **¿Qué está delante de una ventana?**
9. **¿Dónde está el escritorio?**
10. **¿Qué está cerca del escritorio?**
11. **¿Dónde están unas cartas?**
12. **¿Dónde están unos libros?**

REPASO (REVIEW) 1
CAPÍTULOS 1–5 PARTE PRIMERA

Each Review Chapter will begin with a summary of the most important words and expressions that have occurred in the chapters reviewed. Check yourself as follows:

1. Cover up the English words on the right of the page with a piece of paper or blotter. Read one Spanish word at a time aloud and give the English meaning. Uncover the English word of the same number in order to check.

2. Cover up the Spanish words. Say aloud, one at a time, the Spanish for each English word. Uncover the Spanish word to check.

3. Write the words you have difficulty in remembering, three or four times.

Repaso de Palabras (Word Review)

NOUNS

1. el alumno	17. la familia	33. el niño	1. student (m)	17. family	33. child (m)
2. la alumna	18. el hermano	34. la niña	2. student (f)	18. brother	34. child (f)
3. el amigo	19. la hermana	35. el objeto	3. friend (m)	19. sister	35. object
4. el automóvil	20. el hijo	36. el padre	4. automobile	20. son	36. father
5. la calle	21. la hija	37. el papel	5. street	21. daughter	37. paper
6. la casa	22. el hombre	38. la plumafuente	6. house	22. man	38. fountain pen
7. el campo	23. el lápiz	39. la puerta	7. country	23. pencil	39. door
8. la carta	24. la lengua	40. la sala	8. letter	24. language	40. living room
9. la ciudad	25. el lugar	41. el señor	9. city	25. place	41. Mr.
10. el comedor	26. el libro	42. la señora	10. dining room	26. book	42. Mrs.
11. la cosa	27. la madre	43. la silla	11. thing	27. mother	43. chair
12. el cuarto	28. la mesa	44. el tío	12. room	28. table	44. uncle
13. el día	29. la mujer	45. la tía	13. day	29. woman	45. aunt
14. el edificio	30. el maestro	46. el tren	14. building	30. teacher (m)	46. train
15. el escritorio	31. el muchacho	47. la ventana	15. desk	31. boy	47. window
16. la esposa	32. la muchacha	48. el viaje	16. wife	32. girl	48. trip

VERBS

1. es	9. aprende	17. saber	1. he (is)	9. he learns	17. to know
2. está	10. sabe	18. ver	2. he is (place)	10. he knows (how)	18. to see
3. estamos	11. tiene	19. ir	3. we are (place)	11. he has	19. to go
4. están	12. vive	20. pedir	4. they are (place)	12. he lives	20. to ask for
5. espera	13. hablar	21. hay	5. he expects	13. to speak	21. there is
6. estudia	14. visitar	22. dígame	6. he studies	14. to visit	22. tell me
7. habla	15. hacer		7. he speaks	15. to make (do)	
8. va	16. leer		8. he goes	16. to read	

NOTE: The same form of the verb is good for *he, she, it,* and *you* (*usted*). Thus: es = *he, she, it* is, *you* are   espera = *he, she, it* expects, *you* expect.

ADJECTIVES

1. bueno	6. mi	11. sentado	1. good	6. my	11. seated
2. excelente	7. mucho	12. su	2. excellent	7. much	12. his, her, its
3. grande	8. necesario	13. todos	3. great, big	8. necessary	13. all
4. importante	9. otro	14. un poco	4. important	9. other	14. a little
5. malo	10. pequeño		5. bad	10. small	

ADVERBS

1. allí	6. diligentemente	11. además	1. there	6. diligently	11. moreover
2. aquí	7. muy	12. si	2. here	7. very	12. if
3. basta	8. rápidamente	13. sí	3. enough	8. rapidly	13. yes
4. bien	9. siempre	14. ya	4. well	9. always	14. now, already
5. casi	10. también		5. almost	10. also	

PREPOSITIONS

1. a	6. del	11. delante de	1. to, at	6. of the	11. in front of
2. al	7. sobre	12. detrás de	2. to the	7. above	12. behind
3. con	8. alrededor de	13. encima de	3. with	8. around	13. on top of
4. en	9. cerca de	14. por	4. in, on	9. near	14. for, by,
5. de	10. debajo de		5. of, from	10. under	through

QUESTION WORDS

1. cómo	4. dónde	6. cuánto	1. how	4. where	6. how much
2. qué	5. quién	7. cuántos (as)	2. what, which	5. who	7. how many
3. por qué			3. why		

CONJUNCTIONS

1. o	2. pero	3. porque	4. y	1. or	2. but	3. because	4. and

IMPORTANT EXPRESSIONS

1. basta	11. en casa	1. enough	11. at home
2. por hoy	12. es necesario	2. for today	12. it is necessary
3. Buenos días	13. hasta luego	3. Good day	13. so long
4. Buenas noches	14. hasta mañana	4. Good night	14. until tomorrow
5. Buenas tardes	15. hasta la vista	5. Good afternoon	15. so long
6. Adiós	16. por eso	6. Goodbye	16. therefore
7. ¿Cómo está Ud?	17. por favor	7. How are you?	17. please
8. con mucho gusto	18. ¿Qué es esto?	8. with pleasure	18. What is this?
9. muy bien	19. todo el día	9. very well	19. all day
10. gracias	20. tal vez	10. thanks	20. perhaps

PARTE SEGUNDA

Ejercicio 10. From Group II select the antonym (opposite) for each word in Group I.

Group I		Group II	
1. bueno	7. mucho	a. delante de	g. malo
2. sí	8. detrás de	b. el campo	h. grande
3. allí	9. buenos días	c. la muchacha	i. aquí
4. pequeño	10. el muchacho	d. buenas noches	j. debajo de
5. encima de	11. la ciudad	e. no	k. poco
6. padre	12. la mujer	f. el hombre	l. madre

Ejercicio 11. Complete the following sentences in Spanish.

1. **Trabajo** (all day).
2. **Dígame** (please).
3. (Perhaps) **está en la oficina.**
4. (Good-afternoon) **señor.**
5. **Aprende los saludos** (with pleasure).
6. (Therefore) **estudia el español.**
7. ¿(How) **está Ud?**
8. ¿(Where) **vive el señor?**
9. ¿(What) **es esto?**
10. ¿(Who) **es negociante?**

Ejercicio 12. Select the group of words in the right-hand column which best completes each sentence begun in the left-hand column.

Ejemplo: (1 d) **En la familia Adams hay seis personas.**

1. **En la familia Adams**
2. **La casa del Sr. Adams**
3. **El Sr. Adams va por tren**
4. **Estudia el español**
5. **Trabaja todo el día**
6. **Sabe leer el español**
7. **Aprende rápidamente**
8. **Los martes y los jueves**
9. **En la primera conversación**
10. **La esposa del Sr. Adams**
11. **El Sr. Adams va a hacer**

a. **aprende los saludos y las despedidas.**
b. **toca bien el piano.**
c. **porque es muy inteligente.**
d. **hay seis personas.**
e. **un viaje a México.**
f. **está en los suburbios.**
g. **pero no habla la lengua.**
h. **en su oficina.**
i. **a la ciudad.**
j. **los señores tienen una cita.**
k. **porque desea hablar la lengua.**

Ejercicio 13. Complete these sentences in Spanish.

1. **El automóvil está** (in front of the house).
2. **Las sillas están** (near the door).
3. **Los suburbios están** (around the city).
4. **El Sr. Adams está sentado** (behind the desk).
5. **Las lámparas están** (on top of the piano).
6. (The boy's books = the books of the boy) **están en la mesa.**
7. (The girls' mother = the mother of the girls) **está en casa.**
8. (Philip's brother) **es médico.**
9. (Mary's father) **es profesor.**
10. (The children's teacher) **es mexicano.**

PARTE TERCERA

Practice all Spanish dialogues aloud:

Diálogo 1

¿Dónde Está La Calle Lerma?

1. **Por favor, señor, ¿Dónde está la calle Lerma?**
2. **Siga adelante, señorita.**
3. **¿Cuántas cuadras?**
4. **Cinco cuadras, señorita.**
5. **Muchas gracias.**
6. **De nada.**

1. Please sir, where is Lerma Street?
2. Continue straight ahead, Miss.
3. How many blocks?
4. Five blocks, Miss.
5. Many thanks.
6. Don't mention it. (You're welcome)

Diálogo 2

¿Dónde Para El Camión?

1. **Favor de decirme, señor,—¿Dónde para el camión?**
2. **Para en la esquina allá, señorita.**
3. **Muchas gracias, señor.**
4. **No hay de qué.**

1. Please tell me, sir, where does the bus stop?
2. It stops at the corner over there, Miss.
3. Many thanks, sir.
4. Don't mention it (you're welcome).

LECTURA (READING SELECTION)

Exercise No. 14—How to Read the Lecturas

1. Read the passage silently from beginning to end to get the meaning as a whole.

2. Reread the passage looking up any words you may have forgotten, in the Spanish-English dictionary at the end of this book. There are few new words in the Lecturas of the Review Chapters and the meaning of these is given in parentheses.

3. Read the passage silently a third time. Then translate it and check your translation with that given in the answer section of the appendix.

4. Follow this procedure in all succeeding Lecturas.

Exercise No. 14A—El Señor Adams, Comerciante De Nueva York

El señor Adams es un comerciante norteamericano que (who) importa objetos de arte de México. Por eso desea hacer un viaje a México en la primavera. Desea hablar con su agente y visitar unos lugares de interés en México. Pero no sabe hablar español.

El señor Adams tiene un maestro bueno. Es un mexicano que vive en Nueva York y se llama el señor López. Los martes y los jueves el maestro va por tren a la casa de su estudiante. Allí los dos señores hablan un poco en español. El señor Adams es muy inteligente y aprende rápidamente. Por ejemplo (For example), en la primera conversación aprende de memoria los saludos y las despedidas. Ya (already) sabe decir (to say)—Buenos días,—¿Cómo está Ud.?—Hasta la vista—y—Hasta mañana. Ya sabe decir en español los nombres de muchas cosas que (which) están en su sala, y sabe contestar (to answer) bien a las preguntas—¿Qué es esto?—y—¿Dónde está . . .?

El señor López está muy satisfecho (satisfied) con el progreso de su estudiante y dice (says), —Bueno. Basta por hoy. Hasta luego.

CAPÍTULO 6 (SEIS)

PARTE PRIMERA

Los Verbos son Importantes, Señor

1. Los señores Adams y López están sentados en la sala del señor Adams. El Sr. López principia a hablar. El señor Adams le escucha con atención.[1]

2. Ya sabe Ud. que los nombres de las cosas y de las personas son importantes. Pero los verbos son importantes también, señor. No es posible formar una frase sin verbos. Tampoco es posible conversar sin verbos.

3. Vamos a practicar unos verbos corrientes. Voy a hacer unas preguntas. Yo pregunto y Ud. contesta. Si Ud. no sabe la respuesta, diga, por favor—No sé.

4. Bueno, dice el señor Adams. Voy a decir — No sé, si no sé la respuesta.

5. ¿Es Ud. comerciante?

6. Sí, señor, soy comerciante, importador de objetos de arte y otros artículos de varios países hispano-americanos y sobre todo de México.

7. ¿Y por qué estudia Ud. el español?

1. Mr. Lopez and Mr. Adams are seated in the living room of Mr. Adams. Mr. Lopez begins to speak. Mr. Adams listens to him attentively.

2. You already know that the names of things and of persons are important. But verbs are important, too, sir. It is not possible to make a sentence without verbs. Neither is it possible to converse without verbs.

3. We are going to practice some common verbs. I am going to ask some questions. I ask and you answer. If you do not know the answer, please say "I do not know."

4. "Good," says Mr. Adams. "I will say 'I don't know,' if I don't know the answer."

5. Are you a businessman?

6. Yes, sir, I am a businessman, importer of art objects and other things from various Spanish American countries and especially from Mexico.

7. And why are you studying Spanish?

8. Estudio el español porque deseo hacer un viaje a México para visitar a mi agente allí. Deseo hablar con él en español. Él no habla inglés.

9. ¿Espera Ud. visitar otros países?

10. Espero ir además a Guatemala, y tal vez a Colombia.

11. ¿Cuándo sale Ud. de Nueva York para México?

12. Salgo el 31 (treinta y uno) de mayo.

13. ¿Viaja Ud. por tren, por barco o por avión?

14. Viajo por avión porque es el modo más rápido.

15. ¿Cuánto cuesta el vuelo?

16. No sé. Mañana voy a pedir informes y una reservación.

17. Excelente, señor. Ud. aprende el español muy rápidamente.

18. Gracias. Es favor que Ud. me hace.

19. No es favor. Es verdad. Pues, basta por hoy. Hasta luego.

20. Hasta el próximo jueves.

8. I am studying Spanish because I want to take a trip to Mexico to visit my agent there. I want to speak with him in Spanish. He does not speak English.

9. Do you expect to visit other countries?

10. I expect to go besides to Guatemala, and perhaps Colombia.

11. When do you leave New York for Mexico?

12. I am leaving May 31.

13. Are you traveling by train, by boat or by plane?

14. I am traveling by plane because it is the quickest way.

15. How much does the flight cost?

16. I do not know. Tomorrow I am going to ask for information and a reservation.

17. Excellent, sir. You are learning Spanish very quickly.

18. Thank you. You flatter me.[2]

19. It is not flattery. It is the truth. Well, enough for today. So long.

20. Until next Thursday.

NOTE: 1. le *him* or *to him*. It is an object pronoun. Object pronouns usually precede the verb.

NOTE: 2. *Lit.* It is a favor that you are doing me.

Pronunciation and Spelling Aids

1. Practice:

a-ten-ción	ha-**cer**	es-tu-dio	via-jo	a-pren-de	es-tán
re-ser-va-ción	prac-ti-**car**	de-se-o	es-tu-dia	sa-le	co-rrien-tes
con-ver-sar	de-cir	es-pe-ro	es-pe-ra	es-tá	via-ja
vi-si-tar	pre-gun-tar	sal-go	di-ce		

2. pa-í-ses (*pah-ee-says*). The accent mark over the í shows that the í is a separate syllable. Otherwise ai would be pronounced like *ai* in the Eng. word *aisle* and in the Span. word ai-re.

Building Vocabulary

A. **Los Países de Sud-América**

1. La Argentina   3. Colombia   5. El Ecuador   7. El Perú   9. Venezuela
2. Bolivia   4. Chile   6. El Paraguay   8. El Uruguay   10. El Brasil

Los habitantes (inhabitants) del Brasil hablan portugués. Los habitantes de los otros países de Sud-America hablan español.

B. **Algunos Países de Europa** (*ayoo-roh-pah*)   Some Countries of Europe

1. **Inglaterra** England   3. **Alemania** Germany   5. **España** Spain
2. **Francia** France   4. **Italia** Italy   6. **Portugal** Portugal

C. **Los Países de Norte America**   The Countries of North America

1. **Los Estados Unidos** The United States   2. **México** Mexico   3. **El Cánada** Canada

Expresiones Importantes

1. Es favor que Ud. me hace	You flatter me.
2. hacer preguntas	to ask questions
3. hacer un viaje	to take a trip
4. por avión (tren, barco)	by plane (train, boat)
5. sobre todo	above all, especially

Exercise No. 15—Completion of Text

Complete the following sentences based on the text.

1. Los verbos (are important) señor.
2. Vamos a practicar (some common verbs).
3. ¿(Why) estudia Ud. el español?
4. (Because) deseo visitar a (my) agente.
5. Deseo hablar (with him in Spanish).
6. Espero ir (to other countries).
7. ¿Viaja Ud. (by train or by plane)?
8. ¿(How much) cuesta el vuelo?
9. Ud. aprende (very rapidly).
10. Enough for today.

PARTE SEGUNDA

Grammar Notes

1. About Verb Endings

The infinitive is the base form of the verb. In English it is expressed by *to*. Thus: *to* speak, *to* learn, *to* live, etc.

In Spanish there are infinitive endings which mean *to*. Thus:

hablar *to* speak   aprender *to* learn   vivir *to* live

The infinitives of all Spanish verbs end in **-ar -er** or **-ir**. That part of the verb which is left after the ending is removed is called the stem. Thus **habl-, aprend-, viv-,** are the stems of **hablar, aprender,** and **vivir.**

The infinitive endings of the verb are dropped and other endings added to the stem as the verb is used in various persons and tenses.

Let us see how the endings change, and what they mean, in the present tense of the verb **hablar.**

2. Present Tense of **hablar.** Model Regular **-ar** Verb

(yo)	**habl-o**	I speak	(nosotros)	**habl-amos**	we speak
(tú)	**habl-as**	you speak (fam.)	(vosotros)	**habl-áis**	you speak (fam.)
usted ⎤	**habl-a**	you speak	ustedes ⎤	**habl-an**	you speak
(él) ⎬	**habl-a**	he, it speaks	(ellos) ⎬	**habl-an**	they (m) speak
(ella) ⎦	**habl-a**	she, it speaks	(ellas) ⎦	**habl-an**	they (f) speak

a. The endings of a regular **-ar** verb in the present tense are:

singular -o -as -a   plural -amos -áis -an

NOTE: The verb ending **-a** is used with **usted, él** and **ella.**
      The verb ending **-an** is used with **ustedes, ellos** and **ellas.**

b. Since the ending indicates the subject pronoun quite clearly, subject pronouns, except **usted** (**Ud.**) and **ustedes** (**Uds.**) are usually omitted. They may be used for emphasis or to make the meaning clear.

Yo hablo inglés. **Ella** habla francés.   I speak English. She speaks French.

c. The present tense may be translated: I speak, I do speak, I am speaking, etc.

d. **nosotros** and **vosotros** have feminine forms **nosotras, vosotras.**

3. Polite and Familiar *you.*

a. **usted** (*you, sing.*) and **ustedes** (*you, plur.*) are the polite forms of address. They are used most of the time.

¿Habla Ud. francés, Sr. Muñoz?   Do you speak French, Mr. Munoz?
Uds. hablan muy bien, señoras.   You speak very well, ladies.

b. **tú** (*you, sing.*) and **vosotros(as)** (*you, plur.*) are the familiar forms of address. They are used with members of the family, with good friends, and with children. In Latin America (L.A.) the vosotros form is rarely used. ustedes takes its place.

¿Hablas (tú) inglés, papá?	Do you speak English, papa?
(Vosotros) habláis ⎫	
L.A.—Ustedes hablan ⎬ **demasiado alto, niños.**	You speak too loudly, children.

4. The Negative and Interrogative.

a. To form the negative, put the word **no** (*not*) directly before the verb.

No hablamos portugués.	We do not speak Portuguese.

b. To form a question, place the subject after the verb. If the subject is not expressed, the double question mark is sufficient.

¿Platican los alumnos?	Are the students chatting?
¿No van a hacer un viaje?	Are they not going to make a trip?

PARTE TERCERA

Ejercicios (Exercises) No. 16A-16B-16C-16D

16A. Translate the following -ar verbs. They take the same endings as the model **-ar** verb, **hablar**.

1. escuchar	4. formar	7. practicar	10. contestar	13. importar
2. desear	5. esperar	8. viajar	11. platicar	14. tocar (an instrument)
3. principiar	6. conversar	9. preguntar	12. estudiar	15. visitar

16B. Practice aloud the following brief dialogues. Translate them.

1. ¿Habla Ud. español?
   Sí, hablo español.
   ¿Qué lenguas habla su maestro?
   Habla inglés, español y francés.
2. ¿Quién toca el piano?
   María toca el piano.
   ¿No tocas tú el piano, Rosita?
   No, no toco el piano.

3. ¿Estudian los alumnos la lección?
   No, no estudian la lección.
   ¿Platican en español?
   Sí, platican en español.
4. ¿Escuchan Uds. con atención
   cuando el maestro habla?
   Sí, escuchamos con atención
   cuando el maestro habla.

16C. Copy each sentence filling in the correct verb endings.

Ejemplo: El Sr. Adams no habla español.

1. El Sr. Adams no habl ——— español.
2. Nosotros estudi ——— la lección.
3. ¿Quién import ——— objetos de arte?
4. ¿Dese ——— Ud. aprender a hablar español?
5. Yo esper ——— ir a Cuba.
6. Uds. platic ——— mucho.

7. Juan y Carlos (= ellos) practic ——— la pronunciación.
8. ¿Viaj ——— el señor por tren o por avión?
9. Pablo y yo (= nosotros) esper ——— salir mañana.
10. Eva y Ana (= ellas) principi ——— a estudiar.

16D. Complete with the form of the verb that fits the pronoun.

Ejemplo: yo principio

1. yo (principiar)	4. ella (conversar)	7. ellas (contestar)	10. yo no (visitar)
2. él no (escuchar)	5. ellos (practicar)	8. ¿(estudiar) nosotros?	11. yo (viajar)
3. tú (formar)	6. ¿(preguntar) Ud?	9. Uds. (desear)	12. ¿(esperar) Ud?

Exercise No. 17—Preguntas

Answer in complete Spanish sentences.

1. ¿Dónde están sentados los señores?
2. ¿Quién principia a hablar?
3. ¿Quién escucha con atención?

4. ¿Quién pregunta?
5. ¿Quién contesta?
6. ¿Son importantes los verbos?

7. ¿Es comerciante el Sr. Adams?
8. ¿Habla (él) español?
9. ¿Por qué desea hablar español?
10. ¿Qué países espera visitar?

11. ¿Viaja por tren, por avión, o por barco?
12. ¿Aprende el Sr. Adams rápidamente o despacio (slowly)?

CAPÍTULO 7 (SIETE)
PARTE PRIMERA
La Familia del Señor Adams

1. Es jueves, 14 (catorce) de enero a las 8 (ocho) de la noche.

2. El señor López toca el timbre de la casa Adams. La criada abre la puerta y dice — Pase Ud. a la sala, por favor.

3. En la sala el señor Adams espera al señor López, y cuando éste entra, dice — Buenas noches. ¿Cómo está Ud.?

4. Regular. ¿Y cómo está Ud.? ¿Y su familia?

5. Yo estoy muy bien, gracias. Pero mi niña Anita está enferma. Tiene un resfriado.

6. Lo siento mucho. ¿Tiene Ud. otros hijos?

7. Por supuesto. Tengo cuatro hijos, dos muchachos y dos muchachas. Somos una familia de seis personas.

8. ¿Y cómo se llaman sus hijos?

9. Se llaman Felipe, Guillermo, Rosita y Anita.

10. ¿Cuántos años tienen?

11. Felipe tiene diez años. Es el mayor. Guillermo tiene ocho años. Rosita tiene seis años. Anita es la menor. Tiene cinco años.

12. Todos menos Anita van a la escuela.

13. Los señores platican un rato más. Entonces el señor Adams invita al señor López a visitar su oficina el lunes próximo, a las doce y media de la tarde. Éste acepta la invitación con mucho gusto.

14. A las nueve el señor López dice — Hasta la vista.

15. El señor Adams responde — Hasta el lunes a las doce y media de la tarde.

1. It is Thursday, January 14, at 8 o'clock in the evening.

2. Mr. Lopez rings the bell of the Adams house. The maid opens the door and says, "Go to the living room, please."

3. In the living room Mr. Adams is awaiting Mr. Lopez, and when the latter enters, he says: "Good evening. How are you?"

4. So so. And how are you and your family?

5. I am very well, thank you. But my child Annie is ill. She has a cold.

6. I'm very sorry. Have you other children?

7. Surely. I have four children, two boys and two girls. We are a family of six people.

8. And what are the names of your children?

9. Their names are Philip, William, Rosie and Annie.

10. How old are they?

11. Philip is ten years old. He is the oldest. William is eight years old. Rosie is six years old. Annie is the youngest. She is five years old.

12. All except Annie go to school.

13. The two gentlemen chat a while longer. Then Mr. Adams invites Mr. Lopez to visit his office the following Monday at 12:30 p.m. The latter accepts the invitation with much pleasure.

14. At nine o'clock Mr. Lopez says, "So long."

15. Mr. Adams answers, "Till Monday at 12:30 p.m."

Pronunciation and Spelling Aids

1. Practice:

	res-fria-do	Gui-ller-mo	res-pon-de	se-gu-ra-men-te
jue-ves	en-fer-ma	in-vi-tar	a-cep-tar	lue-go
fa-mi-lia	sien-to	in-vi-ta-ción	tie-nen	lla-man (*yah-mahn*)

Building Vocabulary

A. Most Spanish words ending in **-ción** have corresponding English words ending in *-tion*. Words ending in **-ción** are feminine.

1. la invitación
2. pronunciación
3. elección
4. continuación
5. atención
6. dirección
7. aplicación
8. invención
9. prevención
10. solución
11. revolución
12. reservación

B. The ending -*mente* is equal to the ending -*ly* in English.

1. seguramente, surely
2. rápidamente, rapidly
3. generalmente, generally
4. ciertamente, certainly
5. atentamente, attentively
6. probablemente, probably

Important Expressions

1. ¿Cómo se llama Ud.?	1. What is your name?
2. Me llamo Felipe.	2. My name is Philip.
3. ¿Cómo se llama su amigo?	3. What is your friend's name?
4. Mi amigo se llama Pablo.	4. My friend's name is Paul.
5. ¿Cuántos años tiene Ud?[1]	5. How old are you?
6. Tengo 13 (trece) años.[1]	6. I am thirteen years old.
7. ¿Cuántos años tiene Pablo?	7. How old is Paul?
8. Tiene 15 (quince) años.	8. He is fifteen years old.

NOTE: 1. *Lit.* How many years have you. I have 13 years.

Exercise No. 18—Completion of Text

Complete the following sentences based on the text.

1. La criada (opens) la puerta.
2. Dice-(Pass) a la sala, por favor.
3. (Good evening). ¿Cómo está (your) familia?
4. Ella tiene (a cold).
5. ¿Tiene Ud. (other) hijos?
6. (I have) cuatro hijos.
7. (We are) una familia de seis personas.
8. ¿Cuántos (years) tienen sus hijos?
9. Anita es (the youngest).
10. Felipe es (the oldest).
11. Platican (a while longer).
12. El Sr. Adams invita (Mr. Lopez).

PARTE SEGUNDA

Grammar Notes

1. Present Tense of ser to be, estar to be, ir to go.

Singular			Singular			Singular		
	soy	I am		estoy	I am		voy	I go
	eres	you are (fam.)		estás	you are (fam.)		vas	you go (fam.)
Ud.	es	you are	Ud.	está	you are	Ud.	va	you go
	es	he, she, it is		está	he, she, it is		va	he, she, it goes
Plural			Plural			Plural		
	somos	we are		estamos	we are		vamos	we go
	sois	you are (fam.)		estáis	you are (fam.)		vais	you go (fam.)
Uds.	son	you are	Uds.	están	you are	Uds.	van	you go
	son	they are		están	they are		van	they go

NOTE: All forms of estar except estamos are stressed on the last syllable.

2. Use of ir to Indicate Future Time

a. Voy a hacer un viaje a Cuba. — I am going to take a trip to Cuba.
¿Van Uds. a aprender el francés? — Are you going to learn French?

b. Vamos may be translated: *Let us,* or *We are going to,*—whichever makes best sense.
Vamos a principiar.   Vamos a ver. — Let us begin.   Let's see.
Vamos a visitar a nuestro amigo. — We are going to visit our friend.

3. The Personal a. This is placed before the direct object, if the direct object is a person or proper name. The personal a is not translated.   a quién and a quiénes equal *whom*.

¿A quién espera Ud.? — Whom are you expecting?
Espero a Juan. — I am expecting John.
¿Van Uds. a visitar a México? — Are you going to visit Mexico?

4. The Possessive adjectives mi and su. Observe the forms and meanings of **mi** and **su:**

a. *Mi* niña está enferma. — *My* child is ill.
b. *Mis* niños van a la escuela. — *My* children go to school.
c. Ana, ¿dónde está *su* madre? — Anna, where is *your* mother?
d. Juan, ¿dónde están *sus* libros? — John, where are *your* books?
e. María está aquí. *Su* amiga está ausente. — Marie is here. *Her* friend is absent.
f. Felipe está aquí. *Su* amigo está ausente. — Philip is here. *His* friend is absent.
g. Los alumnos están aquí. *Su* maestro está ausente. — The pupils are here. *Their* teacher is absent.

mi (*my*) is used with a sing. noun; mis (*my*) with a plur. noun.
su (*his, her, its, their, your*) is used with a sing. noun.
sus (*his, her, its, their, your*) is used with a plur. noun.

The sense of the sentence determines which meaning of su (sus) applies.

Ejercicios (Exercises) No. 19A-19B-19C

19A. Fill in the correct forms of **ser** and **estar.**

Remember: ser is used to express *Who is?* or *What is?* estar is used to express *place where* or *health.*

1. ¿Quién (is) el señor Lopez? (He is) maestro.
2. ¿Cómo (are) Ud.? (I am) muy bien.
3. ¿Dónde (are) Uds.? (We are) en la sala.
4. ¿(Are) Ud. negociante? Sí, (I am) negociante.
5. ¿(Is) enferma su hija? Sí, mi hija (is) enferma.
6. ¿Cómo (are) Uds.? (We are) muy bien, gracias.
7. ¿Dónde (are) los libros? (They are) en el estante.
8. ¿(Are) Uds. mexicanos? No, (we are) norteamericanos.
9. ¿Quiénes (are) en la sala? Los dos señores (are) allí.
10. ¿(Are) Uds. amigos del maestro? Sí, (we are) sus amigos.

19B. Complete the following sentences with the words in parenthesis, using the personal **a** whenever necessary.

Ejemplo: Hoy invitamos *al* señor Adams.

1. Hoy invitamos (el señor Adams).
2. No voy a visitar (la escuela).
3. Carlos espera (su amigo) Pablo.
4. Estudian (la lección).
5. Vamos a visitar (la señora de López).
6. Esperan Uds. (el tren)?
7. No, esperamos (Isabel).
8. El Sr. Adams desea ver (su agente).
9. Ellos no visitan (el parque).
10. Hoy visitamos (José).

19C. Translate into Spanish.

1. How are you?
2. So so, thank you.
3. My daughter is sick.
4. I am very sorry.
5. You are a family of six people.
6. Do your children go to school?
7. Do you speak Spanish?
8. No, I do not speak Spanish.
9. I invite Charles to visit my house.
10. We are going to chat a while.
11. Let's begin.
12. I want to study Spanish.

PARTE TERCERA
Exercise No. 20—Preguntas

1. ¿Quién abre la puerta?
2. ¿Quién toca el timbre?
3. ¿Dónde espera el Sr. Adams al Sr. López?
4. ¿Quién está enferma?
5. ¿Qué tiene ella?
6. ¿Cuántos hijos tiene el comerciante?
7. ¿Cuántas personas hay en su familia?
8. ¿Cómo se llaman sus hijos?
9. ¿Cuántos años tiene Felipe?
10. ¿Platican los señores un rato más?
11. ¿A quién (whom) invita el negociante a visitar su oficina?
12. ¿Acepta el maestro la invitación?

CAPÍTULO 8 (OCHO)

PARTE PRIMERA

En la Oficina del Señor Adams

1. La oficina del señor Adams está en el décimo piso de un edificio alto. No es grande, pero es muy cómoda. Hay dos ventanas grandes que dan a la calle. En las paredes grises hay algunos carteles de México en colores vivos y un mapa de México.

2. En el escritorio del señor Adams hay muchos papeles. Cerca de la puerta está un escritorio pequeño con una máquina de escribir. Entre las dos ventanas hay una mesa larga. En la mesa hay periódicos y revistas y un cenicero bonito.

3. El señor Adams, quien está sentado detrás de su escritorio cuando el señor López entra en la oficina, se levanta y va a saludarle.

4. Buenas tardes, señor López. Mucho gusto en verle.

5. El gusto es mío. ¿Cómo está Ud?

6. Muy bien, gracias.

7. Su oficina es hermosa. Me gustan muchísimo este mapa de México y estos carteles. ¡Qué colores tan bonitos! A propósito, Sr. Adams, ¿Qué ve Ud. en ese cartel?

8. Veo el cielo y el sol, unas montañas, un tren y casas blancas con tejados rojos.

9. ¿De qué color es el sol?

10. Es amarillo y muy grande.

11. ¿De qué colores son las montañas, el cielo y el tren?

12. El tren es negro. El cielo es azul. Las montañas son verdes. ¡Dios mío! Es la una. Basta de colores. Tengo hambre. ¿No tiene Ud. hambre?

13. Sí. Tengo hambre también.

14. Bueno. No lejos de aquí hay un restaurante bueno.

15. Pues, ¡vámonos!

1. The office of Mr. Adams is on the tenth floor of a tall building. It is not large, but it is very comfortable. There are two large windows that face the street. On the gray walls there are some posters of Mexico in bright colors and a map of Mexico.

2. On the desk of Mr. Adams there are many papers. Near the door is a small desk with a typewriter. Between the two windows there is a long table. On the table there are newspapers and magazines and a pretty ash tray.

3. Mr. Adams, who is seated behind his desk when Mr. Lopez enters the office, gets up and goes to greet him.

4. Good afternoon, Mr. Lopez. I am very glad to see you.

5. The pleasure is mine. How are you?

6. Very well, thank you.

7. Your office is beautiful. I like this map of Mexico and these posters very much. What pretty colors! By the way, Mr. Adams, what do you see on that poster?

8. I see the sky and the sun, some mountains, a train and white houses with red roofs.

9. What color is the sun?

10. It is yellow and very large.

11. What colors are the mountains, the sky and the train?

12. The train is black. The sky is blue. The mountains are green. My goodness! It's one o'clock. Enough of colors. I am hungry. Are you not hungry?

13. Yes, I am also hungry.

14. Not far from here there is a good restaurant.

15. Well, let's go!

Pronunciation and Spelling Aids

1. Practice:

	pe-rió-di-cos	mu-chí-si-mo	a-ma-ri-llo	ce-ni-ce-ro
e-di-fi-cio	re-vis-tas	pro-pó-si-to	bas-ta	má-qui-na

2. quién, cuándo and other question words drop the accent mark when they are not used as question words. Thus: El Sr. Adams, quien está sentado cuando el Sr. López entra en la sala, se levanta.

Building Vocabulary

A. Common Descriptive Adjectives

amarillo	yellow	malo	bad	corto	short
azul	blue	barato	cheap	largo	long
blanco	white	caro	dear	pobre	poor
negro	black	bonito	pretty	rico	rich
gris	grey	hermoso	beautiful	fácil	easy
rojo	red	simpático	nice	difícil	hard
verde	green	alto	high, tall	cómodo	comfortable
vivo	lively	bajo	low	inteligente	intelligent
enfermo	sick	grande	big	importante	important
bueno	good	pequeño	little	interesante	interesting

B. -ísimo This ending means *very*. Thus:

1. muchísimo	very much	3. pobrísimo	very poor	5. larguísimo	very long
2. altísimo	very high	4. hermosísimo	very beautiful	6. bonísimo	very good

Expresiones Importantes

1. **dan a la calle** they face the street. The usual meaning of **dan** is *they give*.

2. **¿Tiene Ud. hambre?** Are you hungry? (*Lit.* Have you hunger?) **Tengo hambre.** I am hungry. (*Lit.* I have hunger.)

3. **a propósito**, by the way.

4. **¿De qué color es el papel?** What color (*Lit.* of what color) is the paper?

5. Expressions of Liking. In Spanish the idea of liking is expressed by means of the verb **gustar** *to be pleasing to*. The person *to whom* something is pleasing, begins the sentence. The thing which is pleasing follows the verb. Thus: **Me gusta el libro.** I like the book. (*Lit. To me* is pleasing the book.) **Me gustan los carteles.** I like the posters. (*Lit. To me* are pleasing the posters.)

Exercise No. 21—Completion of Text

1. **Dos ventanas** (face the street).
2. **En la mesa hay** (newspapers).
3. **El Sr. Adams está sentado** (behind his desk).
4. **El Sr. López** (enters the office).
5. (I'm very glad to see you).
6. (The pleasure is mine).
7. (I like = to me is pleasing) **ese mapa.**
8. (By the way), **¿ve Ud. ese cartel?**
9. (I see) **el cielo y el sol.**
10. ¿(What color) **es el sol?**
11. ¿(What colors) **son las montañas?**
12. (My goodness!) **Es la una.**
13. (I am hungry).
14. (Not far from here) **está un restaurante.**
15. (Let's go!)

PARTE SEGUNDA

Grammar Notes

1. Agreement of Adjectives

Observe the position of the adjectives in the following examples and how they agree with the nouns they modify.

el hombre **bueno**	the good man	el libro **azul**	the blue book
la mujer **buena**	the good woman	la casa **azul**	the blue house
los hombres **buenos**	the good men	los libros **azules**	the blue books
las mujeres **buenas**	the good women	las casas **azules**	the blue houses

El edificio es **grande** y **hermoso.**	The building is large and beautiful.
La ciudad es **grande** y **hermosa.**	The city is large and beautiful.
Los edificios son **grandes** y **hermosos.**	The buildings are large and beautiful.
Las ciudades son **grandes** y **hermosas.**	The cities are large and beautiful.

a. Adjectives agree with the nouns they modify in number and gender.

b. Adjectives ending in -o change to -a in the feminine. (bueno buena; hermoso hermosa)

c. Adjectives not ending in -o do not change in the feminine. (grande grande; azul azul)

d. Adjectives, like nouns, form their plurals by adding -s if they end in a vowel (bueno buenos) (verde verdes); and by adding -es if they end in a consonant. (azul azules; gris grises)

e. Descriptive adjectives usually follow the noun. Adjectives of quantity precede it.

una mesa larga   a long table   muchas hijas   many daughters

2. More About the Uses of ser and estar.

a. You have learned:

ser is used in answer to such questions as *Who is? What is?*

¿Quién es el maestro? El Sr. López es el maestro.

¿Qué es esto? Es el retrato de mi esposa.

estar is used in expressions of place and health.

¿Dónde está la oficina? Está en la Calle Whitehall.

¿Cómo está su niño? Mi niño está enfermo.

b. Study the following sentences and note:

ser is used with adjectives which indicate *lasting qualities,* that is, qualities not likely to change, such as color, size, shape, personal characteristics.

estar is used with adjectives which indicate *non-lasting qualities*, that is, qualities quite subject to change. Among these are adjectives of health.

Adjectives with ser (*Lasting Qualities*)	Adjectives with estar (*Non-lasting Qualities*)
1. La oficina es pequeña.	1. La cocina está caliente (*hot*).
2. Los libros son azules.	2. La sala está fría (*cold*).
3. La lección es fácil.	3. Estamos listos (*ready*).
4. Mis amigos son inteligentes.	4. ¿Están Uds. contentos (*happy*)?
5. Las cestas son baratas.	5. Las ventanas están limpias (*clean*).
6. María es simpática.	6. El jarro está lleno (*full*).
7. El niño es bueno.	7. Estoy bueno (bien) (*well*).
8. Los cuartos no son malos.	8. Jorge está malo (*sick*).

NOTE: bueno and malo go with ser when they mean *good* and *bad*.

NOTE: bueno and malo go with estar when they mean *well* and *sick*.

c. estar is also used with adjectives indicating a finished action, like sentado seated; escrito written.

Los señores están sentados. La carta está escrita.

PARTE TERCERA

Ejercicios (Exercises) No. 22A-22B-22C

22A. Fill in the correct form of the adjective in parenthesis.

Ejemplo: Los colores de los carteles son *vivos.*

1. Los colores de los carteles son (lively).
2. La oficina es (comfortable).
3. Veo las casas con tejados (red).
4. ¿Dónde están las montañas (green)?
5. Los edificios de mi ciudad son muy (high).
6. Hay (many) carteles en la pared.
7. Las casas son (white).
8. (Many) ventanas dan a la calle.
9. El cielo es (blue).
10. Es una señorita muy (nice).

22B. Fill in the correct form of ser or estar as needed.

1. Los niños ——— simpáticos.
2. Un auto ——— en la esquina.
3. El color de los tejados ——— rojo.
4. ¿Cómo ——— Ud.?
5. ——— muy bien.
6. Mis niños ——— enfermos.
7. Nosotros ———sentados en el comedor.
8. Nosotros ——— los amigos de Felipe.
9. Los alumnos ——— muy inteligentes.
10. ¿——— muy altos los edificios?

22C. Translate:

1. The office of Mr. Adams is very nice.
2. The windows of the office are large.
3. Many papers are on the floor (**suelo**).
4. The roofs of the houses are red.
5. The sky is blue.
6. The mountains are green.
7. The building is very high.
8. How are you, Mr. Adams?
9. I am very well, thank you.
10. The posters are beautiful.

Exercise No. 23—Preguntas

Answer in complete Spanish sentences.

1. ¿Dónde está la oficina del Sr. Adams?
2. ¿Es grande la oficina?
3. ¿Es cómoda la oficina?
4. ¿Dónde hay algunos carteles de México?
5. ¿Dónde están muchos papeles?
6. ¿Dónde está un escritorio pequeño?
7. ¿Qué está entre las dos ventanas?
8. ¿Quién está sentado?
9. ¿De qué color es el sol en el cartel?
10. De qué color es el tren?
11. ¿De qué color son las montañas?
12. ¿Es azul el cielo?
13. ¿De qué color son las casas?
14. ¿Son rojos los tejados?
15. ¿De quién (whose) es la oficina?
    Es la oficina del ———.

CAPÍTULO 9 (NUEVE)

PARTE PRIMERA

Un Amigo Visita la Oficina del señor Adams

1. El señor Gómez, amigo del señor Adams, es un habitante de Nueva York. Sin embargo habla bien el español, porque sus padres son puertorriqueños. Es un caballero de treinta y cinco años de edad.

2. Sabe que su amigo Adams aprende el español. Desea saber cómo su amigo adelanta. Por eso entra un día en la oficina del señor Adams y le saluda en español. Sigue la conversación.

3. ¿Qué tal, amigo?

4. Muy bien, gracias. ¿Y Ud.?

5. Así, así. A propósito, ¿Ud. aprende el español, verdad?

6. ¿Cómo no? Aprendo a hablar, a leer, y a escribir el español.

7. ¿Es difícil el español?

8. Pues, no es difícil. Me gusta la lengua y estudio diligentemente.

9. ¿Quién es su maestro de español?

10. El señor López. Es un maestro muy bueno, y día por día hablo, leo y escribo mejor. Aprendo las palabras y las expresiones de la vida diaria. Yo comprendo al señor López cuando él habla español, y él me[1] comprende cuando yo hablo la lengua. Me gusta mucho el español.

11. Amigo mío, Ud. habla estupendamente bien.

1. Mr. Gomez, a friend of Mr. Adams, is an inhabitant of New York. Nevertheless he speaks Spanish well because his parents are Puerto Ricans. He is a gentleman thirty five years old.

2. He knows that his friend Adams is learning Spanish. He wants to find out how his friend is progressing. Therefore he enters the office of Mr. Adams one day and greets him in Spanish. The conversation follows.

3. How goes it, friend?

4. Very well, thank you. And you?

5. So, so. By the way, you are learning Spanish, aren't you?

6. Of course. I am learning to speak, read and write Spanish.

7. Is Spanish difficult?

8. Well, it's not difficult. I like the language and I study industriously.

9. Who is your Spanish teacher?

10. Mr. Lopez. He is a very good teacher and day by day I speak, read and write better. I learn the words and expressions of daily life. I understand Mr. Lopez when he speaks Spanish, and he understands me when I speak it. I like Spanish very much.

11. My friend, you speak wonderfully well.

12. Es favor que Ud. me hace.

13. No es favor. Es verdad. Mis amigos me dicen que Ud. va a hacer un viaje a México el verano que viene.[2]

14. Espero ir en la primavera, el 31 de mayo. Voy a viajar por avión. Quiero llegar a México cuanto antes.

15. ¡Buen viaje! ¡Y buena suerte! Hasta luego, amigo.

16. Hasta la vista.

12. You flatter me.

13. It is not flattery. It is the truth. My friends tell me that you are going to take a trip to Mexico the coming summer.

14. I hope to go in the spring, the 31st of May. I am going to travel by plane. I want to arrive in Mexico as soon as possible.

15. Happy voyage! And good luck! So long, friend.

16. So long.

NOTE: 1. me me. Object pronouns usually precede the verb.
NOTE: 2. *Lit.* The summer which is coming.

Pronunciation and Spelling Aids

1. Practice:

ha-bi-**tan**-te	con-ver-sa-**ción**	es-tu-pen-da-**men**-te	**bue**-na
puer-to-rri-**que**-ño	di-li-gen-te-**men**-te	**fá**-cil	**suer**-te
a-de-**lan**-ta	ex-pre-**sio**-nes	di-**fí**-cil	buen **via**-je

Building Vocabulary

A. **Palabras Relacionadas** (Related Words)

1. habitar	to inhabit	el habitante	the inhabitant		
2. conversar	to converse	la conversación	the conversation		
3. estudiar	to study	el estudiante	the student	el estudio	the study
4. comprender	to comprehend	la comprensión	the comprehension		
5. viajar	to travel	el viaje	the voyage	el viajero	the traveler

B. More Adverbs Ending in -mente

| 1. diligentemente | diligently | 3. rápidamente | rapidly | 5. ciertamente | certainly |
| 2. estupendamente | wonderfully | 4. seguramente | surely | 6. posiblemente | possibly |

Expresiones Importantes

1. sin embargo	nevertheless	4. ¿cómo no?	of course, why not?
2. por eso	therefore	5. día por día	day by day
3. ¿qué tal?	how goes it?	6. cuanto antes	as soon as possible

7. ¿verdad?, ¿no es verdad? is it not true? Translated in various ways, such as: Isn't he, she, it? Aren't you? etc.

8. **el verano que viene** the coming summer (*Lit.* the summer which is coming).

Exercise No. 24—Completion of Text

1. (His parents) son puertorriqueños.
2. Su amigo (is progressing).
3. ¿Cuando el Sr. Gómez entra, dice — ¿(How goes it?)
4. (By the way) **Ud. aprende el español, (aren't you?)**
5. (Of course).
6. (I am learning) **a hablar, a leer, y a escribir el español.**
7. Es (easy). No es (difficult).
8. (I am studying) **diligentemente, porque (I want) ir a México.**
9. **Cuando él habla, yo (understand).**
10. **¿Aprende Ud. las (words) de la vida** (daily)?
11. **Sí, y aprendo las (expressions) también.**
12. (I like = to me is pleasing) **la lengua.**

PARTE SEGUNDA

Grammar Notes

1. Present Tense of aprender and vivir. Model -er and -ir Verbs.

Singular			Singular	
	aprend-o	I learn	viv-o	I live
	aprend-es	you learn (*fam.*)	viv-es	you live (*fam.*)
Ud.	aprend-e ⎱	you learn	Ud. viv-e ⎱	you live
	aprend-e ⎰	he, she, it learns	viv-e ⎰	he, she, it lives
Plural			Plural	
	aprend-emos	we learn	viv-imos	we live
	aprend-éis	you learn (*fam.*)	viv-ís	you live (*fam.*)
Uds.	aprend-en ⎱	you learn	Uds. viv-en ⎱	you live
	aprend-en ⎰	they learn	viv-en ⎰	they live

a. The endings of **aprender** are like the endings of **hablar**, except that the letter **-e** replaces the letter **-a**.

The endings of **aprender** are the same as those of **vivir**, except in the **nosotros** (*we*) and **vosotros** (*you, fam.*) forms.

b. Some common -er and -ir verbs like **aprender** and **vivir**.

beber	to drink	responder	to answer	dividir	to divide
comer	to eat	ver[1]	to see	recibir	to receive
comprender	to understand	abrir	to open	permitir	to permit
leer	to read	escribir	to write	prohibir	to prohibit

NOTE: The present tense of **ver**: Sing. **veo ves ve** Plur. **vemos veis ven**

2. Verbs followed by an Infinitive with a

Va a hacer un viaje.	He is going to make a trip.	**Principia a hablar.**	He begins to speak.
Aprende a leer.	He learns to read.	**Comenzamos a comer.**	We begin to eat.

After the verbs **ir, aprender, comenzar,** and **principiar,** a complementary infinitive must be preceded by **a**.

PARTE TERCERA

Ejercicios (Exercises) No. 25A-25B

25A. Practice these short dialogues aloud. They will give you a "feeling" for the correct use of verbs in the present tense.

1. ¿Aprenden Uds. el español?
   Sí, aprendemos el español.
   ¿Aprende Carlos el español?
   No aprende el español.
2. ¿Escribe Ud. una carta?
   No escribo una carta.
   ¿Qué escribe Ud.?
   Escribo los ejercicios.

3. ¿Qué lee Ud.?
   Leo el diario.
   ¿Qué lee Ana?
   Ella lee una revista.
4. ¿Quién abre la puerta?
   La criada abre la puerta.
   ¿Quién entra en la casa?
   El Sr. López entra en la casa.

5. ¿Qué ve Ud?
   Veo el mapa.
   ¿Ve Ud. los carteles?
   No veo los carteles.
6. ¿Dónde viven Uds.?
   Vivimos en Nueva York.
   ¿Dónde viven los mexicanos?
   Viven en México.

25B. Fill in the missing endings. -ar, -er and -ir verbs are included in this exercise.

Ejemplo: Aprendo el español.

1. (Yo) aprend— el español.
2. El señor López toc— el timbre.
3. (Nosotros) estudi— diligentemente.
4. (Ellos) no comprend— al maestro.
5. ¿Le— Uds. los periódicos?
6. Los niños beb— leche.
7. ¿Escrib— Ud. los ejercicios?
8. ¿Viv— (ella) en la ciudad?
9. Niño, ¿por qué no beb— la leche?
10. Papá, ¿dese— (tú) la revista?
11. (Ellas) no viaj— en la primavera.
12. La criada abr— la puerta.

Exercise No. 26—Preguntas

1. ¿Quién es un habitante de Nueva York?
2. ¿Habla el Sr. Gómez español bien?
3. ¿Son sus padres norteamericanos?
4. ¿Qué sabe el señor Gómez?
5. ¿En dónde entra un día?
6. ¿A quién saluda el Sr. Gómez en español?
7. ¿Quién aprende a hablar, a leer y a escribir el español?
8. ¿Cómo estudia el Sr. Adams?
9. ¿Quién es su maestro de español?
10. ¿Es un maestro bueno?
11. ¿Comprende el señor Adams cuando el maestro habla español?
12. ¿Qué clase de (what kind of) palabras aprende el señor Adams?
13. ¿Quién va a hacer un viaje a México?
14. ¿Cuándo espera ir a México?
15. ¿Quién dice — Buen viaje y buena suerte?

REPASO 2

(CAPÍTULOS 6–9) PARTE PRIMERA

Repaso de Palabras

NOUNS

1. el año	11. la manera	21. el restaurante	1. year	11. manner	21. restaurant
2. el avión	12. el mapa	22. la revista	2. airplane	12. map	22. magazine
3. el caballero	13. la montaña	23. el sol	3. gentleman	13. mountain	23. sun
4. el cartel	14. la noche	24. la suerte	4. poster	14. night	24. luck
5. la criada	15. el país	25. la tarde	5. servant (f)	15. country	25. afternoon
6. el cielo	16. el parque	26. el tejado	6. sky	16. park	26. roof
7. la escuela	17. el periódico	27. la verdad	7. school	17. magazine	27. truth
8. el estudiante	18. la plaza	28. el viaje	8. student	18. square	28. voyage
9. el habitante	19. la pregunta	29. la vida	9. inhabitant	19. question	29. life
10. la lección	20. la respuesta	30. el vuelo	10. lesson	20. answer	30. flight

VERBS

1. aceptar	14. practicar	27. responder	1. to accept	14. to practice	27. to answer
2. adelantar	15. preguntar	28. tener	2. to progress	15. to ask	28. to have
3. contestar	16. principiar	29. saber	3. to answer	16. to begin	29. to know
4. desear	17. saludar	30. ver	4. to want	17. to greet	30. to see
5. entrar(en)	18. tocar	31. abrir	5. to enter	18. to play (instrument)	31. to open
6. escuchar	19. trabajar	32. escribir	6. to listen	19. to work	32. to write
7. esperar	20. viajar	33. ir	7. to expect	20. to travel	33. to go
8. estudiar	21. visitar	34. pedir	8. to study	21. to visit	34. to ask for
9. hablar	22. aprender	35. seguir	9. to speak	22. to learn	35. to follow
10. invitar	23. beber	36. salir(de)	10. to invite	23. to drink	36. to leave, go out of
11. llegar	24. comprender	37. salgo	11. to arrive	24. to understand	37. I leave
12. pasar	25. hacer	38. no sé	12. to pass	25. to make	38. I do not know
13. platicar	26. leer	39. voy a	13. to chat	26. to read	39. I am going to

ADJECTIVES

1. alto	10. difícil	19. listo	1. high	10. difficult	19. ready
2. amarillo	11. enfermo	20. limpio	2. yellow	11. sick	20. clean
3. azul	12. fácil	21. lleno	3. blue	12. easy	21. full
4. bajo	13. frío	22. próximo	4. low	13. cold	22. next
5. barato	14. gris	23. rápido	5. cheap	14. gray	23. rapid
6. caro	15. hermoso	24. rico	6. dear	15. beautiful	24. rich
7. caliente	16. importante	25. rojo	7. hot	16. important	25. red
8. cómodo	17. inteligente	26. sucio	8. comfortable	17. intelligent	26. dirty
9. corriente	18. largo	27. verde	9. common	18. long	27. green

ADVERBS

1. alto	3. hoy	5. tampoco	1. loudly	3. today	5. neither
2. despacio	4. tan	6. demasiado	2. slowly	4. such, so	6. too much

PREPOSITIONS

1. para	3. lejos de	5. menos	1. for, in order to	3. far from	5. except
2. sin	4. por	6. cerca de	2. without	4. for, by, through	6. near

NOTE: The uses of por and para offer some difficulty in Spanish. You can best get a feeling for their correct use by memorizing por and para phrases as you meet them. Thus: por favor, por barco, tren, etc.; basta por hoy; para visitar (in order to visit)· Sale para México. He leaves for Mexico.

In general **para** is used to indicate *purpose, destination,* **por** is used to indicate *price* (**por peso**); *duration of time* (**por dos meses**); *through* (**por la calle**).

QUESTION WORDS

1. quién	3. a quién	5. de quién	1. who	3. whom, to whom	5. of whom, whose
2. cuál	4. cuáles	6. cuándo	2. which (one)	4. which (ones)	6. when

CONJUNCTIONS

1. pues	3. cuando	1. well	3. when
2. si	4. porque	2. if	4. because

IMPORTANT EXPRESSIONS

1. Buena suerte	13. hacer preguntas	1. good luck	13. to ask questions
2. Buen viaje	14. mucho gusto en verle	2. Happy voyage	14. very glad to see you
3. a propósito	15. lo siento mucho	3. by the way	15. I am very sorry
4. ¿cómo no?	16. pedir informes	4. of course, why not?	16. to ask for information
5. con su permiso	17. por tren	5. if you please	17. by train
6. con mucho gusto	18. por barco	6. with great pleasure	18. by boat
7. ¿Cuánto cuesta?	19. por avión	7. How much does it cost?	19. by airplane
8. ¿Cuántos años tiene Ud?	20. ¿qué tal?	8. How old are you?	20. how goes it?
9. Tengo quince (15) años	21. tengo hambre	9. I am 15 years old.	21. I am hungry
10. ¿de qué color?	22. sin embargo	10. what color?	22. nevertheless
11. ¿(no es) verdad?	23. sobre todo	11. isn't it so?	23. especially
12. hacer un viaje	24. vámonos	12. to take a trip	24. let's go
	25. un rato más		25. a while longer

PARTE SEGUNDA

Ejercicio 27. Give the Spanish words that correspond to these English words. The ending *-tion* becomes *-ción.*

Ejemplo: attention atención

1. civilization	3. instruction	5. revolution	7. application	9. invention
2. reservation	4. exception	6. observation	8. election	10. solution

Ejercicio 28. Answer each of the following questions in complete sentences, using the suggested words in the answer.

Ejemplo: ¿De qué color es el jarro? (azul). El jarro es azul. or Es azul.

1. ¿De qué color es el cielo? (azul)
2. ¿Qué lengua hablan los mexicanos? (español)
3. ¿Quién tiene hambre? (El Sr. Adams)
4. ¿De qué color es la revista? (blanc-y negr-)
5. ¿Dónde vive Ud? (en los Estados Unidos)
6. ¿De qué color son los tejidos? (roj-)
7. ¿Qué beben los niños? (leche)
8. ¿A quién saluda el Sr. Adams? (a su amigo)
9. ¿Cuántos años tiene Ud? (treinta años)
10. ¿Cómo se llama Ud? (your own name)

Ejercicio 29. Select the words in the right-hand column which best complete the sentence begun in the left-hand column.

1. No comprendo bien al maestro
2. El señor dice — Con su permiso —
3. Si Ud. no sabe la respuesta
4. El profesor dice — Lo siento mucho
5. Vamos por avión porque
6. Si estudiamos diligentemente
7. Cuando tengo hambre
8. Las ventanas de la oficina
9. El amigo saluda al señor Adams y dice —
10. No sé cuánto cuesta

a. diga — no sé.
b. es el modo más rápido.
c. voy al restaurante.
d. dan a la calle.
e. cuando habla rápidamente.
f. el vuelo a México.
g. cuando pasa delante de una persona.
h. vamos a adelantar día por día.
i. porque la niña está enferma.
j. Mucho gusto en verle.

Ejercicio 30. Complete each verb with the correct ending.

1. nosotros trabaj ———
2. ellos aprend ———
3. él principi ———
4. Ud. sab ———
5. Uds. escrib ———

6. tú abr ———
7. yo permit ———
8. Ud. beb ———
9. nosotros adelant ———
10. yo ve ———

Ejercicio 31. Answer each of the following questions in the affirmative:

Ejemplo: ¿Habla Ud. inglés? Sí, hablo inglés.

1. ¿Aprende Ud. el español?
2. ¿Estudia Ud. la lección?
3. ¿Trabaja Ud. diligentemente?

4. ¿Espera Ud. viajar?
5. ¿Ve Ud. los carteles?
6. ¿Lee Ud. el periódico?

7. ¿Comprende Ud. la pregunta?
8. ¿Acepta Ud. la invitación?
9. ¿Visita Ud. al maestro?

Ejercicio 32. Complete with the correct forms of **ser** or **estar** (See grammar notes 2a, b, c, page 40).

1. El padre (is) profesor.
2. ¿Cómo (are) Ud.?
3. (I am) enfermo.
4. (We are) contentos.
5. La casa (is) blanca.

6. (He is) sentado.
7. Los niños (are) listos.
8. Ella (is) inteligente.
9. Los muchachos (are) simpáticos.
10. La sala (is) fría.

11. (They are) importantes.
12. Tú (are) bonito, niño.
13. Ud. (are) alto.
14. Uds. no (are) ricos.
15. (I am) bien.

PARTE TERCERA

Diálogo 1

Practice the Spanish aloud.

¿Quién Es Ud?

1. ¿Cómo se llama Ud.?
2. Me llamo Carlos Sánchez.
3. ¿Cuántos años tiene Ud.?
4. Tengo veinte años.
5. ¿Dónde vive Ud.?
6. Vivo en la Calle Orizaba 50.
7. ¿Dónde trabaja Ud.?
8. Trabajo en la casa Velarde y Cía. (Compañía).

Who Are You?

1. What is your name?
2. My name is Charles Sanchez.
3. How old are you?
4. I am 20 years old.
5. Where do you live?
6. I live at 50 Orizaba St.
7. Where do you work?
8. I work for the firm, Velarde & Company.

Diálogo 2

¿Qué Camión Tomo?

1. Dispénseme, señor, ¿qué camión tomo para el Zócalo? (para Coyoacán)? (para el centro)? etc.
2. Tome Ud. el camión número 24. Para aquí mismo en la esquina.
3. Muchas gracias, señor.
4. De nada.

What Bus Do I Take?

1. Excuse me, sir, what bus do I take for the Zocalo? (for Coyoacan)? (for downtown)? etc.
2. Take bus number 24. It stops right here on the corner.
3. Thank you very much, sir.
4. You're welcome.

Diálogo 3

¿Qué Tranvía Va a . . .?

1. Dispénseme, señor, ¿me hace el favor de decirme, qué tranvía va al parque de Chapultepec? (al Palacio de Bellas Artes)? (al Jardin Zoológico)? etc.
2. No, sé, señor. Pero aquel policía en la esquina puede decirle, estoy seguro.
3. Muchas gracias, señor. Voy a preguntarle.

What Street Car Goes to . . . ?

1. Excuse me, sir, would you please tell me, what street car goes to Chapultepec Park? (to the Palace of Fine Arts)? (to the Zoo)? etc.
2. I do not know, sir. But that policeman on the corner can tell you, I am sure.
3. Thank you very much, sir. I am going to ask him.

LECTURA 1

Follow the instructions given in Exercise No. 14.

Exercise No. 33—Dos Amigos Del Señor Adams

El señor Adams ya sabe los nombres de todos los objetos de su casa. Ahora principia a estudiar los verbos porque desea aprender a leer, a escribir y a conversar en español. También desea saber los números en español. Siendo (being) un comerciante que espera visitar a su agente en México, necesita (he needs) la práctica de charlar (chatting) con españoles o hispanoamericanos. Afortunadamente (Luckily) tiene dos amigos que son de México y que trabajan cerca de su oficina en la calle Whitehall.

Un día el señor Adams va a visitar a estos (these) mexicanos. Los dos señores escuchan con atención al señor Adams mientras (while) habla con ellos en español. Después de (After) diez minutos de conversación, los mexicanos hacen muchas preguntas a su (their) amigo y están muy contentos (pleased) de sus (his) respuestas.

LECTURA 2

Exercise No. 34—El Sr. Adams Se Pone Enfermo (gets sick)

El jueves, veinte y dos de abril, a las nueve de la noche, llega (arrives) el señor López[1] a la casa de su estudiante, el señor Adams. El hijo mayor, un muchacho de diez años, abre la puerta y saluda al maestro con gusto. Entran en la sala donde el señor Adams generalmente espera a su profesor.

Pero esta (this) noche no está en la sala. Tampoco (Neither) está allí la señora Adams. El señor López está muy sorprendido (surprised) y pregunta al muchacho, — ¿Dónde está su papá? El hijo responde tristemente, — Mi papá está enfermo y no puede (cannot) salir de su dormitorio. Está en cama (bed) porque tiene un fuerte (severe) resfriado. También tiene dolor de cabeza (headache).

El profesor se pone (becomes) muy triste y dice, —¡Qué lastima! (What a pity!) Hoy no es posible dar lección, pero la semana próxima vamos a estudiar dos horas. Hasta el martes próximo.

NOTE: 1. Quite frequently the subject is placed after the verb in Spanish, even when the sentence is not a question. Thus: **llega el Sr. Adams = el Sr. Adams llega.** Watch out for this inverted word order.

CAPÍTULO 10 (DIEZ)

PARTE PRIMERA

En el Comedor

1. Los señores Adams y López están sentados en el comedor de la casa Adams. Toman café y pan dulce.

2. Dice el señor Adams — ¿Le gustan estas tazas y estos platillos?

3. —¡Qué bonitos son! — contesta el señor López. — Esta taza blanca con dibujos azules es de Puebla, ¿verdad?

4. Sí, este tipo de cerámica se llama Talavera de Puebla. Es conocida por todas partes. Es interesante ver que cada distrito tiene su propio estilo de cerámica.

5. ¿De dónde es ese jarro verde y blanco?

6. Este jarro para crema es de Oaxaca. Mire Ud. los dibujos de pájaros y flores. Ese otro para agua es de Michoacán.

1. Mr. Adams and Mr. Lopez are seated in the dining room of the Adams house. They are having coffee and sweet rolls.

2. Mr. Adams says: "Do you like these cups and saucers?"

3. "How pretty they are!" answers Mr. Lopez. "This white cup with the blue designs is from Puebla, is it not?"

4. Yes, this kind of pottery is called Puebla Talavera. It is known everywhere. It is interesting to see that each district has its own style of pottery.

5. Where does that green and white pitcher come from?

6. This cream pitcher is from Oaxaca. Look at the designs of birds and flowers. That other one for water is from Michoacan.

7. Ya sabe Ud., señor Adams, que los indios son verdaderos artistas. Trabajan despacio. Como cualquier artista, no tienen prisa.

8. Sí, es difícil hoy día obtener un surtido adecuado para el mercado norteamericano.

9. — Pobre artista, — dice el señor López. — Para aquel mercado lejano tiene que trabajar de prisa. Así no es fácil mantener la calidad artística.

10. — Es verdad, — responde el señor Adams. — Pero de todos modos veo mucha cerámica de interés artístico.

11. — ¡Ya lo creo! — contesta el señor López. — Me gustan mucho aquellos platos para frutas en el aparador. ¡Qué finos son los dibujos amarillos y azules en el fondo blanco!

12. Tengo también ejemplares de cerámica corriente. Es muy sencilla. Como ese plato cerca de Ud., muchas veces es color de café.

13. — Es para el uso, — dice el señor López. — Pero también tiene dibujos.

14. ¿Quiere Ud. más café? ¿No quiere Ud. también esa torta?

15. — Gracias. Todo está muy sabroso, — contesta el señor López.

7. You already know, Mr. Adams, that the Indians are true artists. They work slowly. Like any artist, they are not in a hurry.

8. Yes, it is hard nowadays to obtain an adequate assortment for the North American market.

9. "Poor artist," says Mr. Lopez. "For that distant market he has to work fast. Thus it is not easy to maintain artistic quality."

10. "It is true," answers Mr. Adams. "But anyway, I see much pottery of artistic interest."

11. "I should say so!" answers Mr. Lopez. "I like very much those fruit dishes on the sideboard. How fine the yellow and blue designs are on the white background!"

12. I also have samples of ordinary pottery. It is very simple. Like that plate near you, it is often brown.

13. "It is for use," says Mr. Lopez. "But it also has designs."

14. Do you want more coffee? Do you want that cake, too?

15. "Thank you. Everything is very tasty," answers Mr. Lopez.

Pronunciation and Spelling Aids

1. Practice:

pla-ti-llo	co-no-ci-do	ar-te-sa-no	cu-cha-ri-ta	Michoacán (mee-chwah-**cahn**)
di-bu-jo	pá-ja-ro	a-pa-ra-dor	le-ja-no	Oaxaca (wah-**hah**-cah)
ce-rá-mi-ca	a-zu-ca-re-ro	pla-ti-llo	sen-ci-llo	Taxco (**tahs**-koh)

2. Exclamations begin with a reversed exclamation point.

¡Qué finos son los dibujos!   How fine the designs are!

3. When a feminine noun begins with a stressed a the masculine article el is used for the sake of the sound. Thus: el agua, but las aguas; el arte, las artes

Building Vocabulary

A. **En el Comedor**   In the Dining Room

el aparador	buffet	el cuchillo	knife	el plato	plate
el azucarero	sugar bowl	la mesa	table	el platillo	saucer
la cuchara	spoon	el jarro para crema	cream pitcher	el sillón	armchair
la cucharita	tea spoon	el jarro para agua	water pitcher	el vaso	glass

B. The endings -ito, -ita, -illo, -illa, added to a noun, have the meaning *small*. They are also used to indicate affection, friendliness, sympathy, or informality. The Mexicans are very fond of these endings and use them even on adjectives and adverbs.

cuchara	spoon	**Ana**	Anna
cucharita	little (tea) spoon	**Anita**	Annie
plato	plate	**Juan**	John
platillo	saucer	**Juanito**	Johnny, Jack
hijo (a)	son, daughter	ahora	now
hijito (a)	sonny, girlie	ahorita	right away

Expresiones Importantes

1. cada artista	each artist	6. tener que	to have to
2. de todos modos	anyway	7. tiene que trabajar	he has to work
3. hoy día	nowadays	8. tener prisa	to be in a hurry
4. muchas veces	many times, often	9. tengo prisa	I am in a hurry
5. por todas partes	everywhere	10. ¡Ya lo creo!	Of course! I should say so!

Exercise No. 35—Completion of Text

1. (They are having) **café y pan dulce.**
2. **¡Qué bonitos son estos** (designs)!
3. **Este tipo de cerámica es conocido** (everywhere).
4. (Each) **distrito tiene su** (own) **estilo.**
5. **Este jarro es** (for cream).
6. **Ese otro es** (for water).
7. **Cualquier artista trabaja** (slowly).
8. (He has to) **trabajar de prisa.**
9. **Pero** (anyway) **veo mucha cerámica.**
10. (I have) **ejemplares de cerámica corriente.**
11. **Ese plato es** (very simple).
12. (Often) **es color de café.**
13. **Es** (for use), **pero tiene dibujos.**
14. (Do you wish) **más cafe?**
15. (Do you not wish) **esta torta?**

PARTE SEGUNDA

Grammar Notes

1. **The Demonstrative Adjectives.** Note the forms and meanings of **este, ese,** and **aquel** in the following sentences.

Este jarro es de Puebla.	*This* pitcher is from Puebla.
Esta taza es de Oaxaca.	*This* cup is from Oaxaca.
Estos jarros son de Puebla.	*These* pitchers are from Puebla.
Estas tazas son de Oaxaca.	*These* cups are from Oaxaca.
Ese plato es de Puebla.	*That* plate is from Puebla.
Esa cuchara es de Taxco.	*That* spoon is from Taxco.
Esos platos son de Puebla.	*Those* plates are from Puebla.
Esas cucharas son de Taxco.	*Those* spoons are from Taxco.
Mire Ud. **aquel tejado rojo.**	Look at *that* red roof.
Mire Ud. **aquella montaña alta.**	Look at *that* high mountain.
Mire Ud. **aquellos tejados rojos.**	Look at *those* red roofs.
Mire Ud. **aquellas montañas altas.**	Look at *those* high mountains.

a. Demonstrative adjectives agree in number and gender with the nouns they modify.

b. **ese, esa, esos, esas** (*that, those*) are used to point out persons or things near the persons spoken to. **aquel, aquella, aquellos, aquellas** (*that, those*) are used to point out distant persons or things.

2. Present Tense of **tener** to have, **venir** to come

Singular		Plural	
tengo	I have	**tenemos**	we have
tienes (*fam.*)	you have	**tenéis**	you have (*fam.*)
Ud. **tiene** ⎱	you have	Uds. **tienen** ⎱	you have
tiene ⎰	he, she, it has	**tienen** ⎰	they have

Singular		Plural	
vengo	I come	venimos	we come
vienes	you come (*fam.*)	venís	you come (*fam.*)
Ud. viene ⎱	you come	Uds. vienen ⎱	you come
viene ⎰	he, she, it comes	vienen ⎰	they come

Memorize the proverb (el refrán): **Quién primero viene primero tiene.** First come first served. (*Lit.* He who comes first, has first.)

PARTE TERCERA

Ejercicios (Exercises) No. 36A-36B-36C

36A. Complete with the correct form of **este, ese, aquel.** The abbreviation, *dist.* (*distant*) after *that* and *those,* means use the correct form of **aquel,** not of **ese.**

Ejemplo: ¿Ven Uds. *aquellas* montañas verdes?

1. ¿Ven Uds. (those-*dist.*) montañas verdes?
2. (This) taza es de Puebla.
3. (These) señores toman café.
4. (These) sillas son nuevas.
5. (Those) revistas son muy interesantes.
6. (Those) dibujos son muy finos.
7. (That-*dist.*) casa es gris.
8. (This) retrato es de mi esposa.
9. Vamos a visitar (those-*dist.*) ciudades.
10. (This) camisa es de Juan.
11. (That) blusa es de María.
12. Me gustan (these) dibujos.

36B. Read each question and answer aloud several times.

1. ¿Tiene Ud. que escribir una carta? Sí, tengo que escribir una carta.
2. ¿Tienen Uds. que hacer un viaje? No, no tenemos que hacer un viaje.
3. ¿Tienes hambre, hijito? Sí, tengo hambre.
4. ¿Tienes prisa, Carlito? No, no tengo prisa.
5. ¿De dónde viene Ud.? Vengo del cine.
6. ¿De dónde vienen Uds.? Venimos del parque.

36C. Translate into Spanish.

1. These gentlemen are seated in the dining room.
2. These cups are from Puebla.
3. I like (**me gustan**) these designs.
4. Those plates are from Oaxaca.
5. Do those (*dist.*) artists work slowly?
6. Has this family five children?
7. Are you hungry, sonny?
8. No, I am not hungry.
9. Do you have to write a letter, Mr. Adams?
10. Yes, I have to write a letter

PARTE CUARTA

Exercise No. 37—Preguntas

Answer in complete Spanish sentences.

1. ¿Dónde están sentados los señores Adams y López?
2. ¿Qué toman?
3. ¿Qué dice el Sr. Adams?
4. ¿De dónde es la taza blanca con los dibujos azules?
5. ¿Tiene cada distrito su propio estilo?
6. ¿De dónde es el jarro para crema?
7. ¿De dónde es el jarro para agua?
8. ¿Son verdaderos artistas los indios?
9. ¿Cómo trabajan los artesanos indios, despacio o de prisa?
10. ¿Tienen prisa los artistas?
11. ¿Para qué mercado es difícil obtener un surtido adecuado?
12. ¿Quién ve mucha cerámica de interés artístico?
13. ¿Dónde están los platos para frutas?
14. ¿De qué color son los dibujos en los platos para frutas?
15. ¿Tiene el Sr. Adams ejemplares de cerámica corriente?

CAPITULO 11 (ONCE)

PARTE PRIMERA

Números, Números, siempre Números

1. Ya sabe Ud. que los nombres de cosas y de personas son importantes. Ya sabe Ud. que no es posible hacer una frase sin verbos.

2. Es verdad, Sr. López.

3. Pues, hay palabras, señor, que son tan importantes como los nombres y los verbos. En efecto, no es posible imaginar nuestra civilización moderna sin estas palabras. ¿Puede Ud. adivinar en qué pienso?

4. Creo que sí. Ud. quiere decir los números.

5. Ud. tiene razón. ¿Puede Ud. enumerar algunas de las ocasiones en la vida moderna que necesitan números?

6. Seguramente. Nada es más fácil. Necesitamos números para comprar y vender.

7. ¡Ja, Ja, Ja! El comerciante piensa primero en comprar y vender. Pero sin dinero no valen mucho los números ¿no es verdad?

8. ¿Cómo no? Pues, necesitamos números para indicar la fecha, las horas del día, la temperatura; para expresar medidas y cantidades; para telefonear; para la radio; para todas las ciencias, y para mil cosas más.

9. Números, números, siempre números. Sí, Sr. Adams, no es posible pasar sin números. Pero una cosa es saber los números. Otra cosa es usarlos[2] y comprenderlos rápidamente y correctamente en la vida diaria.

10. Ud. tiene razón. Yo voy a hacer todo lo posible para comprenderlos y usarlos perfectamente.

11. Entretanto quiero decir que día por día Ud. adelanta mucho.

12. Es favor que Ud. me hace, señor López.

13. No es favor. Es verdad. Pues basta por hoy. Hasta luego.

14. Hasta el jueves próximo, señor.

1. You already know that the names of things and of persons are important. You already know that it is not possible to make a sentence without verbs.

2. It's true, Mr. Lopez.

3. Well, there are words, sir, that are as important as nouns and verbs. In fact, it is not possible to imagine our modern civilization without these words. Can you guess what I am thinking of?

4. I think so. You mean numbers.[1]

5. You are right. Can you enumerate some of the occasions in modern life that require numbers?

6. Certainly. Nothing is easier. We need numbers for buying and selling.

7. Ha, ha, ha! The businessman thinks first of buying and selling. But without money numbers are not worth much, are they?

8. Of course. Well, we need numbers to indicate the date, the time of day, the temperature; to express measures and quantities; to telephone; for the radio; for all the sciences, and for a thousand more things.

9. Numbers, numbers, always numbers. Yes, Mr. Adams, it is not possible to do without numbers. But it is one thing to know numbers. It is another thing to use them and understand them rapidly and correctly in daily life.

10. You are right. I am going to do everything possible to understand them and use them perfectly.

11. Meanwhile I want to say that day by day you are making much progress.

12. You flatter me, Mr. Lopez.

13. It is not flattery. It is the truth. Well, enough for today. So long.

14. Until next Thursday, sir.

NOTE: 1. *Lit.* you wish to say
NOTE: 2. los them. Pronouns which are objects of infinitives *follow* the verb and are attached to it.

Pronunciation and Spelling Aids

1. Practice:

ci-vi-li-za-ción	ne-ce-si-tar	se-gu-ra-men-te	en-tre-tan-to	can-ti-da-des
e-nu-me-rar	a-di-vi-nar	tem-pe-ra-tu-ra	cien-cias	per-fec-ta-men-te

Building Vocabulary

A. Palabras Relacionadas

1. necesitar	to need	necesario	necessary	la necesidad	necessity
2. enumerar	to enumerate	el número	the number	la enumeración	enumeration
3. civilizar	to civilize	la civilización	civilization		
4. indicar	to indicate	la indicación	indication		

B. El día and el mapa are exceptions to the rule that nouns ending in a are feminine.

Important Expressions

1. basta por hoy	enough for today	6. pensar en	to think of
2. Creo que sí	I think so	7. pasar sin números	to do without numbers
3. Creo que no	I think not	8. no valen mucho	are not worth much
4. Ud. tiene razón	You are right	9. en la vida diaria	in daily life
5. en efecto	in fact	10. todo lo posible	everything possible

Exercise No. 38—Completion of Text

1. ¿(Do you know) los números?
2. ¿Hay palabras que son (as important as) los verbos.
3. (Our civilization) no es posible sin números.
4. (You are right.)
5. ¿(Can you) enumerar unas ocasiones (that) demandan números?
6. Los números sin dinero (are not worth) mucho.
7. (We need) números para indicar (the date).
8. No es posible (to get along) sin números.
9. (In the meantime) quiero decir (that) Ud. adelanta mucho.
10. ¿(What is the meaning of) esta palabra?

PARTE SEGUNDA

Grammar Notes

1. **Verbs With Stem Changes**—pensar to think, querer to wish, contar to count, poder to be able.
The stem of a verb is that part which remains after the infinitive ending -ar, -er or -ir has been removed. Note the stem changes in the following verbs. The endings are regular.

I think, etc.	I wish, etc.	I count, etc.	I am able, etc.
pienso	quiero	cuento	puedo
piensas	quieres	cuentas	puedes
piensa	quiere	cuenta	puede
pensamos	queremos	contamos	podemos
pensáis	queréis	contáis	podéis
piensan	quieren	cuentan	pueden

Many verbs have stem changes from e to ie, like pensar and querer.
Many verbs have stem changes from o to ue, like contar and poder.
They will be indicated in the vocabulary as follows: pensar(ie), querer(ie), poder(ue), contar(ue).

NOTE: The stem changes do not occur in the **nosotros-as** (*we*) and the **vosotros-as** (*you, fam.*) forms.

2. **Los Números Desde uno (1) Hasta ciento (100)**

0	cero	5	cinco	10	diez
1	uno	6	seis	11	once
2	dos	7	siete	12	doce
3	tres	8	ocho	13	trece
4	cuatro	9	nueve	14	catorce

15	quince	26	veinte y seis (veintiséis)	60	sesenta
16	diez y seis (dieciséis)	27	veinte y siete (veintisiete)	65	sesenta y cinco
17	diez y siete (diecisiete)	28	veinte y ocho (veintiocho)	70	setenta
18	diez y ocho (dieciocho)	29	veinte y nueve (veintinueve)	76	setenta y seis
19	diez y nueve (diecinueve)	30	treinta	80	ochenta
20	veinte	31	treinta y uno	87	ochenta y siete
21	veinte y uno (veintiuno)	32	treinta y dos	90	noventa
22	veinte y dos (veintidós)	40	cuarenta	99	noventa y nueve
23	veinte y tres (veintitrés)	43	cuarenta y tres	100	ciento
24	veinte y cuatro (veinticuatro)	50	cincuenta		cien (before a noun)
25	veinte y cinco (veinticinco)	54	cincuenta y cuatro		

a. Before a masculine noun **uno** becomes **un.** Before a feminine noun **uno** becomes **una.**

un amigo   **una** amiga   veinte y **un** amigos   veinte y **una** amigas

b. Like any other adjective, **cuánto** (sing. *how much,* plur. *how many*) must agree with the noun it modifies: **cuánto** dinero   **cuánta** tinta (ink)   **cuántos** niños   **cuántas** niñas

PARTE TERCERA

Ejercicios (Exercises) No. 39A-39B-39C-39D

39A. Read aloud, saying the numbers in Spanish.

Ejemplo: treinta palabras españolas

1. 30 palabras españolas
2. 10 lecciones fáciles
3. 50 personas buenas
4. 49 carteles mexicanos
5. 16 colores vivos
6. 78 señoritas inteligentes
7. 17 casas blancas
8. 15 niños bonitos
9. 62 papeles verdes
10. 97 libros azules
11. 84 ciudades grandes
12. 13 plumas negras

39B. Read aloud and write in Spanish.

$2 + 6 = 8$ dos más seis son ocho $5 \times 4 = 20$ cinco por cuatro son veinte

$10 - 7 = 3$ diez menos siete son tres $12 \div 4 = 3$ doce dividido por cuatro son tres

$4 + 9 = 13$ $7 \times 8 = 56$ $19 - 8 = 11$ $50 \div 10 = 5$

$8 + 7 = 15$ $8 \times 3 = 24$ $16 - 3 = 13$ $80 \div 20 = 4$

39C. Read questions and answers aloud, saying all numbers in Spanish.

Ejemplo: ¿Cuántos días hay en enero?   (31) treinta y un días.

1. ¿Cuántos días hay en junio? (30 días)
2. ¿Cuántos meses hay en el año? (12 meses)
3. ¿Cuántos días hay en la semana? (7 días)
4. ¿Cuántas horas tiene un día? (24 horas)
5. ¿Cuántos minutos hay en una hora? (60 minutos)
6. ¿Cuántos segundos tiene un minuto? (60 segundos)
7. ¿Cuántos libros hay en el estante? (75 libros)
8. ¿Cuántos alumnos hay en la clase? (36 alumnos)
9. ¿Cuántos años tiene Ud? Tengo? (35) años
10. ¿Cuántos años tiene Carlos? Tiene (16) años.

39D. Substitute the correct form of the verb for the infinitive in parenthesis.

Ejemplo: 1. Yo quiero aprender los números.

1. Yo (querer) aprender los números.
2. Yo no (poder) ir a casa.
3. Nosotros (pensar) en los números.
4. ¿(Pensar) Ud. en su maestro?
5. ¿Qué (querer) decir esta palabra?[2]
6. Rosa no (querer) ir a la escuela.
7. ¿(Querer) Uds. hablar español?
8. Ellos no (poder) comprar el automóvil.
9. ¿(Poder) tú adivinar la respuesta?
10. Ellas (pensar) en comprar y vender.
11. Este radio[1] (valer) mucho.
12. Yo (contar) en español.
13. Tú (contar) en inglés.
14. ¿(Contar) ella bien?

NOTE: 1. **el radio** = the radio apparatus. **la radio** = the radio system, broadcasting.

NOTE: 2. What does this word mean? (*Lit.* What does this word wish to say?)

Exercise No. 40—Preguntas

Answer each question in a complete Spanish sentence.

1. ¿Son importantes los números?
2. ¿Son los números tan importantes como los nombres?
3. ¿Qué necesitamos para comprar y vender?
4. ¿En qué piensa primero el negociante?
5. ¿Valen mucho los números sin dinero?
6. ¿Es posible comprar y vender sin dinero?
7. ¿Vende y compra un comerciante?
8. ¿Es un comerciante comprador y vendedor?
9. ¿Quién adelanta día por día?
10. Dígame estos números en español: 10, 20, 30, 40, 50, 100.

CAPÍTULO 12 (DOCE)

PARTE PRIMERA

El Sistema Monetario De Mexico

1. En nuestra última conversación hemos dicho que no es posible imaginar nuestra civilización moderna sin números, es decir sin matemáticas. Igualmente no es posible imaginar un viaje sin matemáticas.

2. ¿Sabe Ud. cuántas veces se usan las matemáticas en un viaje?

3. Creo que sí. Se usan para cambiar dinero, para comprar boletos y comida, para pesar maletas, para medir distancias y tamaños y para ir de compras en tiendas, mercados y almacenes.

4. ¿Sabe Ud. el sistema monetario de México?

5. ¡Qué cosa! Ciertamente lo[1] sé! Yo soy un negociante que importa artículos mexicanos, ¿no es verdad? El peso es el "dólar" de México. El dólar norteamericano vale 12.50 pesos (doce pesos, cincuenta centavos).

6. Si quiere Ud. cambiar en pesos 10 (diez) dólares ¿cuántos pesos va Ud. a recibir?

7. Voy a recibir 125 pesos. (Ciento veinte y cinco pesos.)

8. Si quiere Ud. cambiar en pesos 100 (cien) dólares, ¿cuántos pesos va Ud. a recibir?

9. Voy a recibir 1250 (mil doscientos cincuenta) pesos.

10. ¡Cierto! Ud. va a la estación de ferrocarril. Quiere comprar dos boletos para Guadalajara. Cada boleto cuesta 45 pesos. Ud. da al vendidor 100 pesos. ¿Cuánto recibe Ud. de cambio?

11. Recibo 10 (diez) pesos de cambio.

12. Está bien. En nuestra próxima conversación vamos a continuar este tema importante. El ejercicio hace al maestro.

1. In our last conversation we said that it is not possible to imagine our modern civilization without numbers, that is to say, without mathematics. Likewise, it is not possible to imagine a trip without mathematics.

2. Do you know how many times one uses mathematics on a trip?

3. I think so. One uses it in order to change money, buy tickets and food, to weigh suitcases, to measure distances and sizes and to make purchases in shops, markets and department stores.

4. Do you know the monetary system of Mexico?

5. What an idea! I certainly do know it. I am a businessman who imports Mexican things, am I not? The peso is the "dollar" of Mexico. The North American dollar is worth 12.50 pesos.

6. If you want to change 10 dollars into pesos, how many pesos will you receive?

7. I will receive 125 pesos.

8. If you want to change 100 dollars into pesos, how many pesos will you receive?

9. I will receive 1250 pesos.

10. Right! You go to the railroad station. You want to buy two tickets for Guadalajara. Each ticket costs 45 pesos and you give the ticket agent 100 pesos. How much do you receive in change?

11. I receive 10 pesos change.

12. O.K. In our next conversation let us continue this important topic. Practice makes perfect. (*Lit.* Practice makes the master.)

NOTE: 1. lo (m) it. Object pronouns usually precede the verb.

Pronunciation and Spelling Hints

1. Practice.

i-gual-men-te   dis-tan-cias   Gua-da-la-ja-ra   es-ta-ción de fe-rro-ca-rril   con-ti-nuar

2. Una vez, dos veces. Since the letter **z** is unusual before **e** or **i**, words ending in **z** change **z** to **c** in the plural. Other examples are: **el lápiz** (pencil) **los lápices; la voz** (voice) **las voces; la actriz** (actress) **las actrices**

Building Vocabulary

A. 1. la maleta   el veliz (Mex.)   suitcase   **2. el equipaje**   baggage   **3. el baúl**   trunk

B. El Sistema Monetario de Mexico

The monetary system of Mexico is based on pesos and centavos. There are 100 centavos in a peso just as there are 100 cents in a dollar. However, at the present rate of exchange, one dollar equals twelve and one half pesos. Thus $10 (U.S.) equals 125 pesos. The dollar sign ($) is used in Mexico to indicate pesos. Thus $25 (Mex.) means 25 pesos; but it's well to make sure by asking, whether pesos are meant or U.S. dollars.

Expresiones Importantes

1. es decir	that is to say	**4. ir de compras**	to go shopping
2. ¡Qué cosa!	The idea!	**5. El ejercicio hace al maestro**	Practice makes perfect
3. de cambio	in change		

Exercise No. 41—Completion of Text

1. **Nuestra civilización no es posible sin números** (that is to say) **sin matemáticas.**
2. **¿**(How many times) **usa Ud. las matemáticas en un día?**
3. **Compro** (tickets and meals).
4. **Ud. no puede pesar** (suitcases) **y saber los** (sizes) **y las** (distances).
5. (The monetary system) **de México no es difícil.**
6. (Each) **dólar norteamericano vale 12.50 pesos.**
7. **En cada peso hay cien** (cents).
8. (That's correct). **Ud. va a recibir ocho pesos** (in change).
9. **Dos boletos para Guadalajara cuestan** (ninety) **pesos.**
10. **En nuestra** (next) **conversación vamos a continuar** (this) **tema.**

PARTE SEGUNDA

Grammar Notes

1. Present tense of **dar** to give, and **saber** to know, to know how.

I give, etc.		I know, etc.	
doy	damos	sé	sabemos
das	dais	sabes	sabéis
da	dan	sabe	saben

NOTE: Spanish verbs in the yo (*I*) form, present tense, end in **-o**. There are only five exceptions: soy, estoy, voy, doy and sé.

2. The Numbers 100 to 1000.

100 ciento (cien)	200 doscientos (as)	500 quinientos (as)	800 ochocientos (as)
101 ciento uno (un, una)	300 trescientos (as)	600 seiscientos (as)	900 novecientos (as)
102 ciento dos	400 cuatrocientos (as)	700 setecientos (as)	1000 mil

a. Before a noun **ciento** becomes **cien**. Thus: **cien libros, cien plumas,** etc.
b. **y** is never used between the hundreds and tens. Thus: 342 (**trescientos cuarenta y dos**)

c. Note the formation of numbers over one thousand:

1954 mil novecientos cincuenta y cuatro   2662 dos mil seiscientos sesenta y dos

d. The hundreds agree in gender with the nouns they modify. Thus:

trescientos libros,   trescientas plumas.

3. More about Object Pronouns.

a. **lo** (*it*), direct object pronoun, stands for a thing in the masculine gender.

b. **la** (*it*), direct object pronoun, stands for a thing in the feminine gender.

¿Sabe Ud. el sistema monetario? Lo sé.	Do you know the monetary system? I know it.
¿Sabe Ud. la respuesta? La sé.	Do you know the answer? I know it.

Ejercicios (Exercises) No. 41A-41B-41C

41A. Write out the numbers in Spanish.

Ejemplo: 250 doscientos cincuenta

1. 400	3. 525	5. 627	7. 560	9. 200
2. 350	4. 860	6. 490	8. 780	10. 970

41B. Practice the following table aloud:

$1.00	Un dólar vale	$12.50	doce pesos cincuenta centavos
$2.00	Dos dólares valen	$25.00	veinte y cinco pesos
$3.00	Tres dólares valen	$37.50	treinta y siete pesos cincuenta centavos
$4.00	Cuatro dólares valen	$50.00	cincuenta pesos
$5.00	Cinco dólares valen	$62.50	sesenta y dos pesos cincuenta centavos
$6.00	Seis dólares valen	$75.00	setenta y cinco pesos
$7.00	Siete dólares valen	$87.50	ochenta y siete pesos cincuenta centavos
$8.00	Ocho dólares valen	$100.00	cien pesos
$9.00	Nueve dólares valen	$112.50	ciento doce pesos cincuenta centavos
$10.00	Diez dólares valen	$125.00	ciento veinte y cinco pesos

NOTE: The exchange rate of the peso as of January 1955 was $12.50 to the dollar, or one peso for 8 cents. If it changes you can revise the table.

41C. Translate.

1. I know the numbers.
2. Do you (Ud.) know where he lives?
3. We know what (qué) he wants.
4. We do not give the money.
5. Do they give the tickets?
6. What does John give?
7. She does now know the answer.
8. We are not giving our books.
9. Do you (tú) know the questions?
10. They do not know who (quién) lives here.

Exercise No. 42—Preguntas

Answer each question giving the numbers in full in Spanish.

Ejemplo: Recibo cuarenta pesos de cambio.

1. Si una cosa cuesta 10 pesos y Ud. da un billete de 50 pesos, ¿cuánto recibe Ud. de cambio?
2. Si un boleto cuesta 25 pesos, ¿cuánto da Ud. por tres boletos?
3. Si una revista cuesta 2.50 pesos ¿cuánto da Ud. por dos revistas?
4. Si un diario cuesta un peso y Ud. le[1] da al vendedor un billete de cinco pesos, ¿cuánto recibe Ud. de cambio?
5. Si Ud. tiene un billete de cincuenta pesos, dos billetes de cien pesos, y veinte billetes de un peso, ¿cuánto dinero tiene Ud. en el bolsillo (pocket)?
6. Si un hombre tiene un millon de pesos, ¿es millionario?
7. ¿Qué vale más, $500 (quinientos dolares) norteamericanos o 5000 (cinco mil) pesos?
8. ¿Sabe Ud. cuánto dinero hay en el banco de México?
9. ¿Sabe Ud. el sistema monetario de México?   10. ¿Cuándo vamos a continuar este tema?

NOTE: 1. le = *to him*. Do not translate it. The Spanish often uses a pronoun object, even when the noun object (in this case al vendedor) is expressed.

CAPÍTULO 13 (TRECE)

PARTE PRIMERA

Problemas de Aritmética. En el Restaurante. En la Estación. En la Tienda

1. Vamos a continuar nuestro estudio de los usos de las matemáticas en un viaje.

2. En el restaurante tomamos la cena. Somos cuatro. Las cenas cuestan $3.30 (tres pesos, treinta centavos), $2.80 (dos pesos, ochenta centavos), $5.90 (cinco pesos, noventa centavos), y $4.50. (cuatro pesos, cincuenta centavos). Damos al mesero una propina de diez por ciento. ¿Cuánto es la cuenta? ¿La propina?

3. La cuenta es $16.50 (diez y seis pesos cincuenta centavos). La propina es $1.65 (un peso sesenta y cinco centavos).

4. Está bien. En la estación de ferrocarril tengo una maleta muy pesada. Pongo la maleta en la balanza. Pesa 30 kilos. ¿Qué hago para saber cuánto pesa la maleta en libras?

5. No es difícil. En un kilo hay aproximadamente 2.2 (dos y dos décimos) libras. Ud. multiplica 30 (treinta) por 2.2. La maleta pesa 66 (sesenta y seis) libras.

6. Correcto. En México y en los otros países de Hispanoamérica, no se usan[1] millas sino kilómetros para medir las distancias. ¿Sabe Ud. cambiar kilómetros en millas?

7. Por cierto. Divido por ocho y multiplico por cinco. De este modo ochenta kilómetros son iguales a cincuenta millas. Es fácil, ¿verdad?

8. Ud. calcula muy aprisa. Solamente un problema más. En una tienda Ud. compra un sarape a 40 (cuarenta) pesos, dos rebozos a 32 (treinta y dos) pesos, tres cestas a 12 (doce) pesos y cuatro cinturones a 7 (siete) pesos. ¿Cuál es el precio total?

9. $168 (ciento sesenta y ocho pesos). Y si le doy al comerciante $200 voy a recibir 32 (treinta y dos) pesos de cambio.

10. Bueno. Nada más de matemáticas por hoy. El jueves vamos a platicar sobre la hora. Es un tema de inmensa importancia.

11. Seguramente. Espero una conversación interesante.

12. A propósito, Sr. Adams, el próximo jueves no puedo llegar antes de las ocho y media de la noche.

13. Bien. Más vale tarde que nunca.

14. Bien dicho. Hasta la vista, Sr. Adams.

15. Hasta el jueves, Sr. López.

1. Let us continue our study of the uses of mathematics on a trip.

2. In the restaurant we have dinner. We are four. The dinners cost $3.30 (Mex.), $2.80, $5.90 and $4.50. We give the waiter a ten per cent tip. How much is the bill? The tip?

3. The bill is $16.50 (Mex.). The tip is $1.65.

4. That is correct. In the railroad station I have a very heavy suitcase. I put the suitcase on the scales. It weighs 30 kilos. What do I do to find out how much the suitcase weighs in pounds?

5. It is not difficult. In one kilo there are approximately 2.2 pounds. You multiply 30 by 2.2. The suitcase weighs 66 pounds.

6. Correct. In Mexico and in the other countries of Hispanic America, not miles but kilometers are used[1] to measure distances. Do you know how to change kilometers into miles?

7. Certainly. I divide by eight and multiply by five. Thus eighty kilometers are equal to fifty miles. It's easy, isn't it?

8. You figure very fast. Only one more problem. In a store you buy one sarape for 40 pesos, two shawls at 32 pesos, three baskets at 12 pesos and four belts at seven pesos. What is the total price?

9. 168 pesos. And if I give the merchant $200, I will receive 32 pesos in change.

10. Good. No more mathematics for today. On Thursday we are going to talk about the time of day. It is a topic of great importance.

11. Surely. I am expecting an interesting conversation.

12. By the way Mr. Adams, next Thursday I cannot arrive before 8.30 p.m.

13. That's all right. Better late than never.

14. Well said. Good-bye, Mr. Adams.

15. Until Thursday, Mr. Lopez.

NOTE: 1. The reflexive verb is often used in Spanish to express the passive. Thus: **Sarapes se venden.** Sarapes are sold. *Lit.* Sarapes sell themselves.

Pronunciation and Spelling Helps

1. Practice:

res-tau-**ran**-te   mul-ti-pli-**car**   cin-tu-ro-nes   mul-ti-pli-co   co-mer-**cian**-te   pa-**í**-ses

Remember: **au** is pronounced like *ow* in *cow*.

2. **kilómetro.** A few foreign words borrowed by Spanish are spelled with **k**.

Building Vocabulary

A. **el día, el mapa, el sistema, el problema, el tema,** are masculine. Remember: Most nouns ending in -a are feminine.

B. Synonyms (words of about the same meaning)

1. aprisa   rápidamente   rapidly   3. despacio   lentamente   slowly
2. el negociante   el comerciante   the businessman   4. de este modo   de esta manera   in this way

C. Antonyms (opposites)

1. rápidamente   rapidly   despacio   slowly   3. dar   to give   recibir   to receive
2. comprador   buyer   vendedor   seller   4. multiplicar   to multiply   dividir   to divide

Expresiones Importantes

1. **por ciento**   per cent   6. **Tomamos la cena**   We have dinner
2. **de este modo**   thus, in this way   7. **¿Cuánto es la cuenta?**   How much is the bill?
3. **nada más**   nothing more, that's all   8. **Está bien**   Good, that's right
4. **kilométro**   about ⅝ mile   9. **Refrán (proverb):**   Better late than never.
5. **por cierto**   certainly, surely   **Más vale tarde que nunca.**

PARTE SEGUNDA

Grammar Notes

1. The Present Tense of **hacer** to make, to do; **decir** to say; **poner** to put.

I make, etc.		I say, etc.		I put, etc.	
hago	hacemos	digo	decimos	pongo	ponemos
haces	hacéis	dices	decís	pones	ponéis
hace	hacen	dice	dicen	pone	ponen

a. **salir** to leave, **valer** to be worth, **traer**, to bring and **caer**, to fall have a **g** in the first person, but are regular in the other forms of the present tense.

Sing.	salgo	sales	sale	Plur.	salimos	salís	salen
Sing.	valgo	vales	vale	Plur.	valemos	valéis	valen
Sing.	traigo	traes	trae	Plur.	traemos	traéis	traen
Sing.	caigo	caes	cae	Plur.	caemos	caéis	caen

2. Possessive Adjectives. Summary. You are familiar with the possessive adjective **mi (mis)** and **su (sus).** Learn the meaning and forms of all the possessive adjectives.

	Singular		Plural	
	masc.	fem.	masc.	fem.
(my)	mi hijo	mi hija	mis hijos	mis hijas
(your — fam.)	tu hijo	tu hija	tus hijos	tus hijas
(your, his, her) (its, their)	su hijo	su hija	sus hijos	sus hijas
(our)	nuestro hijo	nuestra hija	nuestros hijos	nuestras hijas
(your — fam.)	vuestro hijo	vuestra hija	vuestros hijos	vuestras hijas

a. Possessive adjectives agree with the nouns they modify in number and gender.

b. **tu (tus)** *your* is used to show possession when one person is addressed familiarly. **tú** (*you*) has an accent mark, **tu** (*your*) has not.

> **Tú no tienes tu libro, hijita.** You haven't your book, girlie.

c. **Vuestro, (-a, -os, -as)** (*your*) is used to show possession when more than one person is addressed familiarly. However, do not use this possessive adjective. Like the subject pronoun **vosotros**, it is rarely used in Spanish America. Use **su (sus)** *your* instead.

> **Uds. no tienen sus libros, niños.** You haven't your books, children.

d. **su (sus)** means *your, his, her, its, their,* according to the sense of the sentence. In cases where the meaning would be in doubt the definite article is used before the noun, and the phrase **de Ud., de él, de ella, de Uds., de ellos,** or **de ellas** after the noun.

el padre de él	his father	**la familia de ellos**	their family
la madre de ella	her mother	**la clase de ellas**	their class
la casa de Ud.	your house	**los hijos de Uds.**	your sons

3. **pero** and **sino**. After a negative, **sino** is used instead of **pero** in the sense of "but on the contrary," "but rather."

> **No es rico *sino* pobre.** He is not rich, *but* poor.
> **No se usan libras *sino* kilos.** Not pounds, *but* kilos are used.

However, **pero** must be used if the subject changes.

> **El no es rico, *pero* su tío es rico.** He is not rich, *but* his uncle is rich.

Ejercicios (Exercises) No. 43A-43B-43C-43D

43A. Complete the following sentences, substituting the correct form of **mi, tu, su** or **nuestro** for the words in parentheses.

> Ejemplo: **No tenemos nuestros boletos.**

1. No tenemos (our) boletos.
2. ¿Cuánto cuesta (your) cena, señor?
3. ¿Son muy pesadas (your) maletas, señorita?
4. No, (my) maletas no son muy pesadas.
5. ¿Es muy interesante (their) conversación?
6. ¿Hay cien pesos en (his) escritorio?
7. (Our) equipaje está en la estación.
8. ¿Dónde está (your) madre, niño?
9. ¿(My) amigos están en el restaurante.
10. ¿(Our) civilización no es posible sin números.

43B. Read the following, giving the numbers in Spanish.

> Ejemplo: **Diez kilos son iguales a veinte y dos libras.**

1. 10 kilos = 22 libras
2. 20 kilos = 44 libras
3. 30 kilos = 66 libras
4. 40 kilos = 88 libras
5. 50 kilos = 110 libras
6. 16 kilómetros = 10 miles
7. 32 kilómetros = 20 miles
8. 48 kilómetros = 30 miles
9. 64 kilómetros = 40 miles
10. 80 kilómetros = 50 miles

43C. Translate into Spanish.

1. I say
2. I do
3. I am going out
4. I have
5. we say
6. we do not put
7. they make
8. they put
9. do you (Ud.) make?
10. do you (Uds.) go out?
11. do you (Uds.) say?
12. you (tú) make
13. do you (Ud.) put?
14. I put
15. it is worth

43D. Complete the following sentences with **pero** or **sino** as the sense requires.

1. El señor no estudia el francés (but) el español.
2. No es comerciante (but) profesor.
3. Yo no estudio el español, (but) mi hermano lo estudia.
4. No ponemos los libros en la mesa (but) en el estante.
5. Es un muchacho inteligente, (but) es perezoso (lazy).

Exercise No. 44—Preguntas

1. ¿Dónde toman Uds. la cena?
2. ¿Qué por ciento dan Uds. al mesero como propina?
3. ¿Cuánto es la propina?
4. ¿Dónde tiene Ud. su maleta pesada?
5. ¿Cuánto pesa la maleta en kilos? ¿En libras?
6. ¿Qué se usa en México para medir las distancias, kilómetros o millas?
7. ¿Quién sabe cambiar kilómetros en millas?
8. ¿Qué artículos compra el Sr. Adams en una tienda?
9. ¿Cuál es el tema de la proxima conversación?
10. ¿Qué refrán (proverb) usa el Sr. Adams?

CAPÍTULO 14 (CATORCE)

PARTE PRIMERA

¿Qué Hora Es?

1. ¡La hora! Todo el mundo quiere saber — ¿Qué hora es? ¿A qué hora llega el avión? ¿A qué hora sale el tren? ¿A qué hora comienzan los exámenes? ¿A qué hora comienza la película? ¿A qué hora comienza la función? Y un millón de otras preguntas.

2. Sr. Adams, yo voy a hacer el papel de boletero en la taquilla de la estación del ferrocarril. Ud. va a hacer el papel de viajero que quiere comprar un boleto y pide informes. Favor de comenzar.

3. Buenos días, señor. Quiero comprar un boleto para Puebla.

4. ¿De primera o de segunda clase?

5. De primera, por favor. ¿Cuánto vale el pasaje?

6. Cincuenta pesos por un boleto sencillo o 95 (noventa y cinco) por boleto de viaje redondo.

7. Favor de darme un boleto de viaje redondo. Quiero salir el lunes.

8. Aquí tiene Ud. el boleto. Cuesta 95 pesos.

9. Gracias. ¿A qué hora sale el tren y cuándo llega a Puebla?

10. Sale a las cuatro menos diez de la tarde y llega a las diez menos doce de la noche.

11. Muchas gracias, señor.

12. De nada.

13. Excelente, Sr. Adams. Ud. puede ir pasando en Mexico.

1. The time! Everybody wants to know: What time is it? At what time does the plane arrive? At what time does the train leave? At what time do the examinations begin. At what time does the film begin? At what time does the performance begin? And a million other questions.

2. I am going to play the role of ticket agent at the window in the railroad station. You are going to take the part of a traveler who wants to buy a ticket and is asking for information. Please begin.

3. Good day, sir. I wish to buy a ticket for Puebla.

4. First or second class?

5. First class, please. How much is the fare?

6. Fifty pesos a one way ticket or 95 pesos for a round trip.

7. Please give me a round trip ticket. I want to leave on Monday.

8. Here is the ticket. It costs 95 pesos.

9. Thanks. At what time does the train leave and when does it arrive at Puebla?

10. It leaves at 3.50 in the afternoon and arrives at 9.48 in the evening.

11. Many thanks, sir.

12. Don't mention it.

13. Excellent, Mr. Adams. You can get along in Mexico.

---

1. Ahora yo hago el papel de boletero de un cine. Ud., Sr. Adams, pide informes sobre la función. Favor de comenzar.

2. Por favor, señor, ¿a qué hora comienzan las funciones del cine?

1. Now I am playing the part of the ticket agent at a motion picture theater. You, Mr. Adams, ask for information about the show. Please begin.

2. Please, sir, at what time do the performances begin.

3. Hay tres funciones. La primera comienza a las 4.20 (las cuatro y veinte) de la tarde, la segunda a las 6.50 (a las siete menos diez), y la tercera a las 9.10 (las nueve y diez) de la noche.

4. ¿Hay noticiero?

5. ¿Cómo no? Veinte minutos antes de cada pelicula.

6. ¿Cuánto cuestan los boletos?

7. Tres pesos cada uno. Si Ud. viene temprano va a obtener asientos buenos.

8. Favor de darme dos boletos para la tercera función.

9. Aquí los tiene. Muchas gracias.

10. Admirable, Sr. Adams. Repito— Ud. puede ir pasando en México.

3. There are three showings. The first begins at 4.20 in the afternoon. The second at 6.50, and the third at 9.10 in the evening.

4. Is there a newsreel?

5. Of course. Twenty minutes before each picture.

6. How much do the tickets cost?

7. Three pesos each. If you come early you will obtain good seats.

8. Please give me two tickets for the third showing.

9. Here they are. Thank you very much.

10. Admirable, Mr. Adams. I repeat: You can get along in Mexico.

Pronunciation and Spelling Helps

1. Practice:

co-mien-za	cual-quie-ra	mi-llas	cum-ple-a-ños	Oa-xa-ca
ex-á-me-nes	va-ca-cio-nes	co-rrec-ta-men-te	ta-qui-lla	(wah-hah-kah)

Vocabulary Building

A. Sinónimos (Synonyms):

1. comenzar (ie)   empezar (ie)   to begin
2. la taquilla   la boletería (Mex.)   ticket office
3. el billete   el boleto   the ticket
4. de nada   no hay de qué   don't mention it
5. el diario   el periódico   newspaper

B. Words Dealing with Trains:

1. ¿A que hora sale el tren para—?
   At what time does the train leave for—?
2. ¿Cuándo llega el tren de—?
   When does the train arrive from—?
3. El tren sale (llega) a las dos.
   The train leaves (arrives) at 2 o'clock.
4. un boleto sencillo
   a one-way ticket

5. un boleto de primera (segunda)
   a first (second) class ticket
6. un boleto de pullman
   a pullman ticket
7. un boleto de viaje redondo
   a round trip ticket
8. ¿Cuanto cuesta (vale) el pasaje?
   How much is the fare?

Expresiones Importantes

1. todo el mundo   everybody
2. desde uno hasta ciento   from 1 to 100
3. hacer el papel de   to play the part (role) of
4. pedir informes   to ask for information

5. favor de comenzar   please begin
6. Aquí tiene Ud. el boleto.   Here is the ticket
7. Ud. puede ir pasando   you can get along
8. La próxima vez   next time

Exercise No. 45—Completion of Text

1. ¿A qué hora comienza (the film)?
2. ¿A qué hora comienza (the performance)?
3. ¿Tienen Uds. (other questions)?
4. ¿El boletero está en la (ticket office).
5. ¿Dónde está (the railroad station)?
6. Ud. es un viajero que (is asking for information).

7. Favor de darme (a round trip ticket).
8. ¿A qué hora (does the train leave)?
9. ¿Llega (at nine in the evening)?
10. (Many thanks.)
11. (Don't mention it.)
12. Ahora (I play the role) de boletero

PARTE SEGUNDA

Grammar Notes

1. Verbs with Stem Changes **e** to **i**—**pedir** to ask for, **repetir** to repeat

I ask for, you ask for, etc.		I repeat, you repeat, etc.	
pido	pedimos	repito	repetimos
pides	pedís	repites	repetís
pide	piden	repite	repiten

a. The stem change **e** to **i** does not occur in the nosotros-as (*we*) and the vosotros-as (*you, fam.*) forms.

b. Verbs with stem changes from **e** to **i**, like **pedir** and **repetir**, will be indicated in the vocabulary as follows: **pedir(i), repetir(i).**

2. Time of Day

¿Qué hora es?	What time is it?	Son las cinco y media.	It is half past five.
Es la una.	It is one o'clock.	Son las seis y cuarto.	It is a quarter past six.
Son las dos.	It is two o'clock.	Son las seis y veinte.	It is twenty minutes past six.
Son las tres.	It is three o'clock.	Son las siete menos cuarto.	It is a quarter to seven.
Son las cuatro	It is four o'clock.	Son las siete menos veinte.	It is twenty minutes to seven.

¿A qué hora? A la una en punto.	At what time? At one o'clock sharp.
A las ocho de la mañana.	At eight o'clock in the morning (A.M.)
A las cinco de la tarde.	At five o'clock in the afternoon (P.M.)
A las nueve de la noche.	At nine o'clock at night (P.M.)
A mediodía. A medianoche.	At noon. At midnight.

a. Use the singular verb **es** in all time expressions involving **la una.**

(1.12) **Es la una y doce.**   (1.30) **Es la una y media.**

b. Use the plural verb **son** for all other time expressions.

c. **y** (*and, after*) is used for time after the hour (**cuarto, media, minutos**)
Menos (*less, to*) is used for time before the hour.

d. Base time expressions after the half hour on the following hour.

(6.40) **Son las siete menos veinte.**   It is twenty minutes to seven.

e. If no clock time is mentioned, use **por la mañana, por la tarde** and **por la noche** for in the morning, in the afternoon, and at night. With clock time use **de la mañana, de la tarde** and **de la noche.**

Trabajo por la mañana.	I work in the morning.
Trabajo a las ocho de la mañana.	I work at 8 o'clock in the morning.

PARTE TERCERA

Ejercicios (Exercises) No. 46A-46B-46C

46A. Read these sentences giving the time in Spanish.

Ejemplo: **El tren de Oaxaca llega a las cinco y media de la tarde.**

1. **El tren de Oaxaca llega a (5:30 P.M.)**
2. **El tren llega a Puebla a (8:15 P.M.)**
3. **El tren para Cuernavaca sale a (9:55 A.M.)**
4. **El tren para Guadalajara sale a (10:50 A.M.)**
5. **La primera función comienza a (2:20 P.M.)**
6. **La segunda función comienza a (4:40 P.M.)**
7. **La tercera función comienza a (7:10 P.M.)**
8. **El noticiero comienza a (6:50 P.M.)**
9. **Vamos a tomar la cena a (7:45 P.M.).**
10. **Tomamos el almuerzo (at noon).**

46B. Fill in the correct form of the verbs in parentheses.

Ejemplo: Yo pido informes.

1. Yo (pedir) informes.
2. Nosotros (comenzar) a comer.
3. Ellos (repetir) las preguntas.
4. ¿Quién (pedir) informes?
5. Yo (comenzar) a trabajar.
6. ¿(Empezar) Ud. a trabajar ahora?
7. ¿Qué (pedir) tú, niña?
8. ¿Qué (pedir) Uds.?
9. El maestro (repetir) la respuesta.
10. ¿Por qué no (comenzar) la función?

46C. Translate into Spanish.

1. I want a round trip ticket.
2. He is asking for information.
3. When does the train for Oaxaca leave?
4. Do you know when the train arrives from Puebla?
5. It arrives at 5.30 in the afternoon.
6. At what time does the first performance begin?
7. It begins at 3.20 in the afternoon.
8. Do they repeat the performance?
9. Yes, they repeat the performance twice (dos veces).
10. Here are the tickets.

Exercise No. 47—Preguntas

1. ¿Qué quiere saber todo el mundo?
2. ¿Quién hace el papel de viajero?
3. ¿Quién hace el papel de boletero?
4. ¿Qué clase de boleto quiere comprar?
5. ¿Cuánto cuesta un boleto de viaje redondo?
6. ¿Quién hace el papel de boletero de un cine?
7. ¿Quién pide informes?
8. ¿Cuántas funciones tiene este cine?
9. ¿Para qué función compra el señor dos boletos?
10. ¿Cuánto paga por los dos boletos?

REPASO 3

CAPÍTULOS 10–14 PARTE PRIMERA

Repaso de Palabras

NOUNS

1. el agua	16. la estación	31. el pasaje	1. water	16. station	31. fare
2. el boleto	17. la fecha	32. el platillo	2. ticket	17. date	32. saucer
3. el bolsillo	18. la flor	33. el plato	3. pocket	18. flower	33. plate
4. la cesta	19. la fruta	34. la propina	4. basket	19. fruit	34. tip
5. la cena	20. la función	35. el pueblo	5. dinner	20. performance	35. people, town
6. el cine	21. la hora	36. el rebozo	6. movies	21. hour	36. shawl
7. la clase	22. el jarro	37. el sarape	7. class	22. jar, pitcher	37. blanket
8. la comida	23. la llegada	38. el tamaño	8. meal	23. arrival	38. size
9. el comprador	24. la maleta	39. la taquilla	9. buyer	24. suitcase	39. ticketwindow
10. el dibujo	25. el mercado	40. el tipo	10. drawing	25. market	40. type
11. la cuenta	26. el mesero	41. la tienda	11. bill	26. waiter	41. store
12. el cumpleaños	27. el modo	42. el vendedor	12. birthday	27. way	42. seller
13. el dinero	28. el número	43. el viajero	13. money	28. number	43. traveler
14. el dólar	29. el pájaro	44. el vaso	14. dollar	29. bird	44. glass
15. el equipaje	30. el pan	45. el uso	15. baggage	30. bread	45. use

VERBS

1. caer	13. hacer	25. saber	1. to fall	13. to make, do	25. to know (how
2. cambiar	14. llegar	26. tomar	2. to change	14. to arrive	26. to take
3. contar (ue)	15. mirar	27. traer	3. to count	15. to look at	27. to bring
4. comprar	16. necesitar	28. telefonear	4. to buy	16. to need	28. to telephone
5. continuar	17. obtener	29. repetir (i)	5. to continue	17. to obtain	29. to repeat
6. comer	18. pagar	30. recibir	6. to eat	18. to pay	30. to receive
7. comenzar (ie)	19. pensar (ie)	31. saber	7. to begin	19. to think	31. to know
8. creer	20. poder (ue)	32. salir (de)	8. to believe	20. to be able	32. to leave
9. dar	21. poner	33. tener	9. to give	21. to put	33. to have
10. decir	22. venir	34. valer	10. to say	22. to come	34. to be worth
11. demandar	23. pedir (i)	35. vender	11. to demand	23. to ask for	35. to sell
12. empezar (ie)	24. querer (ie)	36. hemos dicho	12. to begin	24. to want, wish	36. we have said

ADJECTIVES

1. alguno	8. cualquier	15. mismo	1. some	8. any	15. same
2. antiguo	9. diario	16. necesario	2. old	9. daily	16. necessary
3. cada	10. diligente	17. nuestro	3. each	10. diligent	17. our
4. cierto	11. fino	18. pesado	4. certain	11. fine	18. heavy
5. conocido	12. igual	19. propio	5. known	12. equal	19. own
6. correcto	13. ligero	20. sencillo	6. correct	13. light	20. simple
7. corriente	14. más	21. todo	7. ordinary	14. more	21. all

ADVERBS

1. aprisa	6. lentamente	1. quickly	6. slowly
2. ahora	7. más	2. now	7. more
3. ahorita	8. solamente	3. now, right away	8. only
4. correctamente	9. tan	4. correctly	9. so, as
5. entretanto	10. tan rico como	5. meanwhile	10. as rich as

PREPOSITIONS

1. antes de	3. hasta	5. acerca de	1. before	3. to, until	5. about, concerning
2. desde	4. sobre		2. from	4. on, upon	

IMPORTANT EXPRESSIONS

1. aquí tiene Ud.	15. hoy día	1. here is, are	15. nowadays
2. creo que sí	16. ir de compras	2. I think so	16. to go shopping
3. creo que no	17. ir pasando	3. I think not	17. to get along
4. de cambio	18. nada más	4. in change	18. nothing more
5. de este modo	19. pasar sin	5. in this way	19. to get along without
6. de la misma manera	20. pensar en	6. in the same way	20. to think of
7. ¿Qué quiere decir-?	21. por cierto	7. What is the meaning of . . . ?	21. indeed, certainly
8. ¡qué cosa!	22. por todas partes	8. the idea!	22. everywhere
9. tener prisa	23. todo el mundo	9. to be in a hurry	23. everybody
10. tener que	24. todo lo posible	10. to have to	24. everything possible
11. tener razón	25. ¡ya lo creo!	11. to be right	25. yes indeed!
12. en efecto	26. Más vale tarde que nunca.	12. in fact	26. Better late than never.
13. es decir	27. El ejercicio hace al maestro.	13. that is to say	27. Practice makes perfect.
14. favor de darme		14. please give me	

PARTE SEGUNDA

Ejercicio 48. Answer the following questions in the affirmative in complete sentences.

Ejemplo: 1. Sí, pienso en mi amigo.

1. ¿Piensa Ud. en su amigo?
2. ¿Quiere Ud. hacer un viaje a México?
3. ¿Puede Ud. comprar un automóvil?
4. ¿Pone Ud. la lámpara en el piano?
5. ¿Sale Ud. mañana de la ciudad?
6. ¿Cuenta Ud. siempre el cambio?
7. ¿Dice Ud. las palabras dos veces?
8. ¿Continúa Ud. la lección?
9. ¿Le[1] da Ud. una propina al mesero?
10. Sabe Ud. contar en español?

Note: 1. le *to him*, is not translated here.

Ejercicio 49. Answer the following questions in the negative in complete sentences. Be sure to use the nosotros (*we*) form.

Ejemplo: 1. No repetimos las respuestas.

1. ¿Repiten Uds. las respuestas?
2. ¿Hacen Uds. muchas preguntas?
3. ¿Piden Uds. informes?
4. ¿Tienen Uds. prisa?
5. ¿Vienen Uds. temprano a casa?
6. ¿Creen Uds. el cuento (story)?
7. ¿Traen Uds. el equipaje?
8. ¿Toman Uds. la cena?
9. ¿Necesitan Uds. dinero?
10. ¿Tienen Uds. que trabajar?

Ejercicio 50. Select the phrase in the right hand column which best completes the sentence begun in the left hand column.

1. Este tipo de ceramica
2. Estos dibujos son de flores

a. hace al maestro.
b. es conocido por todas partes.

3. Cada negociante piensa   c. antes de las nueve.
4. Ud. sabe que el ejercicio   d. y ésos son de animalitos.
5. Vamos a continuar   e. para comprar dos boletos.
6. No puedo llegar   f. cuando hablo español.
7. Voy a la boletería   g. primero tiene.
8. Sé a qué hora   h. en comprar y vender.
9. El me comprende   i. este tema interesante.
10. Quien primero viene   j. comienza la función.

jercicio 51. Complete the following sentences by choosing the proper expression from those listed below.

1. (How much does it cost?) **Cada turista** (must know) **esta expresión.**

2. **El turista** (asks for information) **en la estación del ferrocarril.—¿**(At what time) **llega el tren de Oaxaca?** **Dice el empleado—**(At 7.30) **de la noche.**

3. **El turista** (is hungry). **Toma una** (meal) **en un restaurante.** (He pays the bill) **con un billete de diez pesos. Recibe cuatro pesos** (in change). **Le da al mesero** (a tip) **de sesenta centavos,** (that is to say), **diez por ciento.**

4. (Thinks) **el turista—**(Everywhere) **son necesarios los números y** (money).

tiene que saber	tiene hambre	es decir
¿a qué hora?	paga la cuenta	el dinero
¿Cuánto cuesta?	una comida	piensa
a las siete y media	por todas partes	una propina
pide informes	de cambio	tiene sed

Ejercicio 52. Translate the demonstrative adjectives in parentheses.

1. (this) **cena**	5. (this) **tipo**	9. (these) **casas**
2. (these) **rebozos**	6. (that) **estación**	10. (those) **fechas**
3. (that) **viajero**	7. (that-dist.) **montaña**	11. (that-dist.) **cielo**
4. (those) **vasos**	8. (those) **tejidos**	12. (those-dist.) **montañas**

Ejercicio 53. From group II select antonyms for each word in group I.

I		II	
1. comprar	6. dividir	a. recibir	f. ir
2. venir	7. llegar a	b. tarde	g. después de
3. dar	8. más	c. aprisa	h. multiplicar
4. antes de	9. lentamente	d. salir de	i. comprador
5. temprano	10. vendedor	e. vender	j. menos

PARTE TERCERA
Diálogo

Practice the Spanish Aloud.

Una Turista Pide Informes Acerca de la Cerámica Mexicana

1. **Favor de decirme, señor — ¿De qué distritos de México son los mejores ejemplares de la cerámica mexicana? Deseo comprar un juego de tazas, platillos y platos.**

2. **Pues, cada distrito tiene su propio estilo. La cerámica de Puebla, Oaxaca y Michoacán es bien conocida por todas partes.**

3. **¿Tengo que ir a aquellos distritos para obtener los mejores ejemplares?**

4. **De ninguna manera. Ud. puede comprar cerámica de todos los distritos aquí mismo en la capital.**

5. **¿Cuesta más aquí?**

1. Please tell me, sir: From which districts of Mexico come the best examples of Mexican pottery? I want to buy a set of cups, saucers and plates.

2. Well, each district has its own style. The pottery of Puebla, Oaxaca, and Michoacan is well known everywhere.

3. Do I have to go to those districts to obtain the best examples?

4. By no means. You can buy pottery from all the districts right here in the capital.

5. Does it cost more here?

6. Por supuesto cuesta más. Pero hay un surtido excelente.

7. Favor de decirme los nombres de algunas tiendas de cerámica.

8. Hay muchas en la Avenida Juárez. En aquella avenida está también el Museo Nacional de Artes e Industrias Populares.

9. ¿Se vende cerámica allí?

10. ¡Ya lo creo! Lo mejor de México.

11. Muchas gracias, señor.

12. De nada, señorita.

6. Of course it costs more. But there is an excellent assortment.

7. Please tell me the names of a few pottery shops.

8. There are many on Juarez Avenue. On that avenue there is also the National Museum of Popular Arts and Industries.

9. Do they sell pottery there?

10. I should say so! The best in Mexico.

11. Many thanks, sir.

12. Don't mention it, Miss.

LECTURA

Exercise No. 54—La Familia Del Señor Adams Viene a Visitar Su Oficina

Es la primera vez que la familia Adams viene a visitar la oficina del señor Adams. La señora Adams y sus (her) cuatro hijos entran en un edificio muy grande y suben (go up) al décimo piso por ascensor (elevator). Anita, la hija menor, que tiene solamente cinco años, está muy curiosa, y hace muchas preguntas a su mamá sobre la oficina.

Cuando llegan a la oficina, el padre se levanta y dice,—Me gusta mucho verlos (to see you) a todos aquí. ¡Qué agradable (pleasant) sorpresa!

Los niños admiran los objetos que ven en la oficina: la máquina de escribir, los diversos artículos importados (imported) de México, las revistas mexicanas y los carteles de muchos colores. Todos están muy contentos.

Felipe, el hijo mayor, mira por la ventana alta y ve el cielo azul y el sol brillante. Abajo (below) ve los automóviles que pasan por la calle. Desde el décimo piso parecen (they seem) muy pequeños.

Después de (after) la visita toda la familia va a un restaurante que no está lejos de la oficina. Comen con mucho gusto, sobre todo los hijos, porque tienen mucha hambre.

Exercise No. 55—Una Fábula Moderna

A Anita, la menor de los hijos del Sr. Adams, le gustan mucho las fábulas antiguas de Esopo. Le gusta también esta fábula moderna que el Sr. López ha escrito (has written) para ella. Sigue[1] "La Fábula del Automóvil y del Burro."

Un automóvil pasa por el camino y ve un burro. El pobre burro lleva una carga grande y pesada (heavy) de madera.

El automóvil para (stops) y dice al burro — Buenos días. Ud. anda muy despacio. ¿No desea Ud. correr rápidamente como yo?

— Sí, sí, señor! Pero dígame, ¿Cómo es posible?

— No es difícil, dice el automóvil. — En mi tanque hay mucha gasolina. Ud. tiene que beber un poco.

Entonces el burro bebe la gasolina. Ahora no anda despacio. No corre rápidamente. No va al mercado. Se echa (he stretches out) en el camino. Tiene dolor de estómago.

¡Pobre burro! No es muy inteligente, ¿verdad? No sabe que la gasolina es buena para un automóvil, pero no vale nada para un burro.

NOTE: 1. The Fable . . . follows. The infinitive of sigue is seguir.

CAPÍTULO 15 (QUINCE)
PARTE PRIMERA
El Cine

1. Sr. Adams, Ud. sabe pedir informes sobre las funciones del cine. ¿Es Ud. amigo del cine?

1. Mr. Adams, you know how to ask for information about the performances of the movies. Are you fond of the movies?

2. Pues, me gusta una buena película, pero la mayor parte de las cintas no me interesan.

3. ¿Le gusta más a Ud. el teatro?

4. Sí. Mi esposa y yo lo preferimos. Vamos a menudo al teatro para ver un buen drama o una producción musical.

5. Y sus hijos? ¿Prefieren ellos el teatro?

6. ¡Claro que no! Los encantan las farsas detectivescas y las películas musicales en colores que nos aburren.

7. Ellos conocen[1] a todas las estrellas de la pantalla, ¿verdad?

8. Claro está, las conocen. Conocen también a las estrellas de la televisión y de la radio.

9. Uds. viven en los suburbios. ¿Hay un cine cerca de su casa?

10. Sí, cosa de ocho cuadras. Podemos ir allí a pie en quince minutos más a menos.

11. ¿Dónde prefieren Uds. sentarse, en las primeras filas o atrás?

12. Nos gusta más sentarnos en las filas catorce o quince. Desde allí es posible ver y oír bien. Desde allí la luz y los movimientos en la pantalla no hacen daño a los ojos.

13. ¿Qué hacen Uds. si la mayor parte de los asientos están ocupados?

14. Entonces pido ayuda al acomodador. Nos sentamos en cualesquier asientos desocupados, delante, atrás o al lado. Pero no nos gustan aquellos asientos y por eso venimos temprano. Tampoco nos gusta estar de pie en el cine.

15. ¡Estupendo, Sr. Adams! ¡Puede Ud. ir pasando en México!

16. Tengo que darle las gracias a Ud., Sr. López.

2. Well, I like a good picture but most films do not interest me.

3. You prefer the theater?

4. Yes. My wife and I prefer it. We often go to the theater to see a good play or a musical show.

5. And your children? Do they prefer the theater?

6. Of course not! Detective dramas and musical pictures in colors which bore us enchant them.

7. They know all the stars of the screen don't they?

8. Of course, they know them. They also know the stars of television and radio.

9. You live in the suburbs. Is there a movie theater near your house?

10. Yes, about eight blocks. We can go there on foot in fifteen minutes more or less.

11. Where do you prefer to sit, in the first rows or in back?

12. We prefer to sit in rows fourteen or fifteen. From there it is possible to see and hear well. From there the light and the movements on the screen do no harm to the eyes.

13. What do you do if most of the seats are taken?

14. Then I ask the usher for help. We sit in any unoccupied seats, in front, in back or at the side. But we do not like those seats and therefore we come early. Nor do we like to stand in the movies.

15. Marvellous, Mr. Adams! You can get along in Mexico!

16. I have you to thank, Mr. Lopez.

NOTE: 1. **conocer** to know (to be acquainted with persons or things). **saber** to know (facts).

Pronunciation and Spelling Helps

1. Practice:

bo-le-te-ro	a-sien-tos	a-co-mo-da-**dor**	es-tre-**lla**
bo-le-te-**rí**-a	pan-ta-**lla**	pe-**lí**-cu-la	pre-**fie**-ro

2. la función, las funciones; la lección, las lecciones; la estación, las estaciones. Nouns ending in ción drop the accent in the plural.

Vocabulary Building

A. Sinónimas:

1. el noticiero — las actualidades   the newsreel
2. por eso — por consiguiente   therefore
3. prefiero — me gusta más   I prefer
4. la cinta — la película   film
5. a menudo — muchas veces   often

B. Antónimos:

1. antes de	before (time)	despúes de	after
2. delante de	in front of	detrás de	behind
3. ocupado	occupied	desocupado	unoccupied

C. Words Dealing with the Movies:

1. el cine   the movie house
2. la película   the picture
3. la función   the performance
4. el noticiero   the newsreel
5. la taquilla, la boletería (Mex.)   the ticket office
6. el papel   the part, role
7. la estrella   the star
8. la pantalla   the screen
9. el asiento   the seat
10. la fila   the row
11. el acomodador   the usher

Expresiones Importantes

1. **tener que:** tener, to have, followed by que means to have to, must.

Tengo que repetir	I have to (*must*) repeat
Ud. tiene que aprender	You have to (*must*) learn
¿Tiene él que escribir?	Does he have to (*must he*) write
Ella no tiene que ir	She does not have to go

2. **ir a pie**   to go on foot
3. **estar de pie**   to stand

Grammar Notes

1. **Direct Object Pronouns. Summary.** Study the following sentences which summarize the direct object pronouns. Note their meanings and position in relation to the verb.

1. ¿Compra Pablo el pan? *Lo* compra.
2. ¿Compra Ana la crema? *La* compra.
3. ¿Ve Ud. al padre? *Le* veo (a él).
4. ¿Ve Ud. al la madre? *La* veo (a ella).
5. Ve Ud. a los padres? *Los* veo (a ellos).
6. ¿Ve Ud. a las madres? *Las* veo (a ellas).
7. ¿Tiene Ud. los boletos? *Los* tengo.
8. ¿Tienen Uds. las cartas? *Las* tenemos.
9. *Le* esperamos a Ud., Sr. Adams.
10. *La* esperamos a Ud., Sra. López.
11. *Los* esperamos a Uds., señores.
12. *Las* esperamos a Uds., señoras.
13. ¿*Me* buscas, mamá?
14. *Te* busco, hijito.
15. ¿Quién *nos* busca?

1. Does Paul buy the bread? He buys *it*.
2. Does Anna buy the cream? She buys *it*.
3. Do you see the father? I see *him*.
4. Do you see the mother? I see *her*.
5. Do you see the fathers? I see *them*.
6. Do you see the mothers? I see *them*.
7. Have you the tickets. I have *them*.
8. Have you the letters? We have *them*.
9. We are expecting *you*, Mr. Adams.
10. We are expecting *you*, Mrs. Lopez.
11. We are expecting *you*, gentlemen.
12. We are expecting *you*, ladies.
13. Are you looking for *me*, mother?
14. I am looking for *you*, sonny.
15. Who is looking for us?

Chart of Direct Object Pronouns

Singular		Plural	
me	me	nos	us
te	you (*fam.*)	os	you (*fam.*)
lo (*m*)	it	los (*m*)	them, you
le (*m*)	him, you	las (*f*)	them, you
la (*f*)	it, her, you		

a. Object pronouns usually stand directly before the verb.

b. When the pronoun is the object of an infinitive or of an affirmative command, it follows the verb and is attached to it.

El Sr. Adams va a saludar*le*.	Mr. Adams goes to greet *him*.
Díga*me*.	Tell *me*.

c. a Ud. and a Uds. are usually added after the verb to distinguish the meaning *you* from the other meanings of le, la, los, las. a él, a ella, a ellos and a ellas may also be added to make the meaning clear.

d. os (object *you,* fam. plur.) is rare in Latin America. Use los (*you*) and las (*you*) instead

Ejercicios (Exercises) No. 56A-56B-56C

56A. Read each Spanish question. Then read the answer, using the correct direct object pronoun in place of the dash. Be sure the object pronouns have the same number and gender as the nouns for which they stand.

Ejemplo: Sí, *los* compro.

1. ¿Compra Ud. los boletos? — Sí, ———— compro.
2. ¿Comienza Ud. el ejercicio? — Sí, ———— comienzo.
3. ¿Quiénes tienen el radio? — Los niños ———— tienen.
4. ¿Ven Uds. bien la pantalla? — No, no ———— vemos bien.
5. ¿Espera el señor a su amigo? — Sí, ———— espera.
6. ¿Prefieren Uds. las primeras filas? — No, no ———— preferimos.
7. ¿Conocen los niños a la estrella? — Sí, ———— conocen.
8. ¿Conocen Uds. a estos hombres? — Sí, ———— conocemos.
9. ¿Conocen Uds. a estas mujeres? — Sí, ———— conocemos.
10. ¿Quiénes esperan al maestro? — Los niños ———— esperan.

56B. Read each Spanish sentence. Then put the corresponding English sentence into Spanish. Where do the object pronouns go?

Ejemplo: La criada la lleva.

1. La criada lleva la cuchara.
2. Los niños comen el azúcar.
3. Pongo los platillos en la mesa.
4. Digo las frases al estudiante.
5. ¿Por qué no saluda Ud. al hombre?
6. ¿Visitas tú a tu hermana?

1. The maid brings it.
2. The children eat it.
3. I put them on the table.
4. I tell them to the student.
5. Why don't you greet him?
6. Do you visit her?

56C. Translate into Spanish.

1. I see you, Mr. Adams.
2. Do you see me?
3. Who sees us?
4. The teacher sees you (pl.), boys.
5. We see the house. We see it.
6. I take the plate. I take it.
7. She writes the verbs. She writes them.
8. We have the chairs. We have them.
9. I expect you, ladies.
10. We expect you, gentlemen.

Exercise No. 57—Preguntas

1. ¿Quién sabe pedir informes?
2. ¿Qué prefieren los señores Adams, el teatro o el cine?
3. ¿Qué prefieren los niños?
4. ¿Conocen los niños a las estrellas del cine?
5. ¿Dónde vive la familia Adams?
6. ¿A qué distancia está el cine de la casa de ellos?
7. ¿Qué filas del cine prefieren?
8. ¿Es posible ver y oír desde allí?
9. ¿A quién piden ayuda en el cine?
10. ¿Vienen temprano o tarde?

CAPÍTULO 16 (DIEZ Y SEIS)

PARTE PRIMERA

Las Calles y las Fechas

1. Si el turista no sabe nada de la historia de México, los nombres de las calles pueden enseñarle mucho. Como en todas las ciudades del mundo, en la ciudad de México hay calles nombradas en memoria de los grandes héroes de la patria.

1. If the tourist knows nothing about the history of Mexico, the names of the streets can teach him a great deal. As in all the cities in the world, so in Mexico there are streets named in memory of the great heroes of the fatherland.

2. Dos de las avenidas más importantes de la ciudad son las avenidas Juárez y Francisco I. Madero. Ud. sabe bien que Benito Juárez es el Abrán Lincoln de México, presidente de México desde 1857 (mil ochocientos cincuenta y siete) hasta 1872 (mil ochocientos setenta y dos), el alma de la resistencia al emperador Maximiliano. Francisco I. Madero fué uno de los líderes contra el dictador Porfirio Díaz en 1910 (mil novecientos diez).

3. Pero en el centro de la ciudad hay otras calles muy interestantes desde el punto de vista histórico. Sus nombres son fechas—16 de septiembre, 20 de noviembre, 5 de febrero, 5 de mayo. ¿Qué significan estas fechas?

4. El 16 de septiembre es el Día de la Independencia de México. Recuerda el año 1810 (mil ochocientos diez) y la lucha contra España. El iniciador de esta revolución fué el cura Hidalgo, el Jorge Washington de México.

5. El 20 de noviembre celebra el comienzo de la revolución de 1910 (mil novecientos diez) contra el dictador Porfirio Díaz.

6. El 5 de mayo es el aniversario de la victoria contra los franceses, partidarios de Maximiliano, en Puebla en el año 1861 (mil ochocientos sesenta y uno).

7. El 5 de febrero es una fiesta también. Se llama esta fiesta el Día de la Constitución.

8. ¿Sr. Adams, le interesan a Ud. estos sucesos de la historia de México?

9. Sí, sí. Me interesan mucho. Un día voy a caminar por las calles cuyos nombres son fechas, y voy a recordar las palabras de mi maestro y amigo, el señor López.

10. Ahora es favor que Ud. me hace a mí.[1]

11. No es favor. Es verdad.

NOTE: 1. a mí *to me*, added for emphasis.

2. Two of the city's most important avenues are Avenue Juarez and Avenue Francisco I. Madero. You know that Benito Juarez is the Abraham Lincoln of Mexico, president of Mexico from 1857 to 1872, the soul of the resistance to Emperor Maximilian. Francisco I. Madero was one of the leaders against the dictator Porfirio Diaz in 1910.

3. But in the center of the city there are other streets, very interesting from a historical point of view. Their names are dates . . . September 16, November 20, February 5, May 5. What do these dates mean?

4. September 16 is Mexico's Independence day. It recalls the year 1810 and the struggle against Spain. The initiator of this revolution was the curate Hidalgo, the George Washington of Mexico.

5. November 20 marks the beginning of the revolution in 1910 against the dictator Porfirio Diaz.

6. The 5th of May is the day of victory against the French, supporters of Maximilian, at Puebla in the year 1861.

7. The 5th of February is a holiday, too. This holiday is called Constitution Day.

8. Mr. Adams, do these events of Mexican history interest you?

9. Yes, yes. They interest me very much. Some day I am going to walk along the streets the names of which are dates, and I will recall the words of my teacher and friend, Mr. Lopez.

10. Now you flatter *me*.

11. It is not flattery. It is the truth.

Pronunciation and Spelling Helps

Practice:

his-to-ria	Fran-cis-co Ma-de-ro	lí-de-res	re-cor-dar
hé-ro-es	Por-fi-rio Dí-az	sig-ni-fi-can	re-cuer-da
Mi-guel Hi-dal-go	em-per-ra-dor	in-de-pen-den-cia	vic-to-ria
Be-ni-to Juá-rez	Ma-xi-mi-lia-no	re-vo-lu-ción	Jor-ge

Vocabulary Building

A. Antónimos:

1. contra   against   por   for   2. enseñar   to teach   aprender   to learn

B. Palabras Relacionadas:

1. interesar   to interest   interesante   interesting
2. la historia   history   histórico   historical
3. dictar   to dictate   el dictador   the dictator

4. luchar	to fight	la lucha	the fight
5. caminar	to walk	el camino	the road
6. recordar	to recall, remember	el recuerdo	the remembrance
7. resistir	to resist	la resistencia	resistance
8. comenzar	to begin	el comienzo	beginning

C. **Los grandes héroes** the great heroes. The adjective **grande** placed before a noun means *great*. After a noun it means *big*. Thus:

un hombre grande   a big man   **un gran hombre**   a great man

Note that **grande** (*not* grandes), before a noun, becomes **gran**.

Expresiones Importantes

1. **en memoria de**   in memory of   2. **desde ... hasta**   from . . . to, until
3. **el Día de la Independencia**   Independence Day

Exercise No. 58—Completion of Text

1. (They know nothing) **de la historia de México.**
2. **Las calles** (can) **enseñarles mucho.**
3. **Hay calles nombradas** (in memory of) **los héroes de la** (fatherland).
4. **Una de las avenidas** (most important) **es la Avenida Juárez.**
5. **Benito Juárez fué presidente de México** (from) 1857 (until) 1872.
6. **Los** (names) **de estas calles son** (dates).
7. **Son interesantes** (from the point of view) **histórico.**
8. **¿Qué** (signify) **estas fechas?**
9. **El** (priest) **Hidalgo fué el** (initiator) **de la revolución contra España en 1810.**
10. (These events) **me interesan mucho.**
11. **Voy a** (walk) **por las calles** (whose) **nombres son fechas.**
12. **Voy a** (recall) **las palabras de mi maestro.**

Grammar Notes

1. The Present Tense of **recordar(ue)** to remember and **oír** to hear

I remember, you remember, etc.

recuerdo	recordamos
recuerdas	recordáis
recuerda	recuerdan

I hear, you hear, etc.

oigo	oímos
oyes	oís
oye	oyen

2. Ordinal Numbers

primero (a)	first	sexto (a)	sixth
segundo (a)	second	séptimo (a)	seventh
tercero (a)	third	octavo (a)	eighth
cuarto (a)	fourth	noveno (a)	ninth
quinto (a)	fifth	décimo (a)	tenth

   a. Ordinal numbers are used much less in Spanish than in English. After the tenth they are seldom used.

   b. Like other adjectives they agree with their nouns in number and gender.

la primera fila   **la segunda fila**   **el décimo piso**

   c. Before a masculine singular noun **primero** and **tercero** drop the -o. When alone, they keep the ending.

el primer año   **el primero**   **el tercer mes**   **el tercero**

3. Dates

1° de mayo de 1954	(el primero de mayo)	May 1, 1954
5 de mayo de 1861	(el cinco de mayo)	May 5, 1861

a. **Primero** is used for the first day of the month. After that the cardinal numbers **dos, tres,** etc. are used.

b. The order for a date is: (day) **de** (month) **de** (year).

c. The numbers in the year are read like numbers in general.

1954 (**mil novecientos cincuenta y cuatro**)   1861 (**mil ochocientos sesenta y uno**)

4. Pronouns with Prepositions

para mí	for me	**para nosotros -as**	for us
para ti	for you (*fam. sing.*)	**para vosotros -as**	for you (*fam. plur.*)
para Ud.	for you	**para Uds.**	for you
para él	for him	**para ellos**	for them (*masc. pl.*)
para ella	for her	**para ellas**	for them (*fem. pl.*)

a. Pronouns with prepositions, except **mí** (*me*) and **ti** (*you*) are the same as the subject pronouns.

b. With the preposition **con, mí** and **ti** become **conmigo** *with me,* and **contigo** *with you.*

c. The accent mark on **mí** (*me*) distinguishes it from **mi** (*my*).

Ejercicios (Exercises) No. 59A-59B

59A. Complete the Spanish sentences so that they correspond fully to the English sentences.

Ejemplo: 1. Hablamos de Ud., señor.

1. We are speaking of you, sir.
2. They do not work for us (m.).
3. He is standing near them (f.).
4. They are seated behind me.
5. You can go with me.
6. I want to go with you, Johnny.
7. We are for them, not against them.
8. We prefer to go without you, Anna.
9. The ash tray is in front of her.
10. We are going to have dinner with him.

1. Hablamos de ———, señor.
2. No trabajan para ———.
3. Está de pie cerca de ———.
4. Están sentados detrás de ———.
5. Ud. puede ir ———.
6. Quiero ir ———, Juanito.
7. Estamos por ———, no contra ———.
8. Preferimos ir sin ———, Ana.
9. El cenicero está delante de ———.
10. Vamos a tomar la cena con ———.

59B. Translate in two ways.

Ejemplo: Where is your book, Anna? ¿Dónde está su libro (el libro de Ud.), Ana?

1. Where is her book?
2. Where is his book?
3. Where are her books?
4. Where are his books?

5. Where are your parents, boys?
6. Where is your house, Mr. A?
7. Where are their chairs?
8. Where is their room?

Exercise No. 60—Preguntas

1. ¿Cuál es la fecha del Día de la Independencia de México?
2. ¿Quién fué (was) el iniciador de la revolución de 1810 contra España?
3. ¿Quién es el Jorge Washington de México?
4. ¿Cuál es la fecha del aniversario de la victoria contra los franceses en Puebla en 1861?
5. ¿Quién es el Abrán Lincoln de México?
6. ¿Cuándo fué presidente?
7. ¿Qué fecha celebra el comienzo de la revolución contra el dictador Porfirio Díaz?
8. ¿Quién fué uno de los líderes de esa revolución?
9. ¿Qué avenidas importantes de la ciudad de México están nombradas en memoria de dos grandes héroes?
10. ¿Cuál es la fecha del Día de la Constitución?
11. ¿Interesan estos sucesos de la historia de México al Sr. Adams?
12. ¿Por dónde va a caminar un día el Sr. Adams?
13. ¿Qué palabras va a recordar?
14. ¿Cuál es la fecha del aniversario del Día de la Independencia de los Estados Unidos?

CAPÍTULO 17 (DIEZ Y SIETE)

PARTE PRIMERA

Calles, Ríos y Montañas

1. Ya sabe Ud., señor Adams, que hay muchas calles en México cuyos nombres recuerdan los grandes héroes de México y otras cuyos nombres son fechas. Estos recuerdan los acontecimientos más notables de la historia de México. Además, en un barrio las calles tienen los nombres de algunos de los escritores franceses más conocidos—Victor Hugo, Anatole France y Eugenio Sue, por ejemplo. En otro barrio los nombres de las calles celebran algunos de los científicos más famosos—por ejemplo, Copernico, Kepler y Galileo.

2. Al sur del Paseo de la Reforma, una de las avenidas más hermosas de México, podemos dar un paseo por algunas de las ciudades más importantes del mundo—"Liverpool, Hamburgo, Florencia, Londres, etc." Al norte del Paseo se encuentran "los ríos Misisipi, Tiber, Rhin, Danubio, etc." De veras una persona que tiene la costumbre de caminar por las calles de México puede educarse bien y barato.

3. A propósito, señor Adams, ¿me permite hacerle a Ud. algunas preguntas acerca de la geografíá del Hemisferio Occidental?

4. Desde luego. ¿Y voy a recibir un premio por las respuestas correctas?

5. No, señor Adams, éste no es un programa de radio. Vamos a empezar. ¿Cuál es el río más largo del Hemisferio Occidental?

6. Por supuesto, el Misisipi es el río más largo.

7. Ud. está equivocado. El Misisipi es mucho más pequeño que el río Amazonas. Éste es el más largo y el más grande, no solamente de nuestro hemisferio, sino también del mundo entero. Tiene más de 4600 millas de largo y cruza todo el Brasil. ¿Y cuál es el pico más alto de la América del Sur?

8. No me acuerdo del nombre pero está en los Andes. Es más alto que cualquier pico de la América del Norte, de Europa o de África. Pero sí hay picos más altos en las Himalayas de Asia.

9. Se llama Aconcagua aquel pico altísimo. Pues bien, una pregunta más. ¿Sabe Ud. los nombres de los dos picos no lejos de México, D.F.?

10. Creo que sí, pero no sé pronunciarlos.

1. You already know, Mr. Adams, that there are many streets in Mexico whose names recall the great heroes of Mexico and others whose names are dates. The latter recall the most outstanding events of the history of Mexico. Besides, in one district the streets have the names of some of the most well-known French writers—Victor Hugo, Anatole France and Eugene Sue, for example. In another district, the names of the streets honor some of the most famous scientists —for example, Copernicus, Kepler and Galileo.

2. South of the Paseo de la Reforma, one of the most beautiful avenues of Mexico, we can take a walk through some of the most important cities in the world—"Liverpool, Hamburg, Florence, London, etc." North of the Paseo are "the rivers Mississippi, Tiber, Rhine, Danube, etc." Indeed a person who has the habit of walking through the streets of Mexico can obtain a good and inexpensive education.

3. By the way, Mr. Adams, will you permit me to ask you a few questions about the geography of the Western Hemisphere?

4. Certainly. And will I receive a prize for correct answers?

5. No, Mr. Adams, this is not a radio program. Let's begin. Which is the longest river in the Western Hemisphere?

6. Of course the Mississippi is the longest river.

7. You are mistaken. The Mississippi is much smaller than the Amazon River. The latter is the longest and the biggest, not only in our hemisphere, but also in the whole world. It is more than 4600 miles long and crosses all Brazil. And which is the highest peak in South America?

8. I do not remember the name but it is in the Andes. It is higher than any mountain in North America, Europe or Africa. But indeed, there are higher peaks in the Himalayas of Asia.

9. That very high peak is called Aconcagua. Well then, one more question. Do you know the names of the two peaks not far from Mexico City?

10. I think so, but I do not know how to pronounce them.

11. **No es difícil. Repita, por favor. Po-po-ca-té-petl. Ix-tac-cí-huatl.**

12. **Po-po-ca-té-petl. Ix-tac-cí-huatl. Ud. tiene razón. No es difícil pronunciarlos sílaba por sílaba.** (poh-poh-ca-*tay*-petl, ees-tah-*see*-wahtl)

11. It is not difficult. Repeat, please. Po-po-ca-te-petl. Ix-tac-ci-huatl.

12. Po-po-ca-te-petl. Ix-tac-ci-huatl. You are right. It is not difficult to pronounce them syllable by syllable.

Pronunciation and Spelling Aids

1. Practice:

cu-yos	Co-pér-ni-co	Mi-si-si-pi	cru-za
re-cuer-dan	Ke-pler	Da-nu-bio	a-cuer-do
a-con-te-ci-**mien**-tos	Ga-li-le-o	Ti-ber	cual-quie-ra
ba-rrio	Pa-se-o	cos-tum-bre	A-sia
fran-ce-ses	de la Re-**for**-ma	con-se-**guir**	Hi-ma-la-yas
es-cri-to-res	en-cuen-tran	ge-o-gra-**fí**-a	A-con-ca-gua
Eu-ge-nio	Flo-ren-cia	he-mis-fe-rio	pro-nun-**ciar**-los
ce-le-brar	Ham-bur-go	oc-ci-den-**tal**	Po-po-ca-té-petl
cien-tí-fi-cos	Li-ver-**pool**	el rí-o A-ma-zo-nas	Ix-tac-cí-huatl (ees-tah-see-wahtl)

2. **francés franceses, inglés ingleses, por-tu-gués portugueses.** The accent mark is dropped in the plural.

3. Remember: In the combination -**guir** (conse**guir**) the **u** is silent. In the combination -**gua** (Acon-cagua) the **u** is pronounced like Eng. *w*.

Building Vocabulary

A. Sinónimos:

1. de veras   verdaderamente   claro está   indeed
2. el sabio   el hombre de ciencia   el científico   the scientist
3. conseguir   obtener   adquirir   to obtain

B. Antónimos:

1. barato   cheap   **caro**   dear   3. **el más largo**   the longest   **el más corto**   the shortest
2. alto   high   **bajo**   low   4. **facíl**   easy   **difícil**   hard

C. Palabras Relacionados:

1. educar   to educate   **educación**   education   3. **historia**   history
2. la ciencia   science   **el científico**   the scientist   **histórico**   historical

Expresiones Importantes

1. **dar un paseo**   to take a walk
2. **hacer preguntas**   to ask questions
3. **cualquier montaña**   any mountain

Exercise No. 61—Completion of Text

1. **Hay muchas calles** (whose) **nombres** (recall) **grandes héroes.**
2. **Otras calles recuerdan** (the most notable events) **de nuestra historia.**
3. **Otras calles tienen los nombres de los escritores franceses** (most well-known).
4. **En un barrio las calles llevan los nombres de los científicos** (most famous).
5. **Podemos dar un paseo por algunas de las ciudades** (most important in the world).
6. (Indeed) **una persona puede** (get a good and inexpensive education) **en las calles de México.**
7. (By the way) **Sr. Adams, quiero hacerle a** Ud. **algunas preguntas** (about) **la geografía del Hemisferio** (Western).
8. **Ud. no va a** (receive) **un premio.**
9. **¿Es** (larger) **el Misisipi que el Amazonas?**
10. **El Misisipi es** (smaller) **que el Amazonas.**
11. **Este río es** (the largest) **y** (the longest) **del mundo.**
12. **El pico de Aconcagua es** (higher) **que cualquier pico de la América del Norte.**
13. **Hay picos** (higher) **en las Himalayas.**
14. **Dos picos** (high) **se encuentran** (not far from) **la capital.**
15. (You are right). **La pronunciación no es difícil.**

PARTE SEGUNDA

Grammar Notes

1. Comparison of Adjectives in Spanish.

grande	large	**más grande**	larger	**el (la) más grande**	largest
notable	notable	**más notable**	more notable	**el (la) más notable**	most notable
notable	notable	**menos notable**	less notable	**el (la) menos notable**	least notable

a. These adjectives follow and agree with their nouns as usual. In the superlative the definite article or a possessive adjective precedes the noun.

las avenidas más hermosas	the most beautiful avenues
mi maestro más amable	my kindest teacher

b. After a superlative use **de** not **en** for *in*.

el río más largo del mundo	the longest river in the world

c. as . . . adj. . . . as, is expressed in Spanish as **tan** . . . adj. . . . **como.**

Carlos es tan alto como Ana.	Charles is as tall as Anna.
El Tiber no es tan largo como el Rhin.	The Tiber is not as long as the Rhine.

d. In comparisons, *than* is usually **que**. Before a number *than* is **de.**

Londres es más grande que Nueva York.	London is larger than New York.
Tenemos más de cien dólares.	We have more than $100.

2. Irregular Comparisons

bueno	good	**mejor**	better	**el (la) mejor**	best
malo	bad	**peor**	worse	**el (la) peor**	worst
grande	big	**mayor**	older	**el (la) mayor**	oldest
		más grande	bigger	**el (la) más grande**	biggest
pequeño	small	**menor**	younger	**el (la) menor**	youngest
		más pequeño	smaller	**el (la) más pequeño**	smallest

a. The irregular forms of grande and pequeño refer to age.
The regular forms of grande and pequeño refer to size.

Felipe es mayor que Guillermo.	Philip is older than William.
Felipe es más grande que Guillermo.	Philip is bigger than William.
Es el mayor de la familia.	He is the oldest in the family.
Es el más grande de la familia.	He is the biggest in the family.
Anita es menor que Rosita.	Annie is younger than Rosie.
Anita es más pequeña que Rosita.	Annie is smaller than Rosie.
Es la menor de la familia.	She is the youngest in the family.
Es la más pequeña de la familia.	She is the smallest in the family.

3. The ending -ísimo(a) may be used instead of **muy.**

alto	tall	**altísimo**	very tall
largo	long	**larguísimo**	very long
bueno	good	**bonísimo**	very good
rico	rich	**requísimo**	very rich
Aconcagua es un pico altísimo.		Aconcagua is a very high peak.	

Exercise No. 62

Complete the Spanish sentences so that they correspond fully to the English sentences.

Ejemplo: Pablo es tan alto como Juan.

1. Paul is as tall as John.
2. My pen is better than John's.
3. Mary is nicer than Elsie.

1. Pablo es ———— alto ———— Juan.
2. Mi pluma es ———— que la de Juan.
3. María es ———— simpática ———— Elsa.

4. I have the best pen of all.
5. The black ink is not as good as the blue.

6. I want the newest book.
7. My exercises are more difficult than yours.

8. Jane is tall. Marie is taller than Jane.
9. Isabel is the tallest girl of the three.
10. Mr. García has the worst luck.
11. Philip is the oldest child.
12. The capital has the most modern buildings.
13. The pen is bad but the pencil is worse.
14. Why are you not as happy as he?

15. He is the laziest man in the office.

16. Annie is the youngest child.

NOTE: 1. **mejor** and **peor** often precede the noun.

4. Tengo la ———— pluma de todas.
5. La tinta negra no es ———— buena ————
la tinta azul.
6. Quiero el libro ———— nuevo.
7. Mis ejercicios son ———— difíciles ————
los de Ud.
8. Juana es alta. María es ————
9. Isabel es la muchacha ———— de las tres.
10. El señor Garcia tiene la ————[1] suerte.
11. Felipe es el hijo ————.
12. La capital tiene los edificios ————.
13. La pluma es mala, pero el lápiz es ————.
14. ¿Por qué no está Ud. ———— contento
———— él?
15. El es el hombre más perezoso ———— la
oficina.
16. Anita es la hija ————.

Exercise No. 63—Preguntas

1. ¿Cuál es el río más largo de Sud América?
2. ¿Cuál es la ciudad más grande del mundo?
3. ¿Cuál es el pico más alto de Sud America?
4. ¿Qué ciudad es más grande que Nueva York?
5. ¿Es Madrid tan grande como Nueva York?
6. ¿Es Nueva York tan antigua como Madrid?
7. ¿Qué ciudad es más antigua—Plymouth o St. Augustine?
8. ¿Qué ciudad tiene los edificios más altos del mundo?
9. ¿Cuál es el país más pequeño de Centro America?
10. El Sr. García es un hombre de cuarenta y cinco años de edad. Tiene $100,000 (cien mil dólares).
El Sr. Rivera es un hombre de cincuenta años. Tiene $80,000 (ochenta mil dólares). El Sr. Torres es un hombre de sesenta años. Tiene $50,000 (cincuenta mil dólares).

a. ¿Quién es el menor de los tres?
b. ¿Quién es el mayor de los tres?
c. ¿Es el Sr. Rivera mayor que el Sr. García?
d. ¿Quién es el más rico?
e. ¿Quién es el menos rico?
f. ¿Es el Sr. Torres tan rico como el Sr. García?

CAPÍTULO 18 (DIEZ Y OCHO)

PARTE PRIMERA

El Día del Señor Adams

1. Sr. Adams, ¿me permite preguntarle cómo pasa Ud. un día típico?
2. ¿Cómo no? Cuando voy a la oficina, me levanto a las seis y media. Ud. ve que soy madrugador. Me lavo y me visto en treinta minutos más o menos. A eso de las siete me siento a la mesa en el comedor para tomar el desayuno. Mi esposa, que también es madrugadora, se levanta temprano y nos desayunamos juntos. Naturalmente me gusta mucho esta costumbre. Tenemos la oportunidad de platicar de los niños y de otras cosas de interés.

1. Mr. Adams, may I ask you how you spend a typical day?
2. Certainly. When I go to the office, I get up at six-thirty. You see that I am an early riser. I wash and dress in thirty minutes more or less. At about seven, I sit down at the table in the dining room to have breakfast. My wife, who is also an early riser, gets up early and we have breakfast together. Naturally I like this custom very much. We have an opportunity to talk about the children and other interesting things.

3. ¿Qué toma Ud. para el desayuno?

4. Para el desayuno tomo jugo de naranja, café, panecillos y huevos. De vez en cuando tomo panqueques en vez de huevos.

5. ¿Y después del desayuno?

6. A las siete y media estoy listo para salir a tomar el tren. Ud. sabe que vivo fuera de la ciudad. Voy en coche a la estación. Dejo allí el automóvil hasta la tarde cuando vuelvo de la ciudad. El tren sale para la ciudad a las ocho menos cuarto en punto. Raras veces sale tarde. Llega a la ciudad a las nueve menos cuarto en punto. Casi siempre llega a tiempo. Desde la estacíon de ferrocarril voy a la oficina por el subterráneo. Llego a eso de las nueve. En la oficina leo las cartas, dicto las respuestas a la taquígrafa, hablo por teléfono a varios clientes y hago una cantidad de cosas que tiene que hacer un negociante.

7. ¿Y cuándo toma Ud. el almuerzo?

8. Casi siempre a la una. Lo tomo en cosa de 20 minutos.

9. Es muy poco tiempo. En México va a ver Ud. que son muy distintas las costumbres. El negociante mexicano pasa mucho más tiempo a las comidas. Pero en otra ocasión vamos a hablar más de esto. ¿Qué toma Ud. al almuerzo?

10. Ordinariamente tomo un sandwich con café y tal o cual postre—una manzana cocida, una torta, o helado.

11. ¿Qué hace Ud. después del almuerzo?

12. Hago lo mismo que por la mañana. Muchas veces algunos clientes vienen a visitarme por la tarde y de vez en cuando salgo a visitar a otros clientes.

13. ¿A qué hora termina Ud. el trabajo?

14. A las cinco en punto salgo de la oficina y tomo el tren de las cinco y media. Llego a casa a eso de las siete menos cuarto y me siento a la mesa para tomar la cena.

15. Ud. debe de estar cansado después de tal día.

16. — ¡Ya lo creo! — responde el señor Adams.

3. What do you have for breakfast?

4. For breakfast I have orange juice, coffee, rolls and eggs. Sometimes I have pancakes instead of eggs.

5. And after breakfast?

6. At seven-thirty I am ready to leave to catch the train. You know that I live outside the city. I go by car to the station. I leave the automobile there until the afternoon, when I return from the city. The train leaves for the city at a quarter to eight sharp. It seldom leaves late. It arrives at the city at quarter to nine sharp. It almost always arrives on time. From the railroad station, I go to my office by subway. I arrive at about nine. In the office I read letters, dictate answers to the stenographer, talk on the telephone to various clients and do a number of things that a business man has to do.

7. And when do you have lunch?

8. Almost always at one. I take it in about 20 minutes.

9. It is very little time. In Mexico you will see that customs are very different. The Mexican businessman spends much more time at meals. But another time we will speak more of this. What do you have for lunch?

10. Usually I have a sandwich and coffee and some dessert or other—a baked apple, a cake or ice cream.

11. What do you do after lunch?

12. I do the same as in the morning. Often some clients come to visit me in the afternoon and from time to time I go out to visit other clients.

13. At what time do you stop work?

14. At five o'clock sharp I leave the office and take the five-thirty train. I arrive home at about a quarter to seven and I sit down at table to have dinner.

15. You must be tired after such a day.

16. "Yes, indeed!" answers Mr. Adams.

Pronunciation and Spelling Aids

1. Practice:

pre-gun-tar	de-sa-yu-nar-se	pan-que-ques	ta-quí-gra-fa
ma-dru-ga-dor	de-sa-yu-na-mos	hue-vos (way-vos)	te-lé-fo-no
ma-dru-ga-do-ra	o-por-tu-ni-dad	a-fue-ra	clien-tes
de-sa-yu-no	pa-ne-ci-llos	sub-te-rrá-ne-o	sand-wich (*sand-weech*)

2. panqueques, sandwich. These have been borrowed by the Mexicans from English. Note the Spanish spelling of the first. The second has retained the English w.

Building Vocabulary

A. Sinónimos:

1. tomar el desayuno   desayunarse   to have breakfast
2. naturalmente   por supuesto   of course
3. platicar   charlar   to chat
4. en coche   en auto   by auto
5. algunas veces   de vez en cuando   sometimes
6. panecillos   bolillos (Mex.)   rolls

B. Antínomos:

1. después del desayuno   after breakfast   antes del desayuno   before breakfast
2. poco tiempo   little time   mucho tiempo   much time

C. Palabras Relacionadas:

1. comer   to eat   **comedor**   dining room   **la comida**   the meal
2. el desayuno   the breakfast   **desayunarse**   to have breakfast

D. Jugos (Juices)

1. jugo de naranja   orange juice   4. jugo de uvas   grape juice
2. jugo de tomate   tomato juice   5. jugo de piña   pineapple juice
3. jugo de toronja   grapefruit juice   6. jugo de limón   lemon juice

Expresiones Importantes

1. a eso de las siete   at about seven   4. ponerse   to become
2. a las cinco en punto   at five o'clock sharp   5. Me pongo enfermo   I become sick
3. de costumbre   generally

B. Expressions with vez:

1. una vez   one time   7. ninguna vez   at no time
2. dos veces   two times   8. cuántas veces   how many times
3. otra vez   another time   9. cada vez   each time
4. algunas veces   sometimes   10. de vez en cuando   from time to time
5. muchas veces   many times   11. en vez de   instead of
6. raras veces   seldom

Exercise No. 64—Completion of Text

1. Sr. Adams, ¿me permite Ud. (to ask you at what time) se levanta Ud.?
2. Me levanto (at 6.30).
3. Soy (an early riser). Mi esposa es (an early riser).
4. Siempre se levanta (early).
5. A las siete y media (I am ready to leave).
6. (I read) las cartas y (I dictate) las respuestas.
7. Para el almuerzo tomo (a sandwich with coffee and some dessert or other.)
8. (Often) algunos clientes vienen (to visit me).
9. Termino el trabajo (at five o'clock sharp.)
10. (The customs) son muy distintas en México.

PARTE SEGUNDA

Grammar Notes

1. Present Tense of Model Reflexive verb. **lavarse** to wash oneself

me lavo	I wash myself	nos lavamos	we wash ourselves
te lavas	you wash yourself (*fam.*)	os laváis	you wash yourselves (*fam.*)
Ud. se lava }	you wash yourself	Uds. se lavan }	you wash yourselves
se lava	he washes himself	se lavan	they wash themselves
	she washes herself		
	it washes itself		

a. Observe that the reflexive pronoun **se** means *oneself, yourself, himself, herself, itself, yourselves,* and *themselves*.

b. Like other object pronouns reflexives usually precede the verb. Used with the infinitive, they follow the verb and are attached to it.

lavarse, to wash oneself   **Quiero lavarme,** I want to wash myself.

2. Present Tense of **sentarse(ie)** to sit down (seat oneself), **vestirse(i)** to dress oneself

I sit down, etc.			I dress myself, etc.	
me siento	nos sentamos		me visto	nos vestimos
te sientas	os sentáis		te vistes	os vestís
Ud. se sienta ⎫	Uds. se sientan ⎫		Ud. se viste ⎫	Uds. se visten ⎫
se sienta ⎭	se sientan ⎭		se viste ⎭	se visten ⎭

3. Other Reflexive Verbs

Some Spanish reflexive verbs are not translated by a reflexive verb in English.

sentarse	to sit down (to seat oneself)	Me siento	I sit down
levantarse	to get up (to raise oneself)	Me levanto	I get up
acostarse(ue)	to go to bed	Me acuesto	I go to bed
llamarse	to be called (to call oneself)	Me llamo	My name is . . .
encontrarse (ue)	to be (to find oneself)	Me encuentro	I am (somewhere)
comerse	to eat up	Me como el pan.	I eat up the bread.
llevarse	to take away	Se lleva el sarape.	He takes away the sarape.
irse	to go away	Me voy de esta ciudad.	I am going away from this city.
acordarse	to remember	Nos acordamos de él.	We remember him.
ponerse	to become	Se ponen enfermos.	They become (get) sick.

Ejercicios (Exercises) No. 65A-65B

65A. Translate the following questions and answers. Then practice the Spanish aloud.

1. ¿A qué hora se acuesta Ud?
   Me acuesto a las once de la noche.
2. ¿A qué hora se levanta Ud?
   Me levanto a las siete de la mañana.
3. ¿Se lava Ud. antes de vestirse?
   Sí, me lavo antes de vestirme.
4. ¿Dónde se encuentra Ud. al mediodía?
   Me encuentro en mi oficina.
5. ¿Cuándo se va Ud. de aquí?
   Mañana me voy de aquí.
6. ¿Se pone Ud. enfermo cuando Ud. come muchos dulces?
   Sí, me pongo enfermo.
7. ¿En qué fila del cine se sientan Uds?
   Nos sentamos en la fila catorce o quince.
8. ¿Se acuerdan Uds. de nuestras conversaciones?
   Sí, nos acordamos de ellas.

65B. Make the Spanish sentences correspond to the English by inserting the correct form of the reflexive pronoun.

Ejemplo: 1. Sr. Adams se sienta en el comedor.

1. Mr. Adams sits down in the dining room.
2. He gets up at seven o'clock.
3. He washes and dresses himself.
4. At what time do you go to bed?
5. I go to bed at 10 o'clock.
6. What is his name?
7. Mr. and Mrs. Adams are (find themselves) in the living room.
8. When do you get up?
9. We get up about seven.
10. I don't remember the name.

1. El Sr. Adams ——— sienta en el comedor.
2. ——— levanta a las siete.
3. ——— lava y ——— viste.
4. ¿A qué hora ——— acuesta Ud.?
5. ——— acuesto a las diez.
6. ¿Cómo ——— llama él?
7. Los señores Adams ——— encuentran en la sala.
8. ¿Cuándo ——— levantan Uds.
9. ——— levantamos a eso de las siete.
10. No ——— acuerdo del nombre.

Exercise No. 66—Preguntas

66. Answer the following in complete sentences.

1. ¿A qué hora se levanta el Sr. Adams?
2. Entonces, ¿qué hace?
3. ¿En cuántos minutos se viste?
4. ¿Qué hace a eso de las siete?
5. ¿Se levanta su esposa temprano?
6. ¿Se desayunan ellos juntos?
7. ¿Qué toma él para el desayuno?
8. ¿Qué toma de vez en cuando en vez de huevos?
9. ¿A qué hora está listo para salir?
10. ¿Cómo va el Sr. Adams a la estación?
11. ¿A qué hora llega a su oficina?
12. ¿Cuándo toma el almuerzo?
13. ¿Qué toma para el almuerzo?
14. ¿Vienen clientes a visitarle por la tarde?
15. ¿A qué hora termina el trabajo?

REPASO 4

CAPÍTULOS 15–18 PARTE PRIMERA

1. Repaso de Palabras

NOUNS

1. el almuerzo	11. la estrella	21. el panecillo	1. lunch	11. star	21. roll
2. el asiento	12. la fiesta	22. los panqueques	2. seat	12. holiday	22. pancakes
3. la cara	13. la historia	23. la película	3. face	13. history	23. film
4. el camino	14. el huevo	24. la pluma	4. road	14. egg	24. pen
5. el cliente	15. el jugo	25. el postre	5. customer	15. juice	25. dessert
6. el coche	16. la luz	26. el recuerdo	6. car, auto	16. light	26. remembrance
7. el comienzo	17. la manzana	27. el río	7. beginning	17. apple	27. river
8. la costumbre	18. la naranja	28. el sur	8. custom	18. orange	28. south
9. el cura	19. el norte	29. el turista	9. priest	19. north	29. tourist
10. el desayuno	20. el ojo	30. el teléfono	10. breakfast	20. eye	30. telephone

VERBS

1. acordarse	15. irse	29. preferir(ie)	1. to remember	15. to go away	29. to prefer
2. buscar	16. hallar	30. reír(i)	2. to look for	16. to find	30. to laugh
3. caminar	17. lavar	31. sonreír(i)	3. to walk	17. to wash	31. to smile
4. celebrar	18. lavarse	32. recordar(ue)	4. to celebrate	18. to wash oneself	32. to recall
5. comer	19. levantar	33. sentarse(ie)	5. to eat	19. to raise	33. to sit down
6. comerse	20. levantarse	34. sentir(ie)	6. to eat up	20. to get up	34. to feel, regret
7. cruzar	21. llevar	35. sentirse(ie)	7. to cross	21. to carry, wear	35. to feel (sad, weak, etc.)
8. deber	22. llevarse	36. significar	8. to owe, ought to	22. to take away	36. to mean
9. dejar	23. llamar	37. tratar	9. to let, to leave	23. to call	37. to try
10. desayunarse	24. llamarse	38. terminar	10. to breakfast	24. to be named	38. to end
11. dormir(ue)	25. poner	39. vestir(i)	11. to sleep	25. to put	39. to dress
12. dormirse	26. ponerse	40. vestirse	12. to fall asleep	26. to become	40. to dress oneself
13. encontrar(ue)	27. oír	41. volver(ue)	13. to meet, to find	27. to hear	41. to return
14. encontrarse	28. permitir	42. fué	14. to be (somewhere)	28. to permit	42. he (she) was

ADJECTIVES

1. ancho	5. chico	9. ocupado	1. wide	5. small	9. busy, occupied
2. barato	6. desocupado	10. obscuro	2. cheap	6. unoccupied	10. dark
3. caro	7. junto	11. raro	3. dear	7. together	11. rare
4. conocido	8. mayor	12. tal	4. well-known	8. older	12. such

ADVERBS

1. ordinariamente	2. naturalmente	3. temprano	1. ordinarily	2. naturally	3. early

PREPOSITIONS

1. contra	2. lejos de	3. en vez de	1. against	2. far from	3. instead of

IMPORTANT EXPRESSIONS

1. a pie	8. desde luego	14. no solamente	1. on foot	8. of course	14. not only
2. a eso de	9. de vez en cuando	15. sino también	2. at about	9. from time to time	15. but also
3. a ver	10. en punto	16. por consiguiente	3. let's see	10. sharp, on the dot	16. consequently
4. a tiempo	11. hacer daño	17. Ud debe de estar	4. on time	11. to hurt	17. you must be tired
5. acabo de + infin.	12. más o menos	cansado	5. I have just	12. more or less	18. to take a walk
6. claro está	13. me gusta más	18. dar un paseo	6. of course	13. I prefer	
7. estar de pie			7. to stand		

PARTE SEGUNDA

Ejercicio 67. Select the group of words in the right-hand column which best completes the sentence begun in the left-hand column.

1. Los niños Adams conocen	a. muy temprano.
2. Desde la fila catorce	b. es el Paseo de la Reforma.
3. En la ciudad de México hay calles	c. es el Amazonas.
4. El 16 de septiembre es	d. el Día de la Independencia de México.
5. Una de las avenidas más hermosas de México	e. se puede ver y oír bien.
6. El río más largo del mundo	f. por tren, por subterráneo, y a pie.
7. La ciudad más antigua de los EEUU	g. toma jugo de naranja.
8. Un madrugador se levanta	h. es San Agustín en la Florida.
9. Para comenzar el desayuno el señor	i. a las estrellas de la pantalla.
10. Para llegar a la oficina viaja	j. nombradas en memoria de los grandes héroes de México.

Ejercicio 68. Read the Spanish questions and then make your answer in Spanish correspond to the English answer following the question:

1. ¿Invita Ud. a sus amigos a su casa?	Yes, I invite them from time to time.
2. ¿Prefiere Ud. el cine?	No, I do not prefer it.
3. ¿Conocen los niños a las estrellas del cine?	Yes, they know them well.
4. ¿Nos esperan Uds.?	Yes, we are waiting for you.
5. ¿Dónde pone la criada las tazas?	She puts them on the table.
6. ¿Me busca Ud.?	No, I am not looking for you, sir.
7. ¿A qué hora se levanta Ud?	I get up at eight o'clock.
8. ¿Se lavan Uds. antes de comer?	Yes, we wash ourselves before eating.
9. ¿En que fila se sientan los Adams?	They sit in row fifteen.
10. ¿Cómo se llama su padre?	My father's name is ————

Ejercicio 69. Complete these sentences by writing all English words in Spanish.

1. El Amazonas es el río (the largest in the world).
2. Nueva York es (bigger than) Los Angeles.
3. Mi padre es (older than) mi madre.
4. No soy (so tall as) mi hermano.
5. Anita es (the youngest in) la familia.
6. El domingo es (the first day) de la semana.
7. Hoy es (January 30, 1955).
8. ¿Desea Ud. ir (with me) al teatro?
9. Pablo prefiere ir (without me).
10. Cuando (I hear) una palabra española (I remember it).

Ejercicio 70. The following expressions are used in the sentences below. See if you can apply them correctly.

tener que + infinitive	hacer preguntas	a eso de	de vez en cuando
darse la mano	dar un paseo	deber de + infinitive	otra vez
por consiguiente	acostarse		

1. Los amigos (shake hands).
2. (We must study) todas los días.
3. (I go to bed) a las once.
4. El profesor (asks many questions).
5. El niño está enfermo. (Consequently) no puede ir a la escuela.
6. Voy el teatro (from time to time).
7. Me gusta (to take a walk) por la noche.
8. (You must be) muy cansado, señor.
9. Dígame su nombre (again), por favor.
10. Me levanto (at about 7.30 a.m.).

PARTE TERCERA
Diálogo

Practice the Spanish Aloud:

En El Mercado

Estamos cerca de un puesto donde se venden sarapes.

We are near a stand where sarapes are sold.

Comprador: ¿Cuánto cuesta éste blanco y negro?

Buyer: How much does this black and white one cost?

Vendedor: 35 (treinta y cinco) pesos.

Seller: 35 pesos.

Comprador: Es demasiado. Le doy a Ud. 25 (veinte y cinco).

Vendedor: Pues no, señor. Éste es muy fino. Por 34 (treinta y cuatro) pesos es de Ud.

Comprador: Es mucho. Le doy 26 (veinte y seis).

Vendedor: Es barato, señor. Mire Ud. Es muy grande. Es para cama de matrimonio. Déme 31 (treinta y uno).

Comprador: Yo soy soltero. No voy a casarme. Le doy 27 (veinte y siete).

Vendedor: No puedo, señor. Tengo mujer y seis niños. Tenemos que vivir. 29 (veinte y nueve) Es el último precio.

Comprador: Muy bien.

Da al vendedor 29 (veinte y nueve) pesos y se lleva el sarape negro y blanco. Es costumbre de regatear y los dos se quedan muy contentos.

NOTE: quedarse to remain may be used instead of estar to be.

Buyer: It's too much. I'll give you 25.

Seller: Well, no sir. It's very fine. For 34 pesos it's yours.

Buyer: It's too much. I'll give you 26.

Seller: It is cheap sir. Look. It's very big. It's for a marriage bed. Give me 31.

Buyer: I am a bachelor. I'm not going to get married. I'll give you 27.

Seller: I cannot do it, sir. I have a wife and six children. We have to live. 29. It's the final price (offer).

Buyer: Very well.

He gives the seller 29 pesos and takes away the black and white sarape. It is customary to bargain and both are (remain) pleased.

LECTURA

Exercise No. 71—Una Visita Al Distrito Puertorriqueño De Nueva York

Es sábado. El señor Adams se levanta a las ocho, y mira por la ventana. El cielo es de color azul. Hay un sol brillante. Dice a su esposa, — Hoy vamos a visitar el distrito (district) puertorriqueño que está cerca del Parque Central en Nueva York.

— Está bien, — dice la señora Adams.

A las nueve suben a (get into) su auto y después de una hora de viaje llegan a la calle 98 (noventa y ocho). Bajan (they get out of) del auto y comienzan a pasearse (to walk) por la calle. Dentro de poco (In a little while) ven a un grupo de muchachos puertorriqueños que están de pie (are standing) cerca de una tienda y que platican muy rápidamente en español.

El señor Adams saluda a los muchachos y principia a charlar con uno de ellos. Sigue la conversación.

— ¡Hola, joven! (young man) ¿Es Ud. puertorriqueño?

— No, señor, soy norteamericano, pero yo sé hablar bien el español. Tengo muchos amigos puertorriqueños y ellos son mis maestros. En casa tengo un libro de español y todas las tardes estudio un poco. A propósito, ¿es Ud. español?

— No, joven, también yo soy norteamericano, y como Ud., estudio el español. Me gusta mucho la lengua. Parece (It seems) que en Nueva York hay muchas personas que estudian el español. Hasta la vista, amigo.

— Hasta luego, señor, — dice el muchacho, y en pocos minutos, desaparece (he disappears) entre su grupo de amigos que siguen (continue) platicando (talking) en español.

¡Qué muchacho tan simpático! — dice el Sr. Adams a su esposa. Y entonces (then) traduce (he translates) la frase, porque ésta (the latter) no comprende el español: "What a nice boy!"

CAPÍTULO 19 (DIEZ Y NUEVE)

PARTE PRIMERA

¡Qué Tiempo Tan Lluvioso!

1. Esta lloviendo mucho. La criada abre la puerta de la casa de los señores[1] Adams. Entra el señor López.

2. La criada dice — Buenas noches, señor López. ¡Qué tiempo tan lluvioso! Pase Ud., pase

1. It is raining hard. The maid opens the door of the house of Mr. and Mrs. Adams. Mr. Lopez enters.

2. The maid says, "Good evening, Mr. Lopez. What rainy weather! Come in, come in. You are

Ud. Está Ud. bastante mojado. Por favor, déme el impermeable y el sombrero. Ponga el paraguas en el paragüero y deje los chanclos en el zaguán.

3. El señor López responde — Gracias. Ahora estoy bien. Llueve a cántaros, pero no hace frío. Estoy seguro de que no voy a atrapar un catarro. ¿Está en casa el señor Adams?

4. Sí, sí. Le espera a Ud. en la sala. Aquí está él mismo.

5. Buenas noches, señor López. Mucho gusto en verle, pero Ud. no debe salir de su casa con este tiempo. Venga conmigo al comedor y tome una taza de té con ron para calentarse un poquito.

6. Gracias, gracias, señor Adams. Tengo un poco de frío. Me gusta mucho tomar una taza de té con Ud., y mientras bebemos el té con ron vamos a charlar sobre el tiempo. Es un tópico de conversación común y en este momento está muy a propósito.

7. Los señores pasan al comedor charlando en voz animada. Se sientan a la mesa y la criada les trae una charola con dos tazas y platillos, una tetera con té caliente, un azucarero y unas cucharitas. Los pone en la mesa junto con una botella de ron que toma del aparador. Entonces sale del comedor.

8. — Permítame servirle a Ud., señor López, — dice el señor Adams. Echa té y una ración generosa de ron en las tazas.

9. Mientras toman el té con ron los señores siguen charlando en voz animada.

10. Afuera sigue lloviendo.

NOTE: 1. señores may mean Mr. and Mrs.

quite wet. Give me, please, your raincoat and hat. Put your umbrella in the umbrella stand and leave your rubbers in the vestibule.

3. Mr. Lopez answers, "Thank you. Now I feel all right. It is raining buckets, but it is not cold. I am sure that I will not catch cold. Is Mr. Adams at home?

4. Yes, yes. He is waiting for you in the living-room. Here he is himself.

5. Good evening, Mr. Lopez. I am very glad to see you, but you should not go out of your house in weather like this. Come with me to the dining room and drink a cup of tea with rum to warm yourself a bit.

6. Thank you, thank you, Mr. Adams. I am a little cold. I am very glad to take a cup of tea with you and while we drink the tea with rum, we will chat about the weather. It is a common topic of conversation and just now is very appropriate.

7. The gentlemen go into the dining room chatting in an animated voice. They sit down and the maid brings them a tray with two cups and saucers, a tea pot with hot tea, a sugar bowl and some teaspoons. She puts them on the table together with a bottle of rum which she takes from the sideboard. Then she leaves the dining room.

8. "Allow me to serve you, Mr. Lopez," says Mr. Adams. He pours tea and a generous portion of rum in the cups.

9. While they are drinking the tea with rum the gentlemen continue chatting in an animated voice.

10. Outside it continues raining.

Pronunciation and Spelling Aids

1. In the combinations gua, guo (*gwah, guo*), the u is pronounced: za-guán, pa-ra-guas (*pah-rah-gwahs*)

2. In the combination gue, gui, the u is silent. It is there to show that the g is hard (not like g in gente). si-guen, se-guir (*say-geer*).

3. In the combinations güe, güi (*gway, gwee*), the ¨ (diaerisis) over the u shows that the u is pronounced: paragüero (*pah-rah-gway-roh*)

Building Vocabulary

A.				
1. él mismo	he himself		3. ellos mismos	they themselves (*m*)
2. ella misma	she herself		4. ellas mismas	they themselves (*f*)

B.   tomar may mean to take, to eat, to drink

Expresiones Importantes

A. Expressions of Weather.

In Spanish we say: What weather does it *make* (hace)? It *makes* (hace) heat, cold, etc., not What is the weather? It is hot, cold, etc.

In Spanish we say *I have* (**tengo**) warmth, cold, etc.; not *I am* warm, cold, etc.

1. ¿Qué tiempo hace? — What's the weather?
2. Hace buen (mal) tiempo. — The weather is (bad) nice.

3. Hace calor, hace frío, hace fresco.	It is warm (hot), it is cold, it is cool.
4. Hace mucho calor. Hace mucho frío.	It is very hot. It is very cold.
5. Hace viento. Hace sol (hay sol).	It is windy. It is sunny.
6. Hay polvo (lodo).	It is dusty (muddy).
7. Llueve (está lloviendo).	It is raining.
8. Nieva (está nevando).	It is snowing.
9. Tengo calor, frío.	I am warm (hot), cold.
10. Tengo mucho calor, mucho frío.	I am very warm (hot), very cold.

Exercise No. 72—Completion of Text

1. La criada dice — ¡(What rainy weather)!
2. (Come in, come in). Ud. está bastante (wet).
3. (Give me) el impermeable y el sombrero.
4. (Put) el paraguas en el paragüero.
5. (Leave) los chanclos en el zaguán.
6. (Come with me) al comedor.
7. (Drink) una taza de té con ron.
8. (Permit me) servirle a Ud.
9. (While they are drinking) el té siguen charlando.
10. Afuera (it continues raining).

PARTE SEGUNDA

Grammar Notes

1. The Imperative or Command Forms of the Verb.

Infinitive	1st Person Singular		Imperative Singular		Imperative Plural	
hablar	hablo	I speak	hable Ud.	speak	hablen Uds.	speak
pensar (ie)	pienso	I think	piense Ud.	think	piensen Uds.	think
contar (ue)	cuento	I count	cuente Ud.	count	cuenten Uds.	count
comer	como	I eat	coma Ud.	eat	coman Uds.	eat
poner	pongo	I put	ponga Ud.	put	pongan Uds.	put
abrir	abro	I open	abra Ud.	open	abran Uds.	open
venir	vengo	I come	venga Ud.	come	vengan Uds.	come
repetir (i)	repito	I repeat	repita Ud.	repeat	repitan Uds.	repeat
oír	oigo	I hear	oiga Ud.	hear	oigan Uds.	hear
traer	traigo	I bring	traiga Ud.	bring	traigan Uds.	bring

a. To form the imperative take these steps:

1. Remove the -o from the first person singular.
2. For the imperative singular add -e to the stem of -ar verbs, and -a to the stem of -er and -ir verbs.
3. For the imperative plural add -en to the stem of -ar verbs, and -an to the stem of -er and -ir verbs.

   Thus the endings of the imperative are the reverse of the endings of the present tense, where -ar verbs have -a and -an, and -er and -ir verbs have -e and -en.
4. Use Ud. and Uds. after the verb. They may, however, be omitted like *you* in English.

2. Irregular Imperatives

Infinitive	Imperative Singular		Imperative Plural	
dar	dé Ud.	give	den Uds.	give
estar	esté Ud.	be	estén Uds.	be
ser	sea Ud.	be	sean Uds.	be
ir	vaya Ud.	go	vayan Uds.	go

3. The Imperative with Object Pronouns.

a. Object pronouns follow and are attached to the affirmative imperative form.
An accent mark must be added to hold the verb stress where it was before the pronoun was added.

Abra Ud. la puerta.	Open the door.	Ábrala Ud.	Open *it*.
Dejen Uds. los platos.	Leave the plates.	Déjenlos Uds.	Leave *them*.
Óigame.	Hear *me*.	Dígame.	Tell *me*.

b. In the negative imperative, object pronouns precede the verb.

No abra Ud. la puerta.	Do not open the door.	No *la* abra.	Do not open *it*.
No tomen Uds. los platos.	Do not take the plates.	No *los* tomen.	Do not take *them*.

Ejercicios (Exercises) No. 73A-73B

73A. Rewrite each sentence, changing the direct object noun into an object pronoun. First, review "Grammar Notes 3."

Ejemplo: **Póng*ala* Ud. en la mesa.**

1. Ponga Ud. *la tetera* en la mesa.
2. No abra Ud. *la puerta.*
3. Repita Ud. *las preguntas.*
4. No deje Ud. *el paraguas* en el zaguán.
5. Traiga Ud. *los platos* al comedor.
6. No tomen Uds. *el pan.*
7. Saluden Uds. *a sus amigos.*
8. Compren Uds. *los boletos.*
9. Inviten Uds. *al maestro.*
10. Hagan Uds. *el ejercicio.*

73B. Write the first person singular, present; and the imperative, singular and plural, of the following verbs. Give the meaning of each form.

Ejemplo: entrar, entro I enter   entre Ud. entren Uds. enter.

1. escribir
2. leer
3. tener
4. ver
5. preguntar
6. recibir
7. repetir
8. ir
9. dar
10. ser

Exercise No. 74—Preguntas

1. ¿Hace buen o mal tiempo?
2. ¿Quién abre la puerta?
3. ¿Dónde pone el Sr. López el paraguas?
4. ¿Dónde deja él los chanclos?
5. ¿A dónde pasan los señores Adams y López?
6. ¿Qué toman en el comedor?
7. ¿Qué pone la criada en la mesa?
8. ¿Qué hace ella entonces?
9. ¿Quién sirve al Sr. López?
10. ¿Qué echa el Sr. Adams en las tazas?

CAPÍTULO 20 (VEINTE)

PARTE PRIMERA

El Clima de México

1. Todavía están sentados los dos señores en el comedor. Todavía están charlando y tomando el té con ron. Todavía está lloviendo afuera. Ya no tiene frío el Sr. López.

2. El señor Adams dice — El clima de los Estados Unidos y el de México son muy distintos ¿verdad? Aquí en los Estados Unidos tenemos cuatro estaciones y cada estación es diferente.

3. Es cierto. En el verano hace calor; muchas veces hace mucho calor. En el invierno hace frío; muchas veces hace mucho frío y de vez en cuando nieva. En la primavera comienza a hacer buen tiempo pero a menudo llueve como esta noche. Usualmente hace tiempo agradable y hay mucho sol. En el otoño hace fresco y hace viento. ¿Qué estación prefiere Ud.?

4. Prefiero la primavera cuando toda la naturaleza se pone verde; pero me gusta también el otoño con sus colores vivos. Pues, basta del

1. The two gentlemen are still seated in the dining room. They are still chatting and drinking tea with rum. It is still raining outside. Mr. Lopez is no longer cold.

2. Mr. Adams says, "The climate of the United States and that of Mexico are very different, are they not? Here in the United States we have four seasons and each season is different."

3. That's true. In summer it is hot; often it is very hot. In winter it is cold; often it is very cold and from time to time it snows. In spring it begins to be good weather but often it rains like tonight. Usually the weather is pleasant and the sun shines a great deal. In autumn it is cool and windy. Which season do you prefer?

4. I prefer the spring when all nature turns green; but I also like autumn with its bright colors. Well, enough of the climate of the United

clima de los Estados Unidos. Dígame algo del clima de México.

5. Bueno. Oiga Ud. bien.

6. Acabamos de hablar del clima de los Estados Unidos. Ahora vamos a hablar del clima de México. Ud. va a viajar por avión. Va a ver abajo el gran panorama de sierras y picos altos. México le va a parecer una tierra de montañas y volcanes. Es la verdad. Al atravesar a México en coche por la Carretera Panamericana, se sube hasta una altura de casi 8000 pies cerca de México, D.F. La ciudad está situada en la Mesa Central, una mesa inmensa cuya altura varía desde 4000 (cuatro mil) hasta 8000 (ocho mil) pies más o menos. Desde esta mesa se elevan grandes montañas y volcanes como Ixtaccíhuatl y Popocatépetl. En el estado de Vera Cruz está el Pico de Orizaba, la cima más alta de México.

7. El señor Adams dice — ¡De veras! México sí es una tierra de montañas. Y este hecho en gran parte determina el clima de México, ¿verdad?

8. — Ud. tiene razon, — responde el señor López. La mitad de México esta situada en la zona tórrida. Son solamente las costas que tienen un clima caliente y húmedo. En la Mesa Central siempre reina la primavera. En las montañas altas naturalmente hace mucho frío y el Pico de Orizaba está coronado de nieve todo el año.

9. Así hay en efecto tres climas en México — el de las tierras frías en las sierras altas, el de las tierras calientes en las costas, y el de las tierras templadas en la Mesa Central.

10. ¿Y las estaciones?

11. Ya es tarde. Vamos a continuar este tópico la próxima vez.

States. Tell me something about the climate of Mexico.

5. Good. Listen carefully.

6. We have just talked about the climate of the United States. Now we are going to talk about the climate of Mexico. You are going to travel by plane. You will see below the great panorama of ranges and high peaks. Mexico will seem a land of mountains and volcanoes. It is a fact. In crossing Mexico by car along the Pan American Highway, one climbs to an altitude of almost 8000 feet near Mexico City. The city is located on the Central Plateau, an immense tableland whose altitude varies from 4000 to 8000 feet more or less. From this tableland rise up great mountains and volcanoes like Ixtaccihuatl y Popocatepetl. In the state of Vera Cruz is the peak of Orizaba, the highest summit in Mexico.

7. Mr. Adams says, "Really! Mexico is indeed a land of mountains. And this fact in large part determines the climate of Mexico, does it not?"

8. "You are right," answers Mr. Lopez. Half of Mexico is located in the torrid zone. Only the coasts have a hot and humid climate. On the Central Plateau spring always reigns. In the high mountains naturally it is very cold and the peak of Orizaba is crowned with snow all year.

9. So there are in fact three climates in Mexico—that of the frigid zone in the high ranges, that of the torrid zone on the coasts and that of the temperate zone on the Central Plateau.

10. And the seasons?

11. It's already late. We shall continue this topic next time.

Pronunciation and Spelling Aids

Practice: pa-no-ra-ma   Ixtaccíhuatl (ees-tah-see-wahtl)   O-ri-za-ba
           Po-po-ca-té-petl   Ve-ra Cruz   na-tu-ra-le-za

Vocabulary Building

1. **Las cuatro estaciones**   (the four seasons)
   la primavera   spring   **el verano**   summer   **el otoño**   autumn   **el invierno**   winter
2. **Los EE. UU.** is the abbreviation for **los Estados Unidos.**

Expresiones Importantes

1. **no importa**   it doesn't matter   2. **en efecto**   in fact
3. **ponerse**   to become   **La naturaleza se pone verde**   Nature becomes green
4. **todavía**   still   5. **ya no**   no longer   **Ya no tiene frío**   He is no longer cold.

Exercise No. 75—Completion of Text

1. (It is raining) **afuera.**
2. **Todavía los señores** (are chatting and drinking) **té con ron.**
3. **En el verano** (it is hot); **en el invierno** (it is cold).
4. **¿Qué estación** (do you prefer)?
5. (Tell me) **algo del clima de México. Bueno.** (Listen well.)
6. (We have just spoken) **del clima de los EE.UU.**
7. (In crossing) **México** (one climbs) **hasta una altura de ocho mil (8000) pies.**
8. **Desde la mesa central** (rise) **grandes montañas.**
9. **El Pico de Orizaba es la cima** (highest in Mexico).
10. (Half) **de México está situada en la zona** (torrid).

PARTE SEGUNDA

Grammar Notes

1. The Present Tense of **seguir (i)** to follow, **servir (i)** to serve.

I follow, continue, etc.

sigo	seguimos
sigues	seguís
sigue	siguen

Imperative

siga Ud.	sigan Uds.

I serve, etc.

sirvo	servimos
sirves	servís
sirve	sirven

Imperative

sirva Ud.	sirvan Uds.

a. Verbs ending in **-guir**, like **seguir**, drop the silent **u** before the ending **-o** and **-a.**

b. **seguir(i)** and **servir(i)** belong in the same stem-changing group as **pedir(i)**, **repetir(i).**

2. The Present Progressive Tense of **hablar, aprender, vivir.**

Singular

estoy hablando (aprendiendo, viviendo)	I am speaking (learning, living)
estás hablando (aprendiendo, viviendo)	you are speaking (learning, living)
Ud. **está hablando (aprendiendo, viviendo)**	you are speaking (learning, living)
está hablando (aprendiendo, viviendo)	he, she, it is speaking (learning, living)

Plural

estamos hablando (aprendiendo, viviendo)	we are speaking (learning, living)
estáis hablando (aprendiendo, viviendo)	you are speaking (learning, living)
Uds. **están hablando (aprendiendo, viviendo)**	you are speaking (learning, living)
están hablando (aprendiendo, viviendo)	they are speaking (learning, living)

a. The present progressive tense in Spanish is formed by the present tense of **estar** and the present participle of a verb.

b. To form the present participle: remove the infinitive ending **-ar**, **-er**, or **-ir**. Add **-ando** to the remaining stem of **-ar** verbs; add **-iendo** to the stem of **-er** verbs and **-ir** verbs. The endings **-ando** and **-iendo** are equivalent to the English ending *-ing*.

hablando speaking　　　**aprendiendo** learning　　　**viviendo** living

c. The simple present tense in Spanish may be translated into the English progressive form. However, to stress continuing action use the progressive tense:

No **están saliendo ahora.**　　They are not leaving now.

3. Present Participle of Some Common Verbs

desear	to want	deseando	wanting
estudiar	to study	estudiando	studying
pensar(ie)	to think	pensando	thinking
contar	to count	contando	counting

hacer	to make, do	haciendo	making, doing
poner	to put	poniendo	putting
querer(ie)	to wish	queriendo	wishing
abrir	to open	abriendo	opening
leer	to read	leyendo	reading
creer	to believe	creyendo	believing
traer	to bring	trayendo	bringing
caer	to fall	cayendo	falling
ir	to go	yendo	going
repetir(i)	to repeat	repitiendo	repeating
pedir(i)	to ask for	pidiendo	asking for
ser	to be	siendo	being

a. The Spanish does not permit an unaccented **i** between two vowels. Therefore, -**iendo** becomes -**yendo** in the following verbs.

    leer, leyendo   **creer, creyendo**   **oír, oyendo**   **caer, cayendo**   **trae, trayendo**

b. No Spanish word may begin with ie. Therefore: **yendo,** going.

4. Position of Object Pronouns with Present Participles

Object pronouns follow the present participle and are attached to it, as in the case of the infinitive. An accent mark must be added to hold the stress on the first syllable of -**ando** and -**iendo**:

Está escribiendo la carta.	He is writing the letter.
Está escribiéndola.	He is writing it.
Estamos esperando al maestro.	We are expecting the teacher.
Estamos esperándole.	We are expecting him.
Estoy sentándome.	I am seating myself.

Ejercicios (Exercises) No. 76A-76B-76C

76A. Rewrite each sentence, changing the direct object noun into an object pronoun.

Ejemplo: **Estamos estudiándolas.**

1. **Estamos estudiando** *las lecciones.*
2. **Carlos está escribiendo** *la carta.*
3. **¿Estás leyendo** *el cuento,* **niño?**
4. **La criada está poniendo** *la mesa.*
5. **Los señores están tomando** *el té.*
6. **Juan y yo estamos contando** *el dinero.*
7. **¿Están comprando Uds.** *los boletos?*
8. **No estoy leyendo** *las revistas.*
9. **¿Quién está escribiendo** *las cartas?*
10. **Están vendiendo** *los rebozos.*

76B. Rewrite each sentence replacing the English direct object pronouns by the correct Spanish pronouns.

Ejemplo: **No estamos esperándola a Ud., señora.**

1. **No estamos esperando** (you), **señora.**
2. **No estamos esperando** (you), **señor.**
3. **No están mirando** (you), **señores.**
4. **No están mirando** (you), **señoras.**
5. **¿Quién está buscando** (me)?
6. **Yo estoy buscando** (you), **hijita.**
7. **El señor López está enseñando** (us) **a hablar español.**

76C. Translate, using the present progressive tense. Omit all subject pronouns except Ud. and Uds.

1. We are studying
2. He is putting
3. We are opening
4. Are you (**Ud.**) reading?
5. She is bringing
6. Who is waiting?
7. Are you (**Ud.**) taking?
8. You (**tú**) are speaking
9. I am not writing
10. Is Mary working?
11. He is looking for
12. They are teaching

Exercise No. 77—Preguntas

1. ¿De qué están hablando los señores?
2. ¿Qué tiempo hace usualmente en la primavera?
3. ¿Se pone verde la naturaleza en el invierno?
4. ¿Qué ve abajo un viajero que viaja por avión en México?
5. ¿Dónde está situada México, D.F.?
6. ¿Qué altura tiene la Mesa Central?
7. ¿Cuál es la cima más alta de México?
8. ¿Qué determina en gran parte el clima de México?
9. ¿En qué zona está situada la mitad de México?
10. ¿En qué zona hace mucho calor?

CAPÍTULO 21 (VEINTE Y UNO)

PARTE PRIMERA

El Clima de México (continuación)

1. Esta noche seguimos charlando del clima de México y primero de las estaciones.

2. En México hay solamente dos estaciones, la estación de lluvias y la estación seca. La estación de lluvias comienza en el mes de junio y termina en el mes de septiembre.

3. Voy a llegar a México el primero o el dos de junio, es decir, al comienzo de la estación de lluvias.

4. No importa. Todas las estaciones allí son agradables.

5. ¿Y es posible ser sorprendido por la lluvia?

6. A veces. Pero en la estación de lluvias acostumbra llover más o menos a la misma hora cada día, es decir, a eso de las cuatro de la tarde. Por lo tanto vale la pena llevar consigo un impermeable o un paraguas si uno quiere pasearse durante esas horas.

7. ¿Y nunca hace frío?

8. Por la noche hace fresco a veces, y un abrigo ligero o un suéter son de utilidad. Nunca hace frío excepto en las montañas altas. Pero tenga cuidado con el sol tropical. Es muy fuerte y es peligroso caminar o quedarse al sol sin sombrero.

9. Muchas gracias por estos consejos.[1] Voy a acordarme de ellos. Y al hacer la maleta no voy a olvidar el impermeable, un suéter y un abrigo ligero.

10. La próxima vez vamos a platicar de los efectos de la altura, de los alimentos, y de las bebidas.

11. Se relacionan ¿verdad? señor López.

12. Claro está, señor Adams.

NOTE: 1. Spanish says: *advices.*

1. Tonight, we continue chatting about the climate of Mexico and first of the seasons.

2. In Mexico there are only two seasons, the rainy season and the dry season. The rainy season begins in the month of June and ends in the month of September.

3. I will arrive in Mexico the first or second of June, that is to say, at the beginning of the rainy season.

4. It doesn't matter. All the seasons there are pleasant.

5. And may one be surprised by the rain?

6. Sometimes. But in the rainy season it usuall rains at more or less the same time every day, that is to say, at about four in the afternoon. Therefore it is worth the trouble to take with you (oneself) a raincoat or umbrella if you want to go for a walk during those hours.

7. And it is never cold?

8. At night it is cool at times, and a light overcoat or a sweater is useful. It is never cold except in the high mountains. But watch out for the tropical sun. It is very strong and it is dangerous to walk or remain in the sun without a hat.

9. Many thanks for this advice. I am going to remember it. And on packing my bag I am not going to forget my raincoat, a sweater and a light overcoat.

10. Next time we will talk about the effects of the altitude, of food, and of drink.

11. They are related, are they not?

12. Yes, indeed, Mr. Adams.

Pronunciation and Spelling Aids

1. Practice: llu-vias (*yoo-vyahs*)   sor-pren-di-do   ve-ces   cui-da-do
                     llo-ver   es-ta-cio-nes   a-cos-tum-bra   li-ge-ro

Vocabulary Building

A. Antínomos:

1. algo	something	nada	nothing
2. antes de mi llegada	before my arrival	después de mi llegada	after my arrival
3. comenzar	to begin	terminar	to end
4. siempre	always	nunca	never
5. alguien	somebody	nadie	nobody

Expresiones Importantes

1. no importa — it doesn't matter
2. por lo tanto, por eso — therefore
3. esta noche — tonight
4. tenga cuidado (con) — be careful (of)
5. al hacer mi maleta — on packing my valise

6. Refrán (Proverb) **Más vale algo que nada.** Literally: Something is worth more than nothing. *English proverb*. Half a loaf is better than none.

Exercise No. 78—Completion of Text

1. **Esta noche** (we continue speaking) **del clima.**
2. **La estación de lluvias comienza** (in the month of June).
3. **Acostumbra llover** (at the same hour) **cada día.**
4. (Therefore) **lleve Ud. un paraguas consigo.**
5. (It's worth the trouble) **llevar un impermeable.**
6. (Never) **hace frío** (except) **en las montañas.**
7. (Be careful of) **el sol tropical.**
8. **Es peligroso** (to remain) **en el sol** (without) **sombrero.**
9. **Voy a** (remember) **de estos consejos.**
10. (On packing) **mi maleta no voy** (to forget) **el impermeable.**

PARTE SEGUNDA

Grammar Notes

1. Negative Words.

a. Common negative words are:

nadie	nobody	**nunca (jamás)**	never
ninguno	no, none, not any	**ni . . . ni**	neither . . . nor
nada	nothing	**tampoco**	neither, not . . . either

b. If these negative words follow the verb, **no** must precede the verb. If the negative words precede the verb or stand alone, **no** is not required.

Nadie viene hoy.	No viene **nadie** hoy.	*Nobody* is coming today.
Ningún cliente viene.	No viene **ningún** cliente.	*No* customer is coming.
Nunca (jamás) hace frío.	No hace nunca (jamás) frío.	It is *never* cold.
Nada tengo.	No tengo **nada.**	I have *nothing*.

No tiene ni amigos **ni** dinero.   He has *neither* friends *nor* money.

¿Qué quiere Ud.? **Nada.**   What do you want? *Nothing*.

Pablo no desea ir. **Tampoco** yo. (**Ni yo tampoco**)   Paul doesn't want to go. *Neither* do I.

NOTE: **ninguno** becomes **ningún** before a noun.

2. Infinitives after Prepositions.

After prepositions the Spanish uses an infinitive where the English uses a present participle.

al cruzar a México	on crossing Mexico	**después de comer**	after eating
sin trabajar	without working	**antes de comer**	before eating

3. Consigo, with oneself (himself, herself, yourself, yourselves, themselves)

Lo trae consigo.	He brings it with him (self).
Uds. lo traen consigo.	You bring it with you (yourselves).

Exercise No. 79

Complete the following, replacing the English words by **nadie, ningun (o, a, os, as), nunca, nada, ni . . . ni, tampoco**, as needed.

1. Muchos turistas no saben (nothing) de la historia de México.
2. (Nothing) es más fácil.
3. (Never) hace frío en la capital.
4. No es posible pasar sin números. (Nor) es posible comprar sin dinero.
5. (Nobody) puede vivir sin comer.
6. No hay (nobody) en la taquilla.
7. Más vale tarde que (never).
8. No anda (never) en el sol sin sombrero.
9. El hombre no está bien. (Neither) está contento.
10. No tenemos (neither) tiempo (nor) dinero.
11. (No) hombre puede vivir sin comer.
12. No vemos a (no) niños en la calle.
13. Tiene Ud. dinero. No tengo (any).
14. No hay (any) fajas en esta cesta.
15. Más vale algo que (nothing).

Exercise No. 80—Preguntas

1. ¿Cuáles son las dos estaciones en México?
2. ¿Cuándo comienza la estación de lluvias?
3. ¿Cuándo termina la estación de lluvias?
4. ¿A qué hora acostumbra llover cada día?
5. ¿Hace frío en la ciudad?
6. ¿Por qué es de utilidad un abrigo ligero.
7. ¿Por qué es peligroso caminar en el sol sin sombrero?
8. ¿Qué no va a olvidar el Sr. Adams al hacer su maleta?
9. ¿De qué van a platicar la próxima vez?
10. ¿Se relacionan los efectos de la altura y los de los alimentos?

CAPÍTULO 22

PARTE PRIMERA

Los Alimentos de México

1. México D.F. tiene una altura de cerca de 7500 (siete mil quinientos) pies sobre el nivel del mar. Mucha gente no acostumbrada a la altura se siente un poco débil y sin ambición.

2. Es costumbre echar a la altura la culpa de todos los malestares. ¿Tiene un turista un dolor de cabeza? Se dice — es la altura. ¿Tiene dolor de estómago? Se dice — Es la altura. ¿Tiene dolor de muelas? Otra vez — Es la altura.

3. Pero ¿qué se puede hacer para acostumbrarse a la altura?

4. No se preocupe. Al principio es mejor no apresurarse. Camine despacio. Descanse varias horas por la tarde.

5. ¿Y qué me aconseja sobre los alimentos?

6. Tenga cuidado con las frutas típicas de México—los mangos, las papayas, los zapotes, etc.

1. Mexico City has an altitude of about 7500 feet above sea level. Many people unaccustomed to the altitude feel a little weak and unambitious.

2. It is the custom to place the blame for all indispositions on the altitude. Does a tourist have a headache? They say—it's the altitude. Does he have a stomach ache? They say—it's the altitude. Does he have a toothache? Again—it's the altitude.

3. But what can one do to accustom oneself to the altitude?

4. Don't worry. At first it is better not to hurry. Walk slowly. Rest several hours in the afternoon.

5. And what do you advise me about the food?

6. Be careful with the typical fruits of Mexico —mangos, papayas, zapotes, etc. They are very

Son muy sabrosas pero al principio es mejor tomar frutas ordinarias—las naranjas, los plátanos, las peras, los melones y las manzanas que se venden en todos los mercados. Acostúmbrese poco a poco a las otras.

7. ¿Hay muchos alimentos típicos de México?

8. Claro está. Hay muchos. Estos alimentos nos parecen raros a nosotros. El hot dog y los corn-flakes les parecen raros a los mexicanos. ¿Conoce Ud. el pan de México?

9. Sí, lo conozco. Es la tortilla.

10. Eso es. La tortilla se parece al panqueque. La hacen del maíz. La usan para hacer los tacos y las enchiladas.

11. ¿Qué clase de carne comen los mexicanos?

12. Comen filete, jamón, pollo, guajalote, varias clases de chuletas, etc. Toman también varias clases de pescado. Les gusta mucho una salsa picante. Y casi no hay comida sin arroz y frijoles.

13. ¿Y hay muchas clases de postres?

14. A los mexicanos les gusta comer un dulce, flan o una de las muchas frutas que se venden en el mercado.

15. Debo saber leer el menú en un restaurante, ¿verdad?

16. Sí, y también debe Ud. probar los alimentos de México. Pero todo con moderación. El estómago norteamericano no se acostumbra rápidamente a los alimentos picantes de México. No lo olvide—Comemos para vivir; no vivimos para comer.

17. No voy a olvidarlo. Y no voy a olvidar ninguno de sus buenos consejos.

tasty but at first it is better to eat ordinary fruits —oranges, bananas, pears, melons and apples which are sold in all the markets. Accustom yourself little by little to the others.

7. Are there many foods typical of Mexico?

8. Of course. There are many. These foods seem strange to us. Hot dogs and corn flakes seem strange to the Mexicans. Do you know the bread of Mexico?

9. Yes, I know it. It is the tortilla.

10. That's right. The tortilla looks like a pancake. They make it of corn. They use it to make tacos and enchiladas.

11. What kind of meat do Mexicans eat?

12. They eat steak, ham, chicken, turkey, several kinds of chops, etc. They also eat several kinds of fish. They like a sharp sauce very much. And there is almost no meal without rice and beans.

13. And are there many kinds of desserts?

14. Mexicans like to eat a sweet, custard or one of the many fruits that are sold in the market.

15. I should know how to read the menu in a restaurant, shouldn't I?

16. Yes, and you should also try the Mexican foods. But everything in moderation. The North American stomach does not accustom itself quickly to the sharp foods of Mexico. Don't forget. We eat to live; we do not live to eat.

17. I will not forget. And I will not forget any of your good advice.

Pronunciation and Spelling Aids

1. Practice:

a-cos-tum-bra-da	a-con-se-ja	pa-re-cen	fri-jo-les
ma-les-ta-res	gua-ja-lo-te	res-tau-**ran**-te	es-pá-rra-gos
a-cos-tum-**brar**-se	es-tó-ma-go	ma-íz	le-gum-bres
a-pre-su-rar-se			

Vocabulary Building

A. Frutas Fruits

la banana	banana	la lima	lime	la piña	pineapple
el plátano	banana (Mex.)	el limón	lemon	la toronja	grapefruit
la cereza	cherry	la naranja	orange	la uva	grape
el melocotón	peach	la pera	pear		

B. Carne Meat Pescados Fish

la chuleta	chop	el pato	duck	el puerco	pork
el cordero	lamb	el pavo	turkey	el rosbif	steak
la hamburguesa	hamburger	el guajalote	turkey (Mex.)	el filete	steak (Mex.)
el jamón	ham	el pescado	fish	la ternera	veal
la langosta	lobster	el pollo	chicken	el tocino	bacon

C. Legumbres y Verduras   Vegetables

el camote	sweet potato (Mex.)	el elote	ear of corn (Mex.)	la lechuga	lettuce
la cebolla	onion	los chícharos	peas	la patata	potato
la col	cabbage	los espárragos	asparagus	la papa	potato (Mex.)
la coliflor	cauliflower	los frijoles	beans	el pepino	cucumber

Expresiones Importantes

1. dolor de cabeza   headache
2. dolor de muelas   toothache
3. dolor de estómago   stomach ache
4. eso es   that's right

Exercise No. 81—Completion of Text

1. Mucha gente (feel a bit weak) **a causa de la altura.**
2. ¿Tiene Ud. (a headache)? **a** (toothache)? (a stomach ache?)
3. (People say) — **Es la altura.**
4. (What can one do) **si se siente un poco débil?**
5. (Rest) **varias horas cada día.** (Walk slowly).
6. ¿(What do you advise me) **sobre los alimentos?**
7. (Be careful) **con las frutas típicas de México.**
8. Estas frutas (are sold) **en todos los mercados.**
9. Estos alimentos nos (seem) **raros a nosotros.**
10. La tortilla (is like) **al panqueque.**
11. ¿Sabe Ud. (what kind of meat) **comen los mexicanos?**
12. (They like) **mucho una salsa picante.**
13. Ud. (should) **probar los alimentos.**
14. (We eat) **para vivir.** (We do not live) **para comer.**
15. No voy (to forget) **sus consejos.**

PARTE SEGUNDA

Grammar Notes

1. The Present Tense of **sentir (ie)** to feel, to regret, **conocer** to know

I feel, etc.			I know, etc.	
siento	sentimos		conozco	conocemos
sientes	sentís		conoces	conocéis
siente	sienten		conoce	conocen

a. **parecer** to seem, and **traducir** to translate, are irregular in the first person singular, like **conocer.** Thus: parezco, pareces, etc.; traduzco, traduces, etc.

2. Special Uses of the Reflexive Verb.

a. The reflexive verb is often used instead of the passive.

Se venden frutas.	Fruits are sold (fruits sell themselves).
Se abre la puerta.	The door is opened (the door opens itself).
Aquí se habla español.	Here Spanish is spoken.
Se ve mucha gente en el parque.	Many people are seen in the park.

b. The reflexive verb is used in certain impersonal constructions where the English has an indefinite subject such as one, people, they or you.

se dice	one says	people say	they say	it is said
¿cómo se dice?	how does one say?	how do you say?		
se puede	one may	can		
se sube	one goes up			

c. The reflexive verb is at times used with a different meaning than the simple verb.

comer	to eat		ir	to go
comerse	to eat up		irse	to go away
parecer	to seem		encontrar	to meet
parecerse	to resemble		encontrarse	to be (somewhere)

3. conocer, saber

a. **saber** means to know facts and things (never persons) by means of the mind. **saber** also means *to know how.*

Sabemos dónde vive Juan.	We know where John lives.
Sabemos cuántos años tiene.	We know how old he is.
Sabemos los números en español.	We know the numbers in Spanish.
Sé cantar esta canción.	I know how to sing this song.

b. **conocer** means to know in the sense of to be acquainted with a person or thing; to recognize; to know by sight, hearing or any of the senses.

Conozco a Juan.	I know (am acquainted with) John.
Conozco esta casa.	I know (recognize by sight) this house.
Conocemos este restaurante. Es muy bueno.	We know this restaurant. It is very good.
Conozco esta canción.	I know (recognize on hearing) this song.

Ejercicios (Exercises) No. 82A-82B

82A. Replace the English words by the correct Spanish reflexive verbs.

1. ¿(May one) **entrar en el parque?**
2. ¿(How does one say) **en inglés—Permítame.**
3. Aquí (are sold) **flores.**
4. Muchos burros (are seen) **en los caminos.**
5. (People say) **que el presidente viene hoy.**
6. Aquí (Spanish is spoken).
7. (They eat up) **todos los alimentos.**
8. ¿(Do you know) **a aquellos profesores?**
9. (I do not know them).
10. (Do you know how) **contar hasta ciento?**
11. Mañana (I go away).
12. (We know how) **cantar estas canciones.**
13. La tortilla (resembles) **a nuestros panqueques.**
14. Tengo (a toothache).

82B. Match up the Spanish words in Group II with the English words in Group I.

Group I

1. the banana	9. the meat
2. the steak	10. the chicken
3. the pear	11. the bread
4. the corn	12. the sauce
5. the dessert	13. the chops
6. the rice	14. the foods
7. the beans	15. the orange
8. the ham	16. the apple

Group II

a. el postre	i. el plátano
b. los frijoles	j. las chuletas
c. el arroz	k. el maíz
d. la carne	l. la naranja
e. el jamón	m. el filete
f. la pera	n. el pollo
g. el pan	o. la manzana
h. la salsa	p. los alimentos

Exercise No. 83—Preguntas

1. ¿Qué altura tiene México D.F.?
2. ¿Cuáles son dos frutas típicas de México?
3. ¿Cuáles son cuatro frutas ordinarias?
4. ¿Dónde se venden todas clases de frutas?
5. Al principio ¿qué es mejor, tomar frutas ordinarias o frutas típicas de México?
6. ¿Cúal es el pan de México?
7. ¿De qué hacen la tortilla?
8. ¿Qué usan para hacer los tacos y las enchiladas?
9. ¿Qué clase de postres comen los mexicanos?
10. ¿Por qué es mejor probar los alimentos típicos de México con moderación?

REPASO 5

(CAPÍTULOS 19–22) PARTE PRIMERA

Repaso de Palabras

NOUNS

1. el abrigo	14. los frijoles	27. el otoño	1. overcoat	14. beans	27. autumn
2. la altura	15. la gente	28. el paraguas	2. height	15. people	28. umbrella
3. el arroz	16. el hecho	29. la pera	3. rice	16. fact	29. pear
4. la botella	17. el impermeable	30. el pie	4. bottle	17. raincoat	30. foot
5. la bebida	18. el invierno	31. el plátano	5. drink	18. winter	31. banana
6. la carne	19. el jamón	32. el pollo	6. meat	19. ham	32. chicken
7. el clima	20. el menú	33. el pico	7. climate	20. menu	33. peak
8. el consejo	21. la lluvia	34. la primavera	8. advice	21. rain	34. spring
9. las chuletas	22. el maíz	35. la tortilla	9. chops	22. corn	35. tortilla
10. el estado	23. el mar	36. la sierra	10. state	23. sea	36. mountain range
11. la estación	24. el melón	37. el sombrero	11. season	24. melon	37. hat
12. el filete	25. la naturaleza	38. el verano	12. steak	25. nature	38. summer
13. el flan	26. la nieve		13. custard	26. snow	

VERBS

1. acostumbrarse	7. llover(ue)	14. quedar	1. to accustom oneself	7. to rain	14. to remain
2. aconsejar	8. olvidar	15. seguir	2. to advise	8. to forget	15. to follow, continue
3. apresurarse	9. parecer	16. servir(i)	3. to hurry	9. to seem	16. to serve
4. conocer	10. parecerse	17. sentirse(ie)	4. to know	10. to resemble	17. to feel (weak, ill, etc.)
5. charlar	11. ponerse	18. subir	5. to chat	11. to become	18. to go up
6. descansar	12. preocuparse	19. traer	6. to rest	12. to worry	19. to bring, carry
	13. probar			13. to try	

ADJECTIVES

1. agradable	7. frío	13. mismo	1. pleasant	7. cold	13. same
2. caliente	8. fuerte	14. peligroso	2. hot	8. strong	14. dangerous
3. común	9. húmedo	15. picante	3. common	9. damp	15. sharp, spicy
4. débil	10. ligero	16. sabroso	4. weak	10. light	16. tasty
5. diferente	11. lluvioso	17. seguro	5. different	11. rainy	17. certain
6. distinto	12. mojado	18. seco	6. different	12. wet	18. dry

ADVERBS

1. afuera	3. entonces	5. todavía	1. outside	3. then	5. still
2. abajo	4. solamente	6. todavía no	2. below	4. only	6. not yet

PREPOSITIONS

1. junto con	2. antes de	3. cerca de	1. together with	2. before	3. near

PRONOUNS

1. algo	2. alguien	3. consigo	1. something	2. somebody	3. with himself, herself, themselves

NEGATIVES

1. nada	4. nunca	7. jamás	1. nothing	4. never	7. never
2. nadie	5. ni … ni	8. todavía no	2. nobody	5. neither … nor	8. not yet
3. ninguno	6. tampoco		3. no, none, not any	6. neither, not … either	

IMPORTANT EXPRESSIONS

1. a menudo	6. es cierto	11. por lo tanto	1. often	6. it is true	11. therefore
2. acabar de	7. dolor de cabeza	12. tener cuidado	2. to have just	7. headache	12. to be careful
3. con su permiso	8. dolor de muelas	13. vale la pena	3. with your permission	8. toothache	13. it is worth the trouble
4. de veras	9. hacer la maleta	14. eso es	4. indeed	9. to pack the trunk	14. that's right
5. en coche	10. no importa		5. by automobile	10. it does not matter	

PARTE SEGUNDA

Ejercicio 84. From Group 2 select the opposite for each word in Group 1.

Group 1		Group 2	
1. antes de comer	7. fuerte	a. caliente	g. nunca
2. frío	8. trabajar	b. después de comer	h. olvidar
3. siempre	9. lluvioso	c. nada	i. débil
4. alguien	10. despacio	d. de prisa	j. terminar
5. comenzar	11. algo	e. seco	k. nadie
6. recordar	12. ahora	f. entonces	l. descansar

Ejercicio 85. Complete the following sentences in Spanish.

1. Cuando hace frío (I am cold).
2. Cuando hace calor (I am warm).
3. En el verano (the weather is nice).
4. En la primavera (it rains a great deal).
5. En el otoño (it is cool).

6. En el invierno (it is cold).
7. Cuando llueve (I wear rubbers).
8. Cuando nieva (I wear an overcoat).
9. Cuando hace calor (it is dusty).
10. Me gustan (all the seasons).

Ejercicio 86. Select the group words in the right hand column which best complete the sentences begun in the left hand column.

1. Prefiero la primavera
2. No me gusta el invierno
3. Voy a decir algo sobre
4. Es verdad que México
5. Se venden frutas
6. Lleve Ud. un paraguas consigo
7. A los mexicanos les gusta
8. No voy a olvidar
9. Sabemos
10. Conocemos bien

a. el clima de México.
b. es una tierra de montañas.
c. en todos los mercados.
d. porque hace buen tiempo.
e. comer los mangos y plátanos.
f. porque hace mucho frío.
g. contar en español.
h. porque está lloviendo.
i. a los alumnos de esta clase.
j. ningunos de sus consejos.

Ejercicio 87. Read each command. Then translate the sentence that follows it. Watch out for the position of the object pronoun!

Ejemplo: **Cuenta Ud. el dinero.** I count it. **Lo cuento.**

1. Abra Ud. la puerta. I open it.
2. Cuente Ud. los picos. I count them.
3. Coma Ud. la carne. I eat it.
4. Ponga Ud. la mesa. I set it.
5. Repita Ud. las preguntas. I repeat them.
6. Dejen Uds. los platos. We leave them.

7. Tomen Uds. las tazas. We take them.
8. Aprendan Uds. las lecciones. We learn them.
9. Escriban Uds. el ejercicio. We write it.
10. Lean Uds. el periódico. We read it.

Ejercicio 88. Substitute the present participle for the infinitive in parentheses to make the present progressive tense.

Ejemplo: 1. **Está lloviendo a cántaros.**

1. Está (llover) a cántaros.
2. Estamos (echar) el café.
3. Están (pedir) informes.
4. Estoy (leer) las cartas.
5. ¿Está (pensar) Ud. en su padre?

6. ¿Quién está (traer) la tetera?
7. ¿Quiénes están (oír) al maestro?
8. ¿No están (contar) el dinero?
9. ¿La criada está (poner) la mesa.
10. ¿Qué está (hacer) Carlos?

PARTE TERCERA

Diálogo

Practice the Spanish Aloud:

En el Restaurante

— ¿Qué hay en la comida corrida? — pregunta el Sr. Adams al mozo.

¿Quiere Ud. tomar algunos platos mexicanos, Sr. Adams?

Pues, todavía no. Acabo de llegar a México y es mejor, al principio, comer platos acostumbrados.

¿Me permite Ud. recomendar el filete mignon a la parrilla?

"What is there on the table d'hote?" Mr. Adams asks the waiter.

Do you want to eat some Mexican dishes, Mr. Adams?

Well, not yet. I have just arrived in Mexico and it is better, at first, to eat customary dishes.

Will you permit me to recommend the broiled filet mignon?

Debe de estar muy bueno pero prefiero probar las chuletas.	It must be very good but I prefer to try the chops.
Chuletas de ternera, entonces. Y Ud. puede escoger dos legumbres.	Veal chops, then. And you may choose two vegetables.
El arroz y las zanahorias. Como postre, déme flan, por favor. Es un postre mexicano que me gusta mucho.	Rice and carrots. As dessert, give me custard, please. It is a Mexican dessert that I like very much.
¿Y de beber?	And to drink?
Café con leche, por favor.	Coffee with milk, please.
Muy bien, Sr. Adams.	Very well, Mr. Adams.
Y favor de traer la cuenta.	And please bring me the check.
Aquí la tiene, Sr. Adams.	Here it is, Mr. Adams.
Muchas gracias.	Many thanks.
A Ud., señor.	Thank you, sir.

LECTURA

Exercise No. 89—A Felipe No Le Gusta Estudiar La Aritmética

Un día, al volver (upon returning) de la escuela, dice Felipe a su madre, — No me gusta estudiar la aritmética. Es tan difícil. ¿Para que necesitamos tantos (so many) ejercicios y problemas hoy día? ¿No es verdad que tenemos máquinas calculadoras (adding machines)?

La señora Adams mira a su hijo y dice, — No tienes razón, hijito. No es posible pasar sin números. Por ejemplo, siempre es necesario cambiar dinero, hacer compras, calcular distancias y . . . y . . .

La madre deja de (stops) hablar al ver (on seeing) que Felipe no presta atención a lo que (what) ella dice

— A propósito, continúa la madre con una sonrisa (smile), — el béisbol no te interesa tampoco (either), hijo mío?

— Ya lo creo, mamacita.

— Pues, si los Dodgers han ganado (have won) ochenta juegos (games) y han perdido (have lost) treinta, ¿sabes qué por ciento de los juegos han ganado?

Al oír (On hearing) esto Felipe abre la boca y exclama, — Tienes razon, mamá. Los números, la aritmética y las matemáticas son muy importantes. Creo que voy a estudiar mucho más.

CAPÍTULO 23 (VEINTE Y TRES)

PARTE PRIMERA

El Pueblo de Mexico

1. Voy a hacerle algunas preguntas acerca del pueblo de México, dice el señor Adams. ¿Está Ud. listo? ¿Quiere Ud. otro puro? Aquí tiene los cerillos y el cenicero.	1. I am going to ask you some questions about the people of Mexico, says Mr. Adams. Are you ready? Do you want another cigar? Here are the matches and the ashtray.
2. Gracias, señor Adams. Estoy muy bien. Continúe, por favor.	2. Thank you, Mr. Adams. I am very comfortable. Continue, please.
3. Ante todo ¿quiénes son los mexicanos?	3. First of all, who are the Mexicans?
4. Son los descendientes de los españoles, conquistadores de México y de la América del Sur, y de los indios indígenas.	4. They are descendants of the Spaniards, conquerors of Mexico and of South America, and of the native Indians.
5. ¿Cuántos habitantes hay ahora en México?	5. How many inhabitants are there today in Mexico?

6. Hoy día viven en México más o menos 28 millones de personas. No todos hablan español. De los 12 millones llamados "indios" muchos todavía hablan varias lenguas indígenas.

7. ¿Dónde vive la mayor parte de los habitantes, en la ciudad o en el campo?

8. Hay ciudades grandes muy modernas e industrias grandes. Tres millones de personas viven en el Distrito Federal, una ciudad hermosa y cosmopolita. Pero la mayor parte vive en el campo y trabaja en la agricultura.

9. ¿Cuáles son los productos más importantes?

10. A causa de la variedad de climas y la extensión del territorio, México produce una variedad de productos, desde el trigo hasta la caña de azúcar. Pero el maíz es el producto más importante de todos.

11. Además de ser agricultores los mexicanos son artistas y artesanos ¿verdad?

12. Tratan siempre de embellecer una vida dura. Son muy trabajadores pero saben también vivir. Y saben a fondo hacer cosas artísticas.

13. ¿De qué artes se ocupan?

14. Mucha gente se ocupa de las artes populares — la cerámica, el tejido; hace cestas, artículos de cuero, de cobre, de hojalata, de oro, de plata y de laca.

15. A propósito, acabo de recibir un envío de algunos artículos de México. ¿Quiere Ud. venir a mi oficina el jueves a las tres de la tarde para verlos? Entonces volvemos a platicar de las artes populares.

16. Con todo gusto, Sr. Adams. Tenemos cita para el jueves a las tres, ¿verdad?

17. Hasta el jueves, entonces.

18. Hasta luego. Que Ud. lo pase bien.

6. Today more or less 28 million people live in Mexico. Not all speak Spanish. Of the 12 million called "Indians" many still speak various native languages.

7. Where do the majority of the inhabitants live, in the city or in the country?

8. There are big, very modern cities and big industries. Three million people live in the Federal District, a beautiful and cosmopolitan city. But the majority live in the country and work in agriculture.

9. What are the most important products?

10. Because of the variety of climates and the extent of territory, Mexico produces a variety of products from wheat to sugar cane. But corn is the most important product of all.

11. Besides being agriculturists Mexicans are artists, are they not?

12. They always try to beautify a hard life. They are very hard working but they also know how to live. And they know thoroughly how to make artistic things.

13. What arts are they engaged in?

14. Many people are engaged in the popular arts—ceramics, weaving; they make baskets, leather goods, things of copper, tin, gold, silver and lacquer.

15. By the way, I have just received a shipment of some articles from Mexico. Do you want to come to my office Thursday at three in the afternoon to look at them? Then we will talk again about the popular arts.

16. With pleasure, Mr. Adams. We have an appointment for Thursday at three, do we not?

17. Until Thursday, then.

18. So long. Good luck to you.

Pronunciation and Spelling Aids

1. Practice:

	con-ti-nen-te	Fe-de-ral	em-be-lle-cer	las Ar-tes	en-ví-o
con-ti-nú-e	in-dí-ge-nas	cos-mo-po-li-ta	tra-ba-ja-do-res	Po-pu-la-res	ho-ja-la-ta
des-cen-dien-tes	in-dus-trias	ex-ten-sión	a-gri-cul-to-res	ce-rá-mi-ca	cue-ro
conquis-ta-do-res	Dis-tri-to	va-rie-dad	ar-tís-ti-cos	te-ji-do	co-bre

2. y and e mean *and*. e is used instead of y when the next word begins with the letter i, to avoid repetition of the i (ee) sound; agricultura e industria.

o and u mean *or*. u is used instead of o when the next word begins with o to avoid repetition of the o sound. septiembre u octubre.

Vocabulary Building

A. Materias Primas (Raw Materials)

el algodón	cotton	la lana	wool	el petróleo	petroleum
el cobre	copper	la madera	wood	la plata	silver
el cuero	leather	el oro	gold	el plomo	lead
el hierro	iron	la paja	straw	la seda	silk

B. Sinónimos

el idioma	la lengua	language
acabar	terminar	to finish
el cigarro	el puro (Mex.)	cigar
el cerillo	el fósforo	match
con todo gusto	con mucho gusto	with great pleasure

Expresiones Importantes

a causa de	because of	a fondo	fully, completely, thoroughly
ante todo	first of all	ocuparse de	to be engaged in (to busy oneself with)

que Ud. lo pase bien   good luck to you (may you get along well).

Exercise No. 90—Completion of Text

1. Voy a (ask you) algunas preguntas.
2. Son (about the people) de México.
3. (Here are) los cerillos. (Continue), por favor.
4. ¿(Who) son los méxicanos?
5. ¿Cuántas personas viven (nowadays) en México?
6. El Distrito Federal es una ciudad (beautiful and cosmopolitan).
7. (Because of the variety) de climas, hay (a variety) de productos.
8. El maíz es (the most important product) del todo.
9. Son (artists and artisans).
10. ¿De qué artes (are they engaged)?
11. (They are engaged) de las artes populares.
12. Hacen (baskets and leather articles).
13. (I have just received) un envío de México.
14. (We will talk again) de las artes populares.
15. (Good luck to you).

PARTE SEGUNDA

Grammar Notes

1. Present Tense of volver (ue) to return, go back; volver a hablar, to speak again

I return, etc.		I speak again, etc.	
vuelvo	volvemos	vuelvo a hablar	volvemos a hablar
vuelves	volvéis	vuelves a hablar	volvéis a hablar
vuelve	vuelven	vuelve a hablar	vuelven a hablar

a. Vuelvo a casa.   I return home.   Volvemos al cine.   We return to the movies.

b. Volver a, plus an infinitive, means to do something again.

Vuelvo a escribir la carta.   I am writing the letter again.
Hoy volvemos a platicar de las artes.   Today we shall speak again of the arts.

Another way of expressing the same idea:
Escribo la carta otra vez.   Hoy platicamos de las artes otra vez.

2. acabar to finish, acabar de recibir to have just received

a. Acabo el trabajo.   I finish the work.   ¿Acaban Uds. la lección?   Are you finishing the lesson?

b. acabar de plus an infinitive, means to have just done something.

Acabo de recibir un envío.   I have just received a shipment.
Acaba de enseñar la lección.   He has just taught the lesson.

Ejercicios (Exercises) No. 91A-91B

91A. Repeat aloud the Spanish sentences many times.

1. ¿Acaba Ud. de comer? Have you just eaten?
2. Sí, acabo de comer. Yes, I have just eaten.
3. ¿Acaba de dormir el niño? Has the child just slept?
4. No, no acaba de dormir. No, he has not just slept.
5. ¿Acaban de tomar la cena? Have they just eaten supper?

6. **Sí, acaban de tomarla.** Yes, they have just eaten it.

7. **¿Cuándo vuelve Ud. a casa?** When do you return home?

8. **Vuelvo a casa a las siete.** I return home at seven.

9. **Vuelven a leer el libro.** They are reading the book again.

10. **Carlos vuelve a venir acá.** Charles is coming here again.

NOTE: **acá** here, and **allá** there, are used instead of **aquí** and **allí** with verbs of motion.

91B. Translate:

1. When do they return home?
2. They return home at ten o'clock in the evening.
3. The students are writing the exercises again.
4. I am reading the guide book (**la guía de viajero**) again.
5. We have just received a shipment of merchandise (**mercancía**).
6. I have just spoken about the climate.
7. She has just returned from the jewelry shop (**joyería**).
8. They have just bought silver earrings (**aretes de plata**).
9. Have you just come from the movies?
10. We are finishing the work (**el trabajo**).

Exercise No. 92—Preguntas

1. ¿Quién va a hacer algunas preguntas?
2. ¿Cuál es la primera pregunta?
3. ¿De quiénes son descendientes los mexicanos de hoy?
4. ¿Cuántos habitantes tiene México?
5. ¿Qué lenguas hablan muchos de los doce millones de indios?
6. ¿Dónde vive la mayor parte de los habitantes, en la ciudad o en el campo?
7. ¿Cuál es el producto más importante de México?
8. ¿De qué artes se ocupan muchas personas?
9. ¿De qué materiales hacen cosas artísticas?
10. ¿Quién acaba de recibir un envío de mercancía de México?

CAPÍTULO 24 (VEINTE Y CUATRO)

PARTE PRIMERA

Las Artes Populares

1. **En la oficina del Sr. Adams.** Este acaba de recibir una caja de mercancía de México y ha invitado al Sr. López a verla con él.

2. Vamos a ver los artículos de México, Sr. López. Acabo de recibirlos.

3. Con mucho gusto. Y entretanto podemos hablar de las artes populares.

4. Sabemos, Sr. López, que algunos de los artículos más artísticos que hacen los artesanos mexicanos son los de uso diario. Así es que el vestido es también un arte popular, ¿verdad?

5. Es cierto. El vestido típico da a los indios un aspecto pintoresco. Las mujeres llevan faldas largas y blusas con bordados sencillos. Lejos de las ciudades visten todavía de blusas, faldas y fajas de antaño. Los hombres llevan traje blanco o de color claro. El sombrero de paja es de uso general.

1. In the office of Mr. Adams. The latter has just received a box of merchandise from Mexico and has invited Mr. Lopez to look at it with him.

2. Let us look at the things from Mexico, Mr. Lopez. I have just received them.

3. With pleasure. And meanwhile we can talk about the popular arts.

4. We know, Mr. Lopez, that some of the most artistic things that the Mexican craftsmen make are those articles of daily use. So it is that the clothing is also a popular art, is it not?

5. Yes, indeed. The typical dress gives the Indians a picturesque appearance. The women wear long skirts and blouses with simple embroidery. Far from the cities they still dress in the blouses and skirts and sashes of olden times. The men wear a white or light colored costume. The straw hat is in general use.

6. Aquí tiene Ud. algunos sarapes de lugares distintos. El sarape es un artículo de ropa ¿verdad?

7. Sí, los hombres llevan el sarape para abrigo o para adorno. Sirve también para manta. ¡Qué bien tejidos son estos sarapes grises! ¡Me gustan los dibujos geométricos! Son de Oaxaca ¿verdad?

8. Sí. Y mire Ud. las fajas. Estas rojas son de Toluca. Tanto los hombres como las mujeres llevan la faja. Es tejida de lana o de algodón.

9. ¡Qué graciosos son los dibujos!—éstos de pajaros y ésos de animalitos que adornan la bolsa que tiene Ud. en la mano. ¿Y le mandan también rebozos?

10. Desgraciadamente, no.

11. Ud. sabe que el rebozo es para la mujer lo que es el sarape para el hombre. Sirve para todo—para sombrero y abrigo, para envolver bultos; para manta y cuna del nene.

12. —Van a mandarme también cestas de varios tamaños y estilos y, desde luego, todas clases de cerámica, — dice el señor Adams.

13. ¿Ha visto Ud. las máscaras que hacen los indios para sus bailes durante las fiestas?

14. No las he visto. Y sé muy poco de las fiestas.

15. Entonces tenemos que hablar de las fiestas la próxima vez. ¿Le parece bien el martes a las ocho?

16. Me parece bien.

17. Hasta el martes, Sr. Adams.

18. Que Ud. lo pase bien, Sr. López.

6. Here are some sarapes from different places. The sarape is an article of clothing, is it not?

7. Yes, the men wear the sarape for an overcoat or for adornment. It serves also as a blanket. How well these gray sarapes are woven! I like the geometric designs! They are from Oaxaca are they not?

8. Yes. And look at the sashes. These red ones are from Toluca. The men as well as the women wear sashes. It is woven of wool or cotton.

9. How pleasing the designs are!—these of birds and those of little animals which adorn the purse that you have in your hand. And they also send you rebozos? (shawls)

10. Unfortunately, no.

11. You know that the rebozo (shawl) is for the woman what the sarape is for the man. It serves for all purposes: as a hat and an overcoat; to wrap packages; as a blanket and cradle for the baby.

12. "They are going to send me also baskets of various sizes and styles and of course, all kinds of pottery," says Mr. Adams.

13. Have you seen the masks that the Indians make for their dances during the fiestas?

14. I have not seen them. And I know very little about fiestas.

15. Then, we must talk about fiestas the next time. Is Tuesday at eight all right with you?

16. It is all right with me.

17. Until Tuesday, Mr. Adams.

18. Good luck to you, Mr. Lopez.

Spelling and Punctuation Aids

1. Practice:

| en-tre-tan-to | des-gra-cia-da-men-te | ge-o-mé-tri-co | as-pec-to |
| pin-to-res-co | ves-ti-do | más-ca-ra | gra-cio-so |

Vocabulary Building

A. la mano, the hand. Nouns ending in -o are masculine. La mano is an exception.

B. La Ropa   Clothing, Wearing Apparel

el abrigo	overcoat	la falda	skirt	el rebozo	shawl
la blusa	blouse	los guantes	gloves	el sarape	blanket
los calcetines	socks	el impermeable	raincoat	el sombrero	hat
la camisa	shirt	las medias	stockings	el traje	suit, costume
la corbata	tie	los pantalones	pants	el vestido	dress
la faja	sash	el pañuelo	handkerchief	los zapatos	shoes

Expresiones Importantes

1. entretanto   meanwhile
2. de seguro   certainly
3. ¿Le parece (a Ud.) bien?   Is it all right with you?
4. Me parece bien   It's all right with me.
5. Se visten de blusas   They dress in blouses.

Exercise No. 93—Completion of Text

1. Vamos (to look at) los artículos de México.
2. (In the meanwhile) vamos a hablar de (the folk arts).
3. Estos artículos son (in common use).
4. (The typical dress) da a los indios un aspecto (picturesque).
5. Las mujeres se visten de (long skirts).
6. Los hombres llevan (a white costume).
7. (The straw hat) es de uso general.
8. El sarape es (an article of clothing).
9. (I like) los dibujos geométricos.
10. La faja es tejida (of wool or cotton).
11. El rebozo (serves for everything).
12. (Of course) van a mandarme (baskets of various sizes).
13. (We must talk) de las fiestas.
14. Is Tuesday all right with you?
15. It's all right with me.

PARTE SEGUNDA

Grammar Notes

1. Demonstrative Pronouns

a.

este dibujo y ése	*this* sketch and *that* (*one*)	esa tienda y ésta	*that* shop and *this* (*one*)
esta casa y aquélla	*this* house and *that* (*one*)	esos trajes y éstos	*those* costumes and *these*.
estos libros y ésos	*these* books and *those*	aquel coche y éste	*that* car and *this one*

When the noun is omitted after a demonstrative adjective, the adjective becomes a demonstrative pronoun. The demonstrative pronoun takes an acccent mark and agrees in number and gender with the omitted noun.

b. **esto, eso, aquello.** These are neuter forms of the demonstrative pronoun. They are used to point out a thing not yet mentioned, and to refer to a whole sentence or idea. They do not have an accent mark.

¿Qué es *esto*? What's *this*? (pointing to it) Es perezoso. *Eso* es verdad. He is lazy. *That* is true.

2. The Former, the Latter.

éste means the latter; **aquél** and **ése**, the former. They agree in number and gender with the nouns to which they refer. The accent mark is usually omitted over capitals.

El Sr. Adams y su esposa están en casa.	Mr. Adams and his wife are at home.
Esta lee una revista.	*The latter* is reading a magazine.
Aquél escribe una carta.	*The former* is writing a letter.

Ejercicios (Exercises) No. 94A-94B-94C

94A. Write each sentence putting the verbs into Spanish. Remember: vestir(i) to dress, vestir de to dress in, vestirse to dress oneself, llevar to wear.

1. (I dress) al niño.
2. I dress myself.
3. (They dress in) faldas bordadas.
4. (We dress) a los niños.
5. Las niñas (dress themselves).
6. ¿Qué (do you wear) los domingos?
7. (I wear) mi vestido nuevo.
8. ¿Quiénes (wear) sarapes?
9. Las señoritas (wear) guantes.
10. (We are wearing) zapatos nuevos.

94B. Complete these sentences using the correct demonstrative adjectives and pronouns.

Ejemplo: Este dibujo es antiguo, ése es moderno.

1. (This) dibujo es antiguo, (that one) es moderno.
2. (These) sarapes tienen dibujos de animalitos, (those) tienen dibujos de pájaros.
3. (Those) faldas son de lana, (these) son de algodón.
4. (This) blusa tiene bordados sencillos, (that one) es moderna.
5. (That—*distant*) casa es antigua, (this one) es moderna.
6. El Sr. López y el Sr. Adams son amigos. (The latter) es negociante, (the former) es profesor.
7. Ana y María son alumnas. (The latter) aprende el español, (the former) aprende el francés.
8. ¿Qué es (this)? ¿Qué es (that)?
9. El hombre es rico. (That) es verdad.
10. Felipe trabaja diligentemente. Todos saben (that).

94C. Repeat the Spanish sentences aloud many times.

1. ¿Qué está comprando Ud.?	1. What are you buying?
2. Estoy comprando un sombrero.	2. I am buying a hat.
3. ¿Qué está comprando su hermana?	3. What is your sister buying?
4. Está comprando una faja.	4. She is buying a sash.

1. ¿Tiene Ud. un rebozo?	1. Have you a shawl?
2. No tengo rebozo.	2. I have no shawl.
3. ¿Tiene Ud. un pañuelo?	3. Have you a handkerchief?
4. No tengo pañuelo.	4. I have no handkerchief.

1. ¿Lleva Ud. guantes en el invierno?	1. Do you wear gloves in winter?
2. Sí, llevo guantes en el invierno.	2. Yes, I wear gloves in winter.
3. ¿Lleva Ud. abrigo?	3. Do you wear an overcoat?
4. Llevo abrigo cuando hace frío.	4. I wear an overcoat when it is cold.

Exercise No. 95—Preguntas

1. ¿Quién acaba de recibir una caja de mercancía de México?
2. ¿Quiénes llevan el sarape, los hombres o las mujeres?
3. ¿De dónde son los sarapes con los dibujos geométricos?
4. ¿De dónde son las fajas rojas?
5. ¿Qué llevan tanto los hombres como las mujeres?
6. ¿Qué clase de dibujos adorna la bolsa?
7. ¿Qué artículo sirve para manta y cuna del nene?
8. ¿Qué hacen los indios para los bailes?
9. ¿De qué sabe muy poco el Sr. Adams?
10. ¿Qué dice el Sr. Adams al Sr. López cuando éste sale de su casa?

CAPÍTULO 25 (VEINTE Y CINCO)

PARTE PRIMERA

Los Días de Fiesta

1. — ¿Cuáles son los días de fiesta en México? — pregunta el Sr. Adams al Sr. López.

2. Hay fiestas casi todos los días en algún pueblo u otro. Hay fiestas nacionales y fiestas dedicadas a varios santos. Todas se celebran con bailes, cohetes, juegos, y dramas.

3. Por supuesto, celebran la Navidad.

4. Sí, la celebración de la Navidad dura diez días, desde el 16 de diciembre hasta el 25. Grupos de personas van de casa en casa cantando canciones y pidiendo "posada." Entran en las casas y allí pasan un buen rato. Cantan, bailan y rompen la piñata tradicional.

5. ¿Qué es la piñata?

6. Es un jarro grande cubierto de papel de colores vivos. Puede representar un animalito o un pájaro. Contiene dulces y juguetes. Un niño con los ojos vendados trata de romperlo con un palo. Al fin llega a romperlo. Todos se apresuran a coger los dulces y juguetes.

1. "What are the fiesta days in Mexico?" Mr. Adams asks Mr. Lopez.

2. There are fiestas almost every day in some town or other. There are national fiestas and fiestas dedicated to various saints. All are celebrated with dances, fireworks, games and plays.

3. Of course, they celebrate Christmas.

4. Yes, the celebration of Christmas lasts ten days, from the 16th of December to the 25th. Groups of people go from house to house singing songs and asking for "lodging." They enter the houses and there spend a pleasant time. They sing, they dance and they break the traditional "piñata."

5. What is the "piñata"?

6. It is a big jar covered with paper in bright colors. It may represent an animal or bird. It contains candy and toys. A child with his eyes blindfolded tries to break it with a stick. At last he succeeds in breaking it. Everybody rushes to gather up the candy and toys.

7. ¿Reciben regalos los niños?

8. Los reciben el seis de enero, el día de los Reyes Magos.

9. ¿Qué fiestas hay en la primavera?

10. Ud. debe ver la fiesta de la Semana Santa en Tzintzuntzan, cerca de Pátzcuaro. Es el drama de la Pasión y dura tres días. Los actores son los habitantes del pueblo. Hacen los papeles con mucha emoción.

11. ¿Cómo celebran el 5 de mayo?

12. Hay una gran batalla simulada cerca de Puebla para celebrar la victoria de los mexicanos contra los franceses.

13. He oído hablar también del Día de los Difuntos.

14. Sí, el 2 de noviembre es el Día de los Difuntos. Los panaderos venden "panes de los muertos." Se pueden comprar en los mercados todas clases de juguetes apropiados—esqueletos danzantes, máscaras, etc. La gente visita los cementerios y prepara ofrendas de comida para los muertos de la familia.

15. Hay fiestas en el Día de Corpus Christi?

16. ¡Claro está! En los pueblos cerca de Pátzcuaro, Michoacán, hay mercados simulados. Cada vendedor vende miniaturas de la mercancía que vende en el mercado ordinariamente—tortillas, ropa o cualquiera cosa que sea. Los compradores usan moneda falsa—hecha por los panaderos.

17. Me acuerdo de otra fecha importante. Es el 16 de septiembre, el Día de la Independencia.

18. Sí, es el día del Grito de Dolores, pronunciado por el padre Miguel Hidalgo para dar comienzo a la revolución de 1810 contra España.

19. Yo sé muy poco de la historia de México.

20. Pero Ud. sí va aprendiendo, Sr. Adams.

7. Do the children receive presents?

8. They receive them on the sixth of January, the Day of the Wise Kings.

9. What fiestas are there in spring?

10. You should see the fiesta of Holy Week in Tzintzuntzan, near Patzcuaro. It is the Passion Play and it lasts three days. The actors are the inhabitants of the town. They act the roles with much feeling.

11. How do they celebrate the fifth of May?

12. There is a great sham battle near Puebla to celebrate the victory of the Mexicans over the French.

13. I have also heard speak of the Day of the Dead.

14. Yes, November 2 is the Day of the Dead. The bakers sell "cakes of the dead." One can buy in the markets all kinds of appropriate toys—dancing skeletons, masks, etc. People visit the cemeteries and prepare offerings of food for the dead of the family.

15. Are there fiestas on Corpus Christi Day?

16. Yes indeed! In the towns near Patzcuaro, Michoacan, there are sham markets. Each seller sells miniatures of the merchandise that he sells in the market ordinarily—tortillas, clothing or whatever it may be. The buyers use counterfeit money—made by the bakers.

17. I remember another important date. It is the 16th of September, Independence Day.

18. Yes, it is the day of the Proclamation of Dolores made by Father Miguel Hidalgo to set off the revolution of 1810 against Spain.

19. I know very little about the history of Mexico.

20. But you are certainly learning, Mr. Adams.

NOTE: 1. **ir** may be used instead of **estar** to express the progressive tense. **va aprendiendo = está aprendiendo.** 2. **sí** = yes, indeed, certainly.

Pronunciation and Spelling Aids

1. Practice:

Na-vi-dad	a-pro-pia-dos	Mi-choa-cán (meech-wah-**cahn**)
di-ciem-bre	ce-men-te-rios	Tzin-tzun-tzan (seen-soon-**sahn**)
ce-re-mo-nia	mi-nia-tu-ras	Pátz-cua-ro (pahts-kwah-roh)
a-pre-su-ran	or-di-na-ria-men-te	Mi-guel (mee-gel)
e-mo-ción	in-de-pen-den-cia	Hi-dal-go (ee-dahl-goh)
ju-gue-tes		

Building Vocabulary

A. Palabras Relacionadas

1.	pan	bread	2.	zapato	shoe
	panadero	baker		zapatero	shoemaker
	panadería	bakery		zapatería	shoe shop

3. plata	silver	4. sastre	tailor
platero	silversmith	sastrería	tailor's shop
platería	silversmith's shop		

B. Partes de la Cara Parts of the Face

la boca	mouth	los oídos	ears (internal)
los dientes	teeth	las orejas	ears (external)
los labios	lips	los ojos	eyes
la nariz	nose	las mejíllas	cheeks

Expresiones Importantes

1. al fin   finally
2. al principio   at first
3. Ud. debe ver   you should see
4. llegar a   to succeed in
5. Llega a romper   He succeeds in breaking.
6. Pasan un buen rato.   They have a good time.

Exercise No. 96—Completion of Text

1. **Hay fiestas** (in some town or other).
2. **Todos** (are celebrated) **con danzas y juegos.**
3. (Of course) **celebran la Navidad.**
4. **Van de casa en casa** (singing songs and asking for lodging).
5. **En las casas** (they have a good time).
6. **La piñata es un jarro** (covered with paper).
7. **Uno niño** (tries to break it).
8. **Llega** (in breaking it).
9. (You should see) **el drama de la Pasión.**
10. **El dos de noviembre es** (the Day of the Dead).
11. (The bakers sell) **"panes de los muertos."**
12. (One may buy) **todas clases de juguetes.**
13. **Hay** (sham markets) **en el día de Corpus Christi.**
14. (The buyers) **emplean moneda falsa** (made by) **los panaderos.**
15. (The 16th of September) **es el día del** (Proclamation of Dolores).

PARTE SEGUNDA

Grammar Notes

1. Present Tense of **coger**   to catch, pick up
I catch, etc.

cojo	cogemos
coges	cogéis
coge	cogen

Imperative

coja Ud.	cojan Uds.

escoger   to choose
I choose, etc.

escojo	escogemos
escoges	escogéis
escoge	escogen

Imperative

escoja Ud.	escojan Uds.

NOTE: Before the endings -o and -a, g becomes **j**, so as to keep the same sound as is found in the infinitive (-ger).

2. Shortened Adjectives

The following adjectives drop the ending -o when used before a masculine noun:

(uno)	un hombre	one man	(malo)	un mal hombre	a bad man
(alguno)	algún pueblo	some town	(primero)	el primer día	the first day
(ninguno)	ningún padre	no father	(tercero)	el tercer año	the third year
(bueno)	un buen hombre	a good man			

NOTE: **algún** and **ningún** have an accent mark to hold the stress on the syllable -**gún**.

3. Present Participle of Stem-Changing Verbs. **pedir** (i), and verbs like it, which have the stem change **e** to **i** in the present tense, have the same change in the present participle.

Infinitive	Present Tense	Present Participle
pedir	(yo) pido	pidiendo
repetir	(yo) repito	repitiendo
servir	(yo) sirvo	sirviendo
despedirse	(yo) me despido	despidiéndome

Ejercicios (Exercises) No. 97A-97B

97A. Complete these sentences in Spanish.

1. Enero es el (first) mes del año.
2. Marzo es el (third) mes del año.
3. Vamos a pasar un (good) rato.
4. Tenemos un maestro (good).
5. El científico Einstein es un (great) hombre. No es un hombre (big, tall).
6. Tenemos asientos en la (third) fila.
7. Hace (bad) tiempo en el invierno.
8. El (first) de enero.
9. Ellos tienen asientos (good).
10. (Some) día Ud. irá a México.

97B. Write each sentence putting all the verbs into Spanish.

1. (They sing) canciones.
2. (We celebrate) la Navidad.
3. (They visit) los cementerios.
4. La celebración (lasts) nueve días.
5. (I am preparing) la comida.
6. ¿(Do you use) moneda falsa?
7. La piñata (contains) dulces y juguetes.
8. Un niño (tries) de romper la piñata.
9. Todos (pick up) los dulces.
10. Los Reyes Magos (bring) los regalos.

Exercise No. 98—Preguntas

1. ¿Cómo está titulada (entitled) esta lectura (reading selection)?
2. ¿Qué clase de fiestas hay en México?
3. ¿Cómo se celebran estas fiestas?
4. ¿Cuántos días dura la celebración de la Navidad?
5. ¿Quiénes van de casa en casa?
6. ¿Qué piden?
7. ¿Cómo pasan ellos un buen rato en las casas?
8. ¿Qué es la piñata?
9. ¿Qué contiene?
10. ¿Quién trata de romperla con un palo?
11. ¿Qué cogen todos cuando un niño llega a romperla?
12. ¿De quiénes reciben los niños regalos?
13. ¿Qué fiesta debe ver el Sr. Adams?
14. ¿Quiénes hacen los papeles en el drama de la Pasión?
15. ¿Cuál es la fecha del "Grito de Dolores?"

CAPÍTULO 26 (VEINTE Y SEIS)

PARTE PRIMERA

¿Qué Lugares Quiere Ud. Visitar, Sr. Adams?

1. Pronto Ud. va a salir para México, Sr. Adams. ¿Ha decidido qué lugares quiere visitar?

2. No pienso en nada más y estoy leyendo mucho en las varias guías del viajero.

3. Viajaré por avión a la capital. Usando el centro de la ciudad como punto de partida, visitaré lugares de interés en el Distrito Federal, en los alrededores y en otras partes del país.

4. En la capital, veré la Alameda con sus grandes árboles; muy cerca está el Museo Nacional de Artes e Industrias Populares. Visitaré la Secretaria de Educación Publica y la Escuela Nacional Preparatoria para ver las pinturas murales. Voy a ver el Zócalo, donde están situados la Catedral, el Palacio Nacional y muchas cosas más de interés. Pasaré un día en el parque de Chapultepec. Tengo ganas también de ir a

1. Soon you are going to leave for Mexico, Mr. Adams. Have you decided what places you want to visit?

2. I think of nothing else and I am reading a great deal in the various guide books.

3. I will travel by plane to the capital. Using the center of the city as a point of departure, I will visit places of interest in the Federal District, in the surrounding area and in other parts of the country.

4. In the capital, I will see the Alameda with its great trees; very near is the National Museum of Folk Arts and Industries. I will visit the Secretariat of Public Education and the National Preparatory School to see the murals. I am going to see the Zocalo, where the Cathedral, the National Palace and many more things of interest are located. I will spend a day in Chapultepec Park. I also have a desire to go to see the markets.

ver los mercados. Oigo hablar a mucha gente del mercado de la Merced y del mercado de Lagunilla.

5. En los alrededores visitaré las pirámides de Teotihuacán. Veré la gran pirámide del Sol y la de la Luna. Se dice que son tan imponentes como las de Egipto. Y mientras estoy en la capital visitaré los suburbios como, por ejemplo, Coyoacan, y algunos de los pueblos cercanos.

6. ¿No quiere Ud. ir a una corrida de toros, Sr. Adams?

7. — Sí, y no — responde el señor Adams. — Tal vez.

8. Estoy seguro de que Ud. irá al mercado de Toluca y a Cuernavaca. Esta ciudad tiene siempre un clima de primavera, edificios bonitos con jardines y patios llenos de flores, muchos árboles y hermosas vistas de las montañas. Ud. irá a Taxco, el pueblo de los plateros y de casas antiguas.

9. Sí, e iré a Pátzcuaro y a los otros pueblos conocidos por sus artes populares.

10. Siempre es Ud. el negociante, Sr. Adams.

11. No es eso. Me interesa el pueblo de México que vive fuera de los grandes centros. Pero claro está que también quiero visitar a Guadalajara y otros lugares bien conocidos.

12. No deje Ud. de ver a Guanajuato, una ciudad colonial con callejones tortuosos que suben las montañas entre casas chicas de varios colores.

13. Y he leído que en Oaxaca también hay una cantidad de cosas interesantes,—los restos de las culturas de los Mixtecas y los Zapotecos, el pueblo de Mitla y la zona arqueológica de Monte Albán.

14. Tengo ganas de acompañarle, Sr. Adams, pero no es posible.

15. ¡Qué lástima, Sr. López!

I hear many people speak of the Merced market and the market of Langunilla.

5. In the surrounding area I will visit the pyramids of Teotihuacan. I will see the great pyramid of the Sun and that of the Moon. It is said that they are as impressive as those of Egypt. And while I am in the capital, I will visit the suburbs like, for example, Coyoacan, and some of the nearby towns.

6. Do you not want to go to a bullfight, Mr. Adams?

7. "Yes and no," answers Mr. Adams. "Perhaps."

8. I am sure that you will go to the market of Toluca and to Cuernavaca. The latter city has a spring climate, pretty buildings with gardens and patios full of flowers, many trees and beautiful views of the mountains. You will go to Taxco, the town of the silversmiths and of ancient houses.

9. Yes, and I will go to Patzcuaro and to other towns known for their folk arts.

10. You are always the business man, Mr. Adams.

11. It is not that. I am interested in the Mexican people who live outside the great centers. But of course I also want to visit Guadalajara and other well-known places.

12. Do not fail to see Guanajuato, a colonial city with winding lanes that climb the mountains among small houses of various colors.

13. And I have read that in Oaxaca also there are a number of interesting things—the remains of the cultures of the Mixtec and the Zapotec Indians, the town of Mitla and the archeological zone of Monte Albán.

14. I have a desire to go with you, Mr. Adams, but it is not possible.

15. What a pity, Mr. Lopez.

Pronunciation and Spelling Aids

1. Practice:

na-cio-nal	ca-lle-jo-nes	Cuer-na-va-ca
se-cre-ta-ria	tor-tuo-so	Tax-co (*tahs-coh*)
ca-te-dral	ar-que-o-ló-gi-ca	Oa-xa-ca (*wah-hah-cah*)
pi-rá-mi-de	Te-o-ti-hua-cán	Mix-te-cas (*mees-tay-cahs*)
im-po-nen-te	(*tay-oh-tee-wah-cahn*)	Za-po-te-cas
co-rri-da	E-gip-to	Gua-na-jua-to

Building Vocabulary

A. The Alameda is a park along the Avenida Juárez, the most important shopping center for the tourist in Mexico City. Most towns have an Alameda, named for the álamo tree that gives them shade.

B. Sinónimos

1. contestar	responder	to answer		3. estoy seguro	estoy cierto	I am sure
2. desear	querer	to wish, want		4. el lugar	el sitio	place

C. Expressions of Future

1. mañana	tomorrow		4. el próximo año	next year
2. pasado mañana	day after tomorrow		5. el año que viene	next year
3. la próxima vez (semana)	next time (week)		6. mañana por la mañana	tomorrow morning

Expresiones Importantes

1. estoy seguro	I am sure		3. pensar en	to think of
2. No deje Ud. de (ver etc.)	do not fail to (see, etc.)		4. tengo ganas	I have a desire (a mind to)

Exercise No. 99—Completion of Text

1. (I am reading) en las varias guías.
2. (I shall travel) por avión.
3. (I shall visit) lugares de interés.
4. (I shall see) la Alameda.
5. (I shall spend) un día en el parque de Chapultepec.
6. (I am sure) que Ud. irá al mercado de Toluca.
7. Tiene siempre (a spring climate).
8. Los edificios son (pretty) y los jardines están (full of flowers).
9. Hay (many trees) y (beautiful views) de las montañas.
10. Le gustará a Ud. Taxco (the town of the silversmiths).
11. (I shall go) a Pátzcuaro.
12. Me interesa más el pueblo que vive (outside of the great centers).
13. (Do not fail) de ver a Guanajuato, una ciudad (with winding lanes).
14. En Oaxaca hay (a number of interesting things).
15. (I have a desire) de acompañarle, Sr. Adams.

PARTE SEGUNDA

Grammar Notes

1. The Future Tense. Model Verb, hablar.

hablar-é	I shall speak	hablar-emos	we shall speak
hablar-ás	you will speak	hablar-éis	you will speak
hablar-á { you, he she, it } will speak		hablar-án { you (pl.), they } will speak	

a. The future endings of *all* verbs are:

singular   -é   -ás   -á   plural   -emos   -éis   -án

b. To form the regular future add these endings to the *whole infinitive* as a base.

hablaré   hablarás   etc.   aprenderé   aprenderás   etc.   seré   serás   etc.
estaré   estarás   etc.   viviré   vivirás   etc.   abriré   abrirás   etc.

2. The Irregular Future.

In a few common verbs there is a change in the infinitive base when the future endings are added. Thus:

saber to know		tener to have		salir to leave	
I shall know, etc.		I shall have, etc.		I shall leave, etc.	
sabré	sabremos	tendré	tendremos	saldré	saldremos
sabrás	sabréis	tendrás	tendréis	saldrás	saldréis
sabrá	sabrán	tendrá	tendrán	saldrá	saldrán

querer	to wish	venir	to come	valer	to be worth
I shall wish, etc.		I shall come, etc.		I shall be worth	
querré	querremos	vendré	vendremos	valdré	valdremos
querrás	querréis	vendrás	vendréis	valdrás	valdréis
querrá	querrán	vendrá	vendrán	valdrá	valdrán

poder	to be able	decir	to say	hacer	to do, make
I shall be able, etc.		I shall say, etc.		I shall do, make, etc.	
podré	podremos	diré	diremos	haré	haremos
podrás	podréis	dirás	diréis	harás	haréis
podrá	podrán	dirá	dirán	hará	harán

Ejercicios (Exercises) No. 100A-100B-100C

100A. Translate:

1. Visitaremos a Taxco.
2. Pasaré una semana allí.
3. Me gustará ver las pinturas murales.
4. ¿Quién viajará a México?
5. Ellos no trabajarán mucho.
6. ¿Estudiarán Uds. la lección?
7. ¿Tomará Ud. café?
8. Felipe no escribirá la carta.
9. No tendré frío.
10. El no vendrá acá.
11. Saldremos a las ocho.
12. Haré este papel.
13. Querrán comer.
14. Ella lo pondrá en la mesa.
15. No podré ir allá.

100B. Answer these questions in complete sentences (in the future), with the help of the words in parentheses.

Ejemplo: A dónde irá Ud. esta noche? (al cine)   Esta noche iré al cine.

1. ¿Qué comprará Ud.? (una corbata)
2. ¿Cuánto costará? (cinco pesos)
3. ¿A dónde irá Ud. en el verano? (al campo)
4. ¿Quién irá con Ud.? (mi hermano)
5. ¿A qué hora volverá Ud. del cine? (a las nueve de la noche)
6. ¿A quién verá Ud. en la estación? (a mi amigo Guillermo)
7. ¿A qué hora saldrá Ud. de su casa? (a las ocho de la mañana)
8. ¿A qué hora tomarán Uds. la cena? (a las siete)
9. ¿A quiénes visitarán Uds. en la ciudad? (a nuestros amigos)
10. ¿Qué estudiarán Uds. esta tarde? (nuestras lecciones de español)

100C. Translate:

1. I shall learn
2. He will write
3. They will go
4. We shall eat
5. She will speak
6. Will you work?
7. Will John see?
8. Who will visit?
9. I shall not travel
10. Will they study?
11. I shall make
12. He will come
13. You (Ud.) will put
14. They will not want
15. Will you (Ud.) go out?
16. I shall have
17. They will be here.
18. Will you (Uds.) go?

Exercise No. 101—Preguntas

1. ¿Cómo está titulada esta lectura?
2. ¿Quién va a salir pronto para México?
3. ¿Qué clase de libros está leyendo él?
4. ¿Cómo viajará?
5. ¿Qué lugar usará como punto de partida?
6. ¿Dónde está el Museo Nacional de Artes e Industrias Populares?
7. ¿Qué verá el Sr. Adams en la Secretaría de Educación Pública?
8. ¿En qué parque pasará un día?
9. ¿Qué pirámides verá en Teotihuacán?
10. ¿Qué se dice acerca de estas pirámides?
11. ¿Irá el Sr. Adams a una corrida de toros?
12. ¿Qué ciudad tiene un clima de primavera.
13. ¿Cuál es el pueblo de los plateros?
14. ¿Qué le interesa más al Sr. Adams — la gente de las ciudades o la gente del campo?
15. ¿Quién tiene ganas de acompañar al Sr. Adams?

REPASO 6

(CAPÍTULOS 23–26) PARTE PRIMERA

Palabras

NOUNS

1. el artista	14. el cuero	27. el ojo	1. artist	14. leather	27. eye

1. el artista	14. el cuero	27. el ojo	1. artist	14. leather	27. eye
2. el árbol	15. la falda	28. el oro	2. tree	15. skirt	28. gold
3. el arte	16. la guía	29. la plata	3. art	16. guide	29. silver
4. el algodón	17. el idioma	30. el panadero	4. cotton	17. language	30. baker
5. el baile	18. el juego	31. los pantalones	5. dance	18. game	31. trousers
6. la blusa	19. el juguete	32. el pañuelo	6. blouse	19. toy	32. handkerchief
7. la boca	20. el jardín	33. el platero	7. mouth	20. garden	33. silversmith
8. la caña de azucar	21. la lana	34. la ropa	8. sugar cane	21. wool	34. clothing
9. la camisa	22. la madera	35. el sastre	9. shirt	22. wood	35. tailor
10. la canción	23. la mano	36. el tejido	10. song	23. hand	36. cloth
11. los calcetines	24. las medias	37. el traje	11. socks	24. stockings	37. suit
12. la cara	25. la moneda	38. el vestido	12. face	25. coin	38. dress
13. la corbata	26. la nariz	39. el zapato	13. necktie	26. nose	39. shoe

VERBS

1. bailar	8. durar	15. ocuparse de	1. to dance	8. to last	15. to be busy with
2. cantar	9. emplear	16. representar	2. to sing	9. to employ	16. to represent
3. celebrar	10. escojer	17. romper	3. to celebrate	10. to choose	17. to break
4. cojer	11. llevar	18. vestir	4. to pick up, to catch	11. to bring, wear	18. to dress
5. contener	12. mandar	19. vestirse	5. to contain	12. to send	19. to dress oneself
6. cubrir	13. mirar	20. volver	6. to cover	13. to look at	20. to return
7. decidir	14. observar		7. to decide	14. to observe	

ADJECTIVES

1. cubierto	5. hecho	9. precioso	1. covered	5. made	9. precious
2. cercano	6. imponente	10. popular	2. near	6. impressive	10. folk, popular
3. chico	7. lleno	11. rosado	3. pretty, little	7. full	11. pink
4. falso	8. pintoresco	12. tejido	4. false	8. picturesque	12. woven

ADVERBS

1. de antemano	2. entretanto	3. todavía	1. beforehand	2. in the meantime	3. still

PREPOSITIONS

1. acerca de	2. a causa de	3. fuera de	1. concerning	2. because of	3. outside of

IMPORTANT EXPRESSIONS

1. acabar de + infin.	5. ¿le parece bien?	9. volver a + infin.	1. to have just	5. is it all right with you?	9. to do again
2. al fin	6. me parece bien	10. a la derecha	2. finally	6. it is all right with me	10. to the right
3. al principio	7. pasar un buen rato	11. a la izquierda	3. at first	7. to have a good time	11. to the left
4. llegar a + infin.	8. vestir de		4. to succeed in	8. to dress in	

PARTE SEGUNDA

Ejercicio 102. From Group 2 select the synonym for each word or expression in Group 1.

Group 1			Group 2
1. contestar	7. me acuerdo	a. terminar	g. vestir de
2. desear	8. vuelvo a escribir	b. lengua	h. el año que viene
3. acabar	9. por eso	c. responder	i. recuerdo
4. llevar	10. idioma	d. lugar	j. escribo otra vez
5. sitio	11. por supuesto	e. querer	k. prefiero
6. el año proximo	12. me gusta más	f. por lo tanto	l. claro está

Ejercicio 103. Complete the following sentences by translating the given words.

Remember: 1. ponerse = to put on   2. Use the definite article (el, la, los, las) instead of the possessive adjective (mi, tu, su, etc.) with clothing, when the meaning is clear.

NOTE: Another meaning of ponerse is to become. Los árboles se ponen verdes. The trees become green.

Ejemplo: Me pongo la camisa (*not* mi camisa). I put on my shirt.

1. **Me pongo** (my trousers).
2. **Te pones** (your hat).
3. **El se pone** (his suit).
4. **Ud. se pone** (your tie).
5. **Ella se pone** (her sash).
6. **Nos ponemos** (our shoes).
7. **Uds. se ponen** (your gloves).
8. **Ellos se ponen** (their shirts).
9. **Ellas se ponen** (their dresses).
10. **Póngase** (your overcoat).

Ejercicio 104. Select the group of words in the right-hand column which best completes the sentence in the left-hand column.

Remember: **se lleva** = is worn, one wears   **se llevan** = are worn, one wears

1. **Se lleva abrigo**
2. **Se lleva impermeable**
3. **Se lleva sombrero**
4. **Se llevan zapatos**
5. **Se llevan guantes**
6. **Se lleva traje de deporte**

a. **cuando se juega al tenis.**
b. **para proteger la cabeza.**
c. **cuando hace frío.**
d. **para proteger las manos.**
e. **cuando llueve.**
f. **para proteger los pies.**

Ejercicio 105. Complete these sentences, putting all the English words into Spanish.

1. (The baker) **vende pan en la** (bakery).
2. (The silversmith) **hace artículos de plata en** (the silversmith's shop).
3. (The shoemaker) **vende zapatos en la** (shoe shop).
4. **El** (tailor) **hace trajes en la** (tailor shop).
5. **Quien vende es** (a seller).
6. **Quien compra es** (a buyer).
7. **Comemos y hablamos con la** (mouth).
8. **Oímos con los** (ears).
9. **Vemos con los** (eyes).
10. **Otras partes de la** (face) **son** (the nose) **y** (the lips).

PARTE TERCERA

Diálogo 1

Practice the Spanish Aloud

En el Camión

1. Dispénseme, señor, ¿dónde bajo para el Correo Central? (para la Avenida Juárez)? (para la Alameda)? (para la embajada de los EE. UU.)? (para la estación de ferrocarril)? (para el mercado de la Merced)? etc.

2. Ud. baja en la esquina de Madero y San Juan de Letrán (etc.)

3. ¿Cuántas cuadras de aquí?

4. Más o menos diez (cinco, etc.) cuadras, señor.

5. ¿En cuántos minutos llegaremos?

6. Cerca de quince minutos.

7. Muchas gracias, señor.

In the Bus

1. Excuse me, sir, where do I get off for the Main Post Office? (for Juarez Avenue)? (for the Alameda)? (for the United States embassy)? (for the railroad station)? (for the Merced market)? etc.

2. You get off at the corner of Madero and San Juan de Letran (etc.)

3. How many blocks from here?

4. More or less ten (five, etc.) blocks, sir.

5. In how many minutes will we get there?

6. About fifteen minutes.

7. Thank you very much, sir.

Diálogo 2

Practice the Spanish Aloud

Sobre el Correo

1. Sr. Adams, por supuesto tiene Ud. mucha correspondencia. ¿Hay un buzón en su edificio?

2. Naturalmente. Tenemos un buzón tubular en donde echamos nuestras cartas. Pero enviamos al Correo Central los paquetes postales.

About the Mail

1. Mr. Adams, of course you have much correspondence. Is there a mailbox in your building?

2. Naturally. We have a letter drop where we mail our letters. But we send parcel post packages to the main post office.

3. ¿Quién los lleva allá?

4. Nuestro chico de oficina. Éste nos compra también los muchos timbres que necesitamos—timbres de correo aereo, de entrega inmediata, etc.

5. ¿Dónde está el Correo Central?

6. No está lejos de aquí.

3. Who takes them there?

4. Our office boy. The latter also buys us the many stamps that we need—air mail stamps, special delivery, etc.

5. Where is the main Post Office?

6. It is not far from here.

LECTURA
Exercise No. 106—El Cumpleaños De La Señora Adams

Es el veintidos de marzo, día del cumpleaños (birthday) de la señora Adams. Hoy cumple (she is) treinta y cinco años de edad. Para celebrar este día, la familia Adams va a cenar (dine) en un restaurante elegante en la calle Cincuenta y Dos (52) en la ciudad de Nueva York.

Cuando entran en el restaurante ven una hermosa canasta (basket) llena de (full of) rosas rojas en el centro de la mesa reservada para los Adams. Naturalmente la señora Adams está muy sorprendida y da mil gracias y besos (kisses) a su querido esposo.

Después de una comida sabrosa, Anita, la hijor menor, dice en voz baja (in a low voice) a sus hermanos, — ¡Ya! (Ready) Y cada uno de los cuatro hijos saca (take out) de debajo de la mesa una cajita bonita. Son regalos para su madre.

Anita le da un pañuelo de seda; Rosita, una blusa de algodón; Guillermo, un par de guantes y Felipe, un rebozo de lana.

La semana proxima el papá Adams calcula la cuenta de aquel día, que es como sigue:

Cena—Catorce dólares ochenta y seis centavos	$14.86
Propina—Un dólar cincuenta centavos	1.50
Flores—Seis dólares veinticinco centavos	6.25
Regalos—Doce dólares treinta y nueve centavos	12.39
Total—Treinta y cinco dólares	$35.00

— ¡Qué coincidencia! — dice el señor Adams. — Treinta y cinco dólares; treinta y cinco años!

CAPÍTULO 27 (VEINTE Y SIETE)
PARTE PRIMERA
El Sr. Adams Escribe Una Carta A Su Agente

1. El Sr. Adams y el Sr. López están sentados en la sala del primero. Es la última cita antes de la salida del Sr. Adams para México. El Sr. Adams tiene en la mano una copia de su carta a su agente, el Sr. Carrillo, y la respuesta de éste, que acaba de llegar.

2. Sr. López, voy a leerle mi carta al Sr. Carrillo.

3. Me gustará mucho oírla.

4. El Sr. Adams lee la carta siguiente:

Nueva York, 4 de mayo de 1954

Sr. Rufino Carrillo
Gante 40
Mexico, D.F., Mexico
Muy señor mío,

Tengo el gusto de informarle que voy a hacer un viaje a Mexico. Saldré de Nueva York por avión el 31 de mayo a las ocho menos cuarto de

1. Mr. Adams and Mr. Lopez are seated in the living room of the former. It is the last appointment before the departure of Mr. Adams for Mexico. Mr. Adams has in his hand a copy of his letter to his agent, Mr. Carrillo, and the latter's answer, which has just arrived.

2. Mr. Lopez, I am going to read you my letter to Mr. Carrillo.

3. I will like very much to hear it.

4. Mr. Adams reads the following letter:

New York, May 4, 1954

Mr. Rufino Carrillo
Gante 40
Mexico, D.F., Mexico
Dear Sir,

I am pleased to inform you that I am going to make a trip to Mexico. I will leave New York by plane May 31 at 7:45 A.M. and will arrive at

la mañana y llegaré al aeropuerto de México D.F. a las siete menos cuarto de la tarde. Tengo la intención de quedar en la capital dos meses. Será un viaje de recreo y también de negocios. Usando la capital como punto de partida, haré viajes a lugares de interés en México. Espero también ir por avión a Guatemala, y tal vez a Colombia.

Siempre le he apreciado mucho a causa de sus servicios excelentes por nuestra casa y ahora espero aprovechar la oportunidad de conocerle a Ud. personalmente. Tenga la bondad de informarme la fecha más conveniente para una cita. Sé que Ud. está muy ocupado y que viaja mucho. Por eso le escribo de antemano esperando tener el gusto de verle a Ud.

Ud. estará sorprendido de saber que desde hace cinco meses tomo lecciones de conversación española. Ud. sabe que yo sabía leer el español bastante bien pero no sabía ni escribirlo ni hablarlo. Esta carta, espero, le mostrará a Ud. que he adelantado un poco en escribir. Espero poder conversar con Ud. en su hermoso idioma. Creo que Ud. no tendrá mucha dificultad en entenderme. Mi maestro es el Sr. Eugenio López, compatriota de Ud. Por eso verá Ud. que uso muchos mexicanismos típicos.

En espera de sus gratas noticias quedo de Ud. atto. y s.s.

Juan Adams

5. Estupendo, Sr. Adams. No hay ninguna falta en toda la carta.

6. Sr. López, tengo que confesarle algo. Hay un libro titulado "Correspondencia Comercial." Me ayuda mucho este libro en todas las cosas relacionadas con encabezamientos, saludos, conclusiones y diversas formulas y expresiones de cortesía. Desde luego, tengo que darle a Ud. mis gracias más sinceras.

7. Ud. es muy bondadoso. ¿Y ahora me hará Ud. el favor de leerme la respuesta que ha recibido del Sr. Carrillo?

8. Con todo gusto, señor.

Continuado en el Cápitulo 28

the airport of Mexico City at 6:45 P.M. I intend to remain in the capital two months. It will be a pleasure trip and also a business trip. Using the capital as a point of departure, I will take trips to places of interest in Mexico. I hope also to go by plane to Guatemala and perhaps to Colombia.

I have always appreciated you very much because of your excellent services for our firm and now I hope to take advantage of the opportunity to meet you personally. With this in mind I beg you to let me know the most convenient date for an appointment. I know that you are very busy and that you travel a great deal. For that reason I am writing you beforehand hoping to have the pleasure of seeing you.

You will be surprised to learn that for five months I have been taking lessons in Spanish conversation. You know that I could read Spanish fairly well but I could neither write it nor speak it. This letter, I hope, will show you that I have made a little progress in writing. I hope to be able to talk with you in your beautiful language. I think you won't have much difficulty in understanding me. My teacher is Mr. Eugene Lopez, a fellow-countryman of yours. For that reason, you will see that I use many typical Mexicanisms.

Awaiting your favorable reply I remain, sincerely yours

John Adams

5. Wonderful, Mr. Adams. There is not a single error in the whole letter.

6. Mr. Lopez, I must confess something to you. There is a book entitled "Commercial Correspondence." This book helps me a great deal in all matters relating to headings, salutations, conclusions and various forms and expressions of courtesy. Of course, I must give my most sincere thanks to you.

7. You are very kind. And now, will you kindly read me the answer you have received from Mr. Carrillo?

8. With great pleasure, sir.

Continued in Chapter 28

Pronunciation and Spelling Aids

1. Practice:

a-e-ro-puer-to per-so-nal-men-te en-ten-der-me
a-pre-cia-do con-ve-nien-te com-pa-trio-ta
a-pro-ve-char sor-pren-di-do co-mer-cial

bon-da-do-so o-por-tu-ni-dad co-rres-pon-den-cia
si-guien-te an-te-ma-no en-ca-be-za-mien-to
ser-vi-cios a-de-lan-ta-do con-clu-sio-nes

Building Vocabulary

A. Sinónimos:

1. bello — hermoso — beautiful
2. comprender — entender (ie) — to understand
3. el idioma — la lengua — language
4. mostrar (ue) — enseñar — to show
5. por eso — por lo tanto — therefore

6. Tenga la bondad de . . . }
   Hágame el favor de . . . } please
   (*Lit.* Have the kindness to; do me the favor to)

B. Palabras Relacionadas

1. la mano — the hand
2. la mano derecha — the right hand
3. la mano izquierda — the left hand
4. a la derecha — to the right

5. a la izquierda — to the left
6. de antemano — beforehand
7. hecho a mano — handmade

Expresiones Importantes

A. Salutation: Business Letters

1. Muy señor mío: Dear Sir:
2. Muy señores míos: Gentlemen:

3. Muy señora mía: Dear Madame:

B. Conclusion: Business Letters

En espera de sus gratas noticias, quedo de Ud. — Awaiting your reply, I remain

atto. afmo. y s.s. — sincerely yours, yours very truly.

atto. (atento) — attentive
afmo. (afectísimo) — most affectionate
s.s. (su servidor) — your servant

Exercise No. 107—Completion of Text

1. **Voy** (to read to you) **mi carta.**
2. (I will be very glad) **oírla.**
3. **Tengo el gusto** (to inform you) **que saldré el 31 de mayo.**
4. **Siempre** (I have appreciated you).
5. (Kindly) **informarme de la fecha** (most convenient).
6. **Sé que Ud. está** (very busy).
7. (Therefore) **le escribo** (in advance).
8. **Espero tener el gusto** (of seeing you).
9. **Esta carta** (will show you) **que he adelantado.**
10. **Ud. no tendrá dificultad** (in understanding me).
11. (There is not any) **falta en la carta.**
12. **Un libro** (called) **Correspondencia Comercial** (helps me) **mucho.**
13. **Tengo que** (give my sincere thanks to you).
14. **You are very kind.**
15. ¿(Will you kindly) **leerme la respuesta?**

PARTE SEGUNDA

Grammar Notes

1. The Indirect Object.

As in English the indirect object is the *to* (sometimes *for*) object. It indicates the person or persons *to* whom, sometimes *for* whom, the action is performed.

Escribo una carta a mi agente. — I write a letter to my agent.

2. The Indirect Object Pronouns.

Observe the indirect object pronouns in the following sentences.

Carlos *me* da el vaso. — Charles gives *me* the glass.
Juan *te* escribe una carta. — John writes *you* (fam.) a letter.
Pablo *le* da (a Ud.) el dinero. — Paul gives *you* the money.
Ana *le* lleva (a él) la silla. — Anna brings *him* the chair.

Yo *le* leo (a ella) el cuento.	I read *her* the story.
El maestro *nos* da la lección.	The teacher gives *us* the lesson.
La criada *les* da (*a Uds.*) los platos.	The servant gives *you* the plates.
Nosotros *les* vendemos (*a ellos*) el auto.	We sell *them* (m) the auto.
Los niños *les* traen (*a ellas*) las flores.	The children bring *them* (f) the flowers.

a. The Indirect Object Pronouns Are:

me (to) me	le . . . a Ud. (to) you	les . . . a Uds. (to) you
te (to) you (fam.)	le . . . a él (to) him	les . . . a ellos (to) them (m.)
nos (to) us	le . . . a ella (to) her	les . . . a ellas (to) them (f.)
os (to) you (fam. pl.)		

b. The indirect object pronouns, **me, te, nos, os** are like the direct object pronouns.

c. The indirect object pronoun **le** can mean *to you, to him* or *to her*. The indirect object pronoun **les** can mean *to you* (pl.), *to them* (m), *to them* (f.)

If necessary to make the meaning clear, add: **a Ud., a él, a ella, a Uds., a ellos, a ellas,** immediately after the verb.

d. Like the direct object, the indirect object precedes the verb, except when used with the infinitive, the present participle, or the affirmative imperative.

3. Familiar Verbs Which May Take Indirect Objects

dar	to give	mandar	to send	leer	to read
enseñar	to show, teach	llevar	to bring	escribir	to write
mostrar (ue)	to show	traer	to bring	decir	to say
enviar	to send	entregar	to deliver		

4. Indirect Objects with **gustar, parecer, importar.**

a. gustar, to be pleasing to

Me gusta el cuento	I like the story.	(*Lit.* To me is pleasing the story)
¿Les gustan a Uds. los cuentos?		Do you like the stories?

b. parecer to seem

Me parece bien. It seems (is) all right to me. **Le parece bien a ella.** It seems (is) all right to her.

c. importar to be important to (another meaning of **importar**)

No nos importa. It is not important to us. It does not concern us.
No les importa a ellos. It is not important to them. It does not concern them.

Ejercicios (Exercises) No. 108A-108B

108A. Translate:

1. ¿Le dará Ud. a él las naranjas?
2. Lléveme Ud. los zapatos.
3. Tenga la bondad de leernos la carta.
4. Cuanto antes le escribiré a ella una carta.
5. ¿Me enseñará Ud. las palabras nuevas?
6. No podemos mandarles a Uds. el dinero.
7. ¿Quién nos leerá el cuento?
8. Dígame — ¿qué hace María en la cocina?
9. No me gustará la corrida de toros.
10. ¿Le parece bien esa fecha?
11. No me parece bien.
12. No me importan estas cosas.

108B. Complete the Spanish sentences, filling in the correct indirect object pronouns, so that the Spanish sentences correspond exactly to the English.

Remember: **le** = to you (*sing.*), to him, to her; **les** = to you (*plur.*), to them (*m.* and *f.*)

Ejemplo: I am writing *you* a letter.   *Le* escribo una carta.

1. Will you give *him* the money?
2. They bring *us* the clothing.
3. Will you teach *her* the lesson?
4. I like your hats.
5. They like your garden.

1. ¿——— dará Ud. el dinero?
2. ——— traen la ropa.
3. ¿——— enseñará Ud. la lección?
4. ——— gustan los sombreros de Uds.
5. ——— gusta a ellos su jardín.

6. Tell *me* the truth.
7. It's of no concern *to them*.
8. The ticket-seller will give *you* the tickets.
9. I like sweets.
10. Their parents are buying *them* the toys.

11. I shall speak *to you* on the telephone, Henry.
12. I am bringing *you* the umbrella, sir.

13. Bring us the coffee, please.
14. It seems good to me.
15. They seem good to us.

6. Díga ——— la verdad.
7. No ——— importa a ellos.
8. El boletero ——— dará a Uds. los boletos.
9. ——— gustan los dulces.
10. Sus padres están comprándo ——— los juguetes.

11. ——— hablaré por teléfono, Enrique.
12. Estoy trayendo ——— a Ud. el paraguas, señor.

13. Tráiga ——— Ud. el café, por favor.
14. ——— parece bien.
15. ——— parecen bien.

Exercise No. 109—Preguntas

1. ¿Dónde están sentados los dos señores?
2. ¿Qué tiene en la mano el señor Adams?
3. ¿Qué va a leerle al Sr. López?
4. ¿A quién le gustará mucho oírla?
5. ¿Cuál es la fecha de la carta?
6. ¿A quién escribe la carta el Sr. Adams?
7. ¿Qué saludo usa el Sr. Adams?
8. ¿Quién irá de viaje a México?
9. ¿Cuándo saldrá el Sr. Adams de Nueva York?
10. ¿Cuándo llegará al aeropuerto de México D.F.
11. ¿Cuánto tiempo quedará en la capital?
12. ¿A dónde hará viajes?
13. ¿A dónde irá tal vez por avión?
14. ¿De quién ha apreciado los servicios el Sr. Adams?
15. ¿A quién quiere conocer personalmente?

CAPÍTULO 28 (VEINTE Y OCHO)

PARTE PRIMERA

El Señor Adams Recibe Una Carta.

El Sr. Adams tiene en la mano la respuesta que acaba de recibir de su agente, el Sr. Carrillo. Está leyéndola.

Mr. Adams has in his hand the reply which he has just received from his agent, Mr. Carrillo. He is reading it.

1. Muy señor mío:
2. Estoy muy agradecido por su carta del 4 de mayo en que Ud. tiene la bondad de informarme de su visita a México.
3. Tengo el gusto de informarle que estaré en la capital durante los meses de junio y julio y quiero aprovechar la oportunidad de ponerme enteramente a sus órdenes.
4. Tendré gran placer en saludarle en el aeropuerto el 31 de mayo a las siete menos cuarto de la tarde. Espero poder facilitar su estancia en esta capital tanto en las diversiones como en los negocios.
5. Con mucho gusto, platicaré con Ud. en español y estoy seguro de que Ud. lo habla perfectamente. Por cierto lo escribe Ud. sumamente bien. Quiero felicitarles a Ud. y a su maestro, el

1. Dear Sir:
2. I am much obliged for your letter of May 4 in which you have the kindness to inform me of your visit to Mexico.
3. I take pleasure in informing you that I shall be in the capital during the months of June and July and I want to take advantage of the opportunity to put myself entirely at your service.
4. I will take great pleasure in greeting you at the airport May 31 at 6:45 P.M. I hope to be able to facilitate your stay in this capital in matters of recreation as well as in matters of business.
5. With much pleasure, I will talk with you in Spanish and I am sure that you speak it perfectly. Indeed you write it extremely well. I want to congratulate you and your teacher, Mr. Lopez.

Sr. López. Puesto que es mexicano, entiendo bien que Ud. usará muchos modismos mexicanos. ¿Cómo no?

6. Esperando la pronta oportunidad de conocerle a Ud., le saludo muy atentamente, s.s.

Rufino Carrillo

7. Es una carta muy amable dice el señor López. Hasta ahora Ud. ha conocido y ha apreciado al señor Carrillo solamente como un buen representante. Sin duda alguna, Ud. verá que es también muy simpático, como tantos mexicanos. Perdóneme si estoy orgulloso de mi pueblo. Pero Ud. verá por sí mismo.

8. Estoy seguro de que estaré muy contento entre la gente de México. Y lo mejor es que podré hablar con ellos en su propio idioma.

9. Claro está. Pues, Sr. Adams, el martes que viene es nuestra última cita antes de su salida para México. Nos veremos en su oficina, ¿verdad?

10. Sí. ¿Y me dará Ud. algunos últimos consejos?

11. Con mucho gusto, Sr. Adams.

Since he is Mexican, I understand very well that you will use many Mexican idioms. Why not?

6. Looking forward to meeting you soon, I remain,

Sincerely yours,
Rufino Carrillo

7. It is a very kind letter. Until now you have known and appreciated Mr. Carrillo only as a good representative. Without any doubt, you will find that he is also very nice like so many Mexicans. Pardon me if I am proud of my people. But you will see for yourself.

8. I am sure that I will be very happy among the people of Mexico. And the best is that I shall be able to speak to them in their own language.

9. Very true. Well, Mr. Adams, next Tuesday is our last appointment before your departure for Mexico. We shall meet in your office, shall we not?

10. Yes, and will you give me some final advice?

11. With great pleasure, Mr. Adams.

Pronunciation and Spelling Aids

1. Practice:

a-gra-de-ci-do es-tan-cia su-ma-men-te re-pre-sen-to
a-pro-ve-char di-ver-sio-nes fe-li-ci-tar-les per-dó-ne-me
en-te-ra-men-te per-fec-ta-men-te a-pre-cia-do or-gu-llo-so

Building Vocabulary

Sinónimos:

1. informar—avisar   to inform
2. enteramente—completamente   entirely
3. tendré gran placer en—me gustará mucho   I shall be pleased to
4. dispénseme—perdóneme   pardon me

Expresiones Importantes

A. 1. aprovechar la oportunidad de   to take advantage of the opportunity to
2. esperando la pronta oportunidad de conocerle   looking forward to meeting you soon
3. a sus órdenes   at your service
4. estoy muy agradecido   I am much obliged
5. lo mejor es   the best is   lo peor es   the worst is
6. quiero felicitarle a Ud.   I want to congratulate you
7. sin duda alguna   without any doubt
8. Ud. tiene a bien informarme   you have the kindness to inform me

B. Salutations: Letters to Friends

Querido Pablo; Querida Elena   Dear Paul; dear Ellen
Querido amigo; Querida amiga   Dear Friend
Estimado amigo; Estimada amiga   My esteemed Friend

C. Conclusions: Letters to Friends

Su sincero amigo Su sincera amiga Your sincere friend	
Sinceramente Afectuosamente Sincerely Affectionately	
Le saluda cordialmente su amigo(a)	Cordial greetings from your friend
Reciba un abrazo de su amigo(a)	Receive an embrace from your friend

NOTE: Querido(a) is for relatives and very intimate friends. It is not used freely like the English Dear —, which is the form of address even for business letters.

Exercise No. 110—Completion of Text

A. Complete these sentences by putting all English words into Spanish.

1. El Sr. Adams tiene (a letter in his hand).
2. (I am much obliged) por su carta del 4 de mayo.
3. Ud. tiene la bondad (to inform me) de su visita a México.
4. (I shall take great pleasure) en esperarle en el aeropuerto.
5. (I shall converse) con Ud. en español.
6. Quiero (to congratulate you) a Ud. y a su maestro.
7. (I understand very well) que Ud. usará modismos mexicanos. (Why not?)
8. (Without any doubt) Ud. verá que el Sr. Carrillo es (very congenial).
9. (Pardon me). **Estoy muy** (proud) **de mi pueblo.**
10. Ud. verá (for yourself) que los mexicanos son (very friendly).
11. (I am sure) de que (I will be able) hablar con ellos en su propio idioma.
12. (The best is) que puedo hablar español.
13. (The worst is) que Ud. no puede ir conmigo.
14. (Each other) veremos en su oficina.
15. Le daré a Ud. (some final advice).

PARTE SEGUNDA

Grammar Notes

1. Use of hacer in Time Expressions.

   a. ¿Cuánto tiempo hace que Ud. estudia el español?
   (How much time does it make that you are studying Spanish?)

   1. How long have you been studying Spanish?

   b. Hace cinco meses que estudio el español.
   (It makes five months that I am studying Spanish.)

   2. I have been studying Spanish five months.

   c. Estudio el español hace cinco meses.
   (I am studying Spanish it makes five months.)

   3. I have been studying Spanish for (since) five months.

To express an action which began in the past and is still going on, the Spanish uses hace (it) makes, plus an expression of time, plus que, plus the present tense of the verb (ex. b).

If the hace expression comes after the verb, que is omitted. (ex. c)

2. Use of the Definite Article in Place of the Possessive Adjective.

   1. El señor tiene una carta en la mano.
   2. Ana se pone el sombrero en la cabeza.

   The gentleman has a letter in his hand.
   Anna puts her hat on her head.

The definite article is used instead of the possessive adjective with parts of the body and clothing when there is no doubt who is meant.

3. Reflexive Pronouns with a Reciprocal Meaning.

Nos veremos.	We shall see each other.
No se conocen el uno al otro.	They do not know each other.
Juana y Ana se admiran la una a la otra.	Jane and Anna admire each other.

a. When the reflexive pronoun is used with a reciprocal meaning, **el uno al otro (la una a la otra)**, *one another*, may be added for clarity.

Ejercicios (Exercises) No. 111A-111B-111C

111A. Complete these sentences by putting the English words into Spanish.

Ejemplo: 1. ¿Cuánto tiempo hace que Ud. estudia el español?

1. ¿(How long) hace que Ud. estudia el español?
2. (For six months) que estudio el español.
3. (For ten years) que el Sr. López es profesor.
4. (For 45 minutes) que esperamos.
5. (For three days) que mi madre está enferma.
6. Hace seis meses que (I have known him).
7. Hace cinco semanas que (they have lived in this house).
8. Hace tres horas que (the children have been in the cinema.)
9. Hace diez años que (he has been in this country).
10. Hace cinco días que (I have been here).

111B. Change the following affirmative commands into negative commands.

Remember: 1. In affirmative commands object pronouns follow the verb. 2. In negative commands they precede it.

Ejemplo: Déme el libro. No me dé el libro.

1. Pónganlos Uds. en la mesa.
2. Escríbales Ud. las cartas.
3. Tráiganlos a la casa.
4. Dígame las respuestas.
5. Mándele los artículos.
6. Lléveme la carne y el pescado.
7. Déme un boleto de viaje redondo.
8. Cómpreme una bolsa de cuero.
9. Léanles todos los cuentos.
10. Véndale el automóvil.

NOTE: The singular imperative of **dar, dé Ud.**, takes an accent mark to distinguish it from **de** (of).

111C. Answer the following questions in the future with both **sí** and **no**. Use an object pronoun in each answer.

Remember: If the question has **Ud.** as subject, the answer has (yo) as subject; if the question has **Uds.**, the answer has (nosotros).

Ejemplos: Comerá Ud. la carne? Sí, la comeré. No, no la comeré.
Comerán Uds. la carne? Sí, la comeremos. No, no la comeremos.

1. ¿Visitará Ud. el museo?
2. ¿Escribirá Ud. la carta?
3. ¿Comprará Ud. el coche?
4. ¿Traerá Ud. los cestos?
5. ¿Tomará Ud. el té?
6. ¿Pedirán Uds. los boletos?
7. ¿Venderán Uds. la casa?
8. ¿Querrán Uds. las frutas?
9. ¿Seguirán Uds. a sus amigos?
10. ¿Repetirán Uds. las preguntas?

Exercise No. 112—Preguntas

1. ¿Qué acaba de recibir el Sr. Adams?
2. ¿Cuándo estará en la capital el Sr. Carrillo?
3. ¿Dónde esperará al Sr. Adams?
4. ¿En qué lengua conversará con él?
5. ¿A quiénes quiere felicitar el Sr. Carrillo?
6. ¿Qué entiende bien?
7. ¿Quién está orgulloso de su pueblo?
8. ¿Qué verá el Sr. Adams por sí mismo?
9. ¿Cuándo será la ultima cita de los dos señores?
10. ¿Dónde se verán?

CAPÍTULO 29 (VEINTE Y NUEVE)

PARTE PRIMERA

Los Consejos del Señor López

1. Hace calor en la oficina del señor Adams. No hace viento. Por la ventana abierta se oyen los ruidos de la calle.

2. — Me alegro de salir de la ciudad, — dice el señor Adams al señor López.

3. — Tengo ganas de acompañarle, — contesta el señor López.

4. ¿No puede Ud. ir conmigo?

5. Desgraciadamente, no es posible.

6. Por lo menos, ¿me hace Ud. el favor de darme algunos últimos consejos? ¿Es muy distinta la vida en México de la vida en los EE. UU.?

7. Sí, señor Adams, hay muchas costumbres diferentes. En general, la vida en México es más formal. Son muy importantes las formalidades. Y eso de la cortesía, yo creo, tiene un significado profundo—quiere decir que cada hombre es digno de respeto.

8. — Es verdad, — responde el señor Adams.

9. He notado que entre los negociantes también hay más formalidad en México que en los EE. UU. Les gusta platicar un rato acerca de otras cosas antes de emprender un negocio. Quieren llegar a conocerse el uno al otro.

10. Estaré muy contento allí.

11. Como le he dicho hace algún tiempo hay que acostumbrarse a la altura. Al principio es mejor no apresurarse.

12. Se dice que en general la vida es más tranquila allí. Espero que sí. Estoy cansado de estar de prisa.

13. A propósito, Sr. Adams, ha leído Ud. los libros sobre Mexico que le he recomendado?

14. Sí, los he leído todos. Me han sido muy útiles e interesantes. Pero me gusta sobre todo "Mexican Folkways by Frances Toor."

15. También he leído el excelente librito "Mexico By Motor" publicado por la Asociación Automobilística de América.

16. Bueno. He dicho muchas veces que Ud. irá pasando en México. En cuanto a mí, pasaré el verano en Nueva York. He gozado de nuestras conversaciones y voy a echarle de menos.

17. Pensaré en Ud. a menudo y le escribiré de vez en cuando.

18. Me gustará mucho recibir sus cartas desde México. Pues bien, tenemos que despedirnos.

1. It is hot in Mr. Adams' office. There is no wind. Through the open window are heard the noises of the street.

2. "I am happy to leave the city," says Mr. Adams to Mr. Lopez.

3. "I have a mind to go with you," answers Mr. Lopez.

4. Can you not go with me?

5. Unfortunately, it is not possible.

6. At least, will you please give me some final advice? Is life in Mexico very different from life in the United States?

7. Yes, Mr. Adams, there are many different customs. In general, life in Mexico is more formal. The formalities are very important. And the matter of courtesy, I think, has a profound significance—it means that every man is worthy of respect.

8. "That is true," answers Mr. Adams.

9. I have noticed that among businessmen too there is more formality in Mexico than in the United States. They like to chat a little about other things before taking up business. They want to get to know one another.

10. I shall be very happy there.

11. As I told you some time ago, one must accustom oneself to the altitude. At first it is better not to hurry.

12. They say that in general life is more tranquil there. I hope so. I am tired of being in a hurry.

13. By the way, Mr. Adams, have you read the books on Mexico which I have recommended to you?

14. Yes, I have read them all. They have been very useful and interesting to me. But I like most of all "Mexican Folkways by Frances Toor."

15. I have also read the excellent booklet "Mexico By Motor" published by the Automobile Association of America.

16. Good. I have said many times that you will get along in Mexico. As for me, I shall spend the summer in New York. I have enjoyed our conversations and I am going to miss you.

17. I shall think of you often and I shall write you from time to time.

18. I shall be glad to receive your letters from Mexico. Well then, we have to take leave of each

Hágame el favor de saludarles por mi parte a la señora Adams y a sus hijos.
19. Gracias y mucha suerte, Sr. López.
20. Buen viaje, Sr. Adams.
   Se dan la mano.

other. Kindly give my regards to Mrs. Adams and to your children.
19. Thank you and good luck, Mr. Lopez.
20. Happy voyage, Mr. Adams.
   They shake hands.

Pronunciation and Spelling Aids

1. Practice:

vien-to	des-gra-cia-da-men-te	for-ma-li-dad	des-pe-dir-nos	cre-í-do
rui-dos	cor-te-sí-as	a-cos-tum-brar-se	le-í-do	o-í-do
a-com-pa-ñar-le	sig-ni-fi-ca-do	a-pre-su-rar-se	ca-í-do	

2. The combinations (diphthongs) **ai, oi, ei** become separate vowels, **a-í, o-í,** and **e-í,** when the **í** has an accent mark.

Building Vocabulary

A. Sinónimos
1. alegrarse (de)   estar contento (de)   to be happy (to)
2. a menudo   muchas veces   often
3. estar de prisa   tener prisa   to be in a hurry
4. hay que   es necesario   it is necessary, one must

Expresiones Importantes

1. en cuanto a mí   as for me
2. espero que sí   I hope so
3. espero que no   I hope not
4. He gozado de nuestras conversaciones   I have enjoyed our conversations.
5. Voy a echarle de menos   I am going to miss you.

Exercise No. 113—Completion of Text

1. (I am glad) salir de la ciudad.
2. (I have a mind) de acompañarle.
3. (At least) hágame el favor de (to give me) algunos consejos.
4. (The matter of courtesy) tiene un significado profundo.
5. (It means) que cada hombre (is worthy) de respeto.
6. (They like) platicar un rato (about) otras cosas.
7. Quieren llegar a (to know each other).

8. (As I have told you) es mejor no apresurarse.
9. (People say) que en general la vida es más tranquila. (I hope so).
10. Estoy cansado (of being in a hurry).
11. ¿(Have you read) los libros sobre México?
12. (As for me) quedaré aquí en Nueva York.
13. (I have enjoyed) de nuestras conversaciones.
14. Tenemos que (take leave of each other).
15. They shake hands.

PARTE SEGUNDA

Grammar Notes

1. The Present Perfect Tense—Model Verbs: **hablar, aprender, vivir.** This is one of the tenses used to indicate past time.

Singular

he hablado	(aprendido, vivido)	I have spoken	(learned, lived)
has hablado	(aprendido, vivido)	you have spoken	(learned, lived)
Ud. ha hablado	(aprendido, vivido)	you have spoken	(learned, lived)
ha hablado	(aprendido, vivido)	he, she, it has spoken	(learned, lived)

Plural

hemos hablado	(aprendido, vivido)	we have spoken	(learned, lived)
habéis hablado	(aprendido, vivido)	you have spoken	(learned, lived)
Uds. han hablado	(aprendido, vivido)	you have spoken	(learned, lived)
han hablado	(aprendido, vivido)	they have spoken	(learned, lived)

a. As in English, the present perfect tense in Spanish is formed by the present tense of the auxiliary (helping) verb, **haber** (*to have*) plus the past participle of the verb.

b. The endings of the auxiliary verb haber are: singular -e, -as, -a; plural -emos, -éis, -an. You have learned that these are also the endings in the future tense (See Capítulo 26). In the future, however, all the endings except -emos have an accent mark.

c. To form the regular past participle of an -ar verb, drop the -ar and add -ado. To form the past participle of an -er or -ir verb drop the -er or -ir and add -ido.

d. The subject may never, as in English, come between the auxiliary verb and the past participle. Object pronouns precede the auxiliary verb.

¿Ha escrito Carlos la carta?	Has Charles written the letter?
Sí, la ha escrito.	Yes, he has written it.

2. The Past Participles of Some Familiar Verbs

he comprado	I have bought	he querido	I have wished
he enseñado	I have taught	he vendido	I have sold
he tomado	I have taken	he comido	I have eaten
he trabajado	I have worked	he bebido	I have drunk
he andado	I have walked	he tenido	I have had
he deseado	I have wanted	he ido	I have gone
he pasado	I have passed	he sido	I have been
he estado	I have been	he venido	I have come

3. Past Participles with an Accent Mark

When the stem of the verb ends in a vowel, the i of -ido has an accent mark.

he leído	(le-í-do)	I have read	he traído	(tra-í-do)	I have brought
he caído	(ca-í-do)	I have fallen	he creído	(cre-í-do)	I have believed
he oído	(o-í-do)	I have heard			

4. Irregular Past Participles

Most past participles are regular. The most common irregulars are:

abrir	he *abierto*	I have opened	poner	he *puesto*	I have put
cubrir	he *cubierto*	I have covered	ver	he *visto*	I have seen
decir	he *dicho*	I have said	volver	he *vuelto*	I have returned
escribir	he *escrito*	I have written	morir	ha *muerto*	he has died
hacer	he *hecho*	I have done	romper	he *roto*	I have broken

NOTE the proverb (refrán): **Dicho y hecho** — No sooner said than done. *Lit.* Said and done.

5. haber and tener

haber, to have, as you have seen, is used as an auxiliary verb to form the present perfect tense.
tener, to have, means *to possess*. It is never used as an auxiliary verb.

He vendido la casa.	I have sold the house.	Tengo una casa.	I have (possess) a house.
He tenido una casa.	I have had (possessed) a house.		

Ejercicios (Exercises) No. 114A-114B-114C

114A. Translate:

1. Hemos tenido un buen viaje.
2. Los jarros han caído en el suelo.
3. No han dicho nada.
4. ¿Qué ha hecho Pablo con el dinero?
5. Nadie ha abierto las puertas.

6. No hemos leído esos diarios.
7. ¿Han estado Uds. en el cine?
8. ¿Ha estado enferma la niña?
9. Nunca he creído ese cuento.
10. ¿Qué han dicho ellos?

114B. Translate:

1. I have noted
2. He has said
3. They have not read
4. (ser) They have been
5. (estar) We have been

6. I have not worked
7. Have you taught (Ud.)?
8. Who has not written?
9. What have you done (Uds.)?
10. You (tú) have opened.

11. What has John said?
12. She has taken
13. I have not believed
14. We have heard
15. Have you (Uds.) heard?

114C. Change the following sentences 1. to the future. 2. to the present perfect. Do not change the subject.

Ejemplo: **Compro un sombrero. Compraré un sombrero. He comprado un sombrero.**

1. El Sr. García vende su casa.
2. Trabajo en la ciudad.
3. Escribimos una carta.
4. Leen las revistas.
5. ¿Toma Ud. la cena a las ocho?

6. Tú no aprendes la lección.
7. ¿Busca el niño a su madre?
8. ¿Compran Uds. zapatos nuevos?
9. Salgo de la ciudad.
10. Entran en la casa.

Exercise No. 115—Preguntas

1. ¿Dónde se encuentran los señores Adams y López?
2. ¿Qué tiempo hace?
3. ¿Qué se oyen por la ventana?
4. ¿Quién se alegra de irse de la ciudad?
5. ¿Quién tiene ganas de acompañar al Sr. Adams?
6. ¿Qué responde el Sr. López a la pregunta — ¿No puede Ud. ir conmigo?
7. ¿Es la vida en México más formal que la vida en los Estados Unidos?

8. ¿Qué quiere decir la importancia de la cortesía en México?
9. ¿Qué ha notado el Sr. López entre los negociantes?
10. ¿Quién está cansado de estar de prisa?
11. ¿Quién ha leído libros sobre México?
12. ¿Quién ha recomendado estos libros?
13. En cuanto al Sr. López, ¿dónde pasará el verano?
14. ¿En quién pensará a menudo el Sr. Adams?
15. ¿Le escribirá cartas al Sr. López de vez en cuando?

CAPÍTULO 30 (TREINTA)

PARTE PRIMERA

El Señor Adams Sale Para México

1. Hace cinco meses que el señor Adams estudia el español. Ha pasado muchas horas en conversación con su maestro, el señor López. También ha aprendido la gramática necesaria y ha leído mucho sobre México e Hispano-América. Verdaderamente ha trabajado mucho. Ahora habla español bastante bien y espera ir pasando muy bien en México.

1. Mr. Adams has been studying Spanish for five months. He has spent many hours in conversation with his teacher, Mr. Lopez. Also he has learned the necessary grammar and has read a great deal about Mexico and Hispanic-America. He really has worked very hard. Now he speaks Spanish quite well and he expects to get along very well in Mexico.

2. El señor Adams ha conseguido los boletos para el vuelo, el pasaporte, y el permiso de entrada mexicano. Necesita todo esto porque está en viaje de negocios así como en viaje de recreo. Tiene también el certificado necesario de vacuna. Un turista necesita solamente una tarjeta de turista y el certificado de vacuna. Desde luego, el señor Adams ha escrito una carta a su agente en México haciéndole saber la hora de llegada del avión en la capital. Este ha prometido recibirle en el aeropuerto.

3. Al fin llega el 31 de mayo, día de la salida. El avión del señor Adams sale del Aeropuerto Internacional a las ocho menos cuarto de la mañana. El tiene que estar en el aeropuerto una hora antes para mostrar su boleto y hacer pesar su equipaje. La familia no va a acompañarle a México porque los hijos tienen que terminar el año escolar y su esposa tiene que quedar en casa para cuidar a los hijos. Además, el viajar con cuatro niños desde cinco hasta diez años de edad no es solamente difícil sino también bastante caro.

4. Por supuesto toda la familia está muy animada. Los niños no han dormido mucho y a las cinco de la mañana todos están despiertos.

5. A las seis de la mañana la familia entera está lista para salir para el aeropuerto. El señor Adams ha hecho dos maletas y las pone en el auto. Entonces todos suben al automóvil que se pone en marcha y llega al aeropuerto a eso de las siete. El señor Adams hace revisar su boleto y hace pesar su equipaje. Tiene que pagar tres dólares de exceso porque el peso total excede las 66 libras permitidas gratis.

6. Entonces el señor Adams se despide de su esposa y de sus hijos que le dan "el buen viaje." Sube al avión saludando a su esposa y a sus hijos que están mirándole con mucha emoción. A las ocho menos cuarto en punto se despega el avión.

7. El señor Adams está en camino.

2. Mr. Adams has obtained the tickets for the flight, his passport and the Mexican entry permit. He needs all this because he is on a business trip as well as a pleasure trip. He has also the necessary vaccination certificate. A tourist needs only a tourist card and the vaccination certificate. Of course Mr. Adams has written a letter to his agent in Mexico letting him know the time of arrival of the plane at the capital. The latter has promised to meet him at the airport.

3. At last May 31st, the day of departure, arrives. Mr. Adams' plane leaves the International Airport at a quarter to eight in the morning. He must be at the airport one hour before to show his ticket and have his baggage weighed. His family is not going with him to Mexico because his children have to finish the school year and his wife has to remain at home to take care of the children. Besides, traveling with four children from five to ten years of age is not only difficult but quite expensive.

4. Of course the whole family is very excited. The children have not slept very much and at five in the morning all are awake.

5. At six in the morning the whole family is ready to leave for the airport. Mr. Adams has packed two valises and puts them in the auto. Then all get into the automobile which starts off and arrives at the airport at about seven. Mr. Adams has his ticket checked and has his baggage weighed. He has to pay three dollars extra because the total weight exceeds the 66 pounds allowed free.

6. Then Mr. Adams takes leave of his wife and children, who wish him "a happy voyage." He goes up into the plane waving to his wife and children who are watching him with great emotion. At 7.45 o'clock sharp the plane takes off.

7. Mr. Adams is on his way.

Pronunciation and Spelling Aids

1. Practice:

ver-da-de-ra-men-te	le-í-do	pro-me-ti-do	cer-ti-fi-ca-do	re-vi-sar	se des-pi-de
pa-sa-do	he-cho	dor-mi-do	re-qui-si-to	ha-cién-do-le	e-qui-pa-je
a-pren-di-do	con-se-gui-do	des-pier-to	va-cu-na	des-pe-dir-se	ae-ro-puer-to

Building Vocabulary

A. Antónimos

1. empezar (ie) to begin acabar, terminar to finish
2. abrir to open cerrar to close
3. abierto open cerrado closed
4. acostarse (ue) to go to bed levantarse to get up
5. dormir to sleep estar despierto to be awake

6. **dormirse**   to go to sleep   **despertarse**   to wake up
7. **despedirse (de)**   to take leave (of)   **saludar (a)**   to greet
8. **llegar (a)**   to arrive (at)   **salir (de)**   to leave (from)
9. **la llegada**   the arrival   **la salida**   the departure
10. **suben al auto**   they get into the auto   **bajan del auto**   they get out of the auto

Expresiones Importantes

1. cuidar a los niños   to take care of the children
2. haciéndole saber   letting him know
3. hacer una maleta   to pack a suitcase
4. no sólamente . . . sino también   not only . . . but also
5. quedar en casa   to remain at home

Exercise No. 116—Completion of Text

1. (For five months) que el Sr. Adams estudia el español.
2. El Sr. Adams (has obtained) los boletos.
3. (Of course) el Sr. Adams ha escrito a su agente.
4. (Finally) llega el 31 de mayo.
5. La familia no va (to accompany him).
6. El viajar con cuatro niños (is not only) difícil (but also) bastante caro.
7. La familia (is ready) para salir.
8. El Sr. Adams (has packed two suitcases).
9. Todos (get into the automobile).
10. (It starts off) y llega al aeropuerto (about) las diez.
11. El peso total (of his baggage) excede 66 (pounds).
12. Por eso (he has to) pagar tres dólares extra.
13. El negociante (takes leave of) su esposa y de sus hijos.
14. (At 11 o'clock sharp) se despega el avión.
15. Mr. Adams is on his way.

PARTE SEGUNDA

Grammar Notes

1. **Present Tense of dormir (ue) to sleep, despedirse (i) to take leave**

I sleep, etc.

duermo	dormimos
duermes	dormís
duerme	duermen

Imperative

duerma Ud.	duerman Uds.

I take leave, etc.

me despido	nos despedimos
te despides	os despedís
se despide	se despiden

Imperative

despídase Ud.	despídanse Uds.

2. **Present Perfect of dormir (ue) and despedirse (i)**

I have slept, etc.

he dormido	hemos dormido
has dormido	habéis dormido
ha dormido	han dormido

I have taken leave, etc.

me he despedido	nos hemos despedido
te has despedido	os habéis despedido
se ha despedido	se han despedido

In the present perfect tense of a reflexive verb, the reflexive pronoun must precede the auxiliary verb.

No me he lavado.   I have not washed myself.   **¿Se ha lavado Ud.?**   Have you washed yourself?

3. **Past Participles Used as Adjectives.**

Study the following expressions, noting in each a past participle used as an adjective.

1. **el libro abierto**   the open book
2. **El libro está abierto**   The book is open.
3. **La ventana cerrada**   the closed window
4. **La ventana está cerrada.**   The window is closed.

a. Past participles may be used as adjectives. Like other adjectives they agree in number and gender with the nouns they modify.

b. Past participles as predicate adjectives, are generally used with **estar.**

Ejercicios (Exercises) No. 117A-117B-117C

117A. Translate:

1. Estamos comenzando la lección.
2. Hemos comenzado el ejercicio.
3. No me acuerdo de él.
4. Me he acordado de ella.
5. ¿Están sentándose?
6. ¿Se han sentado?
7. ¿Están repitiendo Uds. las palabras?
8. ¿Han repetido Uds. las palabras?
9. La criada está poniendo la mesa.
10. La criada no ha puesto la mesa.
11. La mesa está puesta.
12. Ella está sirviendo el café.
13. Ella ha servido el té.
14. ¿Qué frutas prefiere Ud.?
15. ¿Qué frutas ha preferido Ud.?
16. Los niños están acostándose.
17. Ya se han acostado.
18. ¿Están pidiendo Uds. informes?
19. ¿Han pedido Uds. informes?
20. El trabajo no está acabado.

117B. Complete by putting the English words into Spanish.

1. La ventana está (open).
2. La puerta está (closed).
3. Los niños están (awake).
4. La mesa está (set).
5. La casa está (sold).
6. Los muchachos están (dressed).
7. Los señores están (seated).
8. Las cartas están (written).
9. El año escolar está (finished).
10. El traje está (made) a mano.

117C. Translate:

1. I sleep.
2. He is sleeping (prog. tense).
3. They sleep.
4. Do you (Ud.) sleep?
5. I take leave.
6. They take leave.
7. We do not take leave.
8. I have slept.
9. Have you slept?
10. We have not slept.
11. I have taken leave.
12. They have not taken leave.
13. Have you (Uds.) taken leave?
14. Sleep (Ud.)
15. Do not sleep (Uds.)

Exercise No. 118—Preguntas

1. ¿Cuánto tiempo hace que el Sr. Adams estudia el español?
2. ¿Con quién ha pasado muchas horas en conversación?
3. ¿Qué ha aprendido?
4. ¿Cómo ha trabajado?
5. ¿Cómo habla español ahora?
6. ¿Qué ha conseguido el Sr. Adams?
7. ¿Qué certificado ha obtenido?
8. ¿A quién ha escrito el Sr. Adams?
9. ¿Qué le ha prometido su agente?
10. ¿A qué hora están despiertos todos los niños?
11. ¿A qué hora sale el avión del aeropuerto?
12. ¿Qué tiene que mostrar cada pasajero?
13. ¿Va a acompañarle al Sr. Adams su familia?
14. ¿Qué tienen que terminar sus niños?
15. ¿Para qué tiene que quedar en casa la señora Adams?

REPASO 7
(CAPÍTULOS 27–30) PARTE PRIMERA
Repaso de Palabras

NOUNS

1. el aeropuerto	9. la entrada	17. el punto	1. airport	9. entrance	17. point
2. el aire	10. la luna	18. un rato	2. air	10. moon	18. a while, time
3. los alrededores	11. el modismo	19. el ruido	3. suburbs	11. idiom	19. noise
4. el cariño	12. las noticias	20. el servicio	4. affection	12. news	20. service
5. la cortesía	13. el negocio	21. tarjeta de turista	5. courtesy	13. business	21. tourist card
6. la corrida de toros	14. la partida	22. el sitio	6. bullfight	14. departure	22. place
7. la cultura	15. el pasaporte	23. la visita	7. culture	15. passport	23. visit
8. la dirección	16. el placer	24. la vista	8. address	16. pleasure	24. view

VERBS

1. acompañar	8. cuidar	15. felicitar	1. to accompany	8. to take care of	15. to congratulate
2. alegrarse	9. despedirse de	16. gozar de	2. to be glad	9. to take leave of	16. to enjoy
3. aprovechar	10. extender(ie)	17. irse	3. to take advantage of	10. to extend	17. to go away
4. apreciar	11. envidar	18. mostrar(ue)	4. to appreciate	11. to envy	18. to show
5. ayudar	12. informar	19. pesar	5. to help	12. to inform	19. to weigh
6. cansarse	13. faltar	20. prometer	6. to get tired	13. to be lacking	20. to promise
7. confesar(ie)	14. facturar	21. usar	7. to confess	14. to check (baggage)	21. to use

ADJECTIVES

1. abierto	6. cierto	11. ocupado	1. open	6. certain	11. busy
2. amable	7. conveniente	12. orgulloso	2. friendly	7. convenient	12. proud
3. bello	8. despierto	13. siguiente	3. beautiful	8. awake	13. following
4. bondadoso	9. digno	14. sorprendido	4. kind	9. worthy	14. surprised
5. caro	10. entero	15. último	5. dear	10. entire	15. final

ADVERBS

1. atentamente	3. enteramente	5. perfectamente	1. attentively	3. entirely	5. perfectly
2. desgraciadamente	4. entretanto	6. sumamente	2. unfortunately	4. meanwhile	6. completely

IMPORTANT EXPRESSIONS

1. a menudo	8. espero que sí	15. por lo menos	1. often	8. I hope so	15. at least
2. bastante bien	9. espero que nó	16. qué lastima	2. quite well	9. I hope not	16. what a pity
3. de antemano	10. estar de prisa	17. ponerse en marcha	3. beforehand	10. to be in a hurry	17. to set out
4. de seguro	11. estar en camino	18. sin duda alguna	4. surely	11. to be on the way	18. without any doubt
5. dispénseme	12. hace algún tiempo	19. tener la intención	5. pardon me	12. some time ago	19. to intend
6. echar de menos	13. hay que	20. la mano izquierda	6. to miss	13. it is necessary	20. the left hand
7. en cuanto a mí	14. hecho a mano	21. la mano derecha	7. as for me	14. hand-made	21. the right hand

PARTE SEGUNDA

Ejercicio 119. From Group II select the antonyms for each word in Group I.

Group I

1. me acuesto	6. abro
2. me despido	7. aprendo
3. duermo	8. mando
4. acabo	9. subo a
5. compro	10. llego a

Group II

a. comienzo	f. me levanto
b. cierro	g. enseño
c. saludo	h. recibo
d. vendo	i. bajo de
e. estoy despierto	j. salgo de

Ejercicio 120. Complete the following sentences by selecting expressions from those listed (a to j). Be sure to use the correct forms of the verbs.

1. (Pardon me), señor, tengo que despedirme.
2. (It is necessary) conseguir un pasaporte.
3. Estudiamos el español (for some time).
4. (They intend to) salir para México mañana.
5. (Often) he pensado en Ud.
6. No puedo hablar más porque (I am in a hurry).
7. María (will remain at home) porque está enferma.
8. ¿(At least) me dará Ud. algunos consejos?
9. (As for me) pasaré todo el verano en la ciudad.
10. Iré pasando en México porque hablo español (quite well).

a. tener la intención de
b. a menudo
c. dispénseme
d. estar de prisa
e. por lo menos
f. hay que
g. quedar en casa
h. bastante bien
i. hace algún tiempo
j. en cuanto a mí.

Ejercicio 121. Select the group of words in the right-hand column which best completes each sentence begun in the left-hand column.

1. Ahora espero aprovechar la oportunidad
2. El Sr. Adams no es solamente un buen negociante
3. Ha aprendido a hablar español
4. La carta que he recibido
5. Si Ud. quiere viajar en México
6. Después de despedirse de su familia
7. El Sr. López tiene ganas de acompañar a su amigo
8. Pensaré a menudo en Ud.
9. Ya no puedo quedar aquí

a. lea Ud. algo de sus costumbres.
b. pero tiene que quedar en Nueva York.
c. porque estoy de prisa.
d. de conocerle personalmente.
e. sino también un hombre de cultura.
f. de mi agente es muy amistosa (friendly).
g. porque quiere visitar a su agente.
h. entra el Sr. Adams en el avión.
i. que estudio el español.
j. porque voy a echarle de menos.

Ejercicio 122. Complete the Spanish sentences so that they correspond to the English sentences. Be careful to use the correct indirect object pronouns.

Ejemplo: Me gusta la carta.

1. I like the letter.
2. They like to travel.
3. We like the airplanes.
4. Do you like the paintings, Madame?
5. He does not like tomatoes.
6. She does not like this style.
7. Do you like to dance, gentlemen?
8. Don't you like to play, Anita?
9. It seems all right to us.
10. It doesn't concern me.

1. ——— gusta la carta.
2. ——— gusta viajar.
3. ——— gustan los aviones.
4. ¿——— gustan las pinturas, señora?
5. No ——— gustan los tomates.
6. No ——— gusta esta moda.
7. ——— gusta bailar, caballeros?
8. ¿No ——— gusta jugar, Anita?
9. ——— parece bien.
10. No ——— importa.

Ejercicio 123. In the following sentences fill in the past participle of the verbs in parentheses.

1. Los pajáros han (cantar) todo el día.
2. ¿Por qué no han (volver) Uds. a casa?
3. ¿Ha (llegar) el tren todavía?
4. ¿Han (put) Uds. los objetos de arte en la mesa?
5. El señor ha (hacer) un viaje de recreo.

6. Los empleados han (abrir) las cajas.
7. Hemos (recibir) una caja de mercancía.
8. Le he (decir) a Ud. la verdad.
9. ¿Han (leer) Uds. muchos libros sobre México?
10. ¿Se han (despedir) todos los viajeros?

Ejercicio 124. Complete the following sentences with a past participle.

Remember: In these sentences the past participle is used as an adjective and therefore must agree with the noun it modifies.

Ejemplo: 1. Las señoritas están sentadas en la sala.

1. Las señoritas están (sentar) en la sala.
2. La tierra está (cubrir) de nieve (snow).
3. El viento viene por la puerta (abrir).
4. Todos los cuartos están (cerrar).
5. Los rebozos están (hacer) a mano.

6. Estas cartas están (written) en español.
7. La mesa está (poner).
8. No hemos visto el ejercicio (escribir).
9. El trabajo está (acabar).
10. Tiene un libro (abrir) en la mano.

Ejercicio 125. Translate the English sentences. Be careful to use the correct direct object pronouns.

Ejemplo: 1. Ha comprado Ud. la cesta? La he comprado.

1. ¿Ha comprado Ud. la cesta?
2. ¿Ha abierto Ud. la ventana?
3. ¿Ha oído Ud. el ruido?
4. ¿Ha conseguido Ud. el pasaporte?
5. ¿Ha ayudado Ud. a sus amigos?
6. ¿Han visto Uds. los rebozos?
7. ¿Han vendido Uds. los boletos?
8. ¿Han completado Uds. el ejercicio?
9. ¿Han escrito Uds. las cartas?
10. ¿Han leído Uds. la revista?

1. I have bought it.
2. I have opened it.
3. I have heard it.
4. I have obtained it.
5. I have helped them.
6. We have seen them.
7. We have sold them.
8. We have completed it.
9. We have written them.
10. We have read it.

Diálogo
En el Aeropuerto

Practice the Spanish Aloud:

— Buenos días, Sr. Carrillo. ¿Espera Ud. a alguien en el próximo avión?

— Sí, estoy esperando al Sr. Adams de Nueva York, jefe de la casa que represento en México.

Good day, Mr. Carrillo. Are you waiting for someone on the next plane?

Yes, I am waiting for Mr. Adams from New York, head of the firm which I represent in Mexico.

— ¿Le conoce Ud. personalmente?

— Le conozco sólamente por correspondencia. Pero tengo su fotografía y debo reconocerle. Es un hombre de cerca de cuarenta años de edad.

— ¿Cuándo llega el vuelo 225 de Houston?

— Debe de llegar a las once y cuarto.

— ¿Llega atrasado?

— No, llega a tiempo. ¡Ah! Ya llega. Está acercándose. Está bajando. Ya está aterrizando.

Dispénseme, señor, voy a saludar al Sr. Adams.

Do you know him personally?

I know him only by correspondence. But I have his photograph and I should recognize him. He is a man of about forty years of age.

When does flight 225 arrive from Houston?

It should arrive at 11:15.

Is it late?

No, it is on time. Ah! It is arriving now. It is approaching. It is coming down. It is landing now.

Excuse me, sir, I am going to greet Mr. Adams.

— Bienvenido a México, Sr. Adams. ¿Ha tenido Ud. un buen viaje?

— ¡Estupendo! Me alegro mucho de estar en México. A menudo he soñado con este momento.

— Bueno. Estoy seguro de que Ud. estará muy contento aquí.

Welcome to Mexico, Mr. Adams. Have you had a good trip?

Stupendous! I am very happy to be in Mexico. I have often dreamed of this moment.

Good. I am sure that you will be very happy here.

LECTURA

Exercise No. 126—Un Programa Extraordinario En El Cine

Esta tarde el señor Adams y su esposa van al cine. Al señor Adams no le gusta la mayor parte de las cintas (films) de Hollywood, sobre todo aquellas en que los vaqueros americanos se disparan tiros (fire shots) los unos a los otros. Tampoco le interesan películas detectivescas.

Pero esta tarde se exhibe (is being shown) un programa extraordinario en un teatro que está a cosa de cuatro cuadras de su casa. La cinta se llama "Un Viaje Por México." Es una cinta sobre el país que nuestro amigo Adams va a visitar dentro de unos meses y que trata de (deals with) su historia, su geografía, sus ríos, montañas, ciudades, etc.; es decir, una cinta que debe interesar mucho a los turistas.

Los Adams entran en el teatro a las ocho y media. Casi todos los asientos están ocupados y por eso tienen que sentarse en la tercera fila. Esto no le gusta al señor Adams porque los movimientos en la pantalla le hacen daño a los ojos. Afortunadamente pueden cambiar de asientos después de quince minutos y se mudan (move) a la fila trece.

Los Adams gozan mucho de esta película y también aprenden mucho acerca de las costumbres de México.

Al salir (On leaving) del teatro, el señor Adams dice a su esposa, ¿Sabes, Carlota? Creo que iré pasando muy bien en México. He entendido (I have understood) casi todas las palabras de los actores y las actrices de esta película.

CAPÍTULO 31 (TREINTA Y UNO)

PARTE PRIMERA

FOREWORD

Mr. Adams is now in Mexico and writes ten letters to Mr. Lopez, about some of the places he visits and about some of his experiences and impressions.

There are many references in his letters to things he has discussed with his teacher so that much of the vocabulary of Chapters 3 to 30 is repeated in the letters.

It is therefore very desirable that you reread all the texts and dialogues of the previous chapters *before* proceeding with Chapter 31. You will be able to do this easily and rapidly, with little or no reference to the English translation. Thus you will in a pleasant manner review the vocabulary and important expressions.

Chapters 2 to 25 are in the present tense which is by far the most important and most used tense in the affairs of daily life. In Chapters 26 to 30 the future and present perfect tenses were introduced. In Chapter 31 Mr. Adams begins to relate his experiences, that is to say, what *happened* to him. He will begin to use the preterite tense which is the chief tense for relating what *happened* in definite past time.

Thus in Chapter 31 you will accompany Mr. Adams not only into the interesting and fascinating country of Mexico, but also into the realm of the preterite tense, which you will find interesting and useful.

You should continue your pronunciation practice by reading aloud as often as possible dialogues and parts of conversational texts from previous chapters.

El ejercicio hace al maestro.

El Señor Adams Llega a México

Primera Carta De México

México D.F. 4 de junio de 1954

Estimado amigo:

1. Después que llegó el avión al aeropuerto de México y me revisaron el equipaje en la aduana, fuí a la sala de espera.

2. De repente un señor guapo se acercó a mí y dijo — Dispénseme ¿Es Ud. el señor Adams?

3. — A sus órdenes, — contesté yo. — Y Ud. es el señor Carrillo, ¿verdad? Mucho gusto en conocerle. (Se dan la mano.)

4. — El gusto es mío, — respondió el señor Carrillo.

5. Ud. recordará, Sr. López, que el Sr. Carrillo es el agente de nuestra casa en Nueva York y que prometió recibirme en el aeropuerto.

6. Cuando salimos juntos a la calle el señor Carrillo llamó un libre (un taxi mexicano). Dijo al chófer — Al Hotel Luma, por favor.

7. Salimos del aeropuerto. Andando a una velocidad espantosa por una gran avenida, pensé — López está muy equivocado en cuanto a la vida tranquila mexicana.

8. Por la ventanilla del libre ví correr por todas partes a la misma velocidad espantosa, camiones, autos, tranvías y ¿quién sabe qué más?

9. Traté de decir al chófer — ¡Por favor, más despacio! Pero olvidé por entero el español.

10. — Yo no tengo prisa — grité al fin al chófer.

11. — Ni yo tampoco, señor — me contestó, doblando la calle a toda velocidad.

12. Pues, al fin llegamos sanos y salvos al hotel. El automóvil paró y bajamos. El Sr. Carrillo y yo entramos en el hotel. Le dije al dependiente — Buenas tardes. ¿Tiene Ud. un cuarto con baño?

Mexico, D.F. June 4, 1954

Dear (Esteemed) Friend:

1. After the airplane arrived at the airport of Mexico and they examined my luggage in the customs house, I went to the waiting room.

2. Suddenly a fine-looking gentleman approached me and asked "Excuse me, are you Mr. Adams?"

3. "At your service," I answered. "And you are Mr. Carrillo, are you not? I am very pleased to meet you." (They shake hands.)

4. "The pleasure is mine," answered Mr. Carrillo.

5. You will remember, Mr. Lopez, that Mr. Carrillo is the agent of our firm in New York and that he promised to meet me at the airport.

6. When we went outside together Mr. Carrillo called a "libre" (a Mexican taxi). He said to the driver, "To the Hotel Luma, please."

7. We left the airport. Traveling with frightful speed along the great avenue, I thought "Lopez is very mistaken as regards the quiet life of Mexico!"

8. Through the window of the taxi I saw on all sides, dashing at the same frightening speed, buses, automobiles, streetcars and who knows what else?

9. I tried to say to the driver, "Please, more slowly." But I forgot my Spanish completely.

10. "I am not in a hurry," at last I shouted to the driver.

11. "Neither am I, sir," he answered me, turning a corner at full speed.

12. Well, at last we arrived safe and sound at the hotel. The automobile stopped and we got out. Mr. Carrillo and I entered the hotel. I said to the clerk "Good day. Have you a room with bath?"

13. Tenemos un cuarto en el segundo piso. Da a la plaza. Es el número 25.

14. ¿Cuánto es?

15. Treinta pesos al día, señor.

16. Muy bien. Voy a quedar aquí varias semanas. Favor de mandar a un muchacho para buscar las maletas.

17. Ahorita, señor. Ud. habla español muy bien. ¿Hace mucho tiempo que Ud. está aquí en México?

18. — Acabo de llegar, — contesté yo, un tanto orgulloso.

19. — ¿Ud. está aquí de turista? — preguntó el dependiente.

20. Estoy aquí en viaje de recreo y de negocios.

21. El Sr. Carrillo y yo platicamos un rato más y después nos despedimos. El señor Carrillo prometió llamarme por teléfono para hacer una cita.

22. Subí en el ascensor al cuarto número 25. Es muy cómodo. No me falta nada. Vuelvo a decirle, señor López, que voy a estar muy contento en México.

13. We have a room on the second floor. It opens onto the plaza. It is number 25.

14. How much is it?

15. Thirty pesos a day, sir.

16. Very well. I am going to remain here several weeks. Please send a bellboy to get my bags.

17. Right away, sir. You speak Spanish very well. You have been in Mexico a long time?

18. "I have just arrived," I answered, somewhat proud.

19. "You are here as a tourist?" asked the clerk.

20. I am here on a pleasure and business trip.

21. Mr. Carrillo and I chatted a while longer and then we said good-bye. Mr. Carrillo promised to telephone me to make an appointment.

22. I went up in the elevator to room number 25. It is very comfortable. I lack nothing. I tell you again, Mr. Lopez, that I am going to be very happy in Mexico.

Le saluda cordialmente su amigo

Juan Adams

Cordial greetings from your friend

John Adams

NOTE: libre really means *free*. It is the name given to Mexican taxis because they show the sign "Libre" when unoccupied.

Pronunciation and Spelling Aids

1. Practice:

chó-fer   es-pan-to-sa   co-rrien-do   ve-lo-ci-dad   or-gu-llo-so

2. Be sure to stress these verbs on the last syllable.

sa-lió	re-spon-dió	pro-me-tió	ba-jé	con-tes-té	gri-té
con-te-stó	se a-cer-có	en-tré	pre-gun-té	ol-vi-dé	

Building Vocabulary

A. Words Indicating Past Time

1. ayer	yesterday	4. el año (mes) pasado	last year (month)
2. anteayer	day before yesterday	5. la semana pasada	last week
3. anoche	last night	6. el verano pasado	last summer

Expresiones Importantes

A.
1. acercarse a   to approach   Se acercó a mí   He approached me
2. doblando la calle   making a turn
3. de repente   suddenly
4. tratar de   to try to
5. pienso visitar   I intend to visit
6. por entero   completely
7. revisar el equipaje   to examine the luggage
8. sano y salvo   safe and sound (*Lit*. sound and safe)
9. se dan la mano   they shake hands (*Lit*. give the hand to each other)

B. Presentaciones (Introductions)

1. Sr. Carrillo: **Quiero presentarle a Ud. un amigo mío.**
2. Sr. Sánchez: **Pedro Sánchez, a sus ordenes. Tengo mucho gusto en conocerle a Ud.**
3. Sr. Adams: **Juan Adams, servidor de Ud. El gusto es mío. (Se dan la mano)**

1. Mr. Carrillo: I want to present to you a friend of mine.
2. Mr. Sanchez: Peter Sanchez, at your service. I'm very glad to meet you.
3. Mr. Adams: John Adams, your servant. The pleasure is mine. (They shake hands)

Notice that the introducer lets the persons introduced say their own names.

Exercise No. 127—Completion of Text

1. **Fuí a** (the waiting room)
2. (Suddenly) **un señor se acercó a mí.**
3. (Excuse me), **¿es Ud. el Sr. Adams?**
4. **Yo contesté,** — (I am pleased to meet you).
5. — (The pleasure is mine), — **respondió el Sr. Carrillo.**
6. **El Sr. Carrillo llamó** (a taxi).
7. **Pensé** — (Lopez is very mistaken).
8. (Who knows what else?)
9. — (I am not in a hurry!) — **grité al chófer.**
10. — (Neither am I), **señor — me contestó.**
11. **Tenemos un cuarto que** (faces the plaza).
12. **¿Cuánto es?** (Thirty pesos a day).

PARTE SEGUNDA

Grammar Notes

1. The Preterite Tense. Model Verbs—**hablar, aprender, vivir**

The preterite tense is used in Spanish to tell of things that happened at a definite time in the past.

hablar, to speak I spoke (did speak), etc.	aprender, to learn I learned (did learn), etc.	vivir, to live I lived (did live), etc.
Singular	Singular	Singular
habl-é	aprend-í	viv-í
habl-aste	aprend-iste	viv-iste
habl-ó	aprend-ió	viv-ió
Plural	Plural	Plural
habl-amos	aprend-imos	viv-imos
habl-asteis	aprend-isteis	viv-isteis
habl-aron	aprend-ieron	viv-ieron

a. To form the regular preterite tense of **-ar** verbs

1. Drop **-ar** from the infinitive
2. Add to the remaining stem the endings:

Singular: **-é, -aste, -ó**　　Plural **-amos, -asteis, -aron**

b. To form the regular preterite tense of **-er** and **-ir** verbs

1. Drop **-er** or **-ir** from the infinitive.
2. Add to the remaining stem the endings:

Singular: **-í, -iste, -ió**　Plural **-imos, -isteis, -ieron**

The preterite endings of **-er** and **-ir** verbs are exactly the same.

c. **-ar** and **-ir** verbs have **-amos** and **-imos** respectively in the **nosotros** (we) form of both the present and preterite.

The sense of the sentence will tell you which is meant.

Hoy hablamos.	Today we speak.	Hoy vivimos.	Today we live.
Ayer hablamos	Yesterday we spoke.	Ayer vivimos.	Yesterday we lived.

d. **dije,** I said and **dijo,** he said are irregular preterites. You will learn more about these and other irregular preterites later.

2. Preterite of **leer, creer, caer, oír**

I read (did read), etc.	I believed, etc.	I fell, etc.	I heard, etc.
leí	creí	caí	oí
leíste	creíste	caíste	oíste
leyó	creyó	cayó	oyó
leímos	creímos	caímos	oímos
leísteis	creísteis	caísteis	oísteis
leyeron	creyeron	cayeron	oyeron

Note carefully the forms:

leyó, leyeron   creyó, creyeron   cayó, cayeron   oyó, oyeron

Ejercicios (Exercises) No. 128A-128B-128C-128D

128A. Conjugate the following verbs in the preterite tense:

1. entrar   2. comer   3. salir   4. ver   5. sentarse.

128B. Translate:

1. ¿Quién olvidó los boletos?
2. Ayer recibimos las cartas.
3. El hombre compró un vestido nuevo.
4. Anoche no oímos el timbre.
5. ¿Llegó a tiempo el tren?
6. Buscaron el equipaje.
7. El niño cayó delante de la casa.
8. Salieron del aeropuerto en un libre.
9. ¿Dónde esperó el Sr. Adams a su amigo?
10. ¿Cuánto costó el impermeable?

128C. Answer in the negative in complete Spanish sentences. Use the preterite.

Remember: A question with **Ud.** requires an answer in the singular (yo). A question with **Uds.** requires an answer in the plural (nosotros)

Ejemplo: ¿Trabajó Ud. anoche?   Did you work last night?
(Yo) No trabajé anoche.   I did not work last night.

1. ¿Compró Ud. ayer un sombrero nuevo?
2. ¿Volvieron Uds. tarde del teatro anoche?
3. ¿Escribió Ud. unas cartas esta mañana?
4. ¿Llegaron Uds. a las ocho en punto?
5. ¿Salió Ud. a las nueve de la noche?
6. ¿Pasó Ud. el verano pasado en el campo?
7. ¿Oyeron Uds. el timbre?
8. ¿Vendió Ud. su casa?
9. ¿Dejaron Uds. el dinero en casa?
10. ¿Trabajaron Uds. toda la noche?

128D. Translate into Spanish, using the verbs indicated in the preterite tense.

1. (salir) I left
2. (llegar) we arrived
3. (examinar) they examined
4. (oír) he heard
5. (responder) you (Ud.) answered
6. (preguntar) I did not ask
7. (llamar) she called
8. (desear) you (Uds.) wanted
9. (salir) we got out
10. (parar) it stopped
11. (olvidar) I did not forget
12. (gritar) he shouted
13. (creer) they believed
14. (vender) we sold
15. (volver) did you (Uds.) return?
16. (leer) did he read?

Exercise No. 129—Preguntas

1. ¿Quiénes revisaron el equipaje?
2. ¿Quién se acercó al Sr. Adams en la sala de espera?
3. ¿Qué dijo el señor?
4. ¿Qué contestó el Sr. Adams?
5. ¿Cómo pasó el libre por una gran avenida?
6. ¿Qué deseó decir el Sr. Adams al chofer?
7. ¿Qué olvidó?
8. ¿Qué vió el Sr. Adams por la ventanilla?
9. ¿Qué gritó al chófer?
10. ¿Qué le contestó el chófer?
11. ¿Cómo llegaron al fin al hotel?
12. ¿Qué dijo el Sr. Adams al dependiente?

CAPÍTULO 32 (TREINTA Y DOS)

PARTE PRIMERA

Una Visita A La Familia Carrillo

Segunda Carta De México

Estimado amigo:

1. El lunes pasado el Sr. Carrillo me llamó por teléfono. Quiso invitarme a tomar la merienda en su casa el día siguiente. Así es que tuve la oportunidad de visitar a una familia mexicana.

2. A las cinco de la tarde llegué a una casa grande de piedra roja en la Colonia Roma. Me acerqué a la puerta enorme de roble pesado.

3. Toqué el timbre e inmediatamente oí pasos rápidos en el zaguán. Una criada me abrió la puerta y me invitó a entrar en la casa.

4. El Sr. Carrillo vino a saludarme. — Ud. está en su casa, — me dijo, según la costumbre mexicana.

5. Le dí las gracias. — Su casa tiene un aspecto verdaderamente romántico. Me parece una casa de un cuento antiguo.

6. — Hay muchas casas semejantes en México, — me respondió. — Esta casa fué construída en el siglo diez y siete.

7. Miré las paredes gruesas, los balcones y las ventanas altas con sus rejas de hierro. Me encantó el patio lleno de árboles y flores. Gran parte del suelo estaba[1] cubierto de azulejos. Admiré la fuente de piedra en el centro del patio.

8. Entramos en una sala grande, uno de los muchos cuartos que dan al patio. El Sr. Carrillo me presentó a su esposa y a sus dos hijos, jóvenes muy serios e inteligentes.

9. Los muchachos me dijeron que asisten a una escuela secundaria. El mayor quiere hacerse médico. El menor quiere ser abogado.

10. Dentro de poco tuvieron que volver a su cuarto para estudiar.

11. La señora de Carrillo me sirvió una taza de chocolate y algunas tortas muy sabrosas. Entretanto el señor Carrillo y yo platicamos de la vida en México, de las costumbres y del arte.

12. Me dijo que vale la pena de ir al mercado de Toluca tanto para ver un mercado típico como para buscar ejemplares del arte popular. Me dijo que el viernes es el mejor día para visitarlo.

13. Le repondí que tenía[1] la intención de ir allá dentro de unos pocos días.

Dear Friend:

1. Last Monday Mr. Carrillo called me on the telephone. He wanted to invite me to take "tea" at his house the following day. So it is that I had the opportunity to visit a Mexican family.

2. At five o'clock in the afternoon I arrived at a big house of red stone in the Roma district. I approached the enormous door of heavy oak.

3. I rang the bell and immediately I heard rapid steps in the vestibule. A servant opened the door and asked me to enter the house.

4. Mr. Carrillo came to greet me. "My house is yours," he said to me, according to the Mexican custom.

5. I thanked him. Your house has a truly romantic appearance. It seems to me a house out of an old story.

6. There are many similar houses in Mexico, he answered me. This house was built in the 17th century.

7. I looked at the thick walls, the balconies and tall windows with their iron gratings. The courtyard full of trees and flowers enchanted me. Most of the ground was covered with tile. I admired the stone fountain in the center of the courtyard.

8. We entered a big living room, one of the many rooms that open onto the courtyard. Mr. Carrillo introduced me to his wife and to his two sons, very serious and intelligent young men.

9. The boys told me that they go to a secondary school. The elder wants to become a doctor. The younger wants to be a lawyer.

10. Within a short time they had to go back to their rooms to study.

11. Mrs. Carrillo served me a cup of chocolate and some very delicious cakes. Meanwhile Mr. Carrillo and I chatted about life in Mexico, about its customs and art.

12. He told me that it is worth the trouble to go to the Toluca market as much to see a typical market as to look for samples of folk art. He told me that Friday is the best day to visit it.

13. I answered that I intended to go there within a few days.

14. Sintió no poder acompañarme.

14. He regretted not to be able to accompany me.

15. Después de una hora y media muy interesante y divertida nos despedimos y volví a casa, es decir, a mi hotel.

15. After a very interesting and pleasant hour and a half we took leave of one another and I returned home, that is to say, to my hotel.

Su sincero amigo

Juan Adams

Your sincere friend

John Adams

NOTE: 1. Imperfect tense. You will learn this tense later.

Pronunciation and Spelling Aids

1. Practice:

lle-gué	sin-tió	hie-rro	se-cun-da-rio
a-cer-qué	re-pi-tió	se-me-jan-te	ver-da-de-ra-men-te
sir-vió	ro-mán-ti-co	in-me-dia-ta-men-te	

2. el joven, los jóvenes. The plural must add an accent mark to hold the stress on the syllable **jo-**.

Building Vocabulary

A.

1.	casa de piedra	stone house	4.	falda de algodón	cotton skirt
2.	reja de hierro	iron grating	5.	guantes de lana	woolen gloves
3.	silla de madera	wooden chair	6.	vestido de seda	silk dress

NOTE: In Spanish, what things are made of, is indicated by **de** plus the material, not by using the material as an adjective. Thus **casa de piedra** (house of stone).

B. la merienda, a light afternoon meal, "tea." The Mexicans eat **la cena**, supper, rather late in the evening, about 8 or 9 o'clock or later.

Expresiones Importantes

1. **al día siguiente**   on the following day
2. **es decir**   that is to say
3. **hacerse**   to become   (*Lit.* to make oneself)
   Se hace médico (abogado, ingeniero).   He becomes a doctor (lawyer, engineer).
4. **llamar por teléfono**   to telephone   **Llamé por teléfono.**   I telephoned.
5. **Tener la intención de**   to intend to   **Tengo la intención de salir.**   I intend to leave.

Exercise No. 130—Completion of Text

1. El Sr. Carrillo (telephoned me).
2. Quiso invitarme (to have "tea") en su casa.
3. (The following day) llegué a su casa.
4. (I approached) a la puerta.
5. Una criada (invited me to enter) en la casa.
6. El Sr. Carrillo (came to greet me).
7. — (You are in your house) — me dijo.
8. Me saludó (according to the Mexican custom).
9. (It looks to me like) una casa de un cuento antiguo.
10. Hay (many similar houses) en México.
11. (I admired) la fuente de piedra.
12. (He presented me) a la señora de Carrillo.
13. El hijo mayor quiere (to become a doctor).
14. (He was sorry) no poder acompañarme.
15. (We took leave) y volví (home).

PARTE SEGUNDA

Grammar Notes

1. The Irregular Preterite with -i Stems.

hacer to do (make)	querer to wish	venir to come	decir to say
I did (made), etc.	I wished, etc.	I came, etc.	I said, etc.
hic-e	quis-e	vin-e	dij-e
hic-iste	quis-iste	vin-iste	dij-iste
hiz-o	quis-o	vin-o	dij-o
hic-imos	quis-imos	vin-imos	dij-imos
hic-isteis	quis-isteis	vin-isteis	dij-isteis
hic-ieron	quis-ieron	vin-ieron	dij-eron

a. Irregular verbs of this group have an -i in the preterite stem.

b. The ending of the (yo) form is unaccented -e instead of -i; the ending of the (Ud., él, ella) form is unaccented -o instead of -ió.

c. In the form hizo, z replaces c.

d. You know that the (yo) form of the present tense of these verbs ends in unaccented -o.

hago, I do   quiero, I wish   vengo, I come   digo, I say

The change of stem prevents the present forms from being confused with the preterite forms:

hizo, you, he, she did   quiso, you, he, she wished   vino, you, he, she came   dijo, you, he, she said

2. The Preterite of Stem-Changing Verbs like pedir (i).

pedir (i), to ask for	servir (i), to serve	repetir (i), to repeat	vestir (i), to dress
I asked for, etc.	I served, etc.	I repeated, etc.	I dressed, etc.
pedí	serví	repetí	vestí
pediste	serviste	repetiste	vestiste
pidió	sirvió	repitió	vistió
pedimos	servimos	repetimos	vestimos
pedisteis	servisteis	repetisteis	vestisteis
pidieron	sirvieron	repitieron	vistieron

a. The preterite of verbs like pedir (i) is formed almost exactly like the regular preterite of -ir verbs. The only differences are in the stem of the (Ud., él, ella) form (pidió) and in the (Uds., ellos, ellas) form (pidieron) where -i- replaces -e- in the stem.

b. Note the same difference in the preterite of sentir to regret.

sentí   sentiste   *sintió*   sentimos   sentisteis   *sintieron*

Ejercicios (Exercises) No. 131A-131B-131C

131A. Translate:

1. La criada nos sirvió la merienda.
2. ¿Por qué no quiso Ud. invitarme?
3. Anoche volvimos tarde del teatro.
4. Quise llamarle a Ud. por teléfono.
5. ¿Qué hizo Ud. después de la comida?
6. Dijeron—No tenemos prisa.
7. Repetí todas las respuestas.
8. Mi amigo no vino a tiempo. Lo sentí.
9. Pidieron informes en la oficina de información.
10. Quisieron comprar boletos de viaje redondo.

131B. Answer in complete sentences the following questions using the suggested words in the answer.

Ejemplo: ¿Qué quiso Ud. comprar? (guantes de lana)
Quise comprar guantes de lana.

1. ¿Qué dijo Ud. al señor? (Pase Ud.)
2. ¿Quién hizo un viaje al Perú. (mi hermano)
3. ¿Cuándo vino Ud. a casa? (a las siete)
4. ¿De qué vistieron las mujeres? (de falda de algodón)
5. ¿Qué quiso hacerse el mayor? (médico)
6. ¿Qué sirvió la criada? (una taza de chocolate)
7. ¿Qué pidió el viajero? (informes)
8. ¿Qué quisieron Uds. ver? (la película nueva)
9. ¿Cuándo hicieron Uds. un viaje a México? (el año pasado)
10. ¿Qué dijeron Uds. cuando salieron de la casa? (hasta la vista)

131C. Translate. Use the correct forms of querer, decir, hacer, servir(i) repetir(i), sentir(ie)

1. I wished
2. I did not say
3. he made
4. they came
5. she served
6. they wished
7. I repeated
8. we made
9. they said
10. they made
11. What did he say?
12. What did you (Uds.) say?
13. we did not wish
14. I did not come
15. they regretted

Exercise No. 132—Preguntas

1. ¿Quién llamó al Sr. Adams por teléfono?
2. ¿A qué hora llegó a la casa del señor Carrillo?
3. ¿Quién le abrió al Sr. Adams la puerta?
4. ¿Quién vino a saludar al Sr. Adams?
5. ¿Qué encantó al Sr. Adams?
6. ¿Qué admiró él?
7. ¿Quiénes son serios e inteligentes?
8. ¿A qué clase de escuela asisten los jóvenes?
9. ¿Qué quiere hacerse el mayor?
10. ¿A dónde tuvieron que volver los jóvenes?
11. ¿De qué platicaron entretanto los señores?
12. ¿Vale la pena de ir al mercado de Toluca?
13. ¿Quién quiso ir allá?
14. ¿Después de una hora quiénes se despidieron?
15. ¿A dónde volvió el Sr. Adams?

CAPÍTULO 33 (TREINTA Y TRES)

PARTE PRIMERA

El Paseo De La Reforma

Tercera Carta De México

Estimado amigo:

1. ¡Qué hermoso es el Paseo de la Reforma! Los árboles son tan grandes, los edificios tan imponentes—algunos de estilo español, algunos de estilo moderno, otros que combinan los dos estilos. La avenida es tan ancha, tan espaciosa que parece un río enorme recibiendo las aguas de muchos tributarios.

2. Naturalmente, tuve que pensar en nuestra conversación sobre las calles de México. Recordé que al norte del Paseo se puede cruzar algunos de los grandes "ríos" del mundo. Al sur del Paseo, como Ud. me dijo, se puede caminar por algunas de las "ciudades" más grandes de Europa.

Dear Friend:

1. How beautiful the Paseo de la Reforma is! The trees are so big, the buildings so impressive —some in Spanish style, some in modern style, others that unite the two styles. The avenue is so wide, so spacious that it seems like an enormous river receiving the waters of many tributaries.

2. Naturally, I had to think of our conversation about the streets of Mexico. I remembered that north of the Paseo one can cross some of the great "rivers" of the world. South of the Paseo, as you told me, one can walk along some of the largest "cities" of Europe.

3. Ayer, pude ver esto por mí mismo. Fué domingo. El Sr. Carrillo y yo nos encontramos cerca del "Caballito."

4. Le pregunté ¿Qué es este "Caballito"? Mi profesor de español, Eugenio López, me dijo que las terminaciones -ito, -cito, e -illo quieren decir— algo pequeño. También se usan estas terminaciones para expresar cariño. Pero, — seguí yo — no veo más que una estatua enorme.

5. El Sr. Carrillo me respondió que precisamente por eso se llama el "Caballito." ¡Es un ejemplo del humor mexicano! Esta estatua, que representa al rey Carlos IV (cuarto) de España montado en su caballo "chico," domina el Paseo.

6. A lo largo del Paseo de la Reforma, que se extiende desde el "Caballito" hasta el Parque de Chapultepec, vimos otros monumentos históricos. Ud. los conoce bien—el monumento de la Independencia, la estatua de Cristóbal Colón y el monumento a Cuauhtémoc.

7. He leído algo sobre este héroe de los aztecas, Cuauhtémoc, que tan valerosamente defendió a su nacion contra los españoles.

8. Cuando ví todos aquellos monumentos comprendí el orgullo de los mexicanos en el pasado de la nación.

9. No lejos del Parque de Chapultepec, el Sr. Carrillo me señaló un edificio casi enteramente de cristal, muy moderno en todos sus detalles. — Es el edificio del Seguro Social, — me dijo. — Aquí tiene Ud. la arquitectura del futuro, ¿verdad?

10. De veras, pude comprender el orgullo de los mexicanos, no sólamente en su pasado, sino también en su porvenir.

Reciba un abrazo de su amigo

Juan Adams

3. Yesterday I could see this for myself. It was Sunday. Mr. Carrillo and I met near the "Caballito."

4. I asked him: "What is this 'Caballito'? My Spanish professor, Eugene Lopez, told me the endings -ito, -cito, and -illo mean something small. These endings are also used to express affection. But, I continued, I only see an enormous statue.

5. Mr. Carrillo replied to me that just for that reason it is called the "Caballito." It is an example of Mexican humor. This statue (which represents King Charles IV) (Fourth) of Spain mounted on his "tiny" horse dominates the Paseo.

6. Along the Paseo de la Reforma, which stretches from the "Caballito" to Chapultepec Park, we saw other historical monuments. You know them well—the monument of Independence, the statue of Christopher Columbus and the monument to Cuauhtemoc.

7. I have read something about this hero of the Aztecs, Cuauhtemoc, who so bravely defended his nation against the Spaniards.

8. When I saw all those monuments I understood the pride of the Mexicans in the nation's past.

9. Not far from Chapultepec Park Mr. Carrillo pointed out to me a building almost entirely of glass, very modern in all its details. "It is the Social Security Building," he told me. "Here is the architecture of the future, isn't it?"

10. Indeed I could understand the pride of the Mexicans not only in their past but also in their future.

Receive an embrace from your friend

John Adams

Pronunciation and Spelling Aids

1. Practice:

im-po-nen-te	es-ta-tua	tri-bu-ta-rio	en-ter-a-men-te	Co-lón
es-pa-cio-so	mo-nu-men-to	pre-ci-sa-men-te	Cuauh-te-moc	Cha-pul-te-pec
ca-ba-lli-to	ter-mi-na-ción	va-le-ro-sa-men-te	Cris-tó-bal	

Building Vocabulary

A. Related Words

1. pasar, to pass
   el paso, the step, passage
   el pasillo, vestibule

   el pase, pass, permit
   pase de turista, tourist's pass

2. pasear or pasearse, to stroll
   el paseo, the walk, promenade

   el paseante, the stroller
   dar un paseo, to take a walk

3. **parecer, to seem, to appear**
   parecerse a, to resemble
   me parece bien. It seems all right to me.
   La avenida se parece a un río. The avenue resembles a river.

Exercise No. 133—Completion of Text

Complete these sentences based in the text.

1. ¡(How beautiful) **es el Paseo de la Reforma!**
2. **La avenida es** (wide and spacious).
3. (It seems like) **un río enorme.**
4. **Al norte** (one may cross) **algunos de los ríos más grandes** (in the world).
5. **Al sur** (one may walk) **por algunas** (of the largest cities).
6. (Yesterday) **fué domingo.**
7. **Juan y yo** (met) **cerca del "Caballito."**
8. **Las terminaciones -ito, -cito y -illo** (mean something small).
9. (I see only) **una estatua enorme.**
10. **Este "Caballito" representa** (King Charles IV of Spain).
11. (You know well) **el monumento a Cuauhtemoc.**
12. (I have read something) **sobre este héroe.**
13. (I saw) **todos aquellos monumentos.**
14. **Aquel edificio es** (almost entirely of glass).
15. (I could understand) **el orgullo de los mexicanos.**

PARTE SEGUNDA

Grammar Notes

1. Irregular Preterites with **u** Stems.

In the last chapter you learned the irregular preterite of some familiar verbs. Here are more familiar verbs with an irregular preterite.

poder, to be able I was able, etc.	poner, to put I put (did put) etc.	tener, to have I had, etc.	estar, to be I was, etc.	saber, to know I knew, etc.
pud-e	pus-e	tuv-e	estuv-e	sup-e
pud-iste	pus-iste	tuv-iste	estuv-iste	sup-iste
pud-o	pus-o	tuv-o	estuv-o	sup-o
pud-imos	pus-imos	tuv-imos	estuv-imos	sup-imos
pud-isteis	pus-isteis	tuv-isteis	estuv-isteis	sup-isteis
pud-ieron	pus-ieron	tuv-ieron	estuv-ieron	sup-ieron

a. Irregular verbs of this group have a **-u** in the preterite stem.
b. The endings are the same as the irregular preterites (of **hacer,** etc.) you have already learned.
c. **saber** to know, in the preterite usually means *learned, found out.*
   Supe el nombre del médico. I learned the name of the doctor.

2. More Irregular Preterites

dar, to give I gave, etc.	ser, to be I was, etc.	ir, to go I went, etc.
dí	fuí	fuí
diste	fuiste	fuiste
dió	fué	fué
dimos	fuimos	fuimos
disteis	fuisteis	fuisteis
dieron	fueron	fueron

The verbs ser and ir have exactly the same forms in the preterite tense. The sense of the sentence will always tell you which verb is meant. Thus:

Isabel fué reina de España.   Isabel was queen of Spain.
Cristóbal Colón fué a la reina.   Christopher Columbus went to the queen.

3. The personal **a** is often used before the names of the more intelligent animals, as well as before persons and proper names (cities, states, etc.).

La estatua representa al rey y a su caballo.

Ejercicios (Exercises) No. 134A-134B-134C

134A. Translate:

1. En Navidad dí regalos a todos los niños.
2. No tuve oportunidad de conocerle. a Ud. personalmente.
3. No pudimos pagar toda la cuenta.
4. Esta casa fué construída en el siglo diez y seis.
5. El domingo dimos un paseo en el Parque de Chapultepec.

6. Pude conversar con él en su bello idioma.
7. El no tuvo dificultad en entenderme.
8. Ella no quiso descansar mucho.
9. La familia del Sr. Adams no pudo acompañarle.
10. Me puse el sombrero nuevo en la cabeza.

134B. Change these sentences from the present to the preterite. Be sure to keep the same person.

Ejemplo: Pongo la mesa. Puse la mesa.

1. Tengo que estudiar la lección.
2. El Sr. Adams está en el comedor.
3. Los árboles se ponen verdes.
4. El da las gracias al Sr. Carrillo.
5. Soy un estudiante atento.

6. Vamos al mercado.
7. Vienen del cine a las once.
8. No digo nada.
9. Uds. no hacen nada.
10. ¿Quieren Uds. comprarlo?

134C. Translate, using the preterite of the given verbs.

1. (tener), I had
2. (poder), you (Ud.) were able
3. (ir), they went
4. (decir), she said
5. (poner), he put

6. (querer), we wished
7. (dar), they gave
8. (ser), I was
9. (estar), you (Uds.) were
10. (encontrarse), we met

Exercise No. 135—Preguntas

1. ¿Cómo está titulada esta lectura?
2. ¿Es ancho o estrecho el Paseo de la Reforma?
3. ¿En qué conversación tuvo que pensar el Sr. Adams?
4. ¿Qué se puede cruzar al norte?
5. ¿Por dónde se puede caminar al sur?
6. ¿Qué día de la semana fué ayer?
7. ¿Dónde se encontraron el Sr. Adams y el Sr. Carrillo?

8. ¿Qué quieren decir las terminaciones -ito, -cito, e -illo?
9. ¿A quién representa el "Caballito"?
10. ¿Es grande o pequeño este "Caballito"?
11. ¿Qué conoce bien el Sr. López?
12. ¿Quién leyó algo sobre Cuauhtemoc?
13. ¿Contra quiénes defendió a su nación?
14. ¿Qué edificio en el Paseo es casi enteramente de cristal?
15. ¿Dónde está este edificio?

CAPÍTULO 34 (TREINTA Y CUATRO)

PARTE PRIMERA

El Mercado De Toluca

Cuarta Carta De México

Querido amigo:

1. La semana pasada fuí al mercado de Toluca.

2. La ciudad de Toluca está situada acerca de cuarenta millas de Mexico D.F.

Dear Friend:

1. Last week I went to the Toluca market.

2. The city of Toluca is located about forty miles from Mexico City.

3. Mientras que nuestro camión pasaba por las montañas ví mujeres que lavaban ropa en los ríos y hombres que cortaban caña para hacer cestas.

4. Era viernes y el mercado estaba lleno de gente. Probablemente la mayor parte de ellos vino del campo pero había también mucha gente de la ciudad y de otras partes del mundo.

5. Se puede fácilmente perderse uno en este mercado tan grande. Pero yo no tenía dificultad porque sabía pedir informes en español.

6. Mientras que caminaba por una calle de puestos donde se vendían ropa, zapatos y sombreros, ví a un muchacho de siete u ocho años, de aspecto muy serio, cuidando un puesto.

7. Se parecía mucho a un viejecito con su sombrero de ala ancha y sus pantalones muy grandes. Como los demás vendedores arreglaba su mercancía con sumo cuidado. También ví que regateaba en serio.

8. En el mercado se vendían todas clases de mercancía—frutas, flores, cerámica, cestas, ropa, sarapes. Había cosas corrientes y artículos de lujo.

9. Por todas partes veía el sentido estético de muchos de los vendedores. Especialmente entre los puestos de comidas encontré color y arte.

10. Por ejemplo, una mujer estaba sentada en la acera. Delante de ella había unas pocas cebollas y chiles. Con sumo cuidado los arreglaba en montones pequeños.

11. Junto a ella ví un puesto de frutas con algunas hojas verdes cerca de los mangos anaranjados y los plátanos amarillos.

12. Cerca de esos puestos escuché la plática de las mujeres y pude aprender algo sobre la vida del campo.

13. Supe que los campesinos vienen al mercado no solamente para vender y comprar sino también para divertirse, para charlar y para visitar a sus amigos.

14. La gente gritaba, charlaba, compraba, vendía, reía, todos con animación y humor.

15. De veras pasé un día muy interesante y muy divertido en el mercado de Toluca.

16. Y mientras iba a casa, es decir, a la capital, recordaba nuestras conversaciones en que hablábamos de los mercados de México y de tantas otras cosas.

Afectuosamente
Juan Adams

3. While our bus passed through the mountains, I saw women who were washing clothes in the rivers and men who were cutting cane to make baskets.

4. It was Friday and the market was full of people. Probably the majority of them came from the country but there were also many people from the town and from other parts of the world.

5. One can easily lose his way in this very big market. But I did not have difficulty because I knew how to ask for information in Spanish.

6. While I was walking through a street of stalls where clothing, shoes and hats were being sold, I saw a boy of seven or eight years with a very serious appearance watching a stall.

7. He looked very much like a little old man with his broad-brimmed hat and his very large trousers. Like the rest of the sellers he was arranging his merchandise with extreme care. Also I saw he was bargaining seriously.

8. All kinds of merchandise were being sold in the market—fruit, flowers, ceramics, baskets, clothing, blankets. There were ordinary things and luxury articles.

9. Everywhere I saw the aesthetic feeling of many of the sellers. Especially among the food stalls I found color and art.

10. For example, a woman was seated on the sidewalk. Before her there were a few onions and chiles. With extreme care, she was arranging them in little piles.

11. Near her I saw a fruit stall with some green leaves near the orange-colored mangos and the yellow bananas.

12. Near those stalls I listened to the chatting of the women and I could learn something about life in the country.

13. I learned that the peasants come to the market not only to sell and to buy but also to enjoy themselves, to chat, and to visit their friends.

14. The people were shouting, chatting, buying, selling, laughing, all with liveliness and humor.

15. Indeed I spent a very interesting and very enjoyable day in the Toluca market.

16. And while I was going home, that is to say to the capital, I kept remembering our conversations in which we used to speak of the markets of Mexico and of so many other things.

Affectionately
John Adams

Pronunciation and Spelling Aids

1. Practice:

es-té-ti-ca	la-va-ba	a-rre-gla-ba	char-la-ba	é-ra-mos	re-í-a
plá-ti-ca	cor-ta-ba	re-ga-te-a-ba	com-pra-ba	í-ba-mos	ven-dí-a
fa-cil-men-te	es-ta-ba	es-cu-cha-ba	ha-blá-ba-mos	ha-bí-a	
pro-ba-ble-men-te	ca-mi-na-ba	gri-ta-ba	com-prá-ba-mos	te-ní-a	

Building Vocabulary

A. Palabras Relacionadas

1. el animo, animation
   animado, animated, lively
2. campo, country, field
   campesino, farmer, peasant
3. difícil, difficult
   la dificultad, difficulty

4. divertirse, to enjoy oneself
   divertido, enjoyable
5. naranja, orange
   anaranjado, orange-colored
6. platicar, to chat
   la plática, chatting, conversation

B. La gente, people, requires a singular verb in Spanish.

La gente del campo estaba allí.   The country people were there.

Exercise No. 136—Completion of Text

1. (Last week) **fuí al mercado.**
2. (I saw) **mujeres** (who) **lavaban ropa.**
3. **El mercado estaba** (full of people).
4. **Vinieron** (from the country).
5. **Se puede facilmente** (lose one's way).
6. **Yo caminaba** (through a street of stalls).
7. (I saw) **a un muchacho** (of seven or eight years).
8. (Like the other sellers) **arreglaba su mercancía.**
9. **Se vendían en el mercado** (flowers, baskets and clothing).
10. (Among the stands) **encontré color y arte.**
11. **Los campesinos vienen** (to enjoy themselves.)
12. **Yo escuché** (the chatting of the women).
13. **Aprendí un poco** (about country life).
14. (I remembered) **nuestras conversaciones.**
15. **Pasé** (a very pleasant day).

PARTE SEGUNDA

Grammar Notes

1. The Imperfect Tense.

You have learned two tenses which indicate past time, the present perfect and the preterite. Of the two the preterite is more commonly used.

You will now learn a third tense that refers also to past time—the imperfect. We may call the imperfect the "*was, were or used to*" tense because it indicates actions that *were* happening or *used to* happen in past time. Thus:

a. *We were working,* when he entered.   b. *He used to do* his lessons in the evening.

In sentence a., *were working* is in the imperfect; *he entered,* which interrupts the working at a definite moment, is in the preterite.

2. The Imperfect of Model Verbs—hablar, aprender, vivir.

Singular	Singular	Singular
I was speaking, etc.	I was learning, etc.	I was living, etc.
habl-aba	**aprend-ía**	**viv-ía**
habl-abas	**aprend-ías**	**viv-ías**
habl-aba	**aprend-ía**	**viv-ía**
Plural	Plural	Plural
habl-ábamos	**aprend-íamos**	**viv-íamos**
habl-abais	**aprend-íais**	**viv-íais**
habl-aban	**aprend-ían**	**viv-ían**

a. To form the imperfect tense of all **-ar** verbs, *without* exception:

1. Drop **-ar** from the infinitive
2. Add the endings **-aba, -abas, -aba; -ábamos, -abais, -aban,** to the remaining stem.

b. To form the imperfect of all **-er** and **-ir** verbs with the exception of **ver, ser,** and **ir:**

1. Drop **-er** or **-ir** from the infinitive.
2. Add the endings **-ía, -ías, -ía; -íamos, -íais, -ían,** to the remaining stem.

c. The stress is on the first syllable (**a**) in all the **-aba** endings. To prevent it from shifting in the **-ábamos** ending the first **-a** must have an accent mark.

The stress in the **-ía** endings is always on the **i**.

d. The endings of the **yo** and the (**Ud. él ella**) forms of the verb are alike in the imperfect. The subject pronoun is used when the meaning is not clear.

3. The Imperfect of ver, ser, ir.

I was seeing, etc.		I was, etc.		I was going, etc.	
veía	veíamos	era	éramos	iba	íbamos
veías	veíais	eras	erais	ibas	ibais
veía	veían	era	eran	iba	iban

a. The endings of **veía** are regular. But the endings are added to **ve-** not to **v-**.

b. In all forms of **era** and **iba** the stress must be on the first syllable. To prevent it from shifting, an accent mark is added to the first syllable of **éramos** and **íbamos**.

Ejercicios (Exercises) No. 137A-137B-137C

137A. Translate.

1. Llovía a cántaros cuando nos despedimos de los jóvenes.
2. Yo pensaba en Ud. cuando me paseaba en coche por las calles cuyos nombres son fechas.
3. Los turistas y los vendedores regateaban y todos parecían divertirse mucho.
4. Me acercaba a la puerta cuando encontré a los hijos del Sr. Carrillo.
5. Mientras hablábamos sobre las artes populares, la señora de Carrillo leía un periódico.
6. Hacía mucho calor cuando volvimos a los Estados Unidos.
7. Cuando el coche se ponía en marcha se acercó un policía (policeman).
8. Los aviones llegaban y salían a todas horas.
9. Estábamos cansados pero no queríamos descansar.
10. Ya eran las cuatro y media de la tarde y teníamos prisa.

137B. Each of these sentences indicates an action that was going on (*imperfect*) and another action which interrupted it at a definite time (*preterite*). Translate the verbs in parentheses, using the correct tense.

1. Mientras (I was eating), me llamó por teléfono.
2. Cuando (we were studying), entraron en nuestro cuarto.
3. Cuando (he was) enfermo, le visitamos.
4. Mientras (you were taking leave), empezó a llover.
5. Cuando (they were taking a walk), se perdieron.
6. Los vendedores (were shouting) cuando llegamos al mercado.
7. Cayó en la acera cuando (he was getting out) del auto.
8. No nos oyeron cuando (we were speaking).
9. Los encontramos cuando (they were going) al mercado.
10. Cuando (we were passing) por una avenida grande, grité—no tengo prisa.

137C. Translate the following verbs in the correct tense, preterite or imperfect, as necessary.

1. (caminar) I was walking
2. (ir) I was going
3. (decir) he said
4. (jugar) they were playing
5. (cantar) they sang
6. (ver) we were seeing
7. (correr) they were running
8. (perder) you (Ud.) lost
9. (vivir) they lived
10. (leer) she read
11. (empezar) it began
12. (llamar) they were calling
13. (entrar) you (Uds.) did not enter
14. (estar) were you (Ud.)? (imperfect)
15. (ser) we were (imperfect)
16. (oír) they heard

Exercise No. 138—Preguntas

1. ¿Por dónde pasaba el camión?
2. ¿Qué lavaban las mujeres?
3. ¿Qué cortaban los hombres?
4. ¿Qué día de la semana era?
5. ¿De dónde vino la mayor parte de la gente?
6. ¿Había[1] también gente de la ciudad?
7. ¿Por qué no tenía dificultad el Sr. Adams?
8. ¿A quién vió mientras que caminaba?
9. ¿A quién se parecía el muchacho?
10. ¿Qué clase de sombrero llevaba?
11. ¿Qué arreglaba el muchacho?
12. ¿Qué veía por todas partes el Sr. Adams?
13. ¿Quién estaba sentada en la acera?
14. ¿Qué había delante de ella?
15. ¿Cuándo recordaba el Sr. Adams sus conversaciones con el Sr. López?

NOTE: 1. The imperfect of hay (there is or there are) is había (there was or there were). The preterite is hubo (there was or there were).

CAPÍTULO 35 (TREINTA Y CINCO)

PARTE PRIMERA

Sobre El Descanso

Quinta Carta De México

Querido amigo:

Ud. recordará, amigo mío, sus últimos consejos antes de mi salida para México. Me dijo Ud. — No tenga prisa. Camine despacio. Descanse varias horas por la tarde. De veras no he olvidado sus consejos acerca del descanso, pero tengo que confesar—no descanso largo rato. Hay tanto que ver, tanto que oír, tanto que descubrir, tanto que hacer.

Ayer, por ejemplo, descansaba al mediodía en la Alameda. Siempre hay allí una brisa y cuando hay mucho sol es muy agradable debajo de los grandes árboles cerca de una fuente de agua fresca.

Pero no pude descansar largo rato. Al otro lado de la Avenida Juárez veía las muchas tiendas donde se venden objetos de arte, libros, artículos de cuero, de paja, de tela, de plata y de cristal. Muchas veces he visitado aquellas tiendas pero no pude resistir la tentación de volver a visitarlas.

Dear Friend:

You will remember, my friend, your final advice before my departure for Mexico. You told me "Don't be in a hurry. Walk slowly. Rest several hours in the afternoon." Indeed I have not forgotten your advice concerning resting, but I must confess—I don't rest very much. There is so much to see, so much to hear, so much to discover, so much to do.

Yesterday, for example, I was resting at noon in the Alameda. There is always a breeze there and when it's very sunny it is very pleasant under the big trees near a fountain of fresh water.

But I was not able to rest very long. On the other side of Juarez Avenue I saw the many shops where they sell art objects, books, things made of leather, straw, cloth, silver and glass. I have often visited those shops but I was not able to resist the temptation to visit them again.

También tuve que visitar otra vez el Museo de Artes e Industrias Populares. Nunca me canso de mirar las artes de los indios, ni de hacer preguntas a los dependientes en la tienda del Museo y al director.

Saliendo del Museo, que está al sur del parque en la Avenida Juárez, volví a visitar el Palacio de Bellas Artes, que está al este del parque. Todavía no he asistido a ningún concierto en el Palacio, pero me gusta mucho mirar los cuadros y las pinturas murales de los grandes artistas de México.

Pues, Sr. López, Ud. ve que voy aprendiendo más cada día, sobre todo porque soy muy hablador. Y sus consejos me han sido muy útiles, excepto (tengo que confesarlo otra vez) los que me dió Ud. sobre el descanso.

Reciba un apretón de manos de su amigo

Juan Adams

I also had to visit once again the Museum of Folk Arts & Industries. I never tire of observing the arts of the Indians, nor of asking questions of the sales people in the shop of the Museum and of the director.

Leaving the Museum, which is to the south of the park on Juarez Avenue, I again visited the Palace of Fine Arts, which is to the east of the park. I have not as yet attended any concert in the Palace, but I enjoy very much looking at the pictures and murals of the great artists of Mexico.

Well, Mr. Lopez, you see I am learning more every day, especially because I am very loquacious. And your advice has been very useful to me, except (I must confess again) that which you gave me about resting.

Receive a handclasp from your friend

John Adams

Exercise No. 139—Completion of Text

1. (Before my departure) para México, me dijo — (Don't be in a hurry).
2. (I have not forgotten) sus consejos.
3. (I do not rest) largo rato.
4. Hay (so much to discover).
5. (Yesterday) descansaba yo (at noon).
6. Objetos de arte (are sold) en la Avenida.
7. (I was not able) resistir la tentación.
8. (I visited again) el Palacio de Bellas Artes.
9. (Not yet) he asistido a un concierto.
10. (I like very much) las pinturas de los grandes (painters).

PARTE SEGUNDA

Grammar Notes

1. The Possessive Pronouns

In Spanish as in English there are possessive adjectives and possessive pronouns. The possessive adjectives **mi, tu, su,** etc. are important and useful words and you have learned and used them a great deal. The possessive pronouns are not of great practical importance because there are good and easy ways of avoiding them. However, you should be sufficiently familiar with these pronouns to understand them when you hear or see them used. Study the following examples:

Possessive Adjectives

(a)

Mi (*my*) libro es rojo.
Mi (*my*) pluma es roja.
Mis (*my*) libros son rojos.
Mis (*my*) plumas son rojas.

(b)

Es mi (*my*) libro.
Es mi (*my*) pluma.
Son mis (*my*) libros.
Son mis (*my*) plumas.

Possessive Pronouns

(a)

El mío (*mine*) es rojo.
La mía (*mine*) es roja.
Los míos (*mine*) son rojos.
Las mías (*mine*) son rojas.

(b)

El libro es **mío** (*mine*).
La pluma es **mía** (*mine*).
Los libros son **míos** (*mine*).
Las plumas son **mías** (*mine*).

a. The possessive pronoun agrees in number and gender with the noun for which it stands. Each form is preceded by el, la, los or las. (Group a)

b. When the possessive pronoun comes after the verb **ser** the definite article is omitted. (Group b)

c. The complete table of possessive pronouns:

Singular		Plural		
el mío	la mía	los míos	las mías	mine
el tuyo	la tuya	los tuyos	las tuyas	yours (fam.)
el suyo	la suya	los suyos	las suyas	yours, his, hers, theirs
el nuestro	la nuestra	los nuestros	las nuestras	ours
el vuestro	la vuestra	los vuestros	las vuestras	yours (fam.)

d. Memorize the following common expressions in which the long form of the possessive follows the noun:

amigo mío, my friend (m.)   un amigo mío, a friend of mine

amiga mía, my friend (f.)   unos amigos míos, some friends of mine

amigos míos, my friends   unos amigos nuestros, some friends of ours

amigas mías, my friends (f.)   unos amigos suyos, some friends of yours

2. The Definite Article as a Pronoun.

a. el libro de Pedro y el libro de Ana.   Peter's book and Anna's book.
  la pluma de Pedro y la pluma de Ana.   Peter's pen and Anna's pen.
  los libros de Pedro y los libros de Ana.   Peter's books and Anna's books.
  las plumas de Pedro y las plumas de Ana.   Peter's pens and Anna's pens.

b. el libro de Pedro y *el* de Ana.   Peter's book and *that* of Anna.
  la pluma de Pedro y *la* de Ana.   Peter's pen and *that* of Anna.
  los libros de Pedro y *los* de Ana.   Peter's books and *those* of Anna.
  las plumas de Pedro y *las* de Ana.   Peter's pens and *those* of Anna.

In group a, the noun is repeated in each sentence. This, as you see, is monotonous. In group b, the noun is not repeated and the article that remains is translated *that* (in the singular) and *those* (in the plural).

PARTE TERCERA

Ejercicios (Exercises) No. 140A-140B

140A. Read each sentence on the left and complete the corresponding sentence on the right with the correct possessive pronoun.

Ejemplo: ¿De quién es esta revista. Es (mine) **mía.**

1. ¿De quién es este traje?   1. Es (mine).
2. ¿De quiénes son estos carteles?   2. Son (yours).
3. Juan y yo tenemos corbatas.   3. Ésta es (mine), ésa es (his).
4. Ana y yo hemos comprado sarapes.   4. Éstos son (mine), ésos son (hers).
5. Ud. y yo hemos recibido cartas.   5. Éstas son (mine), y ésas son (yours).
6. Pablo y yo compramos boletos ayer.   6. Tengo los (mine) pero él perdió los (his).
7. Las revistas han llegado.   7. Yo he leído las (mine); él ha leído las (his).
8. Fuí al cine con mi madre.   8. Ella fué con la (hers).
9. Fuimos al cine con nuestros amigos.   9. Ellos fueron con los (theirs).
10. Ellos llevaron sus juguetes.   10. Nosotros llevamos los (ours).

140B. Change these sentences from the present to the imperfect and preterite. Translate each sentence.

Ejemplo: Respondo a su pregunta.   I answer his question.
        Respondía a su pregunta.   I was answering his question.
        Respondí a su pregunta.   I answered his question.

1. Salgo del cuarto.   5. El chófer me responde.
2. Entramos en el museo.   6. Ellos no aprenden el francés.
3. Vemos las tiendas.   7. Estoy en casa.
4. Uds. no olvidan mis consejos.   8. Los jóvenes van a la corrida.

Exercise No. 141—Preguntas

1. ¿Qué no ha olvidado el Sr. Adams?
2. ¿Por qué no descansa largo rato?
3. ¿Dónde descansaba al mediodía?
4. ¿Qué veía al otro lado de la avenida?
5. ¿Ha visitado el Sr. Adams aquellas tiendas muchas veces o pocas veces?
6. ¿Qué tentación no podía resistir?
7. ¿Se cansa él de mirar las artes de los indios?
8. ¿Qué palacio volvió a visitar el Sr. Adams?
9. ¿Ha asistido a algún concierto en el Palacio de Bellas Artes?
10. ¿Le gusta mucho al Sr. Adams mirar las pinturas de los grandes pintores?

REPASO 8
(CAPÍTULOS 31–35) PARTE PRIMERA
Repaso de Palabras

NOUNS

1. el abogado	9. el cristal	17. el médico	1. lawyer	9. glass	17. doctor
2. el ascensor	10. el chófer	18. el pase de turista	2. elevator	10. driver	18. tourist pass
3. la brisa	11. el dependiente	19. el pintor	3. breeze	11. employee	19. painter
4. el caballo	12. el descanso	20. la pintura	4. horse	12. rest	20. painting
5. el campesino	13. la dificultad	21. la sala de espera	5. farmer	13. difficulty	21. waiting room
6. la cebolla	14. el este	22. la seda	6. onion	14. east	22. silk
7. el corazón	15. la fuente	23. la tela	7. heart	15. fountain	23. cloth
8. el concierto	16. el joven	24. el viejecito	8. concert	16. youth	24. little old man

VERBS

1. acercarse a	8. descubrir	14. hallar	1. to approach	8. to discover	14. to find
2. arreglar	9. descansar	15. perder	2. to arrange	9. to rest	15. to lose
3. asistir a	10. divertirse	16. pintar	3. to attend	10. to enjoy oneself	16. to paint
4. cansarse	11. encantar	17. regatear	4. to get tired	11. to charm	17. to bargain
5. aconsejar	12. expresar	18. señalar	5. to advise	12. to express	18. to point out
6. cortar	13. gritar	19. sonar	6. to cut	13. to shout	19. to sound
7. correr			7. to run		

ADJECTIVES

1. afortunado	8. emocionante	14. sabroso	1. lucky	8. exciting	14. tasty
2. alegre	9. enorme	15. salvo	2. happy	9. enormous	15. safe
3. cansado	10. guapo	16. sano	3. tired	10. handsome	16. sound (healthy)
4. cuadrado	11. grueso	17. semejante	4. square	11. thick	17. similar
5. demasiado	12. impaciente	18. sumo	5. too much	12. impatient	18. greatest
6. deseoso	13. junto	19. vacío	6. eager	13. together	19. empty
7. divertido			7. enjoyable		

ADVERBS

1. ayer	2. anteayer	3. anoche	4. enfrente	1. yesterday	2. day before yesterday	3. last night	4. in front

PREPOSITIONS

1. dentro de	2. excepto	3. junto a	4. según	1. inside of	2. except	3. close to	4. according to

CONJUNCTIONS

1. mientras(que)	2. antes de que	3. puesto que	1. while	2. before	3. since

IMPORTANT EXPRESSIONS

1. al día siguiente	5. largo rato	9. sano y salvo	1. on the following day	5. a long time	9. safe and sane
2. de repente	6. llamar por teléfono	10. darse la mano	2. suddenly	6. to telephone	10. to shake hands
3. dar un paseo	7. pensar (+ infin.)	11. voy aprendiendo	3. to take a walk	7. to intend to	11. I am learning
4. es decir	8. por entero		4. that is to say	8. entirely	

NOTE: voy aprendiendo = estoy aprendiendo. ir is often used like estar to form the present progressive.

PARTE SEGUNDA

Ejercicio 142. For each Spanish word give the related Spanish word suggested by the English word in parentheses.

Ejemplo: 1. comer (the meal)—la comida

1. comer (the meal)
2. difícil (the difficulty)
3. hablar (talkative)
4. platicar (the chatting)
5. divertirse (enjoyable)
6. el caballo (the little horse)

7. el **viaje** (to travel)   11. **pintar** (the painting)   14. **llegar** (the arrival)
8. **segundo** (secondary)   12. **preguntar** (the question)   15. **fácil** (easily)
9. la **ventana** (the little window)   13. **responder** (the answer)   16. el **campo** (the farmer)
10. **caminar** (the road)

Ejercicio 143. Translate each verb form and give the infinitive of the verb.

Ejemplo: dijeron, they said, decir

1. pudo   4. ví   7. tuvimos   10. pidió   13. hizo
2. quise   5. leyeron   8. dí   11. Uds. hicieron 14. tuviste
3. pusieron   6. Ud. dijo   9. fué   12. vine   15. supe

Ejercicio 144. Select the group of words in the right-hand column which best completes each sentence begun in the left-hand column.

1. Mientras nuestro camión pasaba por las montañas,
2. Las mujeres lavaban ropa y
3. Por todas partes había puestos
4. Le gustaba mucho un muchacho
5. Cuando le encontró,
6. Escuchando la plática de las mujeres,
7. ¿Recuerda Ud. las conversaciones
8. Yo estaba sentado al mediodía en el parque
9. Debajo de los árboles en la Alameda
10. Mientras el Sr. Adams se divertía en México,

a. el Sr. Lopez sufría el calor de Nueva York.
b. donde se vendían cosas corrientes.
c. había una brisa fresca.
d. en que hablábamos de los mercados de México?
e. los hombres cortaban caña.
f. charlando con un estudiante.
g. que cuidaba un puesto.
h. el muchacho arreglaba su mercancía.
i. el Sr. Adams podía comprender todo lo que (all that) decían.
j. chocó (it collided) con otro.

Ejercicio 145. Complete each sentence by selecting that tense which makes good sense. Translate each sentence.

Ejemplo: 1. Ayer recibí un paquete.   Yesterday I received a package.

1. Ayer ——— un paquete (recibí, recibiré, recibo).
2. Mañana ——— en casa (quedé, quedaré, quedo)
3. Anoche no ——— al cine (vamos, iremos, fuimos)
4. Ahora ——— las maletas (hicieron, hacen, harán)
5. El maestro habla y los alumnos ——— (escuchan, escucharán, escucharon)
6. ¿——— Uds. de la ciudad pasado mañana? (salen, saldrán, salieron)
7. ¿Le ——— Ud. anteayer? (vió, ve, verá)
8. El año que viene ——— en Europa (viaja, viajé, viajaré)
9. ¿Qué está diciendo él? No ——— oirle (pudimos, podemos, podremos)
10. Yo ——— la semana pasada (llegué, llego, llegaré)

PARTE TERCERA

Diálogo

En la Gasolinera

Practice the Spanish aloud.

El Sr. Adams necesita gasolina y ha entrado en una de las gasolineras de la Pemex.

En seguida se acerca al coche un joven para servirle.

— Buenas tardes, — le saluda el joven.

— Muy buenas, — le contesta Adams. — ¿Me hace el favor de llenarme el tanque de gasolina?

— Regular o super?

Mr. Adams needs gasoline and has gone into one of the Pemex gasoline stations.

Immediately a young man approaches the car to serve him.

"Good afternoon," the young man greets him.

"Good afternoon to you," Adams answers. "Will you please fill the tank with gasoline?"

Regular or super?

— Regular. ¿Y quiere Ud. chequear el aceite, el agua y el aire?

— Con todo gusto, señor, — le contesta el empleado.

El joven llena el tanque, revisa el aceite, el agua y la presión de aire en las llantas. Entonces vuelve al Sr. Adams.

— Todo está bien, — le dice a nuestro turista.

— Muchas gracias, ¿y cuánto le debo?

— Son treinta y cinco pesos cuarenta centavos.

El Sr. Adams le da un billete de cien pesos. El joven se[1] lo cambia, entregándole sesenta y cuatro pesos sesenta centavos. Adams cuenta el cambio y ve que todo está en orden.

— Está bien, — le dice al empleado. — Muchas gracias y muy buenas tardes.

— Muy buenas y feliz viaje, — le contesta el joven.

Regular. And do you want to check the oil, the water and the air?

"With pleasure, sir," the employee replies.

The young man fills the tank, checks the oil, the water and the air pressure in the tires. Then he returns to Mr. Adams.

"Everything is all right," he says to our tourist.

Many thanks, and how much do I owe you?

It is thirty five pesos forty centavos.

Mr. Adams gives him a bill of one hundred pesos. The young man changes it for him, returning to him sixty-four pesos and sixty centavos. Adams counts the change and sees that everything is in order.

"All right," he says to the employee. "Many thanks and very good afternoon."

"Very good afternoon and happy voyage," the young man answers.

NOTE: 1. The indirect objects *le* (*to* or *for him, her, you*) and *les* (*to* or *for them, you*) become **se** before any other object pronoun that begins with the letter l. Complete treatment of *two object pronouns* will be found in Capítulo 39.

LECTURA 1

Exercise No. 146—Una Visita a Xochimilco (Soh-chee-*meel*-koh)

En una ocasión el Sr. Adams llevó a los hijos del Sr. Carrillo en una excursión al pueblo de Xochimilco con sus canales interesantes.

El pueblo no está muy lejos de la capital y nuestro amigo llegó sin dificultad. Al llegar (On arriving) al pueblo, tuvo una idea muy luminosa. Propuso (He proposed) una merienda al aire libre, al lado de uno de los canales. Los muchachos aceptaron el proyecto con entusiasmo.

Adams entró en una tienda de abarrotes (grocery store), compró dos latas (cans) de sardinas con salsa de tomate. Luego compró unas tortas y unos panes dulces en una panadería. Por último, compró unas naranjas y varios tomates en un puesto de verduras.

Quedó (There remained) el problema de refrescos. Ahora una de los chamacos (boys) tuvo una idea luminosa. — ¿Por qué no comprar unas botellas de Seven-Up?[1] Por (Along) los canales siempre hay muchos vendedores de refrescos fríos.

— Estupenda idea, — comentó Adams.

Alquilaron (They rented) una canoa adornada de miles de claveles (carnations). Después de pasear (riding) dos horas explorando los canales, salieron de la canoa en un lugar muy tranquilo. El Sr. Adms abrió las dos latas de sardinas y preparó unos sandwiches que comieron con los tomates. Por refresco tuvieron el Seven Up que han comprado y por fin, tuvieron por postre las sabrosas naranjas. Era una merienda estupenda y los chicos quedaron (were) encantados. No olvidarán esta experiencia en muchos años.

NOTE: 1. A popular Mexican soft drink.

LECTURA 2

Exercise No. 147—En la Avenida Juárez

Al fin caminamos por la Avenida Juárez. Es una avenida ancha en el centro del Distrito Federal. Está a un lado de la Alameda, un parque muy bonito con árboles altos, fuentes y monumentos.

Hay mucha gente en la Avenida Juárez. Ahí vienen todos los turistas. En las tiendas se venden todas clases de artículos típicos de México — joyería, tejidos, artículos de cuero, alfarería (pottery) y varias clases de ropa hecha a mano.

Naturalmente, vamos a visitar el Museo Nacional de Artes e Industrias Populares. Allí se pueden ver varios artículos de todas las regiones del país.

Caminamos por esta Avenida hasta llegar al "Caballito," la estatua del rey Carlos IV en la Plaza de la Reforma. Allí termina la Avenida.

CAPÍTULO 36 (TREINTA Y SEIS)

PARTE PRIMERA

FOREWORD

In Chapters 36–40 there is no parallel translation of the texts. However, the new words and expressions that appear are given in the vocabularies which follow each text. There is also the Spanish-English dictionary in the Appendix to which you can refer for words you may have forgotten.

You should therefore have no difficulty in reading and understanding the texts. As a means of testing your understanding a series of English questions to be answered in English are given under the heading "Test of Reading Comprehension," instead of the usual Spanish Preguntas. You can check your answers in the Answer Section of the Appendix.

La Plaza

Sexta Carta De México

Querido amigo:

En nuestras conversaciones hemos hablado de muchas cosas pero no me acuerdo de ninguna conversación sobre las plazas mexicanas. Tengo ganas de escribirle a Ud. mis impresiones de ellas.

He notado que cada pueblo en México tiene su "corazón." Es la plaza. Todo el mundo va a la plaza para el descanso, para los negocios, para el recreo, para todo.

Así yo pensaba mientras estaba sentado en la plaza de Oaxaca.

Cada plaza es distinta. Algunas son redondas, otras son cuadradas. Arboles grandes crecen en algunas. En otras no se ve nada más que algunas pocas hojas secas de quién sabe qué pobre arbolito.

Cada plaza tiene su kiosco. Este puede ser cuadrado o redondo, elegante o sencillo, bien cuidado o mal cuidado. Está en el centro de la plaza.

Los músicos del pueblo tocan en el kiosco el domingo por la tarde, el jueves por la noche o a cualquiera hora de cualquier día.

Muchas veces hay portales a un lado o a dos lados de la plaza. En los portales se encuentran (are found) todas clases de tiendas—papelerías, farmacias, mercerías, joyerías, librerías. Casi siempre hay un café. Allí se reúnion los hombres (the men get together) por la tarde para charlar o para leer el periódico mientras toman una taza de chocolate o café, una cerveza, o una coca-cola.

El hotel del pueblo puede estar en la plaza principal. También se ve allí una iglesia antigua.

El aspecto de la plaza cambia a cada hora. Por la mañana temprano se ven (one sees) solamente algunos viajeros cansados que van al mercado. Más tarde vienen los niños que son demasiado chicos para ir a la escuela. Las madres se sientan en los bancos para charlar.

Durante las horas de la siesta, desde la una hasta las tres y media de la tarde, hay pocas personas en la plaza. Algunos descansan en los bancos, algunas duermen. Hace calor. A eso de las cuatro comienza otra vez la vida de la plaza.

El domingo por la tarde se reúne todo el mundo en la plaza para "el paseo." Los muchachos caminan de un rumbo (in one direction), las muchachas del contrario (in the other). Mientras tanto los músicos en el kiosco tocan una pieza alegre.

Al fin llega la noche. La plaza se pone tranquila. Se ven sólamente algunos viajeros que vienen del mercado. La plaza duerme.

Reciba un cordial saludo de su amigo,

Juan Adams

Vocabulario

el aspecto	appearance	el paseo	promenade
la cerveza	beer	la pieza	piece (music)
el contrario	opposite	el portal	arcade
el corazón	heart	el rumbo	direction
la farmacia	pharmacy	crecer	to grow
la hoja	leaf	reunirse	to get together
la joyería	jewelry shop	alegre	merry, lively
la iglesia	church	cansado	tired
el kiosco	band stand	cuadrado	square-shaped
la librería	book shop	cuidado	kept, cared for
la mercería	haberdashery	redondo	round
el músico	musician	seco	dry
la papelería	stationery shop	mientras tanto	in the meantime
la plaza	square		

Exercise No. 148—Test of Reading Comprehension

Answer these questions in English. They will test your comprehension of the text.

1. What has every town?
2. Why does everybody go to the plaza?
3. What grows in some plazas?
4. What does one see in others?
5. Where is the bandstand located?
6. When do the musicians play?
7. Name six kinds of shops which are found in the arcades.
8. For what purpose do the men get together in the cafe in the afternoons?
9. What do they drink?
10. What does one see in the main plaza?
11. What do some people do on the plaza during the siesta hour?
12. At what time does the life of the plaza begin again?
13. What happens on Sunday afternoons?
14. How do the boys and girls promenade?
15. Whom does one see in the plaza at night?

Exercise No. 149—Completion of Text

1. (The heart of each town) es la plaza.
2. Así yo pensaba (while I was seated) en la plaza.
3. (One sees nothing more) que algunas pocas hojas secas.
4. El kiosco (may be) cuadrado o redondo.
5. Los músicos tocan (on Sunday afternoon).
6. Hay portales (where one finds) todas clases de tiendas.
7. Los hombres (get together) en el café (in the afternoon).
8. También se ve allí (an old church).
9. (One sees) algunos viajeros (tired).
10. (Later) vienen los niños (who) son (too small) para ir a la escuela.

PARTE SEGUNDA

Grammar Notes

1. The Present and Preterite of dormir (ue) to sleep

Present		Preterite	
I sleep, etc.		I slept, etc.	
duermo	dormimos	dormí	dormimos
duermes	dormís	dormiste	dormisteis
duerme	duermen	durmió	durmieron

Present Participle: durmiendo

2. Relative Pronouns

a. que, who, whom, which, that

que is the most commonly used relative. Like the English *that* it can refer to persons or things, except with prepositions, when it may refer only to things.

El sombrero que compré me sienta mal.	The hat which I bought fits me poorly.
¿Dónde está el muchacho que perdió su libro?	Where is the boy who lost his book.
¿Dónde está la cesta de que Ud. habló?	Where is the basket of which you spoke?

b. quien, quienes (plural), who, whom

quien and quienes refer only to persons. When they are used as a direct object the personal a is required.

Los hombres de quienes hablé son abogados.	The men of whom I spoke are lawyers.
El niño a quien buscábamos está en casa.	The child whom we were looking for is at home.

c. lo que what (that which), todo lo que, all that

Sé lo que dijo.	I know what he said.
Le diré a Ud. todo lo que he aprendido.	I will tell you all that I have learned.

d. cuyo (o, os, as) whose, must immediately precede the noun it modifies, and must agree with it in number and gender.

Buscan las calles *cuyos* nombres son fechas.	They are looking for the streets whose names are dates.
¿Dónde está el hombre *cuya* casa hemos comprado?	Where is the man whose house we have bought?

e. donde, en donde, a donde, de donde may often take the place of a relative pronoun.

La casa *en donde* vive es antigua.	The house in which (where) he lives is old.
No conozco la escuela *a donde* van los niños.	I do not know the school to which (where) the children go.

f. el cual (la cual, los cuales, las cuales), that, which, who, whom

These longer forms of the relative pronouns are used to make clear to which of two possible antecedents the relative clause refers.

Visité a la esposa del Sr. Adams, la cual toca bien el piano.	I visited the wife of Mr. Adams, who plays the piano well.

PARTE TERCERA

Ejercicios (Exercises) No. 150A-150B

150A. Use the correct verb forms with these subjects:

1. (Yo) sleep
2. (Yo) am not sleeping
3. ¿(Quién) sleeps?
4. (Nosotros) sleep
5. Do you sleep (Ud.)?
6. Sleep (Ud.) (*Imperative*)
7. Do not sleep (Uds.)
8. (El niño) sleeps
9. (La niña) is not sleeping
10. ¿(Quiénes) sleep?
11. (Ellos) sleep
12. (Nadie) is sleeping

150B. Complete these sentences by using the correct relative pronoun.

Ejemplo: Déme el lápiz que compré.

1. Déme el lápiz (which) compré.
2. ¿Dónde está el alumno (whose) libro tengo?
3. Los muchachos (who) eran diligentes aprendieron mucho.
4. Aquí está la pintura (of which) hablábamos.
5. Las palabras (which) aprendemos son difíciles.

6. (What, that which) **le dije a Ud. es verdad.**
7. **Me dió** (all that) **quise.**
8. **La casa** (which) **compró es de piedra.**
9. **Allí están las señoritas** (of whom) **hablábamos.**

10. **El Sr. Adams,** (who) **estaba sentado detrás de su escritorio, se levantó.**

NOTE: Use **que** for *who* (sentence 3). If the relative clause can be omitted without changing the sense or clarity of the sentence use **quien** (sentence 10).

CAPÍTULO 37 (TREINTE Y SEITE)

PARTE PRIMERA

Un Paseo A Teotihuacán

Séptima Carta De México

Querido amigo:

Ayer llamé por teléfono a los hijos del Sr. Carrillo y les pregunté — ¿Quieren Uds. pasear en coche conmigo a Teotihuacán? Aceptaron con alegría.

Quería (I wanted) volver a tiempo para ir a un concierto por la noche. Así es que tempranito nos encontramos (we met) los tres delante de mi hotel. Saqué (I took out) el coche del garage donde lo había alquilado (I had rented) para el día. Charlando y riendo con animación nos pusimos en marcha (we set out.)

Pasamos por los suburbios de la ciudad, primero por tierras laboradas, después por tierras desiertas. Vimos de vez en cuando unas casas pequeñas de adobe o un indio con su burro. Más allá (further on) no vimos más que la llanura de la Mesa Central y las montañas a lo lejos.

Yo manejaba el coche y de repente oí un sonido que inmediatamente conocí. — ¿Qué pasó? — preguntaron los jóvenes.

Paré (I stopped) el auto y bajamos. — Tenemos un pinchazo, — contesté yo.

Yo quería cambiar la llanta y los jóvenes estaban muy deseosos de ayudarme. Los dos, muy contentos, comenzaron a buscar el gato. ¡Ay! No había ningún gato (there was no jack) en la cajuela. ¿Qué hacer?

De vez en cuando pasaba un auto a toda velocidad. A pesar de nuestras señales nadie paró. Era casi mediodía y había mucho sol. Nos sentamos debajo de un pequeño árbol al lado del camino para esperar.

Pronto Carlos vió en el horizonte un camión grande. Se acercó (It approached) rápidamente y paró delante de nuestro árbol. El chófer bajó.

— Tienen Uds. un pinchazo? — dijo sonriendo. ¿Me permiten Uds. ayudarles?

— ¡Ya lo creo! — le respondí. Tenemos un pinchazo y nos hace falta un gato.

El chófer nos prestó su gato y nos ayudó a cambiar la llanta. Afortunadamente teníamos una llanta de repuesto (a spare tire).

Le dí mil gracias al hombre y le ofrecí diez pesos, pero no quiso aceptarlos. Entonces nos dimos la mano y nos despedimos.

Seguimos nuestro camino hasta que llegamos a las Pirámides de Teotihuacán. De veras son muy imponentes. Subimos por aquella escalera ancha hasta la cima de la Pirámide del Sol, que tiene 216 pies de altura. Es más grande que cualquier pirámide de Egipto. Los jóvenes subieron corriendo. Yo subí muy despacio pero sin embargo llegué a la cima algo jadeante (somewhat out of breath). Desde allí, como Ud. sabe, hay una vista maravillosa del valle entero. No es necesario describirle a Ud. las otras ruinas imponentes de Teotihuacán, la Pirámide de la Luna y el Templo de Quetzalcoatl, dios de los Aztecas. Ud. los conoce mejor que yo.

Después de tomar la comida que me habían preparado (they had prepared) en el hotel, subimos otra vez al auto y regresamos, cansados pero muy contentos.

Reciba un apretón de manos de su amigo

Juan Adams

Vocabulario

al camión	truck, bus	regresar	to return
el gato	car-jack, cat	reír	to laugh
el dios	god	riendo	laughing
la cajuela	trunk (of car)	sonreír	to smile
la escalera	stairs	ancho	wide
la llanta (de repuesto)	tire (spare)	deseoso	eager
la llanura	plain	jadeante	out of breath
el paseo	walk, stroll, ride	desierto	deserted
el pinchazo	puncture, flat	imponente	imposing
la señal	signal	entero	entire
el sonido	sound	laborado	cultivated
la tierra	land	tempranito	very early
correr	to run	a pesar de	in spite of
ofrecer	to offer	algo	somewhat, something
manejar	to drive	¡ay!	oh!

Teotihuacán	Quetzalcoatl	piramide
(*tay-oh-tee-wah-kahn*)	(*kayt-sahl-koh-ahtl*)	(*pee-rah-mee-day*)

Expresiones Importantes

a lo lejos	in the distance	hacer falta	to be missing
a tiempo	on time	nos hace falta un gato	we lack a jack
a toda velocidad	at full speed	pasear en coche	to go on an auto ride
dar mil gracias	to thank a thousand times	ponerse en marcha	to set out
nada más que	nothing but, only	sin embargo	nevertheless
de vez en cuando	from time to time		

Exercise No. 151—Test of Reading Comprehension

Answer these questions in English.

1. Where did Mr. Adams want to go?
2. Whom did he invite to go with him?
3. Where did they meet at an early hour?
4. How had Mr. Adams obtained a car?
5. What did they see on the road from time to time?
6. What did they see in the distance?
7. What happened when Mr. Adams was driving?
8. Why weren't they able to change the tire?
9. What time of day was it?
10. How did they finally manage to put on the spare tire?
11. How did Mr. Adams try to show his appreciation of the truck driver's help?
12. How did Mr. Adams climb the Pyramid of the Sun, and how did he feel on reaching the top?
13. How did the boys go up?
14. Why isn't it necessary for Mr. Adams to describe the other ruins to Mr. Lopez?
15. How did they feel when they returned?

Exercise No. 152—Completion of Text

1. ¿Irá Ud. (with me by car) a Teotihuacán?
2. (The young men accepted) la invitácion (with joy).
3. (We met) delante de mi hotel.
4. (I took the car) del garage.
5. (I had rented it) para el día.
6. (Chatting and laughing) subimos en el coche.
7. (From time to time) vimos a un indio.
8. (We saw nothing but) la llanura.
9. (Suddenly) oí un sonido.
10. ¿(What happened?)—preguntaron.
11. Yo quería (to change the tire) pero (there was no jack).
12. (In spite of) nuestras señales nadie (stopped).
13. Dijimos al chófer—(We lack a jack).
14. Nos prestó un gato (and helped us change the tire).
15. Entonces (we shook hands) y (took leave of one another).

PARTE SEGUNDA
Grammar Notes

1. The Past Perfect Tense. Model Verbs, hablar, aprender, vivir

Singular

había hablado	(aprendido, vivido)	I had spoken	(learned, lived)
habías hablado	(aprendido, vivido)	you had spoken	(learned, lived)
Ud. él había hablado ella	(aprendido, vivido)	you he, it had spoken she, it	(learned, lived)

Plural

habíamos hablado	(aprendido, vivido)	we had spoken	(learned, lived)
habíais hablado	(aprendido, vivido)	you had spoken	(learned, lived)
Uds. ellos habían hablado ellas	(aprendido, vivido)	you they had spoken	(learned, lived)

a. As in English, the past perfect tense in Spanish is formed by the auxiliary verb **había** (*had*), plus the past participle of the verb. **Había** is the imperfect of **haber**, *to have*.

2. Verbs with Spelling Changes.

Note the Spelling Changes in these verbs.

sacar to take out				llegar to arrive			
present		preterite		present		preterite	
saco	sacamos	*saqué*	sacamos	llego	llegamos	*llegué*	*llegamos*
sacas	sacáis	sacaste	sacasteis	llegas	llegáis	llegaste	llegasteis
saca	sacan	sacó	sacaron	llega	llegan	llegó	llegaron

imperative		imperative	
saque Ud.	*saquen Uds.*	*llegue Ud.*	*lleguen Uds.*

a. In verbs whose infinitives end in -**car** or -**gar**, **c** must become **qu** and **g** must become **gu** before the endings **e** and **en**, in order to keep the pronunciation of **c** and **g**, as found in the infinitive.

b. Other verbs ending in -**car** or -**gar** are: **buscar**, to look for; **acercarse** (*a*) to approach; **pagar** to pay.

PARTE TERCERA

Ejercicios (Exercises) No. 153A-153B

153A. In the following sentences fill in the correct auxiliary verb in the past perfect tense. Translate the sentence.

Ejemplo: 1. (Nosotros) **habíamos aprendido español en México.**

We had learned Spanish in Mexico.

1. (Nosotros) ———— visto la película.
2. ¿———— leído Ud. muchos libros?
3. ¿Quién ———— abierto la ventana?
4. Los hijos no ———— dormido durante la noche.
5. Yo no ———— creído el cuento.
6. (Nosotros) ———— volado sobre las montañas.
7. Ellos ———— ido al teatro.
8. ¿———— tenido Ud. un buen viaje?
9. Uds. no ———— dicho nada.
10. ¿———— comido (tú) los dulces, Juanito?

153B. Complete in Spanish.

1. (He had bought) **los boletos.**
2. (I had seen) **la película.**
3. (We had eaten) **la comida.**
4. ¿(Had they received) **la carta?**
5. (Had you set) **la mesa?**
6. (You (Uds.) had not heard) **el cuento.**

20

7. (You [tú] had not slept) **bien.**
8. **El hombre** (had seated himself) **en el banco.**
9. (They had had) **un pinchazo.**
10. (We had said) **nada.**

11. **¿Qué** (had happened)?
12. (They had not found) **el gato.**
13. **¿Por qué** (had they not changed) **la llanta?**
14. **El chófer** (had approached) **a nosotros.**

CAPÍTULO 38 (TREINTA Y OCHO)
PARTE PRIMERA
El Sr. Adams Compra Un Billete De Lotería
Octava Carta De México

Querido amigo:

Yo no soy jugador, Sr. López. Es decir, hasta la semana pasada nunca había sido (*I had never been*) jugador.

¿Qué pasó? Oiga bien. Le diré a Ud. todo.

Como Ud. sabe mejor que yo, hay en todas las esquinas en el centro de la capital un vendedor, y muchas veces dos vendedores de billetes de lotería. Cuando llegué a México noté inmediatamente que todo el mundo compraba billetes de lotería. ¿Quién no quiere hacerse rico (*to get rich*)? Yo pensaba en la posibilidad de ganar uno de los muchos premios menores o tal vez, el premio gordo. El año que viene, haría (*I would take*) viajes por todos los países de Sud America. Llevaría (*I would take*) conmigo a toda la familia. Los niños aprenderían (*would learn*) a hablar español. Podría (*I would be able*) volver a visitar a mis amigos en México. Pasaría (*I would spend*) mucho tiempo en las ciudades y pueblos de México que todavía no conozco.

Caminaría (*I would walk*) por todos los mercados para hablar con la gente del campo y para aprender más de la vida y de las costumbres de México. Compraría (*I would buy*) objetos de arte, pero no para venderlos, sino para mi casa.

Así soñaba yo.

El miércoles de la semana pasada paseaba por la Avenida Madero. Ví en la esquina como siempre, a una señora que vendía billetes de lotería. Como siempre me dijo la señora—Compre Ud. este billete afortunado.

— Pero, señora, — le respondí, — todos estos billetes son afortunados, ¿verdad?

— No, señor, — me dijo. — Le he guardado a Ud. (*I have kept for you*) éste. Mire Ud. Tiene tres ceros.

Yo no sabía que quería decir "tres ceros." Pero una voz por dentro (*within*) me dijo — ¡Compre! Y me hice jugador.

Al día siguiente yo leía en el periódico los números que ganaron. Naturalmente no esperaba nada. De repente ví un número con tres ceros, el número 26000. ¡Yo había ganado un premio de doscientos mil (200,000) pesos!

Busqué (*I looked for*) mi billete. Y mientras buscaba, hacía (*I was making*) viajes por todos lo países de Sud América con toda la familia. . . .

Al fin encontré el billete en un bolsillo. Muy impaciente lo miré. Había tres ceros. Había un dos. Pero — ¿qué lastima? Había también un "5." Yo tenía el número veinticinco mil (25,000).

¿Pero qué importa? Desde aquel momento, fuí jugador.

Le saluda cordialmente su amigo

Juan Adams

Vocabulario

el billete de lotería	lottery ticket	ganar	to win
el bolsillo	pocket	guardar	to keep
la esquina	corner	hacerse	to become
el cero	zero	pasar	to happen, to pass
el jugador	player, gambler	pasear	to stroll

el premio	prize	sonar (ue)	to dream
el premio gordo	first (grand) prize	afortunado	lucky
la voz	voice	gordo	fat
buscar	to look for	impaciente	impatiently
busqué	I looked for	siguiente	following
	me hice jugador	I became a gambler	

Note the difference between **sonar** (*ue*) to sound, ring; and **soñar** (ue) to dream. **Tengo sueño:** I am sleepy.

Exercise No. 154—Test of Reading Comprehension

Answer these questions in English.

1. What kind of man had Mr. Adams never been?
2. What had he noted when he came to Mexico?
3. What possibility was he thinking of?
4. After winning the first prize, to what countries would he take trips?
5. Whom would he visit again?
6. What would he buy for his house?
7. From whom did Mr. Adams buy a ticket with three zeros?
8. What was he reading in the newspaper next day?
9. What did he suddenly see?
10. What did he think when he saw the number with three zeros?
11. What was he dreaming of doing while he looked for his ticket?
12. What number did Mr. Adams have?
13. What number won the prize?
14. What expression does Mr. Adams use to show that he doesn't take the matter seriously?
15. Translate: **Desde aquel momento, fuí jugador.**

Exercise No. 155—Completion of Text

1. **Cuando** (I arrived) **en México** (everybody) **compraba boletos de lotería.**
2. **Había vendedores** (on all corners).
3. **Tal vez ganaré** (the first prize).
4. **Podría** (to visit again) **a mis amigos.**
5. **Llevaría conmigo** (the whole family).
6. **Así** (I was dreaming).
7. **Compré el boleto** (with three zeros).
8. **No sabía** (what the three zeros meant).
9. (The numbers which won) **estaban en el periódico.**
10. (I looked for) **mi boleto.**
11. (At last) **lo encontré** (in a pocket).
12. **Sí** (there were) **tres ceros, pero** (there was not) **un seis.**

PARTE SEGUNDA

Grammar Notes

1. **The Present Conditional. Model Verbs—hablar, aprender, vivir**
The conditional may be called the *would* form of the verb. Its use in Spanish is much the same as in English.

hablar-ía	I would speak	hablar-íamos	we would speak
hablar-ías	you would speak	hablar-íais	you would speak
Ud. el ella } hablar-ía	you he, it she, it } would speak	Uds. ellos ellas } hablar-ían	you they } would speak

a. The conditional endings of all verbs are:

singular: -ía, -ías, -ía   plural: -íamos, -íais, -ían

b. To form the regular conditional add these endings to the *whole* infinitive just as you do with the endings of the future. Thus: **hablar-ía, aprender-ía, vivir-ía, ser-ía, estar-ía.**

c. The endings of the conditional are the same as those of **-er** and **-ir** verbs in the imperfect. But remember:

The endings of the conditional are added on to the *whole infinitive*. The endings of the imperfect are added to the *stem of the verb* after the infinitive ending has been removed.

imperfect		conditional	
aprendía	I was learning	aprendería	I would learn
vivía	I was living	viviría	I would live

2. The Irregular Conditional.

Those verbs that have a change in the infinitive base for the future have the same changes in the conditional.

Infinitive	Future	Conditional	Infinitive	Future	Conditional
	I shall, etc.	I would, etc.		I shall, etc.	I would, etc.
saber	(yo) sabré	(yo) sabría	venir	(yo) vendré	(yo) vendría
poder	podré	podría	tener	tendré	tendría
querer	querré	querría	salir	saldré	saldría
decir	diré	diría	poner	pondré	pondría
hacer	haré	haría	valer	valdré	valdría
haber	habré	habría			

Ejercicios (Exercises) No. 156A-156B

156A. Change the following sentences from the future to the present conditional. Translate each sentence in the conditional.

Ejemplo: Future: Haremos viajes. We shall take trips.
Conditional: Haríamos viajes. We would take trips.

1. Iremos a la plaza de Oaxaca.
2. Juan venderá sus boletos de sombra.
3. No ganarán el premio gordo.
4. Ud. encontrará a sus amigos.
5. Leeré muchas guías de viajero.

6. ¿Llevará Ud. a su familia a México?
7. ¿Les gustarán a Uds. los mercados?
8. Saldré de mi casa a las siete.
9. No podremos hacer los ejercicios.
10. No dirán nada.

156B. Translate:

1. I would learn
2. he would write
3. they would go
4. we would eat
5. she would speak

6. would you (Ud.) work?
7. would John see?
8. who would visit?
9. I would not travel
10. would they study?

11. I would make
12. he would come
13. they would not want
14. would you (Ud.) go out?
15. you (Uds.) would put

CAPÍTULO 39 (TREINTA Y NUEVE)

PARTE PRIMERA

El Sr. Adams No Es Aficionado A Los Toros

Novena Carta De México

Querido amigo:

Era sábado. Yo había visitado al Sr. Carrillo en su oficina y estábamos para salir (we were about to leave). Me preguntó — ¿Quiere Ud. ir a una corrida de toros? Mañana sería (would be) el mejor día.

Al principio respondí, — sí. Pensé un rato y dije — no. Pues, — posiblemente.

Sonrió y dijo que tendría mucho gusto (he would be very pleased) en comprar los boletos. Por supuesto acepté.

A las tres de la tarde, el Sr. Carrillo y yo llegamos a la plaza de toros. Faltaba una hora para el comienzo de la corrida. Ya había (There were already) mucha gente allí. Todo el mundo estaba de muy buen humor.

El Sr. Carrillo había comprado boletos de sombra. Me explicó que los verdaderos aficionados a los toros no tienen que estar cómodos. Ellos se sientan en los asientos de sol.

Al principio teníamos dificultad en hallar nuestros asientos. Todo el mundo ayudaba, señalando (pointing out) diferentes partes de la plaza. Al fin nos sentamos y esperamos el comienzo de la corrida.

La plaza de toros me hizo pensar en el estadio de fútbol o béisbol en los EE. UU. Oí los gritos de los vendedores de refrescos, los gritos y las risas de los espectadores. Todos esperaban impacientes las cuatro de la tarde.

De repente oí la música muy animada que anunció el comienzo de la corrida. Pasó por el redondel un desfile (a procession) de hombres en trajes relucientes, matadores, banderilleros, picadores a caballo y monosabios. Se fueron (they went away) y salió el toro.

Hasta este momento yo estaba muy contento. Me gustaban la música, los trajes relucientes, los gritos y las risas, y el sol que brillaba tan alegremente.

Pero — allí estaba el toro.

No voy a tratar de describir la corrida. Ud. conoce bien este deporte y sé que le gusta mucho. Solamente quiero darle algunas de mis impresiones.

En breve no me gusta la corrida. Sí, entiendo que la corrida de toros es un deporte muy emocionante. Pero — ¡Los pobres caballos, el pobre toro, y muchas veces, el pobre matador!

He visto una corrida pero no pienso (I do not intend) asistir a otra. Tengo que confesarle — no soy aficionado a los toros y nunca lo seré.

El Sr. Carrillo me preguntó — En el fútbol, no se puede decir (may one not say) — ¡Pobres jugadores! — Sí, estoy de acuerdo (I am in agreement), pero, por mi parte, prefiero un deporte más pacífico. Por ejemplo, el ajedrez.

Vocabulario

el aficionado	amateur, fan	la plaza de toros	bullring
el aficionado a los toros	bullfight fan	el redondel	arena
el ajedrez	chess	la sombra	shade
el asiento de sol	seat in the sun	refrescos	refreshments
el asiento de sombra	seat in the shade	las risas	laughter
el banderillero	thrower of darts (into bull)	brillar	shine
la banderilla	dart	entender	to understand
la corrida de toros	bullfight	señalar	to point out
el deporte	sport	aficionado (adj.)	fond of
el desfile	procession	emocionante	exciting
el espectador	spectator	pacífico	peaceful
el matador	bullfighter who kills bull	reluciente	brilliant
el monosabio	a general helper at bullfight	alegremente	joyously
el picador	man on horseback who jabs bull with a pike	anunciar	to announce

Expresiones Importantes

a caballo	on horseback	estar para + inf.	to be about to
en breve	in short	de buen humor	in good humor
estar de acuerdo	to be in agreement	falta una hora para	it lacks one hour to, it is one hour before

Exercise No. 157—Test of Reading Comprehension

Answer these questions in English

1. What did Mr. Carrillo ask Mr. Adams when they were about to leave the office?
2. How much time before the beginning of the bullfight did they arrive?
3. What kind of tickets had Mr. Carrillo bought?
4. In what seats do the bullfight fans sit?
5. Of what did the bullring remind Mr. Adams?
6. What did Mr. Adams hear?
7. What sort of procession passed through the arena?

8. What happened when the men left?
9. What did Mr. Adams like about the bull-fight?
10. Why does he not try to describe the bull-fight?
11. In short, what does Mr. Adams think of the bullfight?

12. Whom does he pity?
13. What must he confess to Mr. Lopez?
14. In what does he agree with Mr. Carrillo?
15. What sport does Mr. Adams prefer?

Exercise No. 158—Completion of Text

1. (We were about to go).
2. Pensé (a while) y dijo (well, maybe).
3. Por supuesto (I accepted).
4. (It was one hour) para el comienzo de la corrida.
5. El Sr. Carrillo (had bought) boletos de sombra.
6. (Finally) hallamos nuestros asientos y (sat down).
7. La plaza de toros se parece a nuestro (football or baseball stadium).
8. Oímos (the shouts and laughter) de los espectadores.

9. Me gustó el desfile de (men in brilliant costumes).
10. (They went away) y el toro (came out).
11. Sí, entiendo que la corrida de toros es (a very exciting sport).
12. Sin embargo (I must confess to you) la verdad.
13. (I do not intend) asistir a otra corrida.
14. (I am in agreement) si Ud. dice del fútbol—(the poor players!)
15. (I prefer) el ajedrez.

PARTE SEGUNDA

Grammar Notes

1. Two Object Pronouns.

Note in the following Spanish and English sentences the position of the indirect object (a person or persons) and the direct object (a thing or things).

1. Carlos *me lo* da.
2. Ana *me los* trae.
3. Juan *nos la* manda.
4. María no *nos las* presta.
5. *Te lo* damos, hijito.

1. Charles gives *it* (m.) *to me.*
2. Anna brings *them* (m.) *to me.*
3. John sends *it* (f.) *to us.*
4. Mary does not lend *them* (f.) *to us.*
5. We give it *to you*, sonny.

a. In Spanish, when there are two pronoun objects, the indirect object precedes the direct object.

b. In English, the opposite is true.

2. Two Object Pronouns (continued)

Study the following examples and note what happens to the indirect object pronouns le (*to you, to him, to her*) and les (*to you*, pl., *to them*).

1. *Se lo* digo a Ud.
2. *Se la* traigo a él.
3. *Se las* prestamos a ella.
4. *Se lo* mando a ellos.
5. *Se los* doy a Uds.

1. I tell *it to you.*
2. I bring *it* (f.) *to him.*
3. We lend *them to her.*
4. I send *it* (m.) *to them.*
5. I give *them* (m.) *to you* (pl.)

a. Le (*to you, to him, to her*) and les (*to you*, pl., *to them*) may not be used before another object pronoun that begins with the letter l. In such cases le and les must become se.

b. Thus se may mean *to you* (sing. and plural), *to him, to her, to them* (masc. and fem.).

a Ud., a él, a ella, etc., after the verb, make the meaning clear.

3. Two Object Pronouns After the Verb.

Like single object pronouns, two object pronouns follow the verb with the affirmative imperative, with the infinitive and with the present participle. Study the two object pronouns in the following examples.

1. Dígamelo.	1. Tell *it to me.*
2. Dígaselo a él.	2. Tell *it to him.*
3. Désela a ella.	3. Give *it* (f.) *to her.*
4. Dénoslos.	4. Give *them to us.*
5. Mándeselos a ellos.	5. Send *them to them.*

a. When two object pronouns follow the verb they are attached to it and to each other.

b. An accent mark is added to the stressed syllable of the verb to keep the stress from shifting.

Ejercicios (Exercises) No. 159A-159B-159C-159D

159A. Practice the Spanish questions and answers aloud many times. They will give you a "feeling" for the two object pronouns construction.

1. ¿Le ha escrito el Sr. Adams la carta a su agente?
   Sí, se la ha escrito.
2. ¿Le ha dado Ud. el regalo a su madre?
   Sí, se lo he dado.
3. ¿Me prestará Ud. su pluma?
   Sí, se la prestaré.
4. ¿Nos mandarán Uds. las flores?
   Sí, se las mandaremos.
5. ¿Les prestaron el dinero a Uds.?
   Sí, nos lo prestaron
6. ¿Les contó Ud. los cuentos a los niños?
   Sí, se los conté.

1. Has Mr. Adams written the letter to his agent?
   Yes, he has written it to him.
2. Have you given the gift to your mother?
   Yes, I have given it to her.
3. Will you lend me your pen?
   Yes, I will lend it to you.
4. Will you send us the flowers?
   Yes, we will send them to you.
5. Did they lend you the money?
   Yes, they lent it to us.
6. Did you tell the stories to the children?
   Yes, I told them to them.

159B. Before doing this exercise review Grammar Notes 1.

I. Translate into English:
1. Los niños me los traen.
2. Los alumnos nos las mandan.
3. Ellos no nos los venden.
4. Te lo doy, hijito.

II. Translate into Spanish:
1. Charles gives it (*m.*) to me.
2. Anna lends them (*m.*) to us.
3. The teacher says it (*m.*) to us.
4. We give it (*f.*) to you, child.

159C. Before doing this exercise review Grammar Notes 2.

I. Translate into English:
1. Se lo decimos a Ud.
2. Se lo traemos a Uds.
3. Se los damos a él.
4. Se las mandamos a ellos.

II. Translate into Spanish:
1. John tells it (*m.*) to you (*sing.*)
2. Mary writes it (*f.*) to him.
3. The teacher gives them (*m.*) to you (*pl.*)
4. We send them (*f.*) to her.

159D. Before doing this exercise review Grammar Notes 3.

I. Translate into English:
1. Dígamelo.
2. Dénoslo.
3. Préstemelos.
4. Mándeselos a él.

II. Translate into Spanish:
1. Lend them (*m.*) to me.
2. Send it (*m.*) to us.
3. Tell it (*f.*) to him.
4. Give them (*m.*) to her.

CAPÍTULO 40 (CUARENTA)

PARTE PRIMERA

El Señor Adams Sale De México

Décima Carta De México

Muy amigo mío:

Cuando me fuí (I went away) de Nueva York, como Ud. ya sabe, había aprendido algo acerca de México. Había leído varios libros muy interesantes sobre su (its) historia y sus costumbres. Ya sabía hablar español bastante bien.

Aquí en México he visitado muchos lugares. En nuestras conversaciones, que recuerdo bien, hemos hablado de algunos de ellos. En mis cartas podía describirle un poco de lo mucho que he visto y he aprendido. Lo demás (the rest) espero decírselo personalmente.

Como Ud. puede imaginar, me gustan mucho los lugares de interés histórico, el paisaje, el arte y las artes populares. Pero más me interesa el pueblo de México con su cariño y su hospitalidad generosa. Me gustan su humor y su filosofía frente a las dificultades.

Me gusta mucho la vida de México. De veras es más tranquila que la de Nueva York a pesar de (in spite of) mis primeras impresiones en el libre que me llevó con velocidad espantosa desde el aeropuerto hasta mi hotel.

Ud. sabe que vine a México en viaje de recreo y también de negocios. Afortunadamente pronto terminé los negocios y podía dedicarme enteramente al recreo.

No puedo ir ni a Colombia, ni a Guatemala. ¡Qué lástima! Pero preferí llegar a conocer (to get to know) mejor a México. Hay tanto que ver, tanto que hacer, tanto que aprender. Me encantó todo.

Tendré mucho que decirle de las personas muy simpáticas que he conocido, los lugares que he visitado y todo lo que he aprendido de las costumbres, de la vida, del idioma y de las artes de México.

Claro está que pronto volveré a México. Quiero volver el año que viene. Pero entonces llevaré conmigo a la familia entera. Estoy seguro de que (I am sure that) no tendré ninguna dificultad. No he ganado el premio gordo en la lotería; pero, de todos modos, volveré.

Ésta es la última carta que le escribiré antes de salir para Nueva York el primero de agosto. Tendré mucho gusto en telefonearle después de mi llegada, invitándole a tomar la cena con nosotros cuanto antes. Sin duda pasaremos gran parte de la noche hablando de nuestro querido México.

Hasta entonces y afectuosamente,

Juan Adams

Vocabulario

el cariño	affection	dedicar	to dedicate
el paisaje	landscape	encantar	to charm
la filosofía	philosophy	enteramente	entirely
la hospitalidad	hospitality	frente a	in the face of

Expresiones Importantes

de todos modos	anyway
llegar a conocer	to get to know
cuanto antes	as soon as possible

Exercise No. 160—Test of Reading Comprehension

Answer these questions in English

1. Before leaving for Mexico, how had Mr. Adams obtained some knowledge of the country?

2. How much was he able to describe in his letters?

3. What interests Mr. Adams most in Mexico?

4. Mention four qualities of the people that he likes.

5. How does Mr. Adams compare life in New York with that in Mexico?

6. When had he gotten a different impression?

7. Why didn't he go to Colombia or Guatemala?

8. Whom will he take with him on his next trip to Mexico?

9. What is he sure of?

10. When is he leaving for New York?

11. What will he be glad to do after his return to New York?

12. How does he think he and Mr. Lopez will spend much of the night?

PARTE SEGUNDA

Grammar Notes

1. saber and poder

a. saber plus an infinitive means *to know how to do* something.

Sabe escribir el español. — He can (knows how to) write Spanish.

b. poder plus an infinitive means to have the physical ability or the opportunity to do something.

Hoy no puede escribir, porque está enfermo. — Today he cannot (is not able to) write, because he is ill.

2. Untranslated que.

a. You have learned that **tener que** means *to have to*. Thus:

Tengo que estudiar la lección. — I must (have to) study the lesson.

b. que appears in a number of other expressions where it is not translated:

Tendré mucho que decirle. — I will have much to tell you.
Tengo una carta que escribir. — I have a letter to write.
Hay tanto que ver. — There is so much to see.

PARTE TERCERA

Ejercicios (Exercises) No. 161A-161B-161C

161A. Translate the following sentences accurately. Be sure the tense is correct.

Ejemplo:
Me fuí de Nueva York. — I left New York.
Me iré de Nueva York. — I shall leave New York.

1. Leeré varios libros.
2. Había leído varios libros.
3. He leído varios libros.
4. Hemos visitado a México.
5. Habíamos visitado a México.
6. Visitaremos a México.
7. Puedo describirlo.
8. Podía describirlo.
9. Podré describirlo.
10. Me gusta su carta.
11. Me gustó su carta.
12. Me gustará su carta.
13. Terminan los negocios.
14. Terminaron los negocios.
15. Han terminado los negocios.
16. Tienen mucho que decirme.
17. Tendrán mucho que decirme.
18. Tuvieron mucho que decirme.
19. Volveremos a casa.
20. Volvimos a casa.

161B. Complete with the correct form of saber, conocer or poder as needed:

1. ¿Quién (knows) todas las respuestas?
2. (We know) a ese hombre, pero (we do not know) dónde vive.
3. (I cannot) hacer el viaje con Ud.
4. El Sr. Adams quiere (to know) mejor a su agente.
5. Ahora (they know each other) mejor.
6. (I know how) jugar al fútbol.
7. Si (you know) el sistema monetario, (you can) regatear en el mercado.
8. (You know) aquellas ruínas mejor que yo.
9. Mucho gusto en (know you).
10. (They are not able) cambiar la llanta.

161C.

1. Have you learned much about Mexico?
2. Yes, I have been (estado) there, and I have read many books.
3. Can you speak Spanish?
4. Yes, I speak it quite well.
5. Do you remember the places of which (de que) we have spoken?
6. I remember them well.
7. Are you able to describe them in Spanish?
8. Yes, I can describe them.
9. What did you like most in Mexico?
10. I liked the people most.
11. Is the life of Mexico more tranquil than that of New York?
12. Indeed it is more tranquil.
13. Is there much to see in Mexico?
14. There is much to see, much to hear, much to do, much to learn.
15. My trip is finished.

REPASO 9

(CAPÍTULOS 36–40) PARTE PRIMERA

NOUNS

1. la alegría	11. la estación de gasolina	19. el refresco	1. joy	11. gas station	19. refreshment
2. el aficionado		20. la risa	2. amateur		20. smile
3. el banco	12. la librería	21. la señal	3. bench, bank	12. bookstore	21. signal
4. la biblioteca	13. la lotería	22. el sonido	4. library	13. lottery	22. sound
5. el bolsillo	14. la pieza	23. la sombra	5. pocket	14. piece	23. shade
6. la carretera	15. la posibilidad	24. el sueño	6. road, highway	15. possibility	24. sleep, dream
7. los dulces	16. el premio gordo	25. la tela	7. sweets	16. first prize	25. cloth
8. la esquina	17. el paisaje	26. el tabaco	8. corner	17. landscape	26. tobacco
9. el garage	18. el recreo	27. el valle	9. garage	18. recreation	27. valley
10. la joya			10. jewel		

VERBS

1. alquilar	7. manejar	13. regresar	1. to rent	7. to drive	13. to return (go back)
2. anunciar	8. matar	14. reunirse	2. to announce	8. to kill	14. to meet together
3. crecer	9. nombrar	15. sacar	3. to grow	9. to name	15. to take out
4. dormir(ue)	10. ofrecer	16. señalar	4. to sleep	10. to offer	16. to point to
5. dormirse	11. parar	17. soñar	5. to fall asleep	11. to stop	17. to dream
6. ganar	12. prestar		6. to win	12. to lend	

PREPOSITIONS

1. durante	2. a pesar de	3. hacia	1. during	2. inspite of	3. towards

IMPORTANT EXPRESSIONS

1. a lo lejos	7. no me falta nada	1. in the distance	7. I lack nothing
2. de todos modos	8. más allá	2. anyway	8. further on
3. estar de acuerdo con	9. no (verb) más que	3. to be in agreement with	9. (verb) nothing but, only
4. estar para + infin.	10. ¿qué importa?	4. to be about to	10. what does it matter?
5. en seguida	11. sin embargo	5. immediately	11. nevertheless
6. faltaba una hora	12. tener sueño	6. it was one hour before	12. to be sleepy

PARTE SEGUNDA

Ejercicio 162. Translate the following sentences accurately. All the tenses you have learned and the imperative are here illustrated.

1. ¿Quién pedirá informes en la estación de ferrocarril?
2. Pablo ya había tomado el almuerzo cuando le ví.
3. ¿Querrían Uds. hacer un viaje a todos los países de Europa?
4. Conozco a ese hombre pero no sé dónde vive.
5. Escribíamos nuestras cartas cuando el maestro entró en la sala.
6. Tomen Uds. estos papeles y pónganlos en mi escritorio.
7. Hemos comprado los diarios y los hemos leído.
8. Cuando llegué a México noté que todo el mundo compraba billetes de lotería.
9. Compre Ud. este billete y Ud. tendrá suerte.
10. No podía describirles todo lo que había visto.
11. Vine a México y me recibieron con cariño.

12. Guillermo hablaba toda la tarde mientras yo no decía nada.
13. No me gustó la corrida y por eso no asistiré a otra.
14. La tortilla se parece a nuestros panqueques.
15. Los padres trabajaban mientras que los niños dormían.
16. Estábamos en el mercado cuando comenzó a llover.
17. Eran las ocho y media de la mañana y todavía dormían los niños.
18. No vendrán aquí porque no tendrán tiempo.
19. Niños, ¿no jugarán Uds. en el patio?
20. Mi tío viajó por todos los países de Sud América.
21. Le gustaban al Sr. Adams los alimentos picantes, pero recordaba los consejos de su maestro y no los comería.
22. Yo quería los juguetes pero Carlos no me los daría.
23. Si encuentro platos con dibujos de animalitos, se los mandaré a Ud.
24. Él pidió cambio por un billete de mil pesos y el cajero (cashier) se lo dió.
25. Ud. tiene el sombrero de María. Devuélvaselo.

Ejercicio 163. Complete these sentences in Spanish.

1. El Sr. Adams (is a businessman of New York).
2. Hizo (a trip to Mexico in order to visit) a su agente.
3. Quería (to know him better).
4. Antes de salir para México (he learned to speak Spanish).
5. También (he had read many books) sobre México.
6. Desde México escribió cartas (to his friend and teacher, Mr. Lopez).
7. Le gustaron mucho a él (the places of historic interest).
8. A pesar de sus primeras impresiones (Mr. Adams found the life in Mexico more tranquil than that of New York).
9. Pensó (of the taxi which took him to his hotel).
10. No le gustó (the fearful speed of that taxi).
11. Afortunadamente (he finished his business matters quickly).
12. Sin embargo (he was not able to visit either Colombia or Guatemala).
13. Había (so much to see, so much to hear, so much to do, so much to learn).
14. Pero el Sr. Adams (will return to Mexico).
15. Llevará consigo (the whole family).
16. (He has not won the first prize) en la loteria, pero tendrá (enough money).
17. Ésta es (Mr. Adams' last letter) desde México.
18. (No doubt), invitará al Sr. López (to have dinner with his family) después de su llegada a Nueva York.

LECTURA 1

Exercise No. 164—Las Pirámides de Teotihuacán

Se ven en los alrededores de México D.F. los restos (remains) de varias culturas muy desarrolladas (developed) y algo misteriosas—las culturas de las razas de indios que vivían en México hace diez siglos (ten centuries ago).

En el valle de Teotihuacán se encuentran unas pirámides enormes, monumentos de una cultura apenas (scarcely) conocida, la cultura de los Toltecas. Vivían en el valle antes de los Aztecas. Lo que (what) sabemos de ellos no existe ni en los libros de historia ni en las leyendas (legends) sino en pura piedra.

La Pirámide del Sol domina el valle. Tiene 216 pies de altura, y es más grande que cualquier pirámide de Egipto. Se puede subir hasta la cima por una escalera ancha y muy escarpada (steep).

Más al norte, por la Avenida de los Muertos (dead), está la Pirámide de la Luna y al sur se ve el templo de Quetzalcoatl, la Serpiente Plumada (plumed), dios de los Aztecas. Esta pirámide está decorada con esculturas (sculptures) muy interesantes.

La gente que vive hoy día en el valle de Teotihuacán son descendientes de los Aztecas. Los Toltecas, arquitectos de las pirámides, desaparecieron hace mucho tiempo. Sabemos solamente que era una gente imaginativa con un sentido (sense) estético muy avanzado.

LECTURA 2
Exercise No. 165—En el Zócalo

Estamos en el Zócalo. Es la plaza principal de México, D.F. Caminamos al norte hacia (toward) la Catedral. Es del siglo diez y seis. A la derecha está el Palacio Nacional; también es antiguo, del siglo diez y siete. A la izquierda está el Portal de Mercaderes (Merchants). Allí vemos una cuadra de puestos y vendedores de mercancía barata. Más allá (Beyond) del Portal está el Monte de Piedad (Pawnshop), y detrás de nosotros, al sur, están el Palacio Municipal y el Palacio de Justicia. Éste es un nuevo edificio. Aquél es del siglo diez y ocho. Por todos lados, vemos edificios grandes y mucha gente.

A

able, to be poder(ue)
about de, acerca de
  about 2 o'clock a eso de las dos
accept, to aceptar
accompany, to acompañar
ache el dolor
  headache dolor de cabeza
  toothache dolor de muelas
according to según
accustom, to acostumbrar
address la dirección
admire, to admirar
advice el consejo
advise, to aconsejar
affection el cariño
after después de (prep.) después que (conj.)
afternoon la tarde
  in the afternoon por la tarde; p.m. de la tarde
again otra vez;
  to do again volver a + infin.
against contra
ago: two years ago hace dos años
agent el agente
agreeable agradable
aid la ayuda
aid, to ayudar
air el aire
  in the open air al aire libre
airmail: by airmail por correo aéreo
airplane el avión
airport el aeropuerto
almost casi
alone solo
along por
already ya
also también
although aunque
always siempre
amusement la diversión
and y, e (before i or hi)
announce anunciar
another otro, -a
answer la respuesta
answer, to contestar, responder
any cualquier
anyone alguién, alguno, -a
apple la manzana
approach, to acercarse a
arm el brazo
around alrededor de
arrange, to arreglar
arrival la llegada
arrive, to llegar
art el arte (f) and (m)
article el artículo
artist el (la) artista
as . . . as tan . . . como
ask, to preguntar; to ask for pedir(i);
  to ask questions hacer preguntas
assortment el surtido
at a, en
attend, to asistir a
attention la atención
aunt la tía
automobile el automóvil
avenue la avenida

awake, to be estar despierto, -a
awaken, to (arouse) despertar(ie)

B

bacon el tocino
bad malo, -a
badly mal
baggage el equipaje
baker el panadero
banana el plátano
bargain, to regatear
basket la cesta, la canasta
bath el baño; bathroom el cuarto de baño
bathe, to bañar, bañarse
be, to ser, estar;
  to be in a hurry estar de prisa
  to be on the way estar en camino
  to be about to estar para
beans los frijoles
beautiful bello, -a; hermoso; -a
because porque
become, to ponerse, hacerse
  He becomes sick. Se pone enfermo.
  He is becoming rich. Se hace rico.
bed la cama
bedroom la recámara (Mex.), la alcoba; el dormitorio
before (time) antes de
before (place) delante de
begin, to comenzar(ie), empezar(ie), principiar
beginning el principio
  at the beginning al principio
behind detrás de
believe, to creer
belt el cinturón
bench el banco
better mejor
between entre
big grande
bill la cuenta
bird el pájaro
birthday el cumpleaños
black negro, -a
blanket la manta, el sarape
block la cuadra
blouse la blusa
blue azul
boat el barco
body el cuerpo
boiled cocido, -a
book el libro
bookshelf el estante
bookstore la librería
bottle la botella
box la caja
boy el muchacho
bread el pan
break, to romper
breakfast el desayuno
breakfast, to have desayunarse; tomar el desayuno
bring, to traer, llevar
brother el hermano
building el edificio
bundle el bulto
bus el camión (Mex.), autobús
business el negocio

business man el comerciante, el negociante
busy ocupado, -a
but pero; but on the contrary sino
buy, to comprar
buyer el comprador

C

cake la torta, el pastel
call, to llamar
can (be able to) poder(ue)
car el coche; by car en coche
care: Be careful! ¡Cuidado!
carry, to llevar; to carry away llevarse
catch, to coger
  to catch cold coger (atrapar) un resfriado
celebrate, to celebrar
century el siglo
certain cierto, -a
certainly por cierto
certificate el certificado
chair la silla
change el cambio; in change de cambio
change, to cambiar
  to change clothes cambiar de ropa
chat, to platicar, charlar
cheap barato, -a
check, to (baggage) facturar
cheese el queso
chicken el pollo
child el niño, la niña
choose, to escoger
chop la chuleta
church la iglesia
cigar el puro (Mex.), cigarro
city la ciudad
class la clase
clean limpio, -a
clean, to limpiar
clear claro, -a
clerk el dependiente
climate el clima
close, to cerrar(ie)
closed cerrado, -a
cloth la tela
clothing la ropa
coffee el café
cold frío, -a
  It is cold (weather). Hace frío.
  I am cold. Tengo frío.
color el color;
  What is the color of . . . ? ¿De qué color es . . . ?
come, to venir
comprehend, to comprender, entender(ie)
comfortable cómodo, -a
concert el concierto
confess, to confesar(ie)
congratulate, to felicitar
complete, to completar
consequently por consiguiente
contain, to contener
continue, to continuar, seguir(i)
conversation la conversación
converse, to conversar
cooked cocido, -a
cool fresco, -a

It (weather) is cool. Hace fresco.
copper el cobre
corn maíz
corner la esquina
correct correcto, -a
cost, to costar(ue)
costume el traje
cotton el algodón
count, to contar(ue)
course: of course por supuesto; desde luego; Creo que sí.
  Of course not Creo que no.
country el campo, el país (nation)
cross, to cruzar
cousin el primo, la prima
cover, to cubrir
craftsman el artesano
cream la crema
cry el grito
cry, to (shout) gritar
current corriente
custard el flan
culture la cultura
custom la costumbre
cut, to cortar

D

daily diario, -a
dance, to bailar
dangerous peligroso, -a
dark obscuro, -a
date la fecha
  What is the date? ¿Cuál es la fecha?
daughter la hija
day el día; nowadays hoy día
  on the following day al día siguiente
death la muerte
dear caro, -a; querido, -a (beloved)
decide, to decidir
decoration el adorno
defend, to defender
demand, to demandar
descend, to bajar
depart, to partir
describe, to describir
desire, to desear; tener ganas
desk el escritorio
dessert el postre
die, to morir(ue)
different diferente, distinto, -a
difficult difícil
diligent diligente
dine, to tomar la cena, comer
dining room el comedor
dinner la comida
dirty sucio, -a
discover, to discubrir
dish el plato
distant lejano, -a
divide, to dividir
do, to hacer
doctor el médico, el doctor
dollar el dólar
door la puerta
doubt la duda
  without any doubt sin duda alguna
doubt, to dudar

drawing el dibujo
dress el vestido
dress, to vestir(i); to dress in vestirse de
drink la bebida
drink, to beber, tomar
drive manejar
dry seco, -a
dry clean limpiar en seco
during durante

E

each cada; each one cada uno
ear el oído (*hearing*), la oreja
early temprano
earn, to ganar
east el este
eat, to comer
educate, to educar
egg el huevo
elevator el ascensor, el elevador
employ, to emplear
employee el empleado
empty vacío
end el fin; finally al fin
end, to terminar, acabar
English el inglés (*lang.*)
   Englishman el inglés; Englishwoman la inglesa
enjoy, to gozar de
enough basta, bastante
enter, to entrar en
entire entero, -a
entrance la entrada
equal igual
especially sobre todo
everybody todo el mundo
everywhere por (en) todas partes
examination el examen
examine, to examinar, revisar (*baggage*)
excellent excelente
except excepto, menos
excuse, to dispensar, perdonar, excusar; excuse me dispénseme
expect, to esperar
explain, to explicar
exporter el exportador
express, to expresar
eye el ojo

F

fable la fábula
face la cara
fall, to caer
fall asleep, to dormirse(ue)
false falso, -a
family la familia
famous famoso, -a
far from lejos de
fare el pasaje
fat gordo, -a
fast rápido, -a
father el padre
favor el favor
fear, to temer, tener miedo
feel, to (well, ill) sentirse (ie)
few pocos(as)
find, to hallar; to find out averiguar
fine fino, -a
finish, to terminar, acabar
first primero, -a
fish el pescado
flight el vuelo

floor el suelo; el piso (*story*)
flower la flor
follow, to seguir(i)
following: on the following day al día siguiente
food la comida, los alimentos
foot el pie; on foot a pie
for por, para
forget, to olvidar
fork el tenedor
form, to formar
fountain la fuente
fountain pen la plumafuente
French (*lang.*) el francés
Frenchman el francés
Frenchwoman la francesa
friend el amigo, la amiga
from de; from . . . to desde . . . hasta
fruit la fruta
full lleno, -a

G

game el juego
garage el garage
garden el jardín
gentleman (Mr.) el señor
get, to obtener, conseguir
  to get (become) ponerse
  to get up levantarse
  to get on subir a
  to get off salir, bajar de
gift el regalo
give, to dar; to give back devolver
glad alegre
glass el vaso (*for drinking*), el vidrio, el cristal
glove el guante
go, to ir; to go away irse
  to go shopping ir de compras
gold el oro
good bueno, -a
grandfather el abuelo
grandmother la abuela
grape la uva
grapefruit la toronja
gray gris
green verde
greet, to saludar
greeting el saludo
group el grupo
guess, to adivinar

H

hair el pelo
half la mitad; medio, -a
ham el jamón
hand la mano
  handmade hecho a mano
  to shake hands darse la mano
happen, to pasar
happy contento, -a; feliz
hard difícil
hat el sombrero
have, to haber (*auxiliary*); tener (*possess*)
head la cabeza
headache dolor de cabeza
healthy sano, -a
  to be healthy tener salud
hear, to oír
heart el corazón
heavy pesado, -a
help la ayuda
help, to ayudar

here aquí, acá (*usually after a verb of motion*)
Here it is. Aquí lo tiene Ud.
high alto, -a
holiday la fiesta
home: en casa; to go home ir a casa
hope, to esperar
  I hope so. Espero que sí.
  I hope not. Espero que no.
horse el caballo
hot caliente
  It (weather) is hot. Hace calor.
  I am hot. Tengo calor.
hour la hora
house la casa
how como, ¿cómo?
how much ¿cuánto, -a?
how many ¿cuántos, -as?
hungry: to be hungry tener hambre
hurry: to be in a hurry tener prisa
hurry, to apresurarse
hurt, to hacer daño a
husband el esposo

I

ice cream el helado
if si
ill enfermo, -a; malo, -a
imagine imaginar
immediately inmediatamente, en seguida
in en
inside of dentro de
Indian el indio
industry la industria
inform, to informar, avisar
inhabitant el habitante
ink la tinta
instead of en vez de
intelligent inteligente
intend, to pensar + *infinitive*
interest el interés
interest, to interesar
introduce, to presentar
invitation la invitación
invite, to invitar
iron el hierro

J

jar el jarro
jewel la joya
jewelry shop la joyería
juice el jugo

K

keep, to guardar
kill, to matar
kind amable
king el rey
kiss, to besar
kitchen la cocina
knife el cuchillo
know, to saber; to know how saber; to be acquainted with conocer

L

lady (Mrs.) la señora
lamp la lámpara
land la tierra
language la lengua, el idioma
last ultimo, -a
  last year el año pasado
laugh la risa

laugh, to reír(i)
  to laugh at reírse de
lawyer el abogado
lazy perezoso, -a
leaf la hoja
learn, to aprender
leave, to (go out of) salir de
least el menos
  at least por lo menos
leather el cuero
left izquierdo, -a
  to the left a la izquierda
lemon el limón
lend, to prestar
less menos
let, to (permit) permitir, dejar
letter la carta
library la biblioteca
lie down, to acostarse(ue)
life la vida
light la luz
like, to gustar
  I like the game. Me gusta el juego.
listen, to escuchar
little pequeño, -a; a little un poco
live, to vivir
lively vivo, -a
living room la sala
load la carga
long largo, -a
look at, to mirar
look for, to buscar
lose, to perder(ie)
loud alto, -a
love el amor
love, to querer(ie) a, amar a
low bajo, -a
luck la suerte
lucky afortunado, -a
lunch el almuerzo

M

magnificent magnífico, -a
magazine la revista
maid la criada
mail, to echar en el buzón, echar al correo
maintain, to mantener
make, to hacer; to make a trip hacer un viaje
majority la mayor parte, la mayoría
man el hombre
manner la manera; in the same manner de la misma manera
many muchos, -as
market el mercado
marry, to (someone) casarse con
match el cerillo, el fósforo
matter, to importar; It doesn't matter. No importa. What is the matter? ¿Qué hay? What is the matter with you? ¿Qué tiene Ud.?
meal la comida
mean, to significar; querer(ie) decir
meanwhile entretanto
measure la medida
measure, to medir(i)
meat la carne
meet, to (make the acquaintance of) conocer a; Glad to meet you.

Mucho gusto en conocerle.
meet, to (come together with) encontrar(ue)
melon el melón
memory la memoria
menu la lista, el menú
merchandise la mercancía
merry alegre
month el mes
Mexican mexicano, -a
Mexico México
milk la leche
mile la milla
million el millón
Miss (young lady) la señorita
miss, to echar de menos
mistake la falta
mistaken (to be) estar equivocado, -a
modern moderno, -a
money el dinero, la moneda (currency)
moon la luna
more más
morning, la mañana; in the morning por la mañana; a.m. de la mañana
most el(la) más
mother la madre
motion picture la película
mountain la montaña
mouth la boca
move, to mover(ue)
movies el cine
much mucho, -a
music la música
must (ought to) deber; (to have to) tener que; (probably) deber de

N

name el nombre
name, to nombrar
nature la naturaleza
near cerca de (prep.)
necessary necesario, -a; it is necessary es necesario, hay que + infinitive
necessity la necesidad
need, to necesitar
neither tampoco; neither . . . nor ni . . . ni
never nunca, jamás
nevertheless sin embargo
new nuevo, -a
news las noticias
newspaper el periódico, el diario
next próximo, -a
nice bonito, -a, simpático, -a
night la noche; at night por la noche; p.m. de la noche
nobody nadie
noise el ruido
none, no ninguno, -a
north el norte
North American norteamericano, -a
nose la nariz
nothing nada
now ahora, ahorita
number el número

O

obey, to obedecer
object el objeto
observe, to observar

obtain, to obtener, conseguir(i)
occasion la ocasión
of de
offer, to ofrecer
office la oficina
often a menudo, muchas veces
old viejo, -a antiguo, -a
older mayor
oldest el(la) mayor
on (top of) encima de
only sólo, solamente; not only . . . but also no solamente . . . sino también
open abierto, -a
open, to abrir
opportunity la oportunidad
opposite frente a
or o (u before o or ho)
orange la naranja
order, to mandar, pedir(i)
other otro, -a
over sobre
overcoat el abrigo
ought to deber
outside of fuera de
owe, to deber
own propio, -a

P

pack: to pack a trunk hacer una maleta
package el paquete
paint, to pintar
painter el pintor
painting la pintura
pancakes los panqueques
paper el papel
parcel post el paquete postal
parents los padres
park el parque
pass (by), to pasar
passport el pasaporte
pay, to pagar
peach el melocotón
pear la pera
pen la pluma
pencil el lápiz
people la gente, las personas
perfectly perfectamente
permission el permiso
permit, to permitir, dejar
person la persona
pharmacy la farmacia
picture el cuadro
pick up, to cojer, recojer
piece la pieza
pineapple la piña
pink rosado, -a
pity la lástima What a pity! ¡Qué lástima!
place el sitio, el lugar
place, to poner
plane el avión
play el drama, la comedia
play, to tocar (instrument) jugar(ue) (game)
pleasant agradable
please: por favor; hágame Ud. el favor de; tenga la bondad de
pleasure el placer, el gusto; with pleasure con mucho gusto
pocket el bolsillo
point out, to señalar, indicar, mostrar(ue)
policeman el policía

poor pobre
portrait el retratro
poster el cartel
possible posible
post-office el correo
potato la patata
pottery la cerámica, la alfarería
pound la libra
pour, to echar
practice, to practicar
prefer, to preferir(ie)
prepare, to preparar
present, to presentar
pretty bonito, -a
price el precio
priest el cura
prize el premio
produce, to producir
production la producción
professor el profesor, la profesora
program el programa
progress, to adelantar
promenade el paseo
promise, to prometer
proud orgulloso, -a
purchase la compra
purse la bolsa
put, to poner; to put on (clothing) ponerse

Q

quantity la cantidad
question la pregunta
quickly de prisa, aprisa

R

radio el radio (set), la radio (broadcast)
rain la lluvia
rain, to llover(ue)
raincoat el impermeable
rainy lluvioso, -a
rapid rápido, -a
rapidly rápidamente
raise, to levantar
rare raro, -a
read, to leer
ready listo, -a
really! ¡de veras!
receive, to recibir
recognize, to reconocer
recreation el recreo
red rojo, -a
regret, to sentir(ie)
relate, to contar(ue)
relative el pariente
remain, to quedar, quedarse
remember, to recordar(ue), acordarse(ue)
rent, to alquilar
repeat, to repetir(i)
reply, to responder, contestar
representative el representante
request, to pedir(i)
resemble, to parecerse a
resist, to resistir
respect el respeto
rest el descanso
restaurant el restaurante
return, to volver(ue) (to go back); regresar (to go back); devolver (to give back)
rice el arroz
rich rico, -a
ride, to ir (en coche, etc.); to go for a ride pasearse

(en coche, etc.), dar un paseo (en coche, etc.)
right: to be right tener razon
right derecho, -a
river el río
road el camino
roof el tejado
roll el panecillo
room el cuarto
round redondo, -a
round trip ticket el boleto de viaje redondo
row la fila
run, to run

S

salt la sal
same mismo, -a the same thing lo mismo
sash la faja
sauce la salsa
say decir How does one say? ¿Cómo se dice?
scarcely apenas
school la escuela
screen la pantalla
season la estación
seat el asiento
seated sentado, -a
silk la seda
see, to ver; Let's see. A ver.
seek, to buscar
seem, to parecer
sell, to vender
seller el vendedor
send, to mandar, enviar
sense el sentido
sentence la frase
serve, to servir(i)
set, to poner; to set the table poner la mesa
shade la sombra
shawl el rebozo
shine, to brillar
shipment el envío
shirt la camisa
shoe el zapato
short corto -a, breve
shout, to gritar
show, to (point out) mostrar(ue), enseñar
sick enfermo, -a; malo, -a
side el lado; beside al lado de
sidewalk la acera
sight la vista
silk la seda
silver la plata
silversmith el platero
similar semejante
simple sencillo, -a
since (because) puesto que
sing, to cantar
sister la hermana
sit down, to sentarse(ie); to be sitting estar sentado
size el tamaño
skirt la falda
sky el cielo
sleep, to dormir(ue)
sleepy: to be sleepy tener sueño
slowly despacio, lentamente
small pequeño, -a
smile, to sonreír(i)
snow la nieve; it is snowing nieva
so así; so much tanto, -a; so that para que, de modo que

some alguno, -a
someone alguién
something algo
somewhat algo
son el hijo
song la canción
soon pronto
sorry: to be sorry sentir(ie);
    I am very sorry. Lo
    siento mucho.
south el sur
soup la sopa
souvenir el recuerdo
Spain España
Spaniard el español, la es-
    pañola
Spanish (*lang.*) el español
speak, to hablar
spend, to (*time*) pasar
spend, to (*money*) gastar
spicy picante
spite: in spite of a pesar
    de
spoon la cucharita
spring la primavera
square cuadrado, -a
stairway la escalera
stamp el timbre (*Mex.*) la
    estampilla
stand el puesto
stand up, to ponerse en pie;
    to be standing estar de
    pie
star la estrella
state el estado
station (railroad) la esta-
    ción de ferrocarril
statue la estatua
steak (beef) el filete (*Mex.*)
stenographer la taquígrafa
step el paso
still todavía
stop, to parar
store la tienda
story el cuento
story (*of building*) el piso
straw la paja
street la calle
streetcar el tranvía
strong fuerte
student el(la) estudiante
study, to estudiar
style el estilo
subject el tema
suburb el suburbio
suit el traje
suitcase la maleta to pack
    a suitcase hacer una
    maleta
summer el verano
sun el sol; it is sunny
    hay sol
supper la cena
surely de seguro
surprised sorprendido
surrounded rodeado, -a
sweater el suéter
sweet dulce; sweets
    (candy) los dulces

T

table la mesa; to set the
    table poner la mesa
tailor el sastre
take, to tomar; to take
    away llevarse
take out, to sacar
tall also, -a; grande, alto, -a
tank el tanque
taste, to probar(ue)
tasty sabroso, -a
tea el té
teach, to enseñar
teacher el maestro, la
    maestra, el profesor, la
    profesora
telephone el teléfono
telephone, to llamar por
    teléfono, telefonear
tell, to decir
temperate templado
temperature la temperatura
textile el tejido
thankful agradecido, -a
thanks gracias
that ese, -a; aquel, aquella;
    que (*conj.*)
theater el teatro
then entonces
there allí, ahí, allá (*usually
    with a verb of motion*);
    there is (are) hay
therefore por eso, por lo
    tanto
these (*adj.*) estos, -as
thick grueso, -a
thing la cosa
think, to (believe) creer;
    to think of pensar en
thirsty: to be thirsty tener
    sed
this (*adj.*) este, -a
those (*adj.*) esos, -as; aquel-
    los, -as
through por
thus así
ticket window la taquilla
ticket el boleto (*Mex.*); el
    billete
tile el azulejo
time: What time is it? ¿Qué
    hora es? one time, two
    times una vez, dos veces,
    etc.;
    on time a tiempo; to
    have a good time pasar
    un buen rato
time table el horario
tin la hojalata
tip la propina
tire, to cansarse
tired cansado, -a
to a; in order to para
tobacco el tabaco
today hoy
tomato el tomate
tomorrow morning mañana
    por la mañana
too (also) también
too many demasiados, -as

too much demasiado, -a
tooth el diente
toothache dolor de muela
topic el tópico, el tema
tourist el(la) turista
tourist card la tarjeta de
    turista
towards hacia
town el pueblo, la pobla-
    ción
toy el juguete
train el train
travel, to viajar
traveler el viajero
tree el árbol
trip el viaje to take a trip
    hacer un viaje
trousers los pantalones
trunk la baúl
trunk of car el cajuela
truth la verdad
try, to tratar de; to try on
    probar(ue)
turkey el guajalote (*Mex.*)
typewriter la máquina de
    escribir
typical típico, -a

U

umbrella el paraguas
uncle el tío
under debajo de
understand comprender,
    entender(ie)
unfortunately desgracia-
    damente
United States los Estados
    Unidos (*abbreviation*)
    E.U.A.; E.E.U.U.
university la universidad
upon sobre, encima de
use, to usar, emplear
useful útil

V

vacation las vacaciones
valise la valija
valley el valle
very muy
view la vista
visit la visita
visit, to visitar
voice la voz
voyage el viaje

W

wait for, to esperar
waiter el mozo, el mesero
waiting room la sala de
    espera
wake up, to (*somebody*)
    despertar(ie), (*oneself*)
    depertarse
walk, to andar, ir a pie,
    caminar; to take a walk
    dar un paseo, pasearse
wall la pared
want desear, querer(ie)
wash, to lavar

watch el reloj
water el agua(f)
way: by the way a propósito
weak débil
wear llevar, vestir(i) de
weather: What's the
    weather? ¿Qué tiempo
    hace?
week la semana
weigh, to pesar
well pues, bien
    All right. Está bien.
well known conocido, -a
when cuando, ¿cuándo?
where donde, ¿dónde?
where (whither) ¿a dónde?
whether si
which que, ¿qué?
which one (ones) ¿cuál
    (cuáles)?
while mientras
white blanco, -a
who que, quien, ¿quién?
whom que ¿á quien?
whose cuyo, -a, ¿de quién?
why ¿por qué? ¿para qué?
wide ancho, -a
wife la esposa
win, to ganar
wind el viento
    It is windy. Hace viento.
window la ventana
winter el invierno
wise sabio, -a
wish el deseo
wish, to querer(ie), desear
with con
without sin
woman la mujer
wood la madera
wool la lana
word la palabra
work el trabajo
work, to trabajar
world el mundo
worse peor
worth, to be valer
    It is worth while. Vale la
    pena.
worthy digno, -a
worry, to preocuparse
write, to escribir
writer el escritor
wrong: to be wrong no
    tener razón

Y

year el año; last year el
    año pasado; next year el
    año que viene
yellow amarillo, -a
yesterday ayer
    day before yesterday ante-
    ayer
yet todavía; not yet to-
    davía no
young joven
youth el joven
younger menor
youngest el menor

A

a to, at
abajo under, below
abierto, -a open, opened
el abogado lawyer
el abrigo overcoat
abril (m.) April
abrir to open
acá here (usually with a verb of motion)
acabar to finish
  acaba de + infin. = to have just
aceptar to accept
la acera the sidewalk
acerca de about, concerning
acercarse (a) to approach
acompañar to accompany
aconsejar to advise
acordarse (ue) (de) to remember
acostarse (ue) to go to bed
acostumbrar to accustom
el acuerdo agreement
adelantar to progress
adelante straight ahead, forward
además moreover, also
adiós good-by
admirar to admire
el adobe adobe, sun-dried brick
aereo: por correo aereo by air mail
el aeropuerto airport
el aficionado sport fan
afortunado, -a lucky
afuera outside
el agente agent
agosto August
agradable agreeable, pleasant
agradecido, -a thankful, grateful
el agua (f.) water
ahí there
ahora now
ahorita just now, in just a minute
el aire air; al aire libre in the open air
alegrar to gladden
  alegrarse to rejoice, to be glad
alegre lively, merry
la alfarería pottery
algo something; somewhat
el algodón cotton
alguién someone, anyone
alguno (algún), -a someone, any
el alimento food
el alma (f.) soul
el almacén department store
el almuerzo lunch
alquilar to rent
alrededor de around
los alrededores surrounding area
alto, -a tall, high
la altura altitude
el alumno, la alumna student
allá there (usually with a verb of motion)
allí there
amable kind
amar to love

amarillo, -a yellow
el amigo, la amiga friend
el amor love
anaranjado, -a orange-colored
ancho, -a wide
andar to go, to walk
animado, -a lively, animated
el ánimo soul, spirit; courage
anoche last night
de antaño ancient, of long ago
ante before, in face of
anteayer day before yesterday
antes de before (refers to time)
  cuanto antes as soon as possible
antiguo, -a old
anunciar to announce
el año year
  el año que viene next year
el aparador sideboard
aparecer to appear
apenas scarcely
el apetito appetite
apreciar to appreciate
aprender (a) to learn (to)
apresurarse to hurry
aprisa swiftly, quickly
apropiado appropriate
aprovecharse de to take advantage of
aquel, aquella that
aquél, aquélla that (one); the former
aquí here
  Aquí lo tiene Ud. Here it is.
el árbol tree
arreglar to arrange
arriba above, upstairs
el arroz rice
el arte (m. and f.) art
el artículo article
el artesano craftsman
el(la) artista artist
artístico artistic
el ascensor elevator
así thus, so
el asiento seat
asistir (a) to attend
el aspecto appearance
atento attentive
atrás backwards, behind
atravesar (ie) to cross
aun (aún) even, yet, still
aunque although
el automóvil automobile
la avenida avenue
averiguar to find out
el avión airplane
avisar to inform
¡ay! alas!
ayer yesterday
la ayuda aid
ayudar (a) to aid, help (to)
el azúcar sugar
el azucarero sugar-bowl
azul blue
el azulejo tile

B

bailar to dance
el baile dance

bajar (de) to get out (of); to climb (go) down
bajo low
el balcón balcony
el banco bench
bañar to bathe
el baño bath; bathtub; bathroom
barato, -a cheap
¡basta! enough!
bastante quite, enough
la batalla battle
el baúl trunk
beber to drink
la bebida drink
el béisbol baseball
bello, -a beautiful
el beso kiss
la biblioteca library
bien well
bienvenido, -a welcome
el billete bill
blanco, -a white
la blusa blouse
la boca mouth
la boletería ticket-window
el boletero ticket-seller
el boleto (de primera) (de segunda) (first-class) (second-class) ticket
la bolsa purse
el bolsillo pocket
la bondad kindness
bonito, -a pretty, nice
la botella bottle
el brazo arm
brillar to shine
la brisa breeze
bueno (buen), -a good;
  ¡bueno! hello! (on telephone)
el bulto bundle
el burro donkey
buscar to look for
el buzón mailbox
  echar en el buzón to mail

C

el caballo horse
la cabeza head
cada each, every
caer to fall
el café coffee, cafe
la caja box
la cajuela trunk (of car)
el calcetín sock
caliente warm, hot
el calor heat; hace calor it is hot (weather)
  tener calor to be hot (for persons)
la calle street
la cama bed
cambiar to change, exchange
el cambio change
  de cambio in change
caminar to go, to travel, to walk
el camino road
el camión (Mex.) bus, truck
la camisa shirt
el campesino peasant
el campo country
la canasta basket
la canción song
cansado tired
cansarse to grow weary, tired

cantar to sing
la cantidad quantity
la caña de azucar sugar cane
la cara face
la carga load
el cariño affection
la carne meat
la carnicería butchers shop
caro, -a expensive, dear
la carta letter
el cartel poster
el cartero postman
la casa house
en casa at home
  volver a casa to go home
casarse con to marry
casi almost
la causa cause; a causa de because of
la cebolla onion
celebrar to celebrate
la cena supper
cenar to have supper
el centavo cent
el centro center
la cerámica pottery
cerca de (prep.) near
cercano nearby
el cerillo wax match
el cero zero
cerrado, -a closed, shut
cerrar (ie) to close, shut
el certificado certificate
la cerveza beer
la cesta basket
el cielo sky
el científico scientist
ciento (cien) one hundred
  por ciento percent
cierto certain, true
  por cierto certainly
el cigarro cigar
el cine movies
la cinta film
el cinturón belt
la cita appointment
citar to make an appointment with
la ciudad city
claro, -a clear, light
  ¡Claro que sí! Of course!
  ¡Claro que no! Of course not!
la clase class, kind
el clavel carnation
el cliente client
el clima climate
el cobre copper
cocido cooked, boiled
la cocina kitchen
el coche car, automobile (Mex.)
coger to catch, gather, pick up
el color color
  ¿De qué color es . . . ? What color is . . . ?
el comedor dining room
comenzar (ie) to begin
comer to eat
  comerse to "eat up"
el comerciante business man
la comida meal, food, dinner
como like, as, how; ¿cómo? how?
  ¿cómo no? of course, why not?

¿cómo se dice? how do you say?

cómodo, -a comfortable

el compañero companion

el compatriota countryman

completo, -a complete

la compra purchase

    ir de compras to go shopping

el comprador purchaser

comprar to buy

comprender to understand

común common

con with; conmigo with me; con tal que provided that

el concierto concert

condecorado, -a decorated

conducir to lead; to conduct

confesar (ie) to confess

conocer to know, meet, be acquainted with

conocido, -a well-known

conseguir (i) to get, obtain

el consejo advice

consentir (ie) to consent

consiguiente: por consiguiente consequently

consistir en to consist of

contar (ue) to count; to relate

contener to contain

contento, -a contented, happy

contestar (a) to answer

continuar to continue

contra against

conveniente convenient

conversar to converse

la copia copy

el corazón heart

la corbata necktie

coronado crowned

correcto, -a correct

corregir (i) to correct

el correo the post office, mail

    por correo aéreo by air mail

correr to run

la corrida de toros bull fight

corriente current, popular

cortar to cut

la cortesía courtesy

corto, -a short

la cosa thing

    ¡qué cosa! the idea!

la costa coast

costar (ue) to cost

la costumbre custom

es costumbre it's the custom

crecer to grow

creer to believe, "think"

    Creo que no. I think not.

    Creo que sí. I think so.

    ¡Ya lo creo! Yes indeed; I should say so!

la criada maid

el cristal glass

cruzar to cross

la cuadra block

cuadrado, -a square

el cuadro picture

¿cúal? cuáles which (one, ones)? what?

cualquier any

cuando when; ¿cuándo? when?

¿cuánto, -a? how much?

¿cuántos?, -as? how many?

el cuarto room, quarter, fourth

cubierto de covered (with)

cubrir to cover

la cuchara spoon

la cucharita teaspoon

el cuchillo knife

la cuenta bill

el cuento story

el cuero leather

el cuerpo body

cuidar to look after; cuidar de to take care of

¡Cuidado! Take care!

la culpa guilt, fault

la cultura culture

el cumpleaños birthday

cumplir to fulfill

el cura priest

cuyo, -a whose

CH

el chamaco (*Mex.*) boy

charlar to chat

la chuleta chop

chico (a) small

el chico, la chica small boy (girl)

D

el danzante dancer

el daño harm

dar to give

    dar a to face (*the street etc.*)

    dar buen viaje to wish a pleasant journey

    dar las gracias a to give thanks to

    dar un paseo to go out walking or driving

    darse la mano to shake hands

de of, from, about

debajo de under, beneath

deber ought to, be obliged to, must

débil weak

decidir to decide

décimo tenth

decir to tell, say

    es decir that is to say

defender to defend

dejar to let, to leave, allow; dejar de to fail to (do something)

delante de in front of

demandar to demand

los demás the rest

demasiado, -a too (much) *pl.* too many

dentro (de) inside (of)

el dependiente clerk

el deporte sport

derecho, -a right

    a la derecha to the right

    derecho straight ahead

desaparecer to disappear

desayunarse to breakfast

el desayuno breakfast

descansar to rest

el descanso rest

el descendiente descendant

describir to describe

descubrir to discover

desde from, since

    desde luego of course

desear to wish, want

deseoso desirous

el desfile parade, procession

desgraciadamente unfortunately

el desierto desert

desocupado unoccupied

despacio slowly

despedirse (i) de to take leave of

despertar (ie) to wake up (*somebody*)

despertarse to wake up (*oneself*)

despierto, -a awake

después afterwards

después de after

detrás de behind

devolver (ue) to give back, return

el día day

    al día siguiente next day

    hoy día nowadays

diario, -a daily

el dibujo drawing

diciembre December

el diente tooth

diferente different

difícil difficult

el difunto deceased

digno worthy

diligente diligent

el dinero money

el dios god

la dirección address

dirigirse a to go to, to address (a person)

dispensar to excuse

    dispénseme excuse me

distinto different

la diversión amusement

diverso, -a varied

divertido, -a amusing

divertirse (ie) to have a good time, amuse oneself

dividir to divide

el dólar dollar

el dolor de cabeza (muelas), (estómago) headache (toothache) (stomachache)

dominar to dominate

el domingo Sunday

don (*m.*), doña (*f.*) title used with first name

donde where; ¿dónde? where? ¿Por dónde se va a . . . ? How does one get to . . . ?

dormir (ue) to sleep

    dormirse (ue) to fall asleep

el dormitorio bedroom

el drama play

la duda doubt

    sin duda alguna without and doubt

dulce sweet

    los dulces candy

durante during

durar to last

E

echar to pour; echarse to stretch out

    echar de menos to miss

la edad age

efecto: en efecto in fact

elevar to raise; elevarse to rise

la embajada embassy

embargo: sin embargo nevertheless

emocionante touching, thrilling

empezar (ie) (a) to begin (to)

el empleado employee

emplear to use

en in, on; at

    en seguida at once

    en vez de instead of

encantar to enchant, charm

la enchilada a kind of pancake with chile and meat stuffing

encima (de) on top (of)

encontrar (ue) to find; meet

enero January

enfermo, -a sick, ill

enfrente de opposite, facing

enorme enormous

enseñar to teach

entender (ie) to understand

entero whole

entonces then

la entrada entrance

entrar (en) to enter

entre between

entretanto meanwhile

enviar to send

el envío shipment

el equipaje baggage

equivocado, -a mistaken

la escalera stairway

escoger to choose

el escolar scholar, student

escribir to write

el escritor writer

el escritorio desk

escuchar (a) to listen (to)

la escuela school

ese, -a that

ése, -a that (one)

eso that (*referring to a statement or idea*)

    a eso de at about (*time*)

    por eso therefore

espacioso spacious

el español Spanish (*lang.*)

el español Spaniard; la española Spanish woman

el espectador spectator

esperar to wait (for), hope, expect

    Espero que no. I hope not.

    Espero que sí. I hope so.

el esposo husband; la esposa wife

la esquina corner

la estación de ferrocarril railroad station

el estado state

los Estados Unidos (*abbr.* E.U.A. *or* EE.UU.) the United States

el estante shelf, bookcase

estar to be (*place*)

    estar de prisa to be in a hurry

    estar en camino to be on the way

    estar para to be about to

la estatua statue

el este east

este, -a this

éste, -a this (one)

el estilo style

esto this (*referring to a statement or idea*)

estrecho, -a narrow

la estrella star

el estudiante student

el estudio study

estudiar to study

el examen examination

examinar to examine

excelente excellent
excepto except
explicar to explain
expresar to express
la expresión expression
extender (ie) to extend

F

fácil easy
facilitar to facilitate
facilmente easily
facturar to check (baggage)
la faja sash
la falda skirt
falso, -a false
la falta mistake, lack
  Me hace falta I lack, I
    need
faltar to be lacking, need
  me falta I need
la familia family
famoso, -a famous
la farmacia pharmacy
favor: favor de please
  Es favor que Ud. me hace
    You flatter me
  por favor please
febrero February
la fecha date
  ¿Cuál es la fecha? What
    is the date?
felicitar to congratulate
feliz happy
la fiesta holiday
la fila row
el fin end; al fin finally,
    at last
fino, -a fine
firmar to sign
el flan custard
la flor flower
la formalidad formality
la fortuna fortune
el fósforo match
el francés French (lang.),
    Frenchman; la francesa
    Frenchwoman
la frase sentence
la frente front; en frente
    de in front of; frente
    a opposite, facing
fresco cool
los frijoles beans
frío cold
  hacer frío to be cold
    (weather)
  tener frío to be cold
    (persons)
la fruta fruit
la fuente fountain
el fuego fire
fuera de outside of
fuerte strong
la función performance

G

la gana desire; de buena
    gana willingly
ganar to earn, to win
el garage garage
gastar to spend
generoso generous
la gente people
gordo, -a fat
gozar (de) to enjoy
gracias thanks
gracioso, -a graceful, amus-
    ing
grande large, great
gris gray
gritar to shout

el grito shout, cry
grueso, -a thick
el grupo group
el guajalote turkey (Mex.)
el guante glove
guapo, -a neat, elegant,
    handsome
guardar to keep, guard
la guía guide book
gustar to be pleasing to
  me gusta I like
el gusto pleasure
  con mucho gusto with
    much pleasure
  el gusto es mío the pleas-
    ure is mine
  tanto gusto en conocerle
    very pleased to meet you

H

haber to have (auxiliary)
el habitante inhabitant
hablador, -a talkative
hablar to speak
hacer to do, make
  hace algún tiempo some
    time ago
  hace calor, frío, etc. it is
    hot, cold, etc. (weather)
  hacer daño a to hurt
  me hace falta I need
  hacer preguntas to ask
    questions
hallar to find
el hambre hunger; tener
    hambre to be hungry
hasta until, to, as far as,
    even
  hasta luego so long
  hasta mañana until to-
    morrow
  hasta la vista so long
hay there is, there are
  hay que it is necessary to,
    one must
  hay (sol) (viento) (polvo)
    (lodo) it is (sunny)
    (windy) (dusty) (muddy)
hecho made
  hecho a mano handmade
el helado ice cream
el hermano brother; la
    hermana sister
hermoso, -a beautiful
el héroe hero
el hierro iron
el hijo son; la hija
    daughter; los hijos
    children
la hoja leaf, sheet (of
    paper)
la hojalata tin
el hombre man
la hora hour; time
  ¿A qué hora? At what
    time?
el horario timetable
la hospitalidad hospitality
hoy today; hoy día now-
    adays
el huevo egg
huir to flee
húmedo wet

I

el idioma language
la iglesia church
igual equal
igualmente equally, the
    same to you
imaginar to imagine
imitar to imitate

impaciente impatient
el impermeable raincoat
imponente imposing
el importador importer
importante important
importar to matter, to be
    important; to import
  no importa it does not
    matter
la impresión impression
indicar to point out
indígena indigenous, native
el indio, -a Indian
la industria industry
informar to inform
el informe information
  pedir informes to ask for
    information
el inglés English (lang.);
    Englishman; la inglesa
    Englishwoman
el iniciador founder
inmediatamente imme-
    diately
inmenso, -a immense
inteligente intelligent
el interés interest
interesar to interest
el invierno winter
invitar to invite
ir to go
  irse to go away, leave
  ir de compras to go shop-
    ping
  ir de paseo to go out walk-
    ing or riding
izquierdo, -a left
  a la izquierda to the left

J

¡ja! ¡ja! ha! ha!
el jabón soap
jamás never
el jamón ham
el jardín garden
el jarro jar
el jefe chief
la joya jewel
la joyería jewelry shop,
    jewelry
joven young
el joven young man
el juego game, set
el jueves Thursday
el jugador player, gambler
jugar to play (a game)
el jugo juice
el juguete toy
julio July
junio June
juntar to join, unite
junto a near, close to
  junto con together with

K

el kilo kilogram
el kilómetro kilometer

L

el labio lip
laborado worked, tilled
la laca lacquer
el lado side; al lado de
    beside
la lámpara lamp
la lana wool
el lápiz pencil
largo, -a long
la lástima shame, pity
  ¡Qué lástima! What a
    pity!
la lata can

lavar to wash;
  lavarse to wash oneself
la lección lesson
la leche milk
la lechuga lettuce
leer read
la legumbre vegetable
lejano, -a far-off
lejos de far from;
  a lo lejos in the distance
lentamente slowly
levantar to raise, lift;
  levantarse to rise, get up
la libra pound
el libre taxi (Mex.)
la librería bookstore
el libro book
el líder leader
ligero, -a light
la lima lime
el limón lemon
limpiar to clean
la lista menu
listo, -a ready
la lotería lottery
la lucha struggle
luego then
  hasta luego so long
el lugar place
el lujo luxury
luminoso, -a bright
la luna moon
el lunes Monday
la luz light

LL

llamar to call
  llamar por teléfono to
    call up
llamarse to be called
  Me llamo Pablo. My
    name is Paul.
la llanura plain
la llegada arrival
llegar to arrive
llenar to fill
lleno, -a full
llevar to carry; to take, to
    wear;
  llevarse to carry (take)
    away
llover (ue) to rain
la lluvia rain
lluvioso, -a rainy

M

la madera wood
la madre mother
el madrugador early riser
el maestro teacher
magnífico magnificent
el maíz corn
el malestar indisposition
la maleta suitcase;
  hacer una maleta to pack
    a suitcase
malo, -a bad, sick
la mamá mamma
mandar to order, to send
manejar to drive
la manera manner;
  de manera que so that
  de (otra) (la misma) ma-
    nera; in (another) (the
    same) way
la mano hand
  darse la(s) mano(s) to
    shake hands;
  a la mano derecha on the
    right;
  a la mano izquierda on
    the left

la manta blanket
mantener to maintain
la manzana apple
mañana tomorrow
  hasta mañana till tomorrow
la mañana morning
  por la mañana in the morning
la máquina de escribir typewriter
el mar sea
el martes Tuesday
marzo (m) March
más more, most;
  más o menos more or less
la máscara mask
matar to kill
las matemáticas mathematics
mayo (m) May
mayor older
la mayoría majority
la media stocking
el médico doctor
la medida measure
medio, -a half (a, an)
medir (i) to measure
mejor better
  el (la) mejor best
el melocotón peach
el melón melon
la memoria memory
de memoria by heart
menor younger
  el (la) menor youngest
menos less, minus, except;
  por lo menos at least;
  echar de menos to miss
menudo: a menudo often
el mercado market
la mercancía merchandise
la merienda a light supper, "tea"
la mesa table
el mesero waiter
el mexicanismo Mexicanism
mexicano Mexican
México Mexico
mientras while
  mientras tanto meanwhile
miércoles Wednesday
mil thousand
la milla mile
el millón million
mirar to look (at)
mismo, -a same;
  él mismo he himself
  lo mismo the same thing
la mitad half
moderno, -a modern
el modismo idiom
el modo way
  de este modo in this way
  de todos modos anyway
mojado, -a soaked, wet
la moneda currency, money
la montaña mountain
el montón heap, pile
mostrar (ue) to show
el movimiento movement
el mozo waiter
el muchacho boy; la muchacha girl
mucho, -a much
muchos, -as many
mudarse to move (change house)
la muerte death
el muerto corpse, dead man

la mujer woman
el mundo world
  todo el mundo everybody
el museo museum
muy very

N

nada nothing, not anything;
  de nada you're welcome
nadie no one, nobody
la naranja orange
la naturaleza nature
la Navidad Christmas
necesario, -a necessary
la necesidad necessity
necesitar to need
el negociante business man
el negocio business
negro, -a black
la nariz nose
ni . . . ni neither . . . nor'
  ni yo tampoco nor I either, neither do I
la nieve snow
ninguno, -a no, none, nobody
el niño, la niña child
no not
la noche night
  por la noche in the evening;
  esta noche tonight
nombrar to name
el nombre name
el norte north
el norteamericano North American (*usually means a person from the U.S.*)
notable worthy of note
las noticias news
nuevo, -a new
el número number
nunca never

O

o or (u *before* o *or* ho)
obedecer to obey
el objeto object
observar to observe
obtener to obtain
occidental western
octubre October
ocupado, -a busy
el oeste west
la oficina office
ofrecer to offer
el oído ear (*hearing*)
oír to hear
el ojo eye
olvidar to forget
omitir to omit
la oportunidad opportunity
la orden order
a sus órdenes at your service
ordinario, -a ordinary
el orgullo pride
orgulloso, -a proud
el oro gold
oscuro, -a dark
el otoño autumn
otro, -a other, another

P

pacífico peaceful
el padre father
pagar to pay
el país country
la paja straw
el pajaro bird
la palabra word
el palo stick

el pan bread
el panadero baker
el panecillo roll
el panqueque pancake
la pantalla screen
el papá papa
el papel paper, role
el paquete package
  el paquete postal parcel post
el par pair
para in order to, for;
  para que in order that
el paraguas umbrella
parar to stop
parecer to seem
  Le parece bien. It seems all right to him;
  parecerse a to resemble
la pared wall
el pariente relative
la parte part; por todas partes everywhere
la partida departure
el partidario partisan, supporter
partir to leave
el pasaje fare, passage
el pasaporte passport
pasar to pass, spend (*time*), happen;
  pasar sin to get along without
  pasar un buen rato to spend a pleasant time
¿Qué pasa? What is going on?
Pase Ud. Come in: Go ahead.
el pasado past
pasear to take a walk, to walk about
  pasearse (en coche) (a caballo) (en barco) to go for a walk or a ride (in a car) (on horseback) (in a boat)
el paseo promenade
el paso step
la patata potato
el patio courtyard
el pato duck
pedir (i) to ask for
pedir informes to ask for information
la película motion picture
peligroso, -a dangerous
el pelo hair
pensar (ie) to think, to intend to;
  pensar en to think about
peor worse
pequeño, -a small
la pera pear
perder (ie) to lose
perdonar to pardon
perezoso, -a lazy
perfectamente perfectly
el periódico newspaper
el permiso permission
  con su permiso allow me
permitir to permit
pero but
la persona person
pesado, -a heavy
pesar to weigh;
  a pesar de in spite of
el pescado fish
pescar to fish
  pescar un catarro to catch cold

el peso weight; monetary unit of Mexico
picante spicy, "hot" (*of food*)
el pico peak
el pie foot
estar de pie to stand
la piedra stone
la pierna leg
la pieza piece
pintar to paint
el pintor painter
pintoresco, -a picturesque
la pintura painting
la piña pineapple
la piñata pot full of candy and toys, broken by children at Christmas
la pirámide pyramid
el piso story (*of building*)
el placer pleasure
la plata silver
el plátano banana
el platero silversmith
platicar to chat
el platillo saucer
el plato dish
la plaza square, park
la pluma pen
la plumafuente fountain pen
pobre poor
poco, -a little
  dentro de poco in a short time;
  pocos, -as few
poder (ue) to be able, can, may
  (no) se puede one can (not)
el policía policeman
el pollo chicken
poner to put, to place
  poner la mesa to set the table;
  ponerse to put on, to become
  La natura se pone verde. Nature turns green;
  ponerse en marcha to start
por for, in exchange for, by through, along;
  por cierto certainly;
  por eso therefore;
  por lo tanto therefore;
  por supuesto of course;
  por todas partes everywhere
¿por qué? why?
porque because
el portal arcade
el porvenir future
posible possible
postal: el paquete postal parcel post
el postre dessert
practicar to practice
el precio price
precioso, -a exquisite, beautiful
precisamente exactly
preferir (i) to prefer
la pregunta question
preguntar to ask
el premio prize
preocuparse de to worry (about)
presentar to introduce
prestar to lend
la primavera spring
primer (o), -a first

principar to begin
el principio beginning
    al principio at first
prisa: de prisa fast
    quickly;
    tener prisa to be in a
    hurry
probablemente probably
probar (ue) to try, to prove,
    to taste
el problema problem
producir to produce
el profesor professor
profundo, -a profound
el programa program
prometer to promise
pronto soon
la propina tip
propio, -a own
proponer to propose
propósito: a propósito by
    the way
proteger to protect
próximo, -a next (in time)
el pueblo town; people
puertorriqueño Puerto
    Rican
la puerta door
pues well, then
el puesto stand, booth
puesto que since
el punto point, period
    en punto on the dot
    (*time*)

Q

que who, that, which, than;
    lo que that which, what
¿qué? what, which
    ¿Qué tal? How's every-
    thing?
quedar (se) to remain, stay
querer (ie) to wish, want;
    querer a to love;
    ¿Qué quiere decir? What
    does it mean?
querido, -a dear, beloved
quien, -es who
¿quién, -es? who?
    ¿a quién, -es? whom? to
    whom?
    ¿de quién, -es? whose?
    ¿quién sabe? goodness
    knows?
quitar to remove; quitarse
    to take off (*clothing*)

R

el radio radio (set)
la radio radio (broadcast)
la rapidez speed
rápidamente rapidly
rápido, -a rapid, swift
raro, -a strange, rare
el rato while
    largo rato a long time
razón: tener razón to be
    right
    no tener razón to be
    wrong
el rebozo shawl
la recámara bedroom
    (*Mex.*)
recibir to receive
reconocer to recognize
recordar (ue) to remember
el recuerdo souvenir
el recreo recreation
redondo round
    boleto de viaje redondo
    round trip ticket
el refresco soft drink

el regalo gift
regatear to bargain
regresar to return
reír (i) to laugh
    reírse de (i) to laugh at
la reja grating
el reloj watch, clock
reluciendo shining, glitter-
    ing
repente: de repente sud-
    denly
repetir (i) to repeat
el representante representa-
    tive
requisito necessary
el resfriado cold (illness)
resistir to resist
respecto a in regard to
el respeto respect
responder to answer
la respuesta answer
el restaurant(e) restaurant
los restos remains
el retrato portrait, photo-
    graph
revisar to examine
la revista magazine
el rey king
rico, -a rich
el río river
la risa laugh
rodeado, -a surrounded
rojo, -a red
romper to break
la ropa clothing
rosado, -a pink
el ruido noise

S

el sábado Saturday
saber to know, to know how
sabroso, -a tasty, delicious
sacar to take out
la sala living room, hall
    la sala de espera waiting
    room
salir de to leave, to go out
    of;
    salir para to leave for
la salsa sauce
la salud health
saludar to greet
el saludo greeting
el santo saint
santo holy
el sarape blanket
satisfecho, -a satisfied
seco, -a dry
sed: tener sed to be thirsty
la seda silk
seguida: en seguida at once
seguir (i) to continue, to
    follow
según according to
segundo, -a second
    el boleto de segunda clase
    second-class ticket
seguramente surely
seguro sure
    de seguro surely
la semana week
semejante similar
sencillo, -a simple
sentado, -a seated, sitting
    down
sentarse (ie) to sit down
el sentido meaning, sense
sentir (ie) to regret, be sorry
    Lo siento mucho I am
    very sorry
sentirse (ie) to feel
la señal signal

señalar to point out
el señor gentleman; Mr.
la señora lady; Mrs.
la señorita young lady; Miss
septiembre September
ser to be
el servicio service
el servidor servant
servir (i) to serve; servir
    para to serve as;
    ¿En que puedo servirle?
    May I help you?
si if; whether
sí yes; certainly
siempre always
la sierra mountain range
la siesta afternoon nap, rest
el siglo century
significar to mean
siguiente following;
    al día siguiente the fol-
    lowing day
la silla chair
el sillón armchair
simpático pleasant, nice
sin without (*prep.*); sin
    que without (*conj.*)
sino but (on the contrary)
el sistema system
el sitio place
situado, -a situated
sobre upon, over
el sol sun
solamente only
    no solamente . . . sino
    también not only . . .
    but also
sólo, -a alone, only
solo only (*adv.*)
la sombra shade
el sombrero hat
sonar (ue) to sound, ring
el sonido sound
sonreír (i) to smile
soñar (ue) to dream
la sopa soup
sorprendido surprised
subir to go up, to climb, to
    get into (bus, taxi, etc.)
el suburbio suburb
sucio, -a dirty
el suelo floor, ground
el sueño dream
    tener sueño to be sleepy
la suerte fate, luck
    buena suerte good luck
el suéter sweater
sumamente extremely
supuesto: por supuesto of
    course
el sur south
el surtido assortment

T

el tabaco tobacco
el taco a tortilla sandwich
tal such (a);
    tal vez maybe
el tamaño size
también also
tampoco neither, either;
    ni yo tampoco nor I
    either
tan as, so; tan . . . como
    as . . . as
el tanque tank
tanto, -a so much, (*pl.*) so
    many
    tanto . . . como as much
    . . . as, (*pl.*) as many
    . . . as
la taquígrafa stenographer

la taquilla ticket window
la tarde afternoon
    tarde (*adj.*) late
la tarjeta de turista (turismo)
    tourist card
la taza cup
el té tea
el teatro theater
el tejado roof
el tejido textile
la tela cloth
el teléfono telephone
    llamar por teléfono to
    call up
la televisión
el tema theme, subject
temer to fear
la temperatura temperature
templado temperate
temprano early
el tenedor fork
tener to have
    tener calor, frío to be
    warm, cold (person)
    tener cuidado to be care-
    ful
    tener dolor de (cabeza)
    (muelas) to have a
    (head) (tooth) ache
    tener ganas de to have a
    desire to
    tener hambre, sed to be
    hungry, thirsty
    tener prisa to be in a
    hurry
    tener que to have to
    tener razón to be right
    tener sueño to be sleepy
    ¿Qué tiene Ud.? What
    is the matter with you?
teñido dyed
tercer(o), -a third
terminar to end
la ternera veal
el tiempo weather; time
    a tiempo on time
la tienda store
la tierra land
el timbre stamp, bell
la tinta ink
el tío uncle; la tía aunt
típico typical
tocar to play (an instru-
    ment); to ring (a bell)
el tocino bacon
todavía still, yet
    todavía no not yet
todo, -a all, every, whole,
    everything
    ante todo first of all
    todo el mundo everybody
    todo el año all year
    todo lo posible as much as
    possible
    sobre todo especially
tomar to take, to eat, drink;
    tomar la cena to dine
el tomate tomato
el tópico topic
el torero bullfighter
el toro bull
la toronja grapefruit
la torta cake
la tortilla Mexican "pan-
    cake" of corn
trabajador, -a hard-working
trabajar to work
el trabajo work
traducir to translate
traer to bring

el traje   suit, costume
el tranvía   streetcar
tratar (de)   to try (to),
    deal with
el trigo   wheat
triste   sad
el (la) turista   tourist

U

u or *(before words beginning
    with o or ho)*
último   last
unir   to unite; unirse to
    join
la universidad   university
usar   to use
el uso   use
útil   useful
la uva   grape

V

la vaca   cow
las vacaciones   vacation
vacío, -a   empty
la vacuna   vaccination

valer   to be worth;
    no vale nada   it is not
      worth anything
    valer la pena   to be worth
      while
    más vale tarde que nunca
      better late than never
la valija   valise
el valle   valley
la variedad   variety
varios   several
el vaso   glass *(for drinking)*
la velocidad   speed
    a toda velocidad   at full
      speed
vendado   bandaged
el vendedor   seller
vender   to sell
venir   to come
la ventana   window
ver   to see
    ¡a ver!   let's see!
el verano   summer
veras: ¿de veras?   really?
la verdad   truth

¿verdad?   is(n't) that so?
verdaderamente   truly
verde   green
el vestido   dress
vestir (i)   to dress
    vestirse (de)   to dress in
la vez, *pl.* veces   time
    a la vez   at the same time
    a veces   sometimes
    de vez en cuando   from
      time to time
    en vez de   instead of
    otra vez   again
    tal vez   perhaps
el viaje   trip
    dar buen viaje   to wish a
      pleasant journey
la vida   life
el viejito   little old man
viejo, -a   old
el viento   wind
    hace viento   it is windy
el viernes   Friday
la visita   visit, visitor
la vista   view

hasta la vista   so long
vivir   to live; ¡viva! long
    live!
vivo, -a   lively
volver (ue)   to return
    volver a casa   to go home
    volver a + *inf.*   to do
      again
la voz   voice
el vuelo   flight
la vuelta   turn, return;
    change (money)
    a la vuelta   around the
      corner

Y

y   and
ya   already, now
    ¡Ya lo creo!   I should
      say so!

Z

el zapato   shoe
el zapatero   shoemaker
la zapatería   shoe shop

ANSWERS

CAPÍTULO 3

Exercise No. 1

1. comerciante
2. quién
3. con
4. padre
5. madre
6. hay
7. se llaman
8. su
9. particular
10. todos los cuartos
11. piso
12. calle
13. grande
14. allí, todo el día
15. ciudad

Exercise No. 2A

1. la
2. una
3. la, los
4. el, la
5. una, un
6. el
7. los, un
8. unos, la, unas, la
9. los, la
10. los, las, la

Exercise No. 2B

1. las calles
2. los comedores
3. los cuartos
4. los señores
5. las recámaras
6. las cocinas
7. las madres
8. los padres
9. las salas
10. las hijas
11. las ciudades
12. los años
13. las mujeres
14. los hombres
15. los tíos

Exercise No. 2C

1. El señor Adams es norte-americano.
2. Vive en Nueva York.
3. Hay seis personas en la familia.
4. La casa tiene seis cuartos.
5. Es una casa particular.
6. La señora Adams es la madre.
7. El señor Adams es el padre.
8. La oficina está en la calle Whitehall.
9. Va por tren a la ciudad.
10. Allí trabaja todo el día.

CAPÍTULO 4

Exercise No. 4

1. quién
2. un comerciante de Nueva York
3. su oficina
4. otros
5. va
6. desea
7. además (también)
8. pero
9. estudia
10. martes, jueves
11. rápidamente
12. muy inteligente
13. mexicano
14. un maestro bueno
15. en la primera conversación

Exercise No. 5A

1. es
2. está
3. es
4. está
5. es
6. es
7. está
8. está
9. es
10. es

Exercise No. 5B

1. (1d) 2. (2f) 3. (3a) 4. (4b) 5. (5c) 6. (6e)

Exercise No. 5C

1. y
2. en
3. con
4. también
5. a
6. tal vez
7. pero
8. por eso
9. allí
10. aquí
11. casi
12. siempre
13. ¿Cómo está Ud.?
14. muy bien
15. gracias
16. grande
17. pequeño
18. bueno
19. malo
20. rápidamente

CAPÍTULO 5

Exercise No. 7

1. está sentado
2. hay
3. saber
4. Dígame
5. mi esposa
6. sobre el piano
7. un lápiz, una pluma, y algunos papeles
8. están en la mesita
9. basta
10. hasta el jueves

Exercise No. 8A

1. la calle, las calles, street
2. la oficina, las oficinas, office
3. la pared, las paredes, wall
4. la silla, las sillas, chair
5. el señor, los señores, gentleman
6. la mesa, las mesas, table
7. el papel, los papeles, paper
8. la puerta, las puertas, door
9. el estante, los estantes, bookcase
10. la ventana, las ventanas, window

Exercise No. 8B

1. debajo de
2. cerca de
3. encima del
4. sobre
5. entre
6. delante del
7. alrededor de
8. detrás de
9. debajo de
10. cerca del

Exercise No. 8C

1. de la
2. al
3. de las
4. del
5. a la
6. de los
7. a los
8. a la
9. al
10. a las

Exercise No. 9

1. Está sentado en la sala de su casa.
2. El Sr. López está sentado cerca de él.
3. Sí, hay muchas cosas alrededor de nosotros.
4. Sí, hay muchas cosas en la calle.
5. La esposa del Sr. Adams toca bien el piano.
6. Está encima del piano.
7. Está sobre el piano.
8. El estante está delante de una ventana.
9. Está cerca de la puerta.
10. Cerca del escritorio está una silla.
11. Están encima del escritorio.
12. Están en la mesita.

REPASO 1 Capítulos 1–5

Exercise No. 10

(1 g)   (3 i)   (5 j)   (7 k)   (9 d)   (11 b)
(2 e)   (4 h)   (6 l)   (8 a)   (10 c) (12 f)

Exercise No. 11

1. todo el día
2. por favor
3. tal vez
4. Buenas tardes
5. con mucho gusto
6. Por eso
7. Cómo
8. Dónde
9. Qué
10. Quién

Exercise No. 12

(1 d)   (4 k)   (6 g)   (8 j)   (10 b)
(2 f)   (5 h)   (7 c)   (9 a)   (11 e)
(3 i)

Exercise No. 13

1. delante de la casa
2. cerca de la puerta
3. alrededor de la ciudad
4. detrás del escritorio
5. encima del piano
6. Los libros del muchacho
7. La madre de las muchachas
8. El hermano de Felipe
9. El padre de María
10. El maestro de los niños

Exercise No. 14A—Reading Section
Mr. Adams, New York Merchant

Mr. Adams is a North American business man who imports art objects from Mexico. Therefore he wants to take a trip to Mexico in the spring. He wants to talk with his agent and to visit some places of interest in Mexico. But he does not know how to speak Spanish.

Mr. Adams has a good teacher. He is a Mexican who lives in New York, and his name is Mr. Lopez. Tuesdays and Thursdays the teacher goes by train to the house of his student. There the two gentlemen speak a little in Spanish. Mr. Adams is very intelligent and learns rapidly. For example, in the first conversation he learns by heart the salutations and farewells. He already knows how to say "Good day," "How are you?", "So long," "Until tomorrow." He already knows how to say in Spanish the names of many things which are in his living room and he knows how to answer well the questions: "What is this?" and "Where is . . . ?"

Mr. Lopez is very satisfied with the progress of his student and says: "Good. Enough for today. So long."

CAPÍTULO 6

Exercise No. 15

1. son importantes
2. unos verbos corrientes
3. Por qué
4. Porque, mi
5. con él en español
6. a otros países
7. por tren o por avión
8. Cuánto
9. muy rápidamente
10. Basta por hoy

Exercise No. 16A

1. to listen
2. to want
3. to begin
4. to form, make
5. to expect
6. to converse
7. to practice
8. to travel
9. to ask
10. to answer
11. to chat
12. to study
13. to import
14. to play
15. to visit

Exercise No. 16B

1. Do you speak Spanish?
Yes, I speak Spanish.
What languages does your teacher speak?
He speaks English, Spanish and French.
2. Who plays the piano?
Mary plays the piano.
Don't you play the piano, Rosie?
No, I do not play the piano.
3. Are the students studying the lesson?
No, they are not studying the lesson.
Are they chatting in Spanish?
Yes, they are chatting in Spanish.
4. Do you listen attentively when the teacher is speaking?
Yes, we listen attentively when the teacher is speaking.

Exercise No. 16C

1. no habla
2. estudiamos
3. importa
4. desea
5. espero
6. platican
7. practican
8. viaja
9. esperamos
10. principian

Exercise No. 16D

1. principio
2. escucha
3. formas
4. conversa
5. practican
6. ¿pregunta Vd.?
7. contestan
8. ¿estudiamos?
9. desean
10. visito
11. viajo
12. ¿espera Vd.?

Exercise No. 17

1. Están sentados en la sala del Sr. A.
2. El Sr. L. principia a hablar.
3. El Sr. Adams escucha con atención.
4. El Sr. L. pregunta.
5. El Sr. A. contesta.
6. Sí, son importantes.
7. Sí, es comerciante.
8. No, no habla español.
9. Porque desea hacer un viaje a México. or Porque desea hablar con su agente.
10. Espera visitar a México, a Guatemala, y tal vez a Colombia.
11. Viaja por avión.
12. Aprende rápidamente.

CAPÍTULO 7

Exercise No. 18

1. abre
2. Pase
3. Buenas noches, su
4. un resfriado
5. otros
6. tengo
7. somos
8. años
9. la menor
10. el mayor
11. un rato más
12. al Sr. López

Exercise No. 19A

1. es, Es
2. está, Estoy
3. están, Estamos
4. Es, soy
5. Está, está
6. están, estamos
7. están, Están
8. Son, somos
9. están, están
10. Son, somos

Exercise No. 19B

1. al señor
2. la escuela
3. a su amigo
4. la lección
5. a la señora
6. el tren
7. a Isabel
8. a su agente
9. el parque
10. a José

Exercise No. 19C

1. ¿Cómo está Ud.?
2. Regular, gracias.
3. Mi hija está enferma.
4. Lo siento mucho.
5. Uds. son una familia de seis personas.
6. Van sus niños a la escuela?
7. ¿Habla Ud. español?
8. No, no hablo español.
9. Invito a Carlos a visitar mi casa.
10. Vamos a platicar un rato.
11. Vamos a principiar (comenzar) (empezar).
12. Deseo (quiero) estudiar el español.

Exercise No. 20

1. La criada abre la puerta.
2. El Sr. L. toca el timbre.
3. Espera al Sr. L. en la sala.
4. Anita, la hija del Sr. A. está enferma.
5. Tiene un resfriado.
6. Tiene cuatro hijos.
7. Hay seis personas en su familia.
8. Sus hijos se llaman Felipe, Guillermo, Rosita y Anita.
9. Tiene diez años.
10. Sí, platican un rato más.
11. El Sr. A. invita al Sr. L. a visitar su oficina.
12. Sí, acepta la invitación.

CAPÍTULO 8

Exercise No. 21

1. dan a la calle
2. periódicos
3. detrás de su escritorio
4. entra en la oficina
5. Mucho gusto en verle
6. El gusto es mío
7. Me gusta ese mapa
8. A propósito
9. Veo
10. De qué color
11. De qué colores
12. ¡Dios mío!
13. Tengo hambre
14. No lejos de aquí
15. ¡Vámonos!

Exercise No. 22A

1. vivos
2. cómoda
3. rojos
4. verdes
5. altos
6. muchos
7. blancas
8. muchas
9. azul
10. simpática

Exercise No. 22B

1. son
2. está
3. es
4. está
5. estoy
6. están
7. estamos
8. somos
9. son
10. son

Exercise No. 22C

1. La oficina del Sr. A. es muy bonita.
2. Las ventanas de la oficina son grandes.
3. Muchos papeles están en el suelo.
4. Los tejados de las casas son rojos.
5. El cielo es azul.
6. Las montañas son verdes.
7. El edificio es muy alto.
8. ¿Cómo está Ud., Sr. A?
9. Estoy muy bien, gracias.
10. Los carteles son hermosos.

Exercise No. 23

1. Está en el décimo piso de un edificio alto.
2. No es grande.
3. Sí, es cómoda.
4. En las paredes grises hay algunos carteles.
5. En el escritorio del Sr. A hay muchos papeles.
6. Está cerca de la puerta.
7. Una mesa larga está entre las dos ventanas.
8. El Sr. A. está sentado.
9. Es amarillo.
10. Es negro.
11. Son verdes.
12. Sí, es azul.
13. Son blancas.
14. Sí, son rojos.
15. Es la oficina del Sr. Adams.

CAPÍTULO 9

Exercise No. 24

1. sus padres
2. adelanta
3. ¿Qué tal?
4. A propósito, ¿verdad?
5. ¿Cómo no?
6. Aprendo
7. fácil, difícil
8. Estudio, deseo
9. comprendo
10. palabras, diaria
11. las expresiones
12. Me gusta

Exercise No. 25B

1. aprendo
2. toca
3. estudiamos
4. comprenden
5. Leen
6. beben
7. escribe
8. vive
9. bebes
10. deseas
11. viajan
12. abre

Exercise No. 26

1. El Sr. Gómez es un habitante de Nueva York.
2. Sí, habla español bien.
3. No, son puertorriqueños.
4. Sabe que su amigo Adams aprende el español.
5. Entra en la oficina del Sr. Adams.
6. Saluda al Sr. Adams en español.
7. El Sr. Adams aprende a hablar, a leer y a escribir el español.
8. Estudia diligentemente.
9. El Sr. López es su maestro de español.
10. Sí, es un maestro bueno.
11. Sí, comprende.
12. Aprende las palabras de la vida diaria.
13. El Sr. Adams va a hacer un viaje a México.
14. Espera ir a México el verano que viene.
15. El Sr. Gómez dice—Buen viaje y buena suerte. or Lo dice. (He says it.)

REPASO 2 Capítulos 6–9

Exercise No. 27

1. civilización
2. reservación
3. instrucción
4. excepción
5. revolución
6. observación
7. aplicación
8. elección
9. invención
10. solución

Exercise No. 28

1. Es azul.
2. Hablan español.
3. El Sr. A. tiene hambre.
4. Es blanca y negra.
5. Vivo en los Estados Unidos.
6. Son rojos.
7. Beben leche.
8. Saluda a su amigo.
9. Tengo treinta etc. años.
10. Me llamo . . . .

Exercise No. 29

1. (1 e)
2. (2 g)
3. (3 a)
4. (4 i)
5. (5 b)
6. (6 h)
7. (7 c)
8. (8 d)
9. (9 j)
10. (10 f)

Exercise No. 30

1. trabajamos
2. aprenden
3. principia
4. sabe
5. escriben
6. abres
7. permito
8. bebe
9. adelantamos
10. veo

Exercise No. 31

1. Sí, aprendo . . .
2. Sí, estudio . . .
3. Sí, trabajo . . .
4. Sí, espero . . .
5. Sí, veo . . .
6. Sí, leo . . .
7. Sí, comprendo . . .
8. Sí, acepto . . .
9. Sí, visito . . .

Exercise No. 32

1. es
2. está
3. estoy
4. estamos
5. es
6. está
7. están
8. es
9. son
10. está
11. son
12. eres
13. es
14. son
15. estoy

Exercise No. 33—Reading Selection 1

Two Friends of Mr. Adams

Mr. Adams already knows the names of all the objects in his house. Now he is beginning to study the verbs because he wants to learn to read, to write and to converse in Spanish. He also wants to know the numbers in Spanish. Being a merchant who expects to visit his agent in Mexico he needs practice chatting with Spaniards or Spanish-Americans. Fortunately he has two friends who are from Mexico and who work near his office in Whitehall Street.

One day Mr. Adams goes to visit these Mexicans. The two gentlemen listen attentively to Mr. Adams while he speaks with them in Spanish. After ten minutes of conversation the Mexicans ask their friend many questions and are very pleased with his answers.

Exercise No. 34—Reading Selection 2

Mr. Adams Gets Sick

On Thursday, April 22, at nine o'clock in the evening Mr. Lopez arrives at the house of his student, Mr. Adams. The oldest child, a boy of ten, opens the door and greets Mr. Lopez heartily. They enter the living room where Mr. Adams usually awaits his teacher.

But this evening he is not in the living room. Neither is Mrs. Adams there. Mr. Lopez is very surprised and asks the boy: "Where is your papa?" The boy answers sadly: "My papa is sick and cannot leave his bedroom. He is in bed because he has a severe cold. He also has a headache."

The teacher becomes very sad and says: "What a pity! It is not possible to have a lesson today, but next week we are going to study two hours. Until next Tuesday."

CAPÍTULO 10

Exercise No. 35

1. toman
2. dibujos
3. por todas partes
4. cada, propio
5. para crema
6. para agua
7. despacio
8. Tiene que
9. de todos modos
10. tengo
11. muy sencillo
12. muchas veces
13. para el uso
14. Quiere Ud.
15. No quiere Ud.

Exercise No. 36A

1. aquellas
2. Esta
3. Estos
4. Estas
5. Esas
6. Esos
7. Aquella
8. este
9. aquellas
10. esta
11. esa
12. estos

Exercise No. 36C

1. Estos señores están sentados en el comedor.
2. Estas tazas son de Puebla.
3. Me gustan estos dibujos.
4. Esos platos son de Oaxaca.
5. ¿Trabajan despacio aquellos artistas?
6. ¿Tiene esta familia cinco niños?
7. ¿Tienes hambre, hijito?
8. No, no tengo hambre.
9. ¿Tiene Ud. que escribir una carta, Sr. Adams?
10. Sí, tengo que escribir una carta.

Exercise No. 37

1. Están sentados en el comedor.
2. Toman café y pan dulce.
3. Dice—¿Le gustan estas tazas y estos platillos?
4. Es de Puebla.
5. Sí, cada distrito tiene su propio estilo.
6. Es de Oaxaca.
7. Es de Michoacán.
8. Sí, son verdaderos artistas.
9. Trabajan despacio.
10. No tienen prisa.
11. Es difícil obtener un surtido adecuado para el mercado norteamericano.
12. El Sr. Adams ve mucha cerámica de interés artístico.
13. Están en el aparador.
14. Son amarillos y azules.
15. Sí, tiene ejemplares de cerámica corriente, *or* Sí, los tiene. (He has *them*.)

CAPÍTULO 11

Exercise No. 38

1. Sabe Ud.
2. tan importantes como
3. Nuestra civilización
4. Ud. tiene razón
5. Puede Ud., que
6. no valen
7. Necesitamos, la fecha
8. pasar
9. entretanto, que
10. ¿Qué quiere decir . . . ?

Exercise No. 39A

1. treinta
2. diez
3. cincuenta
4. cuarenta y nueve
5. diez y seis
6. setenta y ocho
7. diez y siete
8. quince
9. sesenta y dos
10. noventa y siete
11. ochenta y cuatro
12. trece

Exercise No. 39B

cuatro más nueve son trece
ocho más siete son quince
siete por ocho son cincuenta y seis
ocho por tres son veinte y cuatro
diez y nueve menos ocho son once

diez y seis menos tres son trece
cincuenta dividido por diez son cinco
ochenta dividido por veinte son cuatro

Exercise No. 39C

1. treinta
2. doce
3. siete
4. veinte y cuatro
5. sesenta
6. sesenta
7. setenta y cinco
8. treinta y seis
9. treinta y cinco
10. diez y seis

Exercise No. 39D

1. quiero
2. puedo
3. pensamos
4. piensa Ud.
5. quiere
6. quiere
7. quieren Uds.
8. pueden
9. puedes tú
10. piensan
11. vale
12. cuento
13. tú cuentas
14. cuenta

Exercise No. 40

1. Sí, son importantes.
2. Sí, son tan importantes como los nombres.
3. Necesitamos números.
4. Piensa en comprar y vender.
5. No valen mucho sin dinero.
6. No es posible comprar y vender sin dinero.
7. Sí, vende y compra.
8. Sí, es comprador y vendedor.
9. El Sr. Adams adelanta día por día.
10. diez, veinte, treinta, cuarenta, cincuenta, ciento.

CAPÍTULO 12

Exercise No. 41

1. es decir
2. Cuántas veces
3. boletos y comida
4. maletas, tamaños, distancias
5. El sistema monetario
6. cada
7. centavos
8. Es cierto, de cambio
9. noventa
10. próxima, este

Exercise No. 41A

1. cuatrocientos
2. trescientos cincuenta
3. quinientos veinte y cinco
4. ochocientos sesenta
5. seiscientos veinte y siete
6. cuatrocientos noventá
7. quinientos sesenta
8. setecientos ochenta
9. doscientos
10. novecientos setenta

Exercise No. 41C

1. Sé los números.
2. ¿Sabe Ud. dónde vive?
3. Sabemos qué desea.
4. No damos el dinero.
5. ¿Dan los boletos?
6. ¿Qué da Juan?
7. Ella no sabe la respuesta.
8. No damos nuestros libros.
9. ¿Sabes las preguntas?
10. No saben quién vive aquí.

Exercise No. 42

1. (40) cuarenta pesos
2. (75) setenta y cinco pesos
3. (5) cinco pesos
4. (4) cuatro pesos
5. (270) doscientos setenta pesos
6. Sí, es millonario.
7. $500 (quinientos dólares)
8. No sé
9. Sí, lo sé
10. Vamos a continuar este tema en nuestra próxima conversación.

CAPÍTULO 13

Exercise No. 43A

1. nuestros
2. su
3. sus
4. mis
5. su
6. su
7. nuestro
8. tu
9. mis
10. nuestra

Exercise No. 43B

1. diez, veinte y dos
2. veinte, cuarenta y cuatro
3. treinta, sesenta y seis
4. cuarenta, ochenta y ocho
5. cincuenta, ciento diez
6. diez y seis, diez
7. treinta y dos, veinte
8. cuarenta y ocho, treinta
9. sesenta y cuatro, cuarenta
10. ochenta, cincuenta

Exercise No. 43C

1. digo
2. hago
3. salgo
4. tengo
5. decimos
6. no ponemos
7. hacen
8. ponen
9. ¿hace Ud.?
10. ¿salen Uds.?
11. ¿dicen Uds.?
12. haces
13. ¿pone Ud.?
14. pongo
15. vale

Exercise No. 43D

1. sino   2. sino   3. pero   4. sino   5. pero

Exercise No. 44

1. Tomamos la cena en el restaurante.
2. Damos al mesero diez por ciento.
3. La propina es un peso sesenta y cinco centavos.
4. Tengo mi maleta pesada en la estación del ferrocarril.
5. Pesa treinta kilos. Sesenta y seis libras.
6. Se usan kilómetros.
7. El Sr. Adams sabe cambiar kilómetros en millas.
8. Compra un sarape, dos rebozos, tres cestas, y cuatro cinturones.
9. El tema es "la hora."
10. Usa el refrán—Más vale tarde que nunca.

CAPÍTULO 14

Exercise No. 45

1. la película
2. la función
3. otras preguntas
4. la taquilla (boletería, *Mex.*)
5. la estación de ferrocarril
6. pide informes
7. un boleto de viaje redondo
8. sale el tren
9. a las nueve de la noche
10. Muchas gracias
11. De nada
12. hago el papel

Exercise No. 46A

1. a las cinco y media de la tarde
2. a las ocho y cuarto de la noche
3. a las diez menos cinco de la mañana
4. a las once menos diez de la mañana
5. a las dos y veinte de la tarde
6. a las cinco menos veinte de la tarde
7. a las siete y diez de la noche
8. a las siete menos diez de la noche
9. a las ocho menos cuarto de la noche
10. a mediodía

Exercise No. 46B

1. pido
2. comenzamos
3. repiten
4. ¿pide?
5. comienzo
6. ¿empieza Ud.?
7. pides
8. ¿piden Uds.?
9. repite
10. ¿comienza?

Exercise No. 46C

1. Quiero un boleto de viaje redondo.
2. Pide informes.
3. ¿Cuándo sale el tren para Oaxaca?
4. ¿Sabe Ud. cuándo llega el tren de Puebla?
5. Llega a las cinco y media de la tarde.
6. ¿A qué hora comienza la primera función?
7. Comienza a las tres y veinte de la tarde.
8. ¿Repiten la función?
9. Sí, repiten la función dos veces.
10. Aquí tiene Ud. los boletos.

Exercise No. 47

1. Todo el mundo quiere saber—¿Qué hora es?
2. El Sr. Adams hace el papel de viajero.
3. El Sr. López hace el papel de boletero.
4. Quiere comprar un boleto de pullman.
5. Cuesta noventa y cinco pesos.
6. El Sr. L. hace el papel de boletero de un cine.
7. El Sr. A. pide informes.
8. Tiene tres funciones.
9. Compra dos boletos para la tercera función.
10. Paga seis pesos.

REPASO 3 Capítulos 10–14

Exercise No. 48

1. Sí, pienso . . .
2. Sí, quiero . . .
3. Sí, puedo . . .
4. Sí, pongo . . .
5. Sí, salgo . . .
6. Sí, cuento . . .
7. Sí, digo . . .
8. Si, continúo . . .
9. Sí, le doy . . .
10. Sí, sé contar . . .

Exercise No. 49

1. No repetimos . . .
2. No hacemos . . .
3. No pedimos . . .
4. No tenemos . . .
5. No venimos . . .
6. No creemos . . .
7. No traemos . . .
8. No tomamos . . .
9. No necisitamos . . .
10. No tenemos . . .

Exercise No. 50

1. (1 b)
2. (2 d)
3. (3 h)
4. (4 a)
5. (5 i)
6. (6 c)
7. (7 e)
8. (8 j)
9. (9 f)
10. (10 g)

Exercise No. 51

1. ¿Cuánto cuesta?, tiene que saber
2. pide informes, ¿A qué hora?, a las siete y media.
3. tiene hambre, una comida,
4. paga la cuenta, de cambio, una propina, es decir
5. Piensa, por todas partes, dinero

Exercise No. 52

1. esta
2. estos
3. ese
4. esos
5. este
6. esa
7. aquella
8. esos
9. estas
10. esas
11. aquel
12. aquellas

Exercise No. 53

1. (1 e)
2. (2 f)
3. (3 a)
4. (4 g)
5. (5 b)
6. (6 h)
7. (7 d)
8. (8 j)
9. (9 c)
10. (10 i)

Exercise No. 54—Reading Selection 1
The Family of Mr. Adams Comes to Visit His Office

It is the first time that the Adams family comes to visit Mr. Adams' office. Mrs. Adams and her four children enter a very large building and go up to the tenth floor on the elevator. Annie the younger daughter, who is only five years old, is very curious and asks her mother many questions about the office.

When they arrive in the office the father gets up and says: "I am very happy to see you all here. What a pleasant surprise!"

The children admire the objects which they see in the office, —the typewriter, the various articles imported from Mexico, the Mexican magazines, the many colored posters. All are very happy.

Philip, the older boy, looks out of the high window and sees the blue sky and the bright sun. Below he sees the automobiles which pass through the street. From the tenth floor they seem very small.

After the visit the whole family goes to a restaurant which is not far from the office. They eat with gusto, especially the boys, because they are very hungry.

Exercise No. 55—Reading Selection 2
A Modern Fable

Annie, the youngest of Mr. Adams children, likes the old fables of Aesop very much. She also likes this modern fable which Mr. Lopez has written for her. "The Fable of the Automobile and the Donkey" follows:

An automobile is passing along the road and sees a donkey. The poor donkey is carrying a big, heavy load of wood.

The automobile stops and says to the donkey: "Good morning. You are walking very slowly. Do you not want to run fast like me?"

"Yes, yes sir! But tell me how is it possible?"

"It is not difficult," says the automobile. "In my tank there is much gasoline. You have to drink a little."

Then the donkey drinks the gasoline. Now he does not walk slowly. He does not run fast. He does not go to the market. He stretches out in the road. He has a stomach ache.

Poor donkey! He is not very intelligent, is he? He does not know that gasoline is good for an automobile, but is not at all good for a donkey.

CAPÍTULO 15

Exercise No. 56A
1. los 2. lo 3. lo 4. la 5. le 6. las 7. la 8. los 9. las 10. le

Exercise No. 56B
1. La criada la lleva.
2. Los niños lo comen.
3. Los pongo en la mesa.
4. Las digo al estudiante.
5. ¿Por qué no le saluda Ud.?
6. ¿La visitas?

Exercise No. 56C
1. Le veo a Ud., Sr. A.
2. ¿Me ve Ud.?
3. ¿Quién nos ve?
4. El maestro los ve a Uds., muchachos.
5. Vemos la casa. La vemos.
6. Tomo el plato. Lo tomo.
7. Ella escribe los verbos. Los escribe.
8. Tenemos las sillas. Las tenemos.
9. Las espero a Uds., señoras.
10. Los esperamos a Uds., señores.

Exercise No. 57
1. El Sr. A. sabe pedir informes.
2. Prefieren el teatro.
3. Prefieren las farsas detectivescas.
4. Claro está, las conocen.
5. Vive en los suburbios.
6. Está cosa de ocho cuadras de su casa.
7. Prefieren las filas catorce o quince.
8. Sí, es posible ver y oír bien.
9. Piden ayuda al acomodador.
10. Vienen temprano.

CAPÍTULO 16

Exercise No. 58
1. No saben nada
2. pueden
3. en memoria de, patria
4. más importantes
5. desde, hasta
6. nombres, fechas
7. desde el punto de vista
8. significan
9. cura, iniciador
10. Estos sucesos
11. caminar, cuyos
12. recordar

Exercise No. 59A
1. de Ud. 2. nosotros 3. ellas 4. mí 5. conmigo 6. contigo 7. ellos, ellos 8. usted 9. ella 10. él

Exercise No. 59B
1. ¿Dónde está su libro (el libro de ella)?
2. ¿Dónde está su libro (el libro de él)?
3. ¿Dónde están sus libros (los libros de ella)?
4. ¿Dónde están sus libros (los libros de él)?
5. ¿Dónde están sus padres, muchachos (los padres de Uds.)?
6. ¿Dónde está su casa (la casa de Ud.), Sr. A.?
7. ¿Dónde están sus sillas (las sillas de ellos, or ellas)?
8. ¿Dónde está su cuarto (el cuarto de ellos, or ellas)?

Exercise No. 60
1. El 16 de septiembre es la fecha del Día de la Independencia de México.
2. El cura Hidalgo fué el iniciador de la revolución de 1810.
3. El cura Hidalgo es el Jorge Washington de México.
4. El cinco de mayo es el aniversario de la victoria contra los franceses.
5. Benito Juárez es el Abrán Lincoln de México.
6. Fué presidente de México desde 1857 hasta 1872.
7. El 20 de noviembre celebra el comienzo de la revolución contra Díaz.
8. Francisco I. Madero fué uno de los líderes.
9. Las avenidas Juárez y Francisco I. Madero están nombradas en memoria de dos grandes héroes.
10. El 5 de febrero es la fecha del Día de la Constitución.
11. Sí, le interesan mucho.
12. Va a caminar por las calles cuyos nombres son fechas.
13. Va a recordar las palabras de su maestro y amigo.
14. El 4 de julio es la fecha del aniversario del Día de la Independencia de los Estados Unidos.

CAPÍTULO 17

Exercise No. 61
1. cuyos, recuerdan
2. los acontecimientos más notables
3. más conocidos
4. más famosos
5. más importantes del mundo
6. de veras, puede educarse bien y barato
7. a propósito, acerca de, Occidental
8. recibir
9. más grande
10. más pequeño
11. el más grande y el más largo
12. más alto
13. más altos
14. altos, no lejos de
15. Ud. tiene razon

Exercise No. 62
1. tan alto como
2. mejor
3. más, que
4. mejor
5. tan, como
6. más nuevo
7. más, que
8. más, que
9. más alta
10. peor
11. mayor
12. más modernos
13. peor
14. tan, como
15. de
16. menor

Exercise No. 63
1. El Amazonas es el río más largo de Sud América.
2. Londres es la ciudad más grande del mundo.
3. Aconcagua es el pico más alto de Sud América.
4. Londres es más grande que Nueva York.
5. Madrid no es tan grande como Nueva York.
6. Nueva York no es tan antigua como Madrid.
7. St. Augustine es más antigua.
8. Nueva York tiene los edificios más altos del mundo.
9. El Salvador es el país más pequeño de Centro América.
10. a. El Sr. García es el menor.
b. El Sr. Torres es el mayor.
c. Sí, el Sr. Rivera es mayor que el Sr. García.
d. El Sr. García es el más rico.
e. El Sr. Torres es el menos rico.
f. El Sr. Torres no es tan rico como el Sr. García.

CAPÍTULO 18

Exercise No. 64
1. preguntarle a qué hora
2. a las seis y media
3. madrugador, madrugadora
4. temprano
5. estoy listo para salir
6. Leo, dicto
7. un sandwich con café y tal o cual postre.
8. muchas veces, a visitarme
9. a las cinco en punto
10. Las costumbres

Exercise No. 65A
1. At what time do you go to bed? I go to bed at 11 p.m.
2. At what time do you get up? I get up at 7 a.m.
3. Do you wash (yourself) before dressing (yourself)? Yes, I wash (myself) before dressing (myself).
4. Where will you be at noon? I shall be in my office.

5. When do you go from here?
   I go from here tomorrow.
6. Do you get sick when you eat too many sweets?
   Yes, I get sick.
7. In what row do you sit in the movies?

We sit in the fourteenth or fifteenth row.
8. Do you remember our conversations?
   Yes, we remember them.

Exercise No. 65B

1. se	3. se, se	5. me	7. se	9. nos
2. se	4. se	6. se	8. se	10. me

Exercise No. 66

1. Se levanta a las seis y media.
2. Se lava y se viste.
3. Se viste en treinta minutos.
4. A eso de las siete se sienta a la mesa.
5. Se levanta temprano.
6. Se desayunan juntos.
7. Toma jugo de naranja, café, panecillos y huevos.
8. Toma panqueques en vez de huevos.
9. A las siete y media está listo para salir.
10. Va en coche a la estación.
11. A eso de las nueve llega a su oficina.
12. Lo toma casi siempre a la una.
13. Toma un sandwich, con café y tal o cual postre.
14. Muchas veces vienen clientes a visitarle.
15. Termina el trabajo a las cinco en punto.

REPASO 4 Capítulos 15–18

Exercise No. 67

1. (1 i)	3. (3 j)	5. (5 b)	7. (7 h)	9. (9 g)
2. (2 e)	4. (4 d)	6. (6 c)	8. (8 a)	10. (10 f)

Exercise No. 68

1. Sí, les invito de vez en cuando.
2. No, no lo prefiero.
3. Sí, las conocen bien.
4. Sí, les esperamos a Uds.
5. Las pone en la mesa.
6. No, no le busca a Ud. señor.
7. Me levanto a las ocho.
8. Sí, nos lavamos antes de comer.
9. Se sientan en la fila quince.
10. Mi padre se llama . . .

Exercise No. 69

1. más grande del mundo
2. más grande que
3. mayor que
4. tan alto como
5. la menor de la familia
6. el primer día
7. el 30 de enero de 1955
8. conmigo
9. sin mí
10. oigo (entiendo), la recuerdo

Exercise No. 70

1. se dan la mano
2. Tenemos que estudiar
3. Me acuesto
4. hace muchas preguntas
5. Por consiguiente
6. de vez en cuando
7. dar un paseo
8. Ud. debe de estar
9. otra vez
10. a las siete y media de la mañana

Exercise No. 71—Reading Selection
A Visit to the Puerto Rican District of New York

It is Saturday. Mr. Adams gets up at 8 o'clock and looks out of the window. The sky is blue. There is a bright sun. He says to his wife: "Today we are going to visit the Puerto Rican district which is near Central Park."

"That's fine," says Mrs. Adams.

At nine o'clock they get into their auto and after one hour of riding they arrive at 98th Street. They get out of the auto and begin to walk through the street. In a little while they see a group of Puerto Rican boys who are standing near a shop and who are talking very rapidly in Spanish.

Mr. Adams greets the boys and begins to chat with one of them. The conversation follows:

"Hello, young man! Are you a Puerto Rican?"

"No sir, I am a North American, but I know how to speak Spanish well. I have many Puerto Rican friends and they are my teachers. At home I have a Spanish book and every afternoon I study a little. By the way, are you Spanish?"

"No, young man, I am a North American and like you I am studying Spanish. I like the language very much. It seems that in New York there are many people who are studying Spanish. So long, friend."

"So long, sir," says the boy and in a few minutes he disappears among his group of friends who continue talking in Spanish.

—¡Qué muchacho tan simpático!— says Mr. Adams to his wife. And then he translates the sentence because his wife does not understand Spanish:
"What a nice boy!"

CAPÍTULO 19

Exercise No. 72

1. ¡Qué tiempo tan lluvioso!
2. Pase, pase. mojado
3. Déme
4. Ponga
5. Deje
6. Venga conmigo
7. Tome
8. Permítame
9. Mientras toman
10. Sigue lloviendo

Exercise No. 73A

1. Póngala	5. Tráigalos	8. Cómprenlos
2. No la abra	6. No lo tomen	9. Invítele
3. Repítalas	7. Salúdenlos	10. Háganlo
4. No lo deje		

Exercise No. 73B

1. escribo I write   escriba Ud. escriban Uds. write
2. leo I read   lea Ud. lean Uds. read
3. tengo I have   tenga Ud. tengan Uds. have
4. veo I see   vea Ud. vean Uds. see
5. pregunto I ask   pregunte Ud. pregunten Uds. ask
6. recibo I receive   reciba Ud. reciban Uds. receive
7. repito I repeat   repita Ud. repitan Uds. repeat
8. voy I go   vaya Ud. vayan Uds. go
9. doy I give   dé Ud. den Uds. give
10. soy I am   sea Ud. sean Uds. be

Exercise No. 74

1. Hace mal tiempo.
2. La criada abre la puerta.
3. Lo pone en el paragüero.
4. Los deja en el zaguán.
5. Pasan al comedor.
6. Toman té con ron.
7. Pone en la mesa dos tazas y platillos, una tetera, un azucarero y unas cucharitas.
8. Sale del comedor.
9. El Sr. Adams sirve al Sr. López.
10. Echa té con ron en las tazas.

CAPÍTULO 20

Exercise No. 75

1. está lloviendo
2. están charlando y tomando
3. hace calor, hace frío
4. prefiere Ud.
5. Dígame. Oiga Ud. bien
6. Acabamos de hablar
7. Al atravesar; se sube
8. se elevan
9. más alta de México
10. La mitad, tórrida

Exercise No. 76A

1. Estamos estudiándolas
2. Carlos está escribiéndola
3. ¿Estás leyéndolo?
4. La criada está poniéndola
5. Los señores están tomándolo.
6. Juan y yo estamos contándolo.
7. ¿Están comprándolos Uds.?
8. No estoy leyéndolas.
9. ¿Quién está escribiéndolas?
10. Están vendiéndolos.

Exercise No. 76B

1. No estamos esperándola a Ud. señora.
2. No estamos esperándole a Ud., señor.
3. No están mirándolos a Uds., señores.
4. No están mirándolas a Uds., señoras.
5. ¿Quién está buscándome?
6. Yo estoy buscándote, hijita.
7. El Sr. López está enseñándonos a hablar español.

Exercise No. 76C

1. Estamos estudiando
2. Está poniendo
3. Estamos abriendo
4. ¿Está leyendo Ud.?
5. Está trayendo
6. ¿Quién está esperando?
7. ¿Está tomando Ud.?
8. Estás hablando
9. No estoy escribiendo
10. ¿Está trabajando María?
11. Está buscando
12. Están enseñando

Exercise No. 77

1. Están hablando del clima.
2. Hace buen tiempo.
3. No se pone verde en el invierno.
4. Ve el gran panorama de sierras y picos altos.
5. Está situada en la Mesa Central.
6. Su altura varía desde cuatro mil (4000) hasta ocho mil (8000) pies.
7. El Pico de Orizaba es la cima más alta de México.
8. Las montañas determinan en gran parte el clima.
9. La mitad de Mexico está situada en la zona tórrida.
10. En la zona tórrida hace mucho calor.

CAPÍTULO 21

Exercise No. 78

1. seguimos charlando
2. en el mes de junio
3. a la misma hora
4. Por lo tanto
5. Vale la pena
6. Nunca, excepto
7. Tenga cuidado con
8. quedarse, sin
9. acordarme
10. al hacer, a olvidar

Exercise No. 79

1. nada
2. nada
3. nunca
4. Tampoco
5. Nadie
6. nadie
7. nunca
8. nunca
9. Tampoco
10. ni, ni
11. ningún
12. ningunos
13. ninguno
14. ningunas
15. nada

Exercise No. 80

1. Son la estación de lluvias y la estación seca.
2. La estación de lluvias comienza en el mes de junio.
3. Termina en el mes de septiembre.
4. Acostumbra llover a eso de las cuatro de la tarde.
5. Nunca hace frío en la ciudad.
6. Porque a veces hace fresco por la noche.
7. Porque el sol tropical es muy fuerte.
8. No va a olvidar el impermeable.
9. Van a platicar de los efectos de la altura.
10. Sí, se relacionan.

CAPÍTULO 22

Exercise No. 81

1. se siente un poco débil
2. un dolor de cabeza, dolor de muelas, dolor de estómago
3. Se dice
4. ¿Qué se puede hacer ...?
5. Descanse. Camine despacio
6. ¿Qué me aconseja Ud. ...?
7. Cuidado
8. se venden
9. parecen
10. se parece
11. qué clase de carne
12. Les gusta
13. debe
14. Comemos. No vivimos
15. a olvidar

Exercise No. 82A

1. Se puede
2. Cómo se dice
3. se venden
4. se ven
5. Se dice
6. se habla español
7. Se comen
8. Conoce Ud.
9. No los conozco
10. Sabe Ud.
11. me voy
12. Sabemos
13. se parece
14. un dolor de muelas

Exercise No. 82B

1. i	5. a	9. d	13. j
2. m	6. c	10. n	14. p
3. f	7. b	11. g	15. l
4. k	8. e	12. h	16. o

Exercise No. 83

1. Tiene una altura de cerca de 7500 pies.
2. Son los mangos y las papayas.
3. Son las naranjas, los plátanos, las peras y los melones.
4. Se venden en los mercados.
5. Es mejor tomar frutas ordinarias.
6. Es la tortilla.
7. La hacen del maíz.
8. Usan la tortilla para hacer los tacos y las enchiladas.
9. Comen un dulce, flan o frutas.
10. Porque el estómago norteamericano no se acostumbra rápidamente a los alimentos picantes de México.

REPASO 5 Capítulos 19–22

Exercise No. 84

1. (1 b)	4. (4 k)	7. (7 i)	10. (10 d)
2. (2 a)	5. (5 j)	8. (8 l)	11. (11 c)
3. (3 g)	6. (6 h)	9. (9 e)	12. (12 f)

Exercise No. 85

1. Tengo frío
2. Tengo calor
3. Hace buen tiempo
4. Llueve mucho
5. Hace fresco
6. Hace frío
7. Llevo chanclos
8. Llevo abrigo
9. Hay polvo
10. Todas las estaciones

Exercise No. 86

1. (1 d)	3. (3 a)	5. (5 c)	7. (7 e)	9. (9 g)
2. (2 f)	4. (4 b)	6. (6 h)	8. (8 j)	10. (10 i)

Exercise No. 87

1. La abro
2. Los cuento
3. La como
4. La pongo
5. Las repito
6. Los dejamos
7. Las tomamos
8. Las aprendemos
9. Lo escribimos
10. Lo leemos

Exercise No. 88

1. lloviendo
2. echando
3. pidiendo
4. leyendo
5. pensando
6. trayendo
7. oyendo
8. contando
9. poniendo
10. haciendo

Exercise No. 89—Reading Selection

Philip Does Not Like to Study Arithmetic

One day upon returning from school Philip says to his mother:

"I don't like to study arithmetic. It is so difficult. Why do we need so many exercises and problems nowadays. Is it not a fact that we have adding machines?"

Mrs. Adams looks at her son and says: "You are wrong, sonny. It is not possible to get along without numbers. For example, one must always change money, calculate distances, and . . . and . . ."

The mother stops speaking on seeing that Philip is not paying attention to what she is saying.

"By the way," continues the mother with a smile, "does not baseball interest you either, my son?"

"I should say so, mama."

"Well, if the Dodgers have won eighty games and have lost thirty, do you know what percentage of the games they have won?"

On hearing this Philip opens his mouth and exclaims:

"You are right, mother. Numbers, arithmetic and mathematics are very important. I think I'm going to study much more."

CAPÍTULO 23

Exercise No. 90

1. hacerle
2. acerca del pueblo
3. Aquí tiene Ud., Continúe
4. Quiénes
5. hoy día
6. hermosa y cosmopolita
7. a causa de la variedad, una variedad
8. el producto más importante
9. artistas y artesanos
10. se ocupan
11. Se ocupan
12. cestas y artículos de cuero
13. Acabo de recibir
14. Volvemos a platicar
15. Que Ud. lo pase bien

Exercise No. 91B

1. ¿Cuándo vuelven a casa?
2. Vuelven a casa a las diez de la noche.
3. Los alumnos vuelven a escribir los ejercicios.
4. Vuelvo a leer la guía de viajero.
5. Acabamos de recibir un envío de mercancía.
6. Acabo de hablar sobre el clima.
7. Ella acaba de volver de la joyería.
8. Acaban de comprar aretes de plata.
9. ¿Acaba de venir Ud. del cine?
10. Acabamos el trabajo.

Exercise No. 92

1. El Sr. Adams va a hacer algunas preguntas.
2. La primera pregunta es—¿Quiénes son los mexicanos?
3. Son descendientes de los españoles, conquistadores de México y de los indios indígenas.
4. México tiene 28 millones de personas más o menos.
5. Hablan lenguas indígenas.
6. Viven en el campo.
7. El maíz es el producto más importante.
8. Se ocupan de las artes populares.
9. Hacen artículos artísticos de cuero, de cobre, de hojalata, de plata, etc.
10. El Sr. A. acaba de recibir un envío de México.

CAPÍTULO 24

Exercise No. 93

1. a ver
2. entretanto, las artes populares
3. de uso diario
4. El vestido típico, pintoresco
5. faldas largas
6. un traje blanco
7. El sombrero de paja
8. un artículo de ropa
9. Me gustan
10. de lana o de algodón
11. sirve para todo
12. Por supuesto, cestas de varios tamaños
13. Tenemos que hablar
14. ¿Le parece bien el martes?
15. Me parece bien.

Exercise No. 94A

1. Visto
2. Me visto
3. visten de
4. Vestimos
5. se visten
6. lleva Ud.
7. Llevo
8. llevan
9. llevan
10. llevamos

Exercise No. 94B

1. Este, ése
2. Estos, ésos
3. Esas, éstas
4. Esta, ésa
5. Aquella, ésta
6. Éste, aquél
7. Ésta, aquélla
8. esto, eso
9. Eso
10. Eso

Exercise No. 95

1. El Sr. A. acaba de recibir una caja de mercancía de México.
2. Los hombres llevan el sarape.
3. Son de Oaxaca.
4. Son de Toluca.
5. Llevan la faja.
6. Dibujos de pajaros y de animalitos adornan la bolsa.
7. El rebozo sirve para manta y cuna del nene.
8. Hacen máscaras.
9. Sabe muy poco de las fiestas.
10. Dice—Que Ud. lo pase bien.

CAPÍTULO 25

Exercise No. 96

1. en algún pueblo u otro
2. se celebran
3. Por supuesto
4. cantando canciones y pidiendo "posada"
5. pasan un buen rato
6. cubierto de papel
7. trata de romperlo
8. a romperlo
9. Ud. debe ver
10. El Día de los Difuntos
11. Los panaderos venden
12. Se pueden comprar
13. mercados simulados
14. Los compradores, hecha por
15. El 16 de septiembre, Grito de Dolores

Exercise No. 97A

1. primer
2. tercer
3. buen
4. bueno
5. gran, grande
6. tercera
7. mal
8. primero
9. buenos
10. algún día

Exercise No. 97B

1. Cantan
2. Celebramos
3. Visitan
4. dura
5. Estoy preparando
6. Usa Ud.
7. contiene
8. trata
9. cogen
10. llevan (traen)

Exercise No. 98

1. Está titulada—Los Días de Fiesta.
2. Hay fiestas nacionales y fiestas dedicadas a varios santos.
3. Se celebran con bailes, cohetes, juegos y dramas.
4. Dura nueve días.
5. Grupos de personas van de casa en casa.
6. Piden "posada."
7. Pasan un buen rato, cantando, bailando y rompiendo la piñata.
8. Es un jarro cubierto de papel de colores vivos.
9. Contiene dulces y juguetes.
10. Un niño con los ojos vendados trata de romperlo.
11. Recogen los dulces.
12. Los reciben de los Reyes Magos.
13. Debe ver la fiesta de la Semana Santa en Tzintzuntzan.
14. Los habitantes del pueblo hacen los papeles.
15. Es el 16 de septiembre, el Día de la Independencia.

CAPÍTULO 26

Exercise No. 99

1. Estoy leyendo
2. Viajaré
3. Visitaré
4. Veré
5. Pasaré
6. Estoy seguro
7. un clima de primavera
8. bonitos, llenos de flores
9. muchos árboles, hermosas vistas
10. el pueblo de los plateros
11. Iré
12. fuera de los grandes centros
13. No deje de ver, con callejones tortuosos
14. una cantidad de cosas interesantes
15. Tengo ganas

Exercise No. 100A

1. We shall visit Taxco.
2. I shall spend a week there.
3. I shall be glad to see the murals.
4. Who will travel to Mexico?
5. They will not work hard.
6. Will you study the lesson?
7. Will you have coffee?
8. Philip will not write the letter.
9. I shall not be cold.
10. He will not come here.
11. We shall leave at 8 o'clock.
12. I shall play this role.
13. They will want to eat.
14. She will put it on the table.
15. I shall not be able to go there.

Exercise No. 100B

1. Compraré una corbata.
2. Costará cinco pesos.
3. Iré al campo.
4. Mi hermano irá conmigo.
5. Volveré a las nueve de la noche.
6. Veré a mi amigo Guillermo.
7. Saldré a las ocho de la mañana.
8. Tomaremos la cena a las siete.
9. Visitaremos a nuestros amigos.
10. Estudiaremos nuestras lecciones de español.

Exercise No. 100C

1. Aprenderé
2. Escribirá
3. Irán
4. Comeremos
5. Hablará
6. ¿Trabajará Ud.?
7. ¿Verá Juan?
8. ¿Quién visitará?
9. No viajaré
10. ¿Estudiarán?
11. Haré
12. Vendrá
13. Ud. pondrá
14. No querrán
15. ¿Saldrá Ud.?
16. Tendré
17. Estarán aquí.
18. ¿Irán Uds.?

Exercise No. 101

1. ¿Está titulada— ¿Qué Lugares Quiere Ud. Visitar, Sr. A?
2. El Sr. A. va a salir pronto.
3. Está leyendo guías de viajero.
4. Viajará por avión.
5. Usará el centro de la ciudad.
6. Está cerca de la Alameda.
7. Verá las pinturas murales.
8. Pasará un día en el parque de Chapultepec.
9. Verá la gran pirámide del Sol y la de la Luna.
10. Se dice que son tan imponentes como las de Egipto.
11. Tal vez irá a una corrida de toros.
12. Cuernavaca tiene un clima de primavera.
13. Taxco es el pueblo de los plateros.
14. Le interesa más la gente del campo.
15. El Sr. L. tiene ganas de acompañar al Sr. A.

REPASO 6 Capítulos 23–26

Exercise No. 102

1. (1 c)
2. (2 e)
3. (3 a)
4. (4 g)
5. (5 d)
6. (6 h)
7. (7 i)
8. (8 j)
9. (9 f)
10. (10 b)
11. (11 l)
12. (12 k)

Exercise No. 103

1. los pantalones
2. el sombrero
3. el traje
4. la corbata
5. la faja
6. los zapatos
7. los guantes
8. la camisa
9. el vestido
10. el abrigo

Exercise No. 104

1. (1 c) 2. (2 e) 3. (3 b) 4. (4 f) 5. (5 d) 6. (6 a)

Exercise No. 105

1. El panadero, la panadería
2. El platero, platería
3. El zapatero, zapatería
4. El sastre, sastrería
5. vendedor
6. comprador
7. la boca
8. los oídos
9. los ojos
10. la cara, la nariz, los labios

Exercise No. 106—Reading Selection

Mrs. Adams' Birthday

It is March 22, the birthday of Mrs. Adams. Today she is 35 years old. In order to celebrate this day the Adams family is going to dine in a fine restaurant on 52nd Street in New York City.

When they enter the restaurant they see a beautiful basket full of red roses in the center of the table reserved for the Adamses. Naturally Mrs. Adams is very surprised and gives her dear husband a thousand thanks and kisses.

After a delicious meal, Annie, the younger daughter, says in a low voice to her brothers and sister: "Now!" And each one of the four children takes out from under the table a pretty little box. They are gifts for the mother.

Anita gives her a silk handkerchief; Rosie, a cotton blouse; William, a pair of gloves; and Philip, a woolen shawl.

The following week Mr. Adams figures out the bill for that day, which is as follows:

Supper	$14.86
Tip	1.50
Flowers	6.25
Gifts	12.39
Total	$35.00

"What a coincidence," says Mr. Adams. "Thirty-five dollars; thirty-five years."

CAPÍTULO 27

Exercise No. 107

1. a leerle
2. Me gustará mucho
3. de informarle
4. le he apreciado
5. Tenga la bondad de, más conveniente
6. muy ocupado
7. Por eso, de antemano
8. de verle a Ud.
9. le mostrará a Ud.
10. en entenderme
11. No hay ninguna falta
12. titulado, me ayuda
13. darle a Ud. mis gracias más sinceras
14. Ud. es muy bondadoso
15. ¿Me hará Ud. el favor . . . ?

Exercise No. 108A

1. Will you give him the oranges?
2. Bring me the shoes.
3. Kindly read us the letter.
4. As soon as possible I shall write her a letter.
5. Will you teach me the new words?
6. We are not able to send you the money.
7. Who will read the story to us?
8. Tell me: What is Mary doing in the kitchen?
9. I shall not like the bullfight.
10. Does that date seem all right to you?
11. It suits me.
12. These things don't matter to me.

Exercise No. 108B

1. le
2. nos
3. le
4. me
5. les
6. dígame
7. les
8. les
9. me
10. comprándoles
11. le
12. llevándole
13. Llévanos
14. me
15. Nos

Exercise No. 109

1. Están sentados en la sala del Sr. A.
2. Tiene en la mano una copia de la carta a su agente.
3. Va a leerle al Sr. L. la carta.
4. Le gustará mucho al Sr. L. oírla.
5. La fecha es—4 de mayo de 1954.
6. Escribe la carta al Sr. Rufino Carrillo.
7. Usa el saludo—Muy señor mío:
8. El Sr. A. irá de viaje a México.
9. Saldrá de Nueva York el 31 de mayo.
10. Llegará al aeropuerto de México D.F. a las siete menos cuarto de la tarde.
11. Quedará en la capital dos meses.
12. Hará viajes a lugares de interés en México.
13. Irá a Guatemala y tal vez a Colombia.
14. Ha apreciado los servicios del Sr. Carrillo.
15. Desea conocer al Sr. Carrillo personalmente.

CAPÍTULO 28

Exercise No. 110

1. una carta en la mano
2. Estoy muy agradecido
3. de informarme
4. Tendré gran placer
5. platicaré
6. felicitarles
7. Entiendo bien, ¿Cómo no?
8. sin duda alguna, simpático
9. Perdóneme, orgulloso
10. por sí mismo, muy simpáticos
11. Estoy seguro, podré
12. Lo mejor es
13. Lo peor es
14. Nos
15. algunos últimos consejos

Exercise No. 111A

1. Cuánto tiempo
2. Hace seis meses
3. Hace diez años
4. Hace cuarenta y cinco minutos
5. Hace tres días
6. le conozco
7. viven en esta casa
8. están en el cine
9. está en este país
10. estoy aquí

Exercise No. 111B

1. No los pongan Uds. . . .
2. No les escriba Ud. . . .
3. No los traigan . . .
4. No me diga . . .
5. No le mande . . .
6. No me lleve . . .
7. No me dé . . .
8. No me compre . . .
9. No les lean . . .
10. No le venda . . .

Exercise No. 111C

1. Sí, lo visitaré. No, no lo visitaré.
2. Sí, la escribiré. No, no la escribiré.
3. Sí, lo compraré. No, no lo compraré.
4. Sí, los traeré. No, no los traeré.
5. Sí, lo tomaré. No, no lo tomaré.
6. Sí, los pediremos. No, no los pediremos.
7. Sí, la venderemos. No, no la venderemos.
8. Sí, las querremos. No, no las querremos.
9. Sí, los seguiremos. No, no los seguiremos.
10. Sí, las repetiremos. No, no las repetiremos.

Exercise No. 112

1. Acaba de recibir una carta de su agente en México.
2. Estará en la capital durante los meses de junio y julio.
3. Esperará al Sr. Adams en el aeropuerto.
4. Conversará con él en español.
5. Quiere felicitar al Sr. Adams y a su maestro.
6. Entiende bien que el Sr. Adams usará muchos modismos mexicanos.
7. El Sr. López está orgulloso de su pueblo.
8. Verá que el Sr. Carrillo está muy simpático como tantos mexicanos.
9. Será el martes que viene.
10. Se verán en la oficina del Sr. Adams.

CAPÍTULO 29

Exercise No. 113

1. Me alegro de
2. Tengo ganas
3. Por lo menos, darme
4. Eso de la cortesía
5. Quiere decir, es digno
6. Les gusta, acerca de
7. conocerse el uno a otro
8. Como le he dicho
9. Se dice, Espero que sí
10. de estar de prisa
11. Ha leído Ud.
12. En cuanto a mí
13. He gozado
14. despedirnos
15. Se dan la mano

Exercise No. 114A

1. We have had a good trip.
2. The pitchers have fallen on the floor.
3. They have said nothing.
4. What has Paul done with the money?
5. No one has opened the doors.
6. We have not read those newspapers.
7. Have you been at the movies.
8. Has the child been sick?
9. I have never believed that story.
10. What have they said?

Exercise No. 114B

1. He notado
2. Ha dicho
3. No han leído
4. Han sido
5. Hemos estado
6. Non he trabajado
7. ¿Ha enseñado Ud.?
8. ¿Quién no ha escrito?
9. ¿Qué han hecho Uds.?
10. Has abierto
11. ¿Qué ha dicho Juan?
12. Ha tomado
13. No he creído
14. Hemos oído
15. ¿Han oído Uds.?

Exercise No. 114C

1. El Sr. García venderá . . .
   El Sr. García ha vendido . . .
2. Trabajaré . . .
   He trabajado . . .
3. Escribiremos . . .
   Hemos escrito . . .
4. Leerán . . .
   Han leído . . .
5. ¿Tomará Ud. . . . ?
   ¿Ha tomado Ud. . . . ?
6. Tú no aprenderás . . .
   Tu no has aprendido . . .
7. ¿Buscará el niño . . . ?
   ¿Ha buscado el niño . . . ?
8. ¿Comprarán Uds. . . . ?
   ¿Han comprado Uds. . . . ?
9. Saldré . . .
   He salido . . .
10. Entrarán . . .
    Han entrado . . .

Exercise No. 115

1. Se encuentran en la oficina del Sr. A.
2. Hace color.
3. Se oyen los ruidos de la calle.
4. El Sr. A. se alegra de irse de la ciudad.
5. El Sr. L. tiene ganas de acompañarle.
6. Desgraciadamente, no es posible.
7. Sí, es más formal.
8. Quiere decir que cada hombre es digno de respeto.
9. Ha notado que entre los negociantes hay más formalidad en México que en los EE.UU.
10. El Sr. A. está cansado de estar de prisa.
11. El Sr. A. ha leído libros sobre Mexico.
12. El Sr. L. los ha recomendado.
13. Pasará el verano en Nueva York.
14. Pensará a menudo en su maestro.
15. Sí, le escribirá cartas.

CAPÍTULO 30

Exercise No. 116

1. Hace cinco meses
2. ha conseguido
3. Desde luego
4. Al fin
5. a acompañarle
6. no es solamente, sino también
7. está lista
8. ha hecho dos maletas
9. suben al automóvil
10. Se pone en marcha, a eso de
11. de su equipaje, libras
12. tiene que
13. se despide de
14. A las once en punto
15. El Sr. A. está en camino.

Exercise No. 117A

1. We are beginning the lesson.
2. We have begun the exercise.
3. I do not remember him.
4. I have remembered her.
5. Are they sitting down?
6. Have they sat down?
7. Are you repeating the words?
8. Have you repeated the words?
9. The maid is setting the table.
10. The maid has not set the table.
11. The table is set.
12. She is serving the coffee.
13. She has served the tea.
14. What fruits do you prefer?
15. What fruits have you preferred?
16. The children are going to bed.
17. They have already gone to bed.
18. Are you asking for information?
19. Have you asked for information?
20. The work is not finished.

Exercise No. 117B

1. abierta
2. cerrada
3. despiertos
4. puesta
5. vendida
6. vestidos
7. sentados
8. escritas
9. terminado
10. hecho

Exercise No. 117C

1. Duermo
2. Está durmiendo
3. Duermen
4. ¿Duerme Ud.?
5. Me despido
6. Se despiden
7. No nos despedimos
8. He dormido
9. ¿Ha dormido Ud.?
10. No hemos dormido
11. Me he despedido
12. No se han despedido
13. ¿Se han despedido Uds.?
14. Duerma Ud.
15. No duerman Uds.

Exercise No. 118

1. Hace cinco meses que el Sr. A. estudia el español.
2. Ha pasado muchas horas en conversación con su maestro.
3. Ha aprendido la gramática necesaria.
4. Ha trabajado mucho.
5. Ahora habla español bastante bien.
6. Ha conseguido los boletos para el vuelo.
7. Ha obtenido el certificado de vacuna.
8. Ha escrito a su agente.
9. Su agente ha prometido recibirle en el aeropuerto.
10. Están despiertos a las cinco de la mañana.
11. Sale a las ocho menos cuarto de la mañana.
12. Cada pasajero tiene que mostrar su boleto.
13. No. La familia no va a acompañarle.
14. Tienen que terminar el año escolar.
15. La señora tiene que quedar en casa para cuidar a los niños.

REPASO 7 Capítulos 27–30

Exercise No. 119

1. (1 f)
2. (2 c)
3. (3 e)
4. (4 a)
5. (5 d)
6. (6 b)
7. (7 g)
8. (8 h)
9. (9 i)
10. (10 j)

Exercise No. 120

1. Dispénseme
2. Hay que
3. Hace algún tiempo
4. Tienen la intención de
5. A menudo
6. Estoy de prisa
7. Quederá en casa
8. Por lo menos
9. En cuanto a mí
10. bastante bien

Exercise No. 121

1. (1 d)
2. (2 e)
3. (3 g)
4. (4 f)
5. (5 a)
6. (6 h)
7. (7 b)
8. (8 j)
9. (9 c)
10. (10 i)

Exercise No. 122

1. Me gusta la carta.
2. Les gusta a ellos viajar
3. Nos gustan los aviones
4. ¿Le gustan a Ud. las pinturas?
5. No le gustan a él los tomates.
6. No le gusta a ella esta moda.
7. ¿Les gusta a Uds. bailar?
8. ¿No te gusta jugar?
9. Nos parece bien.
10. No me importa

Exercise No. 123

1. han cantado
2. vuelto
3. llegado
4. puesto
5. hecho
6. abierto
7. recibido
8. dicho
9. leído
10. despedido

Exercise No. 124

1. sentadas
2. cubierta
3. abierta
4. cerrados
5. hechos
6. escritas
7. puesta
8. escrito
9. acabado
10. abierto

Exercise No. 125

1. La he comprado
2. La he abierto
3. Lo he oído.
4. Lo he conseguido.
5. Los he ayudado
6. Los hemos visto
7. Los hemos vendido
8. Lo hemos completado
9. Las hemos escrito
10. La hemos leído.

Exercise No. 126—Reading Selection
An Extraordinary Program in the Movies

This afternoon Mr. Adams and his wife are going to the movies. Mr. Adams does not like the majority of Hollywood films, especially those in which the American cowboys fire shots at each other. Neither do the detective pictures interest him.

But on this afternoon an extraordinary program is being shown in a theater which is about four blocks from his house. The film is called: "A Trip Through Mexico." It is a film about the country which our friend Adams is going to visit within a few months and which deals with its history, geography, rivers, mountains, cities, etc., that is to say a film which ought to interest tourists very much.

The Adamses enter the theater at 8:30. Almost all the seats are occupied and therefore they have to sit in the third row. Mr. Adams does not like this, because the movements on the

screen hurt his eyes. Fortunately, they are able to change seats after fifteen minutes, and move to the thirteenth row.

The Adamses enjoy this picture very much and also learn a great deal about the customs of Mexico.

On leaving the theater Mr. Adams says to his wife:

"Do you know, Charlotte, I believe that I shall get along very well in Mexico. I have understood almost all the words of the actors and actresses in this film."

CAPÍTULO 31

Exercise No. 127

1. la sala de espera
2. de repente
3. Dispénseme
4. Mucho gusto en conocerle.
5. El gusto es mío
6. un libre
7. López está muy equivocado
8. ¿Quién sabe qué más?
9. No tengo prisa
10. Ni yo tampoco
11. da a la plaza
12. treinta pesos al día

Exercise No. 128A

1. entré	2. comí	3. salí	4. ví	5. me senté
entraste	comiste	saliste	viste	te sentaste
entró	comió	salió	vió	se sentó
entramos	comimos	salimos	vimos	nos sentamos
entrasteis	comisteis	salisteis	visteis	os sentasteis
entraron	comieron	salieron	vieron	se sentaron

Exercise No. 128B

1. Who forgot the tickets?
2. Yesterday we received the letters.
3. The man bought a new suit.
4. Last night we did not hear the bell.
5. Did the train arrive on time?
6. They looked for the baggage.
7. The child fell in front of the house.
8. They left the airport in a taxi.
9. Where did Mr. A. wait for his friend?
10. How much did the raincoat cost?

Exercise No. 128C

1. No compré . . .
2. No volvimos . . .
3. No escribí . . .
4. No llegamos . . .
5. No salí . . .
6. No pasé . . .
7. No oímos . . .
8. No vendí . . .
9. No dejamos . . .
10. No trabajamos . . .

Exercise No. 128D

1. salí
2. llegamos
3. examinaron
4. oyó
5. Ud. respondió
6. no pregunté
7. llamó
8. Uds. desearon
9. salimos
10. paró
11. no olvidé
12. gritó
13. creyeron
14. vendimos
15. ¿volvieron Uds.?
16. ¿leyó?

Exercise No. 129

1. Los aduaneros mexicanos lo revisaron.
2. Un señor guapo se acercó á él.
3. Dijo—Dispénseme ¿Es Ud. el Sr. A?
4. Contestó—a sus órdenes.
5. Pasó a una velocidad espantosa.
6. Deseó decir—Por favor, más despacio.
7. Olvidó el espanol.
8. Vió camiones, autos, y tranvías.
9. Gritó— ¡No tengo prisa!
10. Le contestó—Ni yo tampoco.
11. Llegaron al hotel sanos y salvos.
12. Buenos días Tiene Ud. un cuarto con baño?

CAPÍTULO 32

Exercise No. 130

1. me llamó por teléfono
2. a tomar la merienda
3. El día siguiente
4. Me acerqué
5. me invitó a entrar
6. vino a saludarme
7. Ud. está en su casa
8. según la costumbre mexicana
9. Me parece
10. muchas casas semejantes
11. Admiré
12. Me presentó
13. hacerse médico
14. Sintió
15. Nos despedimos, a casa

Exercise No. 131A

1. The maid served us the (late) luncheon.
2. Why did you not wish to invite me?
3. Last night we returned late from the theater.
4. I wanted to telephone you.
5. What did you do after the meal?
6. They said—"We are not in a hurry."
7. I repeated all the answers.
8. My friend did not come on time. I was sorry.
9. They asked for information at the information office.
10. They wanted to buy round trip tickets.

Exercise No. 131B

1. Le dije—Pase Ud.
2. Mi hermano hizo un viaje al Perú.
3. Vine a casa a las siete.
4. Vistieron de falda de algodón.
5. Quiso hacerse médico.
6. Sirvió una taza de chocolate.
7. Pidió informes.
8. Quisimos ver la nueva película.
9. El año pasado hicimos un viaje a México.
10. Dijimos—Hasta la vista.

Exercise No. 131C

1. quise
2. no dije
3. hizo
4. vinieron
5. sirvió
6. quisieron
7. repetí
8. hicimos
9. dijeron
10. hicieron
11. ¿Qué dijo?
12. ¿Que dijeron Uds.?
13. no quisimos
14. no vine
15. sintieron

Exercise No. 132

1. El Sr. Carrillo le llamó por teléfono.
2. Llegó a su casa a las cinco de la tarde.
3. Una criada le abrió la puerta.
4. El Sr. Carrillo vino a saludarle.
5. El patio lleno de árboles y flores le encantó.
6. Admiró la fuente de piedra en el centro del patio.
7. Los dos hijos del Sr. Carrillo son serios e inteligentes.
8. Asisten a una escuela secundaria.
9. Quiere hacerse médico.
10. Tienen que volver a su cuarto.
11. Platicaron de la vida en México, de las costumbres y del arte.
12. Sí, vale la pena de ir allá.
13. El Sr. Adams quiso ir allá.
14. El Sr. Adams y el Sr. Carrillo se despidieron.
15. Volvió a su hotel.

CAPÍTULO 33

Exercise No. 133

1. ¡Qué hermoso!
2. ancha y espaciosa
3. parece
4. se puede cruzar, del mundo
5. se puede caminar, de las ciudades más grandes
6. ayer
7. Nos encontramos
8. quieren decir—algo pequeño
9. No veo más que
10. al rey Carlos IV (Cuarto) de España
11. Ud. conoce bien
12. He leído algo
13. Ví
14. casi enteramente de cristal
15. Pude entender

Exercise No. 134A

1. At Christmas I gave gifts to all the children.
2. I did not have the opportunity to know you personally.
3. We were not able to pay the whole bill.
4. This house was constructed in the 16th century.
5. On Sunday we took a walk in Chapultepec Park.
6. I was able to converse with him in his beautiful language.
7. He had no difficulty in understanding me.
8. She did not wish to rest much.
9. Mr. A's family could not accompany him.
10. I put my new hat on my head.

Exercise No. 134B

Translate:

1. Tuve que estudiar . . .
2. El Sr. A. estuvo . . .
3. Los árboles se pusieron . . .
4. El dió . . .
5. Fuí un estudiante . . .
6. Fuimos al . . .
7. Vinieron . . .
8. No dije nada.
9. Uds. no hicieron nada.
10. Quisieron Uds. . . . ?

Exercise No. 134C

1. tuve
2. Ud. pudo
3. fueron
4. dijo
5. puso
6. quisimos
7. dieron
8. fuí
9. Uds. estuvieron
10. nos encontramos

Exercise No. 135

1. Está titulada "El Paseo de la Reforma."
2. Es muy ancho.
3. Tuvo que pensar en su conversación con el Sr. López sobre las calles de México.
4. Al norte se puede cruzar algunos de los grandes "ríos" del mundo.
5. Al sur se puede caminar por algunas de las "ciudades" más grandes de Europa.
6. Fué domingo.
7. Se encontraron cerca del "Caballito."
8. Quieren decir—algo pequeño.
9. Representa a Carlos IV (Cuarto).
10. Es muy grande.
11. Conoce bien los otros monumentos históricos de México.
12. El Sr. A. leyó algo sobre él.
13. La defendió contra los españoles.
14. El edificio del Seguro Social es casi enteramente de cristal.
15. Está no lejos del Parque de Chapultepec.

CAPÍTULO 34

Exercise No. 136

1. La semana pasada
2. Ví, que
3. lleno de gente
4. del campo
5. perderse
6. por una calle de puestos
7. Ví, de siete u ocho años
8. Como los demás vendedores
9. flores, cestas y ropa
10. Entre los puestos
11. a divertirse
12. la plática de las mujeres
13. sobre la vida del campo
14. recordaba
15. un día muy divertido

Exercise No. 137A

1. It was raining buckets when we took leave of the young men.
2. I was thinking of you when I was riding in an automobile through the streets whose names are dates.
3. The tourists and vendors were bargaining and all seemed to be enjoying themselves greatly.
4. I was approaching the door when I met Mr. Carrillo's sons.
5. While we were speaking about the folk arts, Mrs. Carrillo was reading a newspaper.
6. It was very hot when we returned to the United States.
7. When the car was starting, a policeman approached.
8. The airplanes were coming and going at all hours.
9. We were tired but we did not want to rest.
10. It was already 4:30 P.M. and we were in a hurry.

Exercise No. 137B

1. yo comía
2. estudiábamos
3. estaba
4. Uds. se despedían
5. se paseaban
6. gritaban
7. bajaba
8. hablábamos
9. iban
10. pasábamos

Exercise No. 137C

1. caminaba
2. iba
3. dijo
4. jugaban
5. cantaron
6. veíamos
7. corrían
8. Ud. perdió
9. vivieron
10. leyó
11. empezó
12. llamaban
13. Uds. no entraron
14. ¿estaba Ud.?
15. éramos
16. oyeron

Exercise No. 138

1. Pasaba por las montañas.
2. Lavaban ropa.
3. Cortaban caña.
4. Era viernes.
5. Vino del campo.
6. Sí, había gente de la ciudad.
7. Porque sabía pedir informes en español.
8. Vió a un muchacho de siete u ocho años.
9. Se parecía a un viejecito.
10. Llevaba un sombrero de ala ancha.
11. Arreglaba su mercancía.
12. Veía el sentido estético de muchos de los vendedores.
13. Una mujer estaba sentada en la acera.

14. Delante de ella había unas pocas cebollas y chiles.
15. Mientras iba a casa recordaba sus conversaciones con el Sr. L.

CAPÍTULO 35

Exercise No. 139

1. antes de mi salida, No tenga prisa
2. No he olvidado
3. no descanso
4. tanto que descubrir
5. ayer, al mediodía
6. se venden
7. No pude
8. volví a visitar
9. Todavía no
10. Me gustan mucho, pintores

Exercise No. 140A

1. mío
2. suyos
3. mía, suya
4. míos, suyos
5. mías, suyas
6. los míos, los suyos
7. las mías, las suyas
8. la suya
9. los suyos
10. los nuestros

Exercise No. 140B

1. Salía . . . — I was leaving . . .
   Salí . . . — I left . . .
2. Entrábamos . . . — We were entering . . .
   Entramos . . . — We entered . . .
3. Veíamos . . . — We were seeing . . .
   Vimos . . . — We saw . . .
4. Uds. no olvidaban . . . — You were not forgetting . . .
   Uds. no olvidaron . . . — You did not forget . . .
5. El chófer me respondía. — The driver was answering me.
   El chofer me respondió. — The driver answered me.
6. Ellos no aprendían . . . — They were not learning . . .
   Ellos no aprendieron . . . — They did not learn . . .
7. Estaba . . . — I was . . .
   Estuve . . . — I was . . .
8. Los jóvenes iban . . . — The young men were going
   Los jóvenes fueron . . . — The young men went . . .

Exercise No. 141

1. No ha olvidado los consejos del Sr. L.
2. Hay tanto que ver, tanto que oír, etc.
3. Descansaba en la Alameda.
4. Veía las tiendas en la Avenida Juárez.
5. Las ha visitado muchas veces.
6. No podía resistir la tentación de volver a visitar las tiendas.
7. Nunca se cansa de mirarlas.
8. Volvió a visitar el Palacio de Bellas Artes.
9. No ha asistido a ningún concierto.
10. Le gusta mucho mirarlas.

REPASO 8 Capítulos 31–36

Exercise No. 142

1. la comida
2. la dificultad
3. hablador
4. la plática
5. divertido
6. el caballito
7. viajar
8. secundario
9. la ventanilla
10. el camino
11. la pintura
12. la pregunta
13. la respuesta
14. la llegada
15. facilmente
16. el campesino

Exercise No. 143

1. he (she) was able, poder
2. I wanted, querer
3. they put, poner
4. I saw, ver
5. they read, leer
6. you said, decir
7. we had, tener
8. I gave, dar
9. he was (went), ser, ir
10. he (she) asked, pedir
11. You did (made) hacer
12. I came, venir
13. he, she made (did), hacer
14. you (fam. sing.) had, tener
15. I found out, saber

Exercise No. 144

1. (1 j)
2. (2 e)
3. (3 b)
4. (4 g)
5. (5 h)
6. (6 i)
7. (7 d)
8. (8 f)
9. (9 c)
10. (10 a)

Exercise No. 145

1. recibí, Yesterday I received a package.
2. quedaré, I shall remain at home.
3. fuimos, We did not go to the movies.
4. hacen, Now they are packing the valises.
5. escuchan, The teacher speaks and the students listen.

6. saldrán, Will you leave the city the day after tomorrow?
7. Vió, Did you see him the day before yesterday?
8. Viajaré, Next year I shall travel in Europe.
9. podemos, We are not able to hear him.
10. llegué, I arrived last week.

Exercise No. 146—Reading Selection 1

A Visit To Xochimilco

On one occasion Mr. Adams took the sons of Mr. Carrillo on an excursion to the town of Xochimilco with its interesting canals. The town is not very far from the capital and our friend arrived without difficulty. On arriving at the town he had a very bright idea. He proposed a lunch in the open air. The boys accepted the project with enthusiasm.

Adams entered a grocery store, bought two cans of sardines with tomato sauce. Then he bought some cakes and sweet rolls in a bakery. Finally he bought some oranges and some tomatoes at a vegetable stand.

There remained the problem of cold drinks. Now one of the two boys had a bright idea. "Why not buy some bottles of Seven-Up? Along the canal there are many vendors of cold drinks."

"Wonderful idea," Mr. Adams commented.

They rented a canoe adorned with thousands of carnations. After riding two hours exploring the canals they got out of the canoe in a very quiet spot. Mr. Adams opened the cans of sardines and prepared some sandwiches which they ate with the tomatoes. For refreshment they had the "Seven Up," and finally they had as dessert the delicious oranges. It was a wonderful lunch and the boys were enchanted. They will not forget this experience for many years.

Exercise No. 147—Reading Selection 2

On Juarez Avenue

Finally we walk through Juarez Avenue. It is a wide avenue in the center of the Federal District. It is on one side of the Alameda, a very beautiful park with high trees, fountains and monuments.

There are many people on Juarez Avenue. All the tourists come there. In the shops are sold all kinds of things typical of Mexico,—jewelry, textiles, leather goods, pottery and various kinds of handmade clothing.

Naturally we are going to visit the National Museum of Folk Arts and Industries. There one can see various articles from all parts of the country.

We walk through this avenue until we arrive at the "Caballito," the statue of Charles IV, on the Plaza de la Reforma. There the Avenue ends.

CAPÍTULO 36

Exercise No. 148

1. Every town has a plaza.
2. Everybody goes to the plaza for rest, business, recreation—for everything.
3. Big trees grow on some plazas.
4. In others one sees nothing but dry leaves from some poor little tree.
5. The bandstand is in the center of the plaza.
6. The musicians play Sunday afternoon, Thursday night, or any hour, any day.
7. Six kinds of shops in the arcades are: stationery shops, pharmacies, haberdashers, jewelry shops, and book shops.
8. They get together in the cafe to chat or read the newspapers.
9. They drink a cup of coffee, chocolate, a beer, or a coca-cola.
10. One sees an old church in the main plaza and perhaps the hotel of the town.
11. During the siesta hours some people rest on the benches, others sleep.
12. The life of the plaza begins again about 4 o'clock.
13. On Sunday afternoons everybody gets together on the plaza for the "promenade."
14. The boys walk in one direction and the girls in the opposite direction.
15. At night one sees some travelers who come from the market.

Exercise No. 149

1. El corazón de cada pueblo
2. mientras estaba sentado
3. Se ve nada más
4. puede ser
5. el domingo por la tarde
6. donde se encuentran

7. se reunen, por la tarde
8. una iglesia antigua
9. Se ven, cansados
10. Más tarde, que, demasiado chicos

Exercise No. 150A

1. Duermo
2. No estoy durmiendo
3. ¿Quién duerme?
4. Dormimos
5. ¿Duerme Ud.?
6. Duerma Ud.
7. No duerman Uds.
8. Duerme
9. La niña no está durmiendo
10. ¿Quiénes duermen?
11. duermen
12. está durmiendo

Exercise No. 150B

1. que
2. cuyo
3. que
4. de que
5. que
6. lo que
7. todo lo que
8. que
9. de quienes
10. quien

CAPÍTULO 37

Exercise No. 151—Test of Reading Comprehension

1. He wanted to take an auto trip to Teotihuacan.
2. He invited the sons of Mr. Carrillo to go with him.
3. They met in front of Mr. A's hotel.
4. Mr. A had rented a car.
5. They saw nothing but some small adobe houses or an Indian with his donkey.
6. They saw in the distance the plain of the Central Plateau and the mountains.
7. They had a flat.
8. They could not find a jack in the trunk.
9. It was noon.
10. A truck driver stopped, loaned them a jack and helped them change the tire.
11. He thanked him and offered him ten pesos.
12. He climbed up slowly, but was nevertheless out of breath.
13. The boys ran up.
14. Mr. L. knows these ruins, the Pyramid of the Moon and the Temple of Quetzalcoatl, better than Mr. A.
15. They felt tired but happy.

Exercise No. 152

1. conmigo en coche
2. Los jovenes aceptaron, con alegría
3. Nos encontramos
4. Saqué
5. Lo había alquilado
6. charlando y riendo
7. de vez en cuando
8. No vimos más que
9. De repente
10. ¿Qué pasó?
11. cambiar la llanta, no había gato
12. a pesar de, paró
13. Nos hace falta un gato
14. y nos ayudó a cambiar la llanta
15. Nos dimos la mano y nos despedimos.

Exercise No. 153A

1. habíamos We had seen the movie.
2. había Had you read many books?
3. había Who had opened the window?
4. habían The children had not slept during the night.
5. había I had not believed the story.
6. habíamos We had flown over the mountains.
7. habían They had gone to the theater.
8. Había Had you had a good trip?
9. habían You had said nothing.
10. Habías Had you eaten the sweets, Johnny?

Exercise No. 153B

1. Él había comprado . . .
2. Yo había visto . . .
3. Habíamos comido . . .
4. ¿Habían recibido . . . ?
5. ¿Había puesto Ud. . . . ?
6. Uds. no habían oído . . .
7. No habías dormido . . .
8. se había sentado . . .
9. Habían tenido . . .
10. No habíamos dicho . . .
11. ¿Qué había pasado?
12. No habían hallado . . .
13. no habían cambiado
14. se había acercado

CAPÍTULO 38

Exercise No. 154—Test of Reading Comprehension

1. He had never been a gambler.
2. He had noted that everybody was buying lottery tickets.
3. He was thinking of the possibility of winning one of the lesser prizes or perhaps the first prize.
4. He would take trips to all the countries of South America.
5. He would visit again his friends in Mexico.

6. He would buy art objects for his house.
7. He bought a ticket from the woman vendor on the corner of Madero Avenue.
8. Next day he was reading the winning numbers in the newspaper.
9. He saw a number with three zeros.
10. He thought he had won a prize of 200,000 pesos.
11. He was taking trips with his whole family through all the countries of South America.
12. Mr. A. had the number 25000.
13. The number 26000 won the prize.
14. ¿Qué importa? What does it matter.
15. From that moment I was a gambler.

Exercise No. 155

1. llegué, todo el mundo	8. qué querían decir los tres ceros
2. en todas las esquinas	
3. el premio gordo	9. Los números que ganaron
4. volver a visitar	10. Busqué
5. toda la familia	11. Al fin, en un bolsillo
6. soñaba	12. había, no había
7. con los tres ceros	

Exercise No. 156A

1. Iríamos . . .	We would go . . .
2. Juan vendería . . .	John would sell . . .
3. No ganarían . . .	They would not win . . .
4. Ud. encontraría . . .	You would meet . . .
5. Leería . . .	I would read . . .
6. ¿Llevaría Ud. . . . ?	Would you take . . . ?
7. ¿Les gustarían . . . ?	Would you like . . . ?
8. Saldría . . .	I would leave . . .
9. No podríamos . . .	We would not be able . . .
10. No dirían . . .	They would say nothing . . .

Exercise No. 156B

1. yo aprendería	6. ¿trabajaría Ud.?	11. yo haría
2. él escribiría	7. ¿vería Juan?	12. él vendría
3. irían	8. ¿Quién visitaría?	13. no querrían
4. comeríamos	9. yo no viajaría	14. ¿saldría Ud.?
5. ella hablaría	10. ¿estudiarían?	15. Uds. pondrían

CAPÍTULO 39

Exercise No. 157—Test of Reading Comprehension

1. Do you want to go to a bullfight?
2. They arrived one hour before the beginning of the bullfight.
3. Mr. Carrillo had bought tickets for seats in the shade.
4. The bullfight fans sit in the sun seats (bleachers).
5. The bullring reminded Mr. A. of our football or baseball stadiums.
6. Mr. A. heard the shouts of the refreshment vendors and the cries and laughter of the spectators.
7. A procession of men in brilliant costumes passed through the arena.
8. The bull came out.
9. Mr. A liked the music; the brilliant costumes, the shouts and the laughter, and the cheerful sunlight.
10. He does not try to describe the bullfight because Mr. L. knows this sport well.
11. He doesn't like it.
12. He pities the poor horses, the poor bull, and often the poor bullfighter.
13. He must confess that he is not and never will be a bullfight fan.
14. He agrees that one may say about football: "the poor players."
15. He prefers a more peaceful sport, chess.

Exercise No. 158

1. Estábamos para salir	9. hombres en trajes relucientes
2. un rato, Pues, posiblemente	
3. acepté	10. Se fueron, salió
4. Faltaba una hora	11. un deporte muy emocionante
5. había comprado	
6. Al fin, nos sentamos	12. tengo que confesarle
7. estadio de fútbol o béisbol	13. No pienso
8. los gritos y las risas	14. Estoy de acuerdo, los pobres jugadores
	15. Prefiero

Exercise No. 159B

I. 1. The children bring them to me.
2. The students send them to us.
3. They do not sell them to us.
4. I give it to you, sonny.

II. 1. Carlos me lo da.
2. Ana nos los presta.
3. El maestro nos lo dice.
4. Te la damos, niño.

Exercise No. 159C

I. 1. We say it to you.
2. We bring it to you (pl.)
3. We give them to him.
4. We send them (f) to them.

II. 1. Juan se lo dice a Ud.
2. María se la escribe a él.
3. El maestro se los da a Uds.
4. Se las mandamos a ella.

Exercise No. 159D

I. 1. Tell it to me.
2. Give it to us.
3. Lend them to me.
4. Send them to him.

II. 1. Préstemelos.
2. Mándenoslo.
3. Dígasela a él.
4. Déselos a ella.

CAPÍTULO 40

Exercise No. 160—Test of Reading Comprehension

1. He had read various interesting books about its history and customs.
2. He was able to describe a little of what he had seen and learned.
3. The people interest him most.
4. Four qualities are: affection, generous hospitality, humor, and their philosophy in face of difficulties.
5. He finds life in Mexico more tranquil.
6. He had gotten a different impression in the taxi which brought him to his hotel at fearful speed.
7. He preferred to get a better knowledge of Mexico.
8. He will take his whole family with him.
9. He is sure there will be no difficulties.
10. He leaves for New York August 1.
11. He will be glad to telephone Mr. L. and invite him to supper as soon as possible.
12. They will spend much of the night speaking of their beloved Mexico.

Exercise No. 161A

1. I shall read . . .	12. I shall like your letter.
2. I had read . . .	13. They finish . . .
3. I have read . . .	14. They finished . . .
4. We have visited . . .	15. They have finished . . .
5. We had visited . . .	16. They have much to tell me.
6. We shall visit . . .	
7. I can describe it.	17. They will have . . .
8. I was able to describe it.	18. They had . . .
9. I shall be able . . .	19. We shall return home.
10. I like your letter . . .	20. We returned . . .
11. I liked your letter.	

Exercise No. 161B

1. sabe	6. Sé
2. Conocemos, no sabemos	7. Ud. sabe, Ud. puede
3. No puedo	8. Ud. conoce
4. conocer	9. conocerle
5. se conocen	10. no pueden

Exercise No. 161C

1. ¿Ha aprendido Ud. mucho sobre México?
2. Sí, he estado allí y he leído muchos libros.
3. ¿Sabe Ud. hablar español?
4. Sí, lo hablo bastante bien.
5. ¿Recuerda Ud. los lugares de que hemos hablado?
6. Los recuerdo bien.
7. ¿Puede Ud. describirlos en español?
8. Sí, puedo describirlos.
9. ¿Qué le gustó más a Ud. en México?
10. Me gustó más el pueblo.
11. ¿Es más tranquila la vida de México que la de Nueva York?
12. De veras, es más tranquila.
13. ¿Hay mucho que ver en México?
14. Hay mucho que ver, mucho que oír, mucho que hacer y mucho que aprender.
15. Mi viaje está acabado. (terminado)

REPASO 9 Capítulos 36–40

Exercise No. 162

1. Who will ask for information in the railroad station?
2. Paul had already eaten lunch when I saw him.
3. Would you want to take a trip to all the countries of Europe?
4. I know that man, but I do not know where he lives.
5. We were writing our letters when the teacher entered the room.
6. Take these papers and put them on my desk.
7. We have bought the newspapers and we have read them.
8. When I arrived in Mexico, I noted that everybody was buying lottery tickets.
9. Buy this ticket and you will have luck.
10. I was not able to describe to them everything I had seen.
11. I came to Mexico and they received me with affection.
12. William was speaking all afternoon while I was saying nothing.
13. I did not like the bullfight and therefore I shall not attend another.
14. The tortilla resembles our pancakes.
15. The fathers (parents) were working while the children were sleeping
16. We were in the market when it began to rain.
17. It was 8:30 in the morning and still the children were sleeping.
18. They will not come here because they will not have time.
19. Children, won't you play in the yard?
20. My uncle traveled through all the countries of South America.
21. Mr. Adams liked spicy foods, but he remembered the advice of his teacher and would not eat them.
22. I wanted the toys but Charles would not give them to me.
23. If I find plates with designs of little animals I shall send them to you.
24. He asked for change of a bill of 1000 pesos and the cashier gave it to him.
25. You have Mary's hat. Return it to her.

Exercise No. 163

1. es un comerciante de Nueva York.
2. un viaje a México para visitar
3. conocerle mejor.
4. aprendió a hablar español
5. había leído muchos libros
6. a su amigo y maestro, el Sr. López
7. los lugares de interés histórico
8. el Sr. Adams encontró la vida de México más tranquila que la de Nueva York
9. en el libre que le llevó a su hotel
10. la velocidad espantosa del libre
11. pronto terminó sus negocios
12. no pudo visitar ni a Colombia ni a Guatemala
13. tanto que ver, tanto que oír, tanto que hacer, tanto que aprender.
14. volverá a México
15. toda la familia
16. No ha ganado el premio gordo, bastante dinero
17. la última carta del Sr. Adams
18. Sin duda, tomar la cena con su familia

Exercise No. 164
The Pyramids of Teotihuacan

One sees in the outskirts of Mexico, D.F., the remains of various highly developed and somewhat mysterious cultures—the cultures of the Indian races who lived in Mexico ten centuries ago.

In the valley of Teotihuacan are found some enormous pyramids, monuments of a scarcely known culture, the culture of the Toltecs. They used to live in the valley before the Aztecs. What we know of them exists neither in the history books nor in the legends but in solid stone.

The Pyramid of the Sun dominates the valley. It is 216 feet high and is larger than any pyramid of Egypt. One can climb to the summit by a broad and very steep stairway.

Further to the north, through the Avenue of the Dead, is the Pyramid of the Moon and to the south one sees the Temple of Quetzalcoatl, the Plumed Serpent, God of the Aztecs. This pyramid is decorated with very interesting sculptures.

The people who live nowadays in the valley of Teotihuacan are descendants of the Aztecs. The Toltecs, architects of the pyramids, have disappeared a long time ago. We only know that they were an imaginative people with a very advanced aesthetic sense.

Exercise No. 165—Reading Selection 2
En el Zocalo

We are in the Zocalo. It is the principal plaza of Mexico, D.F. We walk to the north toward the Cathedral. It is of the 16th Century. To the right is the National Palace; it is also old, of the 17th Century. To the left is the Arcade of the Merchants. There we see a block of stands and vendors of cheap merchandise. Beyond the Arcade is the Pawnshop, and behind us to the south are the Municipal Palace and the Palace of Justice. The latter is a modern building. The former is of the 18th Century. On all sides we see big buildings and many people.